Discovering Syntax

Studies in Generative Grammar 93

Editors

Henk van Riemsdijk
Jan Koster
Harry van der Hulst

Mouton de Gruyter
Berlin · New York

Discovering Syntax

Clause Structures of English,
German and Romance

by
Joseph E. Emonds

Mouton de Gruyter
Berlin · New York

Mouton de Gruyter (formerly Mouton, The Hague)
is a Division of Walter de Gruyter GmbH & Co. KG, Berlin.

The series Studies in Generative Grammar was formerly published by
Foris Publications Holland.

♾ Printed on acid-free paper which falls within the guidelines
of the ANSI to ensure permanence and durability.

Library of Congress Cataloging-in-Publication Data

> Emonds, Joseph E.
>   Discovering syntax : clause structures of english, german, and romance / by Joseph E. Emonds.
>   p. cm. − (Studies in generative grammar ; 93)
>   Includes bibliographical references.
>   ISBN 978-3-11-018682-6 (cloth : alk. paper)
>   1. Languages, Modern − Syntax.   I. Title.
>   PB211.E46   2007
>   415−dc22
>   2007007837

Bibliographic information published by the Deutsche Nationalbibliothek

The Deutsche Nationalbibliothek lists this publication in the Deutsche Nationalbibliografie; detailed bibliographic data are available in the Internet at http://dnb.d-nb.de.

ISBN 978-3-11-018682-6
ISSN 0167-4331

© Copyright 2007 by Walter de Gruyter GmbH & Co. KG, D-10785 Berlin.
All rights reserved, including those of translation into foreign languages. No part of this book may be reproduced in any form or by any means, electronic or mechanical, including photocopy, recording, or any information storage and retrieval system, without permission in writing from the publisher.
Cover design: Christopher Schneider, Berlin.
Printed in Germany.

Acknowledgments and dedication

As this volume is a collection of articles written on separate topics and on separate occasions, many important acknowledgments in the initial notes of the various studies are not repeated or summarized here.

Nonetheless, colleagues and friends have been indispensable in bringing to publication this collection taken as a whole. For this project Series Editor Henk van Riemsdijk has, as throughout my career, furnished encouragement, direction and enthusiasm. I hope that the result can in part justify his unflagging support for my research efforts. The editor at Mouton, Ursula Kleinhenz, has from the beginning taken a personal and very perceptive interest in how the volume should be structured. Moreover, she has steadfastly helped overcome pitfalls and setbacks we encountered in bringing material together from so many sources in the needed uniform formats. When many chapters previously produced electronically in fact turned out to exist only in the (ultimately more secure) format of the printed page, a less dedicated manager might well have abandoned the project. Instead, these difficulties served (thankfully) to increase her determination to see the project through.

Several chapters here are reprinted, sometimes in slightly abridged form, from other publishers, who have all generously given their permission for reprinting materials they first published. In particular, John Benjamins Press has granted permission to reprint for Chapter 10, Kaitakusha Press for Chapter 8, Kenkyusha Press for Chapter 4, Kluwer Academic Publishers for reprinting Chapters 3 and 11. As the collection would not be fully coherent without these essays, I am especially grateful for their cooperation.

My continuing appreciation goes out to Lida Veselovská, whose influence has helped shape so many of the chapters in this book. Our continuing interchanges on grammatical analyses and their proper theoretical expression seem to have an ever increasing impact on my work. In addition to the considerable influence of her linguistic ideas, the constant if critical support that emanates from these interchanges has been essential in warding off a dangerous sense of intellectual isolation. She has given me the energy to widen the scope of research topics and to attend carefully to properly integrating them. And to this partner in life as well as linguistics, my gratitude extends far beyond the linguistic.

vi *Acknowledgments and dedication*

I wish to dedicate the work of assembling this volume to my friends Mike Rogin and Ann Banfield, whose 18 years of exemplary partnership were not far from coinciding with the period of writing these essays. Their shared devotion to intellectual excellence has always been an inspiration. The final version of Chapter 10 was written at his Paris desk during what so sadly became his last year with us.

Contents

Acknowledgments and dedication v
Prologue to *Discovering Syntax* 1

Part I: Structures in lexical projections

Chapter 1	Types of syntactic categories and features	9
Appendix	The status of the small clause category	14
1.1	Secondary Predication and Small Clauses	14
1.2	Binary Branching and "Learnability"	15
1.3	Small Clauses: irrelevant or defective syntactic arguments	17
1.4	An Aristotelian legacy	22
Chapter 2	The restricted complement space of lexical frames . . .	27
2.1	The range of single phrase complements to verbs	27
2.1.1	Variations on the frames ___D, ___A and ___P	28
2.1.2	The predicate nominal frame +___N	30
2.1.3	Variations on the frames ___V and ___I	33
2.1.4	Extrinsic features in single frames	38
2.2	Limitations on multiple complements	40
2.2.1	The puzzling descriptive generalizations	40
2.2.2	The role of Abstract Case in Logical Form	47
2.2.3	Confirmation of the LF Case Filter from triple complement structures	50
2.3	The Case of predicate attributes	55
2.4	The restrictive Syntactic Lexicon confronts open-ended Conceptual Space	62
Chapter 3	The autonomy of the (syntactic) lexicon and syntax . . .	71
3.1	The problem of "neutralized" phrases	71
3.2	The uses of *ing*	72
3.2.1	Derived Nominals	72
3.2.2	Derived Adjectives	73
3.2.3	Gerunds	75
3.2.4	Present Participles	76

3.3	A generalized and autonomous lexical entry for *ing*	78
3.3.1	From Midde to Modern English	78
3.3.2	Selection through lexical heads	81
3.4	Defining the lexical head	84
3.5	Lexical selection of non-finite clause types	86
3.5.1	The choice between Participles and Gerunds	89
3.5.2	Why Infinitives and not Gerunds?	93
3.6	Conclusion: all uses of *ing* result from a single entry	95
Chapter 4	Secondary predication, stationary particles, and silent prepositions	99
4.1	Lexical representations of Intransitive Prepositions	99
4.2	Case Transparency and Word Order of Intransitive Prepositions	102
4.3	Stationary Particles and Secondary Predication	104
4.4	Stacked PPs, Silent Ps, and the Revised Theta Criterion	106
Chapter 5	Projecting indirect objects	115
Introduction: a path not followed		115
5.1	The surface structure of the prepositionless dative	118
5.1.1	English double objects	118
5.1.2	Some non-Indo-European prepositionless datives	123
5.2	The deep structure of indirect object constructions	127
5.3	Prepositionless datives: theoretical issues	130
5.3.1	Structure-preserving derivations and the Projection Principle	130
5.3.2	The interpretation of indirect objects and further predictions	133
5.3.3	The passivizability and abstract Case of NPs in P-less datives	136
5.4	Accounting for P-less datives	137
5.4.1	The licensing of the empty P in P-less datives	137
5.4.2	Phrasal antecedents for empty heads	139
5.5	Accounting for crosslinguistic variation	141
5.5.1	Applicative suffixes	141
5.5.2	Accounting for crosslinguistic variation: The English gambit	145
5.6	Conclusion: syntax rules OK	148

Part II: Minimal structures for functional categories

Chapter 6	The flat structure economy of semi-lexical heads	159
6.1	Van Riemsdijk's Categorial Identity Thesis	159
6.2	Expected properties of phrasal XP complements	160
6.3	Defining semi-lexical heads	164
6.4	Flat structures when X = Preposition	165
6.5	Flat structures when X = Adjective/ Adverb	172
6.6	Flat structures when X = Noun	174
6.7	Flat structures when X = Verb	180
6.7.1	Romance restructuring	180
6.7.2	Romance causative structures	186
6.7.3	Concluding remarks on flat V–V structures	192
Chapter 7	How clitics license null phrases: A theory of the lexical interface	199
7.1	The apparent non-local character of clitic placement	199
7.1.1	Five contexts for long distance licensing	199
7.1.2	Problems with the Movement approach	205
7.2	Right dislocation as the key to en/ne	208
7.2.1	Distribution of the genitive clitics	208
7.2.2	The relation of en/ne to subject position	214
7.2.3	Free right dislocations without en/ne	215
7.3	Alternative realisation: Minimising covert syntax	220
7.3.1	The host of clitic placement	220
7.3.2	In situ representations of clitics in trees	221
7.3.3	Realising syntactic features in different positions	223
7.4	The "absolute transparency" of phrases allowing clitic climbing	226
7.4.1	Rizzi's paradigms for restructuring verbs	226
7.4.2	Lexical theory: Late insertion	229
7.4.3	Lexical theory: Satisfying subcategorisation	232
7.4.4	Clitic climbing, dual insertion levels, and the Phrase Mate Hypothesis	235
7.4.5	Causative and perception verbs	238
7.4.6	Restrictions on cliticisation in causative/perception complements	243
7.5	Clitics corresponding to complements of adjectives	244
7.5.1	Two lexical projections for French adjectives	244

x Contents

7.5.2	Two lexical projections for English adjectives	248
7.6	Unresolved issues in the in situ framework	250
7.6.1	Nominative clitics and finite agreement	251
7.6.2	Enclisis	251
7.6.3	Clitic ordering	251
7.6.4	Choice of host V within restructured VPs	252
7.6.5	The historical persistence of clitic case	253
7.6.6	Economy of Derivation	255
Chapter 8	English indirect passives	267
8.1	Characteristics and scope of structures called "Passive"	267
8.2	Indirect Passives: a needed concept in English grammar	269
8.2.1	Genesis of the term "Indirect Passive"	269
8.2.2	The English candidates for Indirect Passive status	270
8.3	The theoretical components of the Indirect Passive	274
8.3.1	Characterizing the "Grammatical V" that trigger the Passive	274
8.3.2	Properties of the Grammatical Lexicon	276
8.3.3	The lexical entries for the participial suffixes	278
8.3.4	The relation of the Syntacticon to levels of Lexical Insertion	281
8.4	Countering possible objections	284
8.4.1	Objection: grouping Japanese and English Indirect Passives	284
8.4.2	Objection: the structures examined aren't really Passives	285
8.4.3	Objection: The structures examined are Passives in Small Clauses	287
8.5	Conclusion: English Indirect Passives confirm Late Insertion	289

Part III: Landing sites of phrasal movements

Chapter 9	A theory of phrase structure based on Extended Projections	297
9.1	Lexical Projections	297
9.2	The Subject as a special phrase: I and IP	298

9.3	The DP Hypothesis and generalizing the definition of Subject	300
9.4	The EPP: explaining the "strong D feature on Tense"	303
9.5	Transformational derivations	305

Chapter 10	The lower operator position with parasitic gaps	309
10.1	Subjacency effects on parasitic gaps	311
10.2	The location of the parasitic operator O_i	312
10.2.1	No operator O_i in finite clauses	312
10.2.2	No operator O_i in infinitives with overt subjects	313
10.2.3	No operataor O_i in bare adverbial participles	313
10.2.4	No operator O_i in absolute constructions	313
10.3	Puzzle: the lower operator O_i is not in SPEC(CP)	314
10.4	The lower operator is in SPEC(IP) or SPEC(DP)	315
10.5	Why parasitic gaps must be DPs	319
10.6	The sequence of T-model operations on a cyclic domain	320
10.7	A generalized definition of subject	324
10.8	Extending the analysis to long distance movement	325

Chapter 11	Unspecified categories as the key to root constructions	331
11.1	Root vs. embedded clause asymmetry	331
11.1.1	Variation in root domains across languages	332
11.1.2	Variation across clausal types	332
11.1.3	An inventory of root transformational operations	334
11.2	Leftward movements without commas	336
11.2.1	The domains of root movements: "Discourse Projections"	336
11.2.2	The landing sites of root movements: "Discourse Shells"	339
11.2.3	Cross-linguistic variation in Discourse Projections?	343
11.3	Extending Structure Preservation	344
11.3.1	Deriving local and root operations from structure preservation	345
11.3.2	Unique landing sites for frontings without comma intonation	349
11.3.3	Exclusion or rarity of French frontings without verb inversion	352
11.4	Licensing the root X^0 position: English Ø vs. German V	353
11.4.1	Lexical entries for Complementisers	354
11.4.2	A grammatical moral based on Germanic Verb Second	357

11.4.3	"Residual" English verb inversions in root and root-like clauses	358
11.5	Left dislocations with commas	361
11.5.1	Iterative a-categorial root clauses	361
11.5.2	Parentheticals in apparently final position	365
11.5.3	Clausal remnants in apparently final position	368
11.6	Summary of proposed hypotheses	369
References		381

Prologue to *Discovering Syntax*

This volume brings together a set of essays in formal syntax published over 15 years. Each essay offers solutions to some much studied yet still quite puzzling construction(s) of English, German or Romance languages (Standard French, Italian and Spanish). Each essay has been designed as self-contained and can be read in isolation, with the proviso that all take for granted the syntactic category system described in Chapters 1 and 9.

Nonetheless, certain general hypotheses appear in several or even most of the essays; for instance, *(only) grammatical items are inserted late in transformational derivations*. These main hypotheses are justified precisely because they help account for recalcitrant paradigms in several apparently diverse areas. Because of their generality, they serve to unify the separate topics covered, so that a particular and rather comprehensive approach to grammar emerges. We might call it "Tri-level Lexical Insertion" or "The Syntacticon Model of Minimalism," i.e. a specific theory of grammar based on most, perhaps not all, minimalist assumptions. By bringing these essays together in one volume, readers hopefully can more easily understand its advantages and adopt aspects of it in their own work.[1]

Taken together, the essays cover a coherent range of topics, but their cohesion will not be apparent from simply examining titles or introductory passages. I therefore next spell out the design behind my choice of topics and their order of presentation. By happy accident, this ordering is also not too far from chronological, so that it additionally takes advantage of the natural property of later written material referring to earlier work

The grammatically practiced reader will recognize the following schematic and pre-theoretic phrase structure for underlying head-initial clauses (e.g. in English or French), using the functional categories of Chomsky (1986).

(i)
$XP - [_{CP} (YP) C [_{SPEC(IP)} NP (Clitics +) v_{AUX} - v_{AUX} \ldots [_{VP} V - ZP_1 - ZP_2 \ldots]]]$
<= Part III =>| <========Part II========>| <= Part I =>

Part I of this volume treats the most embedded (bold) area in (i), that of *complement structures*, and focuses on the English system. Chapter 2 develops a general theory of complementation based solely on case and *syntactic sub-*

categorization; it encompasses single and double complements, explaining asymmetries and even predicting the very limited range of triple complementation (*describe Clinton to them as a genus, bring John Hamlet to peruse on the train*). Subsequent chapters deal separately with three less transparent complement constructions: Chapter 3 accounts for the variety and differing distributions of non-finite complements. Chapter 4 analyzes contrasting types of post-verbal particle structures, and Chapter 5 provides a cross-linguistically motivated analysis of double objects.

Part II turns to the VP-external functional category structures in what are called "extended projections" of VP, namely vP and IP, the area in normal font in (i) above. Chapter 6 generalizes over structures for functional or "semi-lexical" x^0 for all values of X^0: V, N, A and P. It concludes, counter to widespread assumptions, that these structures are "flat." Chapter 7 analyzes the bound verbal clitics of 3 Standard Romance languages, again concluding against the grain: the independently justified flat structures of Chapter 6 crucially permit characterizing all Romance clitics as "clause bound." Chapter 8 studies properties of so-called auxiliary verbs ("small v") as seen in both the familiar (direct) passives and a construction here characterized for the first time, the English indirect passive.

Part III then moves on to the "high peripheries" of extended projections, underlined in the schema (i). After Chapter 9 briefly introduces the needed category system, Chapter 10 analyzes English parasitic gaps, concluding that the evidence of many paradigms points to SPEC(IP) and SPEC(DP) as the loci for "lower operators" in these constructions. Chapter 11 investigates the consequences of introducing "label-less" root projections for the contrasting main clause phenomena of German and English.

We can summarize the chapter sequence then as moving through the generalized tree schema in (i) from the bottom to the top. Part I treats the internal structure of the lexical VP in English; Part II analyzes the intermediate structures linking subject and predicate across English and Romance languages; Part III focuses on constructions involving movements and "landing sites" in non-argument or "A-bar" positions, contrasting especially English and German. This progression of topics may lend itself to use in advanced syntax courses with a similar progression of topics.

The domain of investigation in this book is thus all the many subparts of the single finite clause, in particular as they are elaborated in Standard Language grammars of English, German, and the Romance languages French, Italian, and Spanish. The study of finite clauses might these days sound like a limited domain, but the wide-range of topics and conclusions in the above synopsis demonstrates the contrary; indeed, such a focus encompasses most of traditional grammar.² The paradigms and analyses presented here in fact have led to unflinching revisions of many currently common presuppositions. In the end, I think the reader will be convinced that my challenges to these presuppositions are well justified.

Notes

1. Another reason for publishing a single volume is that most of the essays here are scattered in festschrifts and thematic collections that are often not easily located, and which stand little chance of staying in print.
2. The real oversimplification would be to consider that single finite clauses are "grammatically simple." Complex examples such as (i)–(ii) are actually single finite clauses. In order to understand how they fit together, we need analyses of all the English grammar topics studied in this volume
   (i) Which bunch of boys could getting them jobs help without insulting?
   (ii) The people out in the field the boss may want sent their bonuses early.

Part I
Structures in lexical projections

Chapter 1: "Types of syntactic categories and features." Reprinted from Sections 1.1 and 1.2 of *Lexicon and Grammar,* Mouton de Gruyter, 2000a, 1–12. **Appendix: "The status of the small clause category."**

Chapter 2: "The restricted complement space of lexical frames." Reprinted from Chapter 8, *Lexicon and Grammar,* Mouton de Gruyter, 2000a.

Chapter 2, a revised abridgement of Emonds (2000a, Ch. 8), illustrates the main results of that book's theory of complementation, based on Economy of Representation and a "Logical Form Case Filter." This theory permits all and only the subcategorization frames that correspond to classically discussed constructions. Certain less transparent complement structures left aside here are analyzed in the following chapters in Part I.

Chapter 3. "The autonomy of the (syntactic) lexicon and syntax." Abridged from the original version in *Interdisciplinary Approaches to Language,* edited by C. Georgopoulos and R. Ishihara, Kluwer Publications, 1991a. (permission obtained)

Chapter 3 develops a system of Economy of Representation and late (PF) lexical insertion that predicts the distribution of **non-finite clausal types** in English, eliminating the need for ad hoc diacritics. It constructs non-trivial explanations for these variations that other analyses treat as ad hoc. The argumentation leads smoothly into the Revised Theta Criterion, the keystone of the following chapter.

Chapter 4: "Secondary predication, stationary particles, and silent prepositions." Abridged from the original version in *Essays in Linguistics and Philology presented to Professor Kinsuke Hasegawa*, edited by A. Baba et al., Kenkyusha Press, 1996. (permission obtained)

In Chapter 4, **standard post-verbal particles** are contrasted with true resultative constructions containing the same particles, showing among other things that the former have *no secondary predication*. Thus if secondary predication supports small clause structure (in *I want [those shoes on]*), then this article's paradigms show that post-verbal particles (*Put those shoes on*) *empirically contrast* with it hence must be analyzed differently.

Chapter 5: "Projecting indirect objects." Abridged from *The Linguistic Review* 10, 211–263, 1993.

Chapter 5, again an abridgment of a longer essay "Projecting indirect objects" (*Linguistic Review* 10, 1993), provides empirical and cross-linguistic argument for a non-obvious yet theoretically satisfying analysis for **double object constructions**. Nonetheless, the version here omits no data or argumentation that directly concerns indirect objects.

Chapter 1:
Types of syntactic categories and features*

Any framework purporting to characterize syntactic well-formedness requires an approximate inventory of the categories whose co-occurrence is to be determined.[1] Since language clearly distinguishes four "open" or "lexical" categories whose members number in the hundreds or thousands (nouns, verbs, adjectives, and pre/post-positions: N, V, A, P), these categories must play a central role.

Moreover, the great membership of these lexical categories never fails to astonish; informal sampling today still confirms Jespersen's (1905, 227) observation: "People who had never been to college, but, … were regular readers of books and periodicals, … reported generally from 25,000 to 30,000 words …" That is, the combined membership of the four lexical categories X must typically be well over 20,000. In a well-formed syntactic structure, each of these lexical categories X has a "maximal projection" XP which obligatorily contains ("dominates") its structural head X as well as any modifiers and complements of X.

In addition to and in contrast to the open categories, a number of syntactic categories of limited membership modify and help extend the projections of the lexical categories. Each of these non-lexical "closed" or "functional" categories seem to contain at most twenty or so morphemes. The most prominent functional categories are the elements I making a verb phrase into a finite Fregean judgment and a class of quantificational and/or definite items D determining the referential properties of noun phrases. I and VP together form an "extended projection" IP of V, while D and NP together form an extended projection DP of N.

For a number of other closed class elements which are characteristic modifiers of at least the four lexical categories X, I continue to use the early term cover specifier SPEC(XP) as in Chomsky (1970); in this study, specifiers can include both closed classes of grammatical elements and/or phrases. For example, there seems to be a single "slot" in which modifiers of English adjectives appear: certain degree words such as *very* and *so*, measure phrases (*two hours, ten feet*) and short adjective phrases (*less believably, somewhat tolerably*) are in complementary distribution:

(1.1) *That lecture was {very two hours/ two hours very} long.
(1.2) *That {unbelievably too/ too unbelievably} optimistic estimate was foolish.
(1.3) *Be sure to install a {tolerably ten feet/ ten feet tolerably} deep pool.

I will consider all these elements to be in SPEC(AP) and do not commit myself to analyzing morphemes such as *very* as either a head or a phrase; but little if anything in my arguments hinges on this decision. Nonetheless, this use of SPEC does not conform to the practice of authors who reserve this symbol for phrasal positions.[2]

Syntactic categories thus fall into two separate classes, whose diverging nature can be derived from five properties of Universal Grammar ("UG"):

a. UG provides a restricted set of morpheme categories {B}: lexical heads X, specifiers SPEC(XP), I, D and perhaps a few others.[3]

b. UG matches a small range of *cognitive syntactic features* F (upper case) with each B whose combinations [B, ±F] characterize up to a maximum of twenty or so members of B.[4]

c. The cognitive syntactic features F on B contribute *centrally* to meaning (that is, to "Logical Form") in all syntactic classes.

d. Finer distinctions of meaning in terms of purely semantic features f (lower case script) which play no role in syntax (Chomsky, 1965, Ch. 4) appear *only in the four open lexical classes N, A, V and P.*

e. All non-lexical categories are "closed" because they crucially lack these purely semantic features f, which apparently proliferate and recombine fairly freely. Hence, the closed categories have few members and disallow coining (Emonds, 1985, Ch. 4).

Some plausible examples of purely semantic features f: (i) I would imagine that color terms share a feature f_i, permitting for example unexceptional compound adjectives such as *dark pink* and *light magenta*, in contrast to (compounds) **dark smooth* or **light dirty*. (ii) Among verbs of say "harm" (which itself might be a semantic feature), some exclude further normal use of an object *(!He destroyed/ ruined/ totaled/ wrecked the bicycle and then rode away on it)* while others don't (*He damaged/ harmed/ messed up/ misused the bicycle and then rode away on it*). Plausibly, some feature f meaning roughly "usable for intended purpose" seems involved. It seems incontrovertible that elaboration of syntactic theory does not in general depend on such features f.

I now discuss properties (a-e) in more detail. Properties (a-b) are reflected in the partial and tentative table (1.4), which may well be modified as research proceeds. Most of these matches are inherited from traditional grammar, with generative grammar providing a number of non-trivial modifications. Many features F have unique canonical positions in which they are realized, such as PAST on I, but for some F, UG may provide more than one possible host. Thus, POTENTIAL is matched with I and A in English (*can, able*) but with V in French (*pouv-*), and COMPARATIVE features occur in several specifier positions (Bresnan, 1973: *more into Zen, more of a man*).

(1.4) Examples of *probable* UG matches:
      syntactic features F   categories B
      tense and modal features   I
      quantifier features   D or NUM
      space-time co-ordinates   P
      ACTIVITY   V
      PERFECTIVE (aspect)   V
      ANIMATE, COUNT   N
      comparative features   SPEC(XP)
      EVAL(uative)   A

Certain features F may cross-classify the syntactic categories B. Thus, a [+N] feature subsumes N, D, and A, while [-N] subsumes V, I, and P.[5] The much discussed feature ±WH most plausibly occurs on the "specifier" (SPEC) of both the marked [+N] categories D and A in e.g. *which, what, how*, and so also does ±PROXIMATE; e.g. *{this / that} + {bread / tall}*.

A central tenet in this study's approach to the lexicon is thus a general condition on syntactic features (1.5), which expresses (b) and also (c).

(1.5) *Canonical Realization. UG associates a few cognitive syntactic features F with each syntactic category B. These features F contribute to semantic interpretation (Logical Form) only in these "canonical positions" on B, and appear elsewhere only via lexical stipulation.*

Emonds (2000a, Chapter 4) treats a range of syntactic features which are *not* canonically realized and two mechanisms which severely limit the distribution of these uninterpreted features.

Notice that properties (a-c) do *not* distinguish open from closed classes; the distinction follows rather from properties (d-e). These two properties which set off closed class categories can be formally linked as follows:

(1.6) *Functional Categories. Outside the lexical categories N, V, A, and P, the only features allowed are the cognitive syntactic features F (and the small sets of morphemes they generate).*

Observe now that the lexical categories are defined as those whose features *may* extend beyond the inventory F; this possibility of additional semantic features *f* makes these classes "open." The question arises as to whether every N, V, A and P *must* have *f* distinct from F. In fact, there is no reason to assume this, i.e., Canonical Realization (1.5) can apply as its stands to the four lexical categories. Indeed, certain subclasses of N, V, A and P have properties characteristic of the non-lexical classes, such as post s-structure insertion and unique syntactic behavior (cf. Emonds, 1985, Ch. 4, and 1987). *The lexical categories are in this way like the others: each has a subset of say up to twenty or so elements fully characterized by cognitive syntactic features F and entirely lacking purely semantic features f.*

These closed subsets of open categories can be called "grammatical" N, V, A or P; in contrast, open class subsets which have purely semantic features will be called "lexical" N, V, A, or P. English grammatical verbs include *be, have, do, get, go, come, let, make, say*, etc. Its grammatical nouns include *one, self, thing, stuff, people, other(s), place, time, way, reason*. A widely acknowledged distinction between grammatical and lexical or "contentful" prepositions also falls into place as a predicted subcase of a more general property in this theory of lexical categories: lexical P are specified with purely semantic *f* and grammatical P are not.[6]

(1.7) *Definition. A closed grammatical class X (including N, V, A, P) is one whose members have no purely semantic features f, but only cognitive syntactic features F.*

In Emonds (2000a: Chapter 3), I define the subpart of the lexicon which contains all and only the closed grammatical classes of elements as the "Syntacticon" of a language, and show that it has properties quite distinct from an open class "Dictionary." Explanatory accounts throughout this study will repeatedly utilize the distinctions between grammatical and lexical X and between features in canonical and non-canonical positions.

As we proceed, it will become evident that among the syntactic features F (the only features within closed classes), three subclasses are not interpreted in LF: (i) purely contextual features, (ii) copies of a feature F outside of F's canonical position(s), referred to subsequently as "alternatively realized F," and (iii) features which specify a marked "absence of content." These three classes of syntactic F which are not used at LF will be called "purely syntactic" or uninterpreted. Other cognitive syntactic features which are used at LF, for instance those discussed above, will be called "cognitive syntactic" or simply cognitive or interpreted features notated in upper case. Lexical elements will turn out to have very different syntactic properties depending on which of these types of features they realize.

There are thus three main types of features on categories which interact differently with respect to lexical insertion, syntactic derivation, and logical form ("LF"):

(1.8) Purely semantic features f, which are present *only* on the head categories X = N, V, A, and P. They are not used in syntax and are not present on closed subclasses of grammatical X.

(1.9) Cognitive syntactic features F in canonical positions, which can occur with all syntactic categories. They play a central role in both syntax and at Logical Form.

(1.10) Purely syntactic features F, also occurring with all syntactic categories. They indicate contexts, realize the features in (1.19) in noncanonical positions, or stipulate a marked lack of content (e.g, +STATIVE on V, -LOCATION on P). They are used only in syntax.

Summarizing, as stated earlier, both the types of features used in syntax, i.e. in (1.9) and (1.10), are uniformly notated with upper case F.

Appendix. The status of the small clause category

1.1 Secondary Predication and Small Clauses

Part I of this volume presents a theory of complementation, focusing on the domain where the variety of complement types is greatest, the verb phrase. A common type of verb complementation involves what traditional grammar calls "secondary predication," whereby some XP modifies or is "predicated" of an NP, with both constituents being inside VP:

(1.11) a. Mary ate [$_{NP}$ the carrots] [$_{AP}$ raw].
      b. Mary found [$_{NP}$ the cat] [$_{PP}$ inside (the cupboard)].
(1.12) a. Mary considered [$_{NP}$ John] { [$_{AP}$ available]/ [$_{NP}$ my best friend]}.
      b. Mary wanted [$_{NP}$ the cat] [$_{PP}$ inside (the cupboard)].

The NP is the subject of the XP; hence it must be the lowest NP that c-commands XP (using the definition of "subject" in this volume) or XP's actual sister (the widely used "mutual c-command" definition). Sometimes NP but not XP receives a theta role from V, as in (1.11), and sometimes as in (1.12) the XP but not the NP receives a theta role (cf. Stowell, 1981).[7]

A typical contemporary view on secondary predication, with origins in Kayne (1981) and Stowell (1981), is that some additional "small clause" node unites a post-verbal NP with its predicate XP. From this perspective, a study of verb complementation should include small clauses. As they do not appear in this volume, I of course should explain why. In fact, I will go further; this section argues that syntactic theory utilizes *no such construct*.

The issue is thus whether to represent the secondary predications (1.11b)–(1.12b) minimally as (1.13) or less parsimoniously as (1.14):

(1.13)

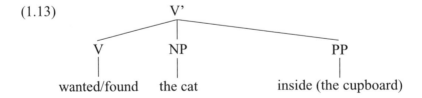

(1.14)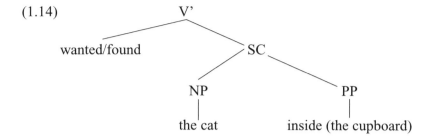

For discussion, I adopt the neutral notation SC of many authors. Significantly, in 25 years no SC proponent has successfully imposed on the field a restrictive theory of categories to replace this ad hoc notation.

In examining arguments for SC nodes, let us keep in mind that, counter to a widespread impression, SCs are *irrelevant* for locating the subject of a secondary predicate. As noted above, either definition of subject (based on closest c-command or mutual c-command) successfully picks out [$_{NP}$ *the cat*] in both (1.13) and (1.14) as the subject of [$_{PP}$ *inside*]. SCs are equally superfluous for the purposes of binding theory. The local domain required for binding anaphors, e.g., in Chomsky's (1981) Principle A, crucially refers only to "smallest domains containing a subject." Since SCs are not needed to locate subjects, they are not needed for binding domains either. Only an additional redundant requirement, that subjects be *unique* sisters of predicates, could motivate using SCs to house subjects; section 1.3 looks into such a requirement.

What then are the motivations for small clauses? Why are they so popular? Even among proponents, it is indeed generally understood that SCs are a somehow aberrant category. For example they are the only type of phrase that never undergoes movement, not even Scrambling (Haegemann, 1991: 545), which nonetheless seems completely unconditioned. But SCs are not abandoned even though they fail this classic generative diagnostic for constituenthood from Ross (1967).[8]

1.2 Binary Branching and "Learnability"

The most influential support for small clause structures is that they extend the range of binary branching; tree (1.14) but not tree (1.13) is binary branching. But even so, small clause predication structures are not *sufficient* for establishing fully binary trees. In this regard, section 2.2.1 in this volume

16   *Structures in lexical projections*

discusses eight *different types* of verbs with two complement phrases that cannot be plausibly construed as subject-predicate pairs. Some examples are the differing dual complement structures with *look, prevent, promise, require, rob, speak, strike* and *suggest* (*John looks **ill to her**; I promised **Sam to shave myself**; suggest **to him how Mary did it**,* etc.). Using small clause predication structures for establishing binary branching is thus a bit like using airplanes to fly to the moon; they get part way, but something additional is surely needed (perhaps rendering them irrelevant).

Such difficulties notwithstanding, one widely accepted argument for binary branching concerns learnability. Kayne (1983a: IX) claims that uniform binary branching

> ... constitutes a step towards a solution to the learnability problem for phrase structure. (How does the language learner know what tree representation, of all those available in theory, to associate with a given sentence?)

This remark has impressed later researchers, for example den Dikken (1995: 27). But in fact binary branching does *not* reduce the set of grammars; learned parts of grammars, probably consisting of the lexicons of functional categories, contain *no information about branching*. Thus, the above comment has no relation to any "learnability" in language acquisition. Rather, what binary branching can facilitate, as Kayne's rhetorical question openly indicates, is *processing*. It can help associate given sentences with appropriate trees in *performance* models.

But to my knowledge, successfully implemented processing procedures invariably *give priority to the argument-taking devices of heads*, whether these be thought of as argument structures, theta-grids, lexical conceptual structures, event structures, or subcategorization frames. An absolutely central step in models of either producing or comprehending a sentence of any complexity is always (1.15):

(1.15) *Economy of Representation (computational first try). To construct a syntactic tree, first use the lexical argument information of a head building as little phrase structure as possible.*

Binary branching suggests no way to eliminate or supplant (1.15). So processing Economy motivates associating (merging) a head with arguments by sisterhood, not by binary branching trees.[9]

Outside the realm of head-complement relations, binary branching can be a serviceable principle for projecting adjuncts, coordination structures, external arguments, or the X^0-internal structure of compounds. That is, it can function as a kind of "Elsewhere Condition" for processing when (1.15) is irrelevant. We can therefore supplement Economy with a default principle of tree construction, in line with Kayne's quote above.

(1.16) *Binary Branching (computational default). Lacking lexical argument information, construct syntactic trees with binary branching.*

In sum, I cannot agree with den Dikken (1995: 28), who claims that small clause complements "are available at no cost whatsoever." Their additional structure must be empirically justified like all other phrasal structures. In the next subsection, I review several syntactic advantages claimed for them and find them to be irrelevant at best. Thus, in the absence syntactic advantages of SCs (and in view of the additional stipulations they require), the essays on complementation in Part I of this volume retain Economy (1.15) and sisterhood structures for multiple complements.

1.3 Small Clauses: irrelevant or defective syntactic arguments

(i) Unambiguous Paths. Kayne's (1981a: section 1) initial argument for binary branching is a purely formal exercise. A type of tree relation alluringly named an "unambiguous path" is shown to be compatible only with binary branching trees. He then proposes his principle (3):

(1.17) An anaphor that falls under the binding principles must be connected to its antecedent by an unambiguous path. (Kayne, 1981a: 145)

However, there is nothing unambiguous in binary trees about the actual location of an anaphor's antecedent. In order to find an antecedent, the direction "up or down" in a tree must be specified independently at each dominating node. To the extent that c-command mimics linear order, as is frequent in binary branching analyses, unambiguous paths simply amount to saying that an anaphor's antecedent precedes it somewhere in the string. That is, specifying unambiguous paths to an antecedent is exactly the same as specifying c-command; nothing is gained by imposing an unambiguous path requirement.

(ii) Connectedness. In impressive studies of transformational movement, Kayne (1981a, 1981b, 1983c) develops a theory of "connectedness" in trees which accounts for a number of paradigms involving long distance extractions, parasitic gaps, multiple questions, etc. for deeply embedded constituents. These papers do not discuss binary branching but it is true enough that researchers often conceptualize or explicate this theory in terms of binary trees (den Dikken, 1995: 28). A usual catch phrase is something like, "one can't extract from a left-branching subject (inside an SC),"

In fact, Kayne's connectedness results can be recast without binary branching, although a detailed demonstration would be outside the scope of this study. Informally, his final statement of Connectedness (1983c: 181) requires the deepest variables bound by operators to be *terminal right branches*; nothing in this formulation mentions a left branch. Hence, it *treats left and center branches exactly the same way* and makes the same predictions for both.

Moreover, Kayne (1981b: note 36) cites an alternative statement of his results in Koster (1978a), which that author in other work calls the "Nesting Hypothesis" (Koster, 1978b: Ch. 2).[10] The latter prohibits material to the right of the most embedded bound category in "nested configurations" and does not refer to branching at all. Thus, even as we grant the correctness of the Kayne/ Koster approach to deeply embedded empty categories (they must be on right branches), we conclude that their theories of extraction and movement neither benefit from nor crucially use binary trees.

(iii) Case marking in double NP small clauses. Kayne (1981a: section 2) hypothesizes that English double objects form a clause-like constituent rather than each being a sister to V. Kayne (1983a) later advances two empirical arguments for this SC grouping of double NP complements. The first involves an ordering restriction by which English *post-verbal particles must precede all but a first NP complement.*[11]

(1.18) a. They are trying to make John out a liar.
        b. The secretary sent a memo out to the committee.
        c. The secretary sent the committee out a memo.

(1.19) a. *They are trying to make John a liar out.
        b. *The secretary sent a memo to the committee out.
        c. *The secretary sent the committee a memo out.

(1.20) a. ?They are trying to make out John a liar.
        b. The secretary sent out a memo to the committee.
        c. The secretary sent out the committee a memo.

Focusing on double NPs that contain secondary predication (the a examples), Kayne accounts for (1.19a) by means of "recursive small clauses": *make [$_{YP}$ [$_{XP}$ [$_{NP}$ John] [$_{X'}$ a liar]] [$_Y$ out]]*. Since *make* is not a sister of XP, the latter's subject *John* is ungoverned, hence not assigned case, hence ungrammatical. Presumably, the argument is meant to cover all examples in (1.19), for if it doesn't, it loses force due to its ad hoc coverage.

Kayne treats *out* here as the higher SC head. Assuming his solution is general, the underlying structure for the other alternations should therefore also be [$_{SC}$ [$_{SPEC}$ Ø] [$_{PRT}$ *out*] [$_{SC}$ NP – XP]] Overall, it would appear that V casemarks any NPs moved in front of particles (over one SC boundary), while those NP remaining in the deepest SC receive case from PRT (again over one SC).

In this case, the complements in the examples b–c should start out uniformly as [$_{SC}$ [$_{SPEC}$ Ø] *out* [$_{SC}$ [$_{NP}$ *the memo*]–[$_{PP}$ *to* [$_{NP}$ *the committee*]]]], with those NPs ending up in SPEC of the inner SC receiving case from *out*. However, this leaves the direct object *a memo* in the grammatical (1.20c) with no source for its case. Hence another ad hoc step is needed somewhere, so to my mind the approach loses any appeal as support for SCs. Moreover, nowhere does Kayne indicate how his account limits the distribution of these recursively nested SCs.

(iv) Deriving the adjacency condition on Case Assignment. Kayne (1983a) suggests that Stowell's (1981), perhaps English-particular adjacency requirement on V-object case assignment can be derived from requiring binary branching. He claims that assigning an NP a Θ-role is impossible for both the bracketings "[V Adv] NP" and "V [Adv NP]." Consequently, binary branching and Θ-role assignment principles together correctly exclude adverbs between a V and an NP it case-marks.

But these statements equally well exclude grammatical V-PP combinations such as *glance quickly into the room* and (idiomatic) *decide quickly on the boat*. In order for V to assign a Θ-role to PP, we now need either ternary branching or some other stipulation about Θ-roles equivalent to (or less general than) Stowell's (1981) adjacency condition on case-marking. Clearly nothing has been gained, so we may as well maintain the original adjacency condition. All told, there are no convincing arguments in Kayne (1983a) for small clause complement structures.

(v) Exclusion of Small Clauses in Nominalizations. Perhaps the most extensive and detailed syntactic defense of SC structures is Kayne's (1981a:

sections 3 and 4) study of their *absence* in English nominalizations. It is of course quite a tour de force to turn the complete absence of a category in a range of constructions into an argument for its *existence* elsewhere, but this is indeed the logic, and perhaps the appeal of Kayne's presentation.

For space reasons, I will not reproduce his many paradigms but only his numbering for them, since my judgments usually agree with his. Using data from various sources, he finds the following English configurations acceptable as verb complements but *not* as noun complements:

(1.21) a. Exceptional Case-Marking infinitives: paradigm (71)
 b. Secondary Predication: paradigm (73)
 c. NPs + obligatory control infinitives, e.g. after *persuade/ persuasion, compel/compulsion, encourage/encouragement*: paradigms (79), (84) and (86)
 d. Prepositionless double objects: paradigm (74)
 e. Complex Event Nominals with two NP complements, the first of which has a Goal role: paradigms (75), (76), (94) and (102)

In my view, however, independent and general reasons explain the ill-formed paradigms in all these nominalizations. In a framework with no small clauses, when Vs take either ECM clauses (a), secondary predication (b) or obligatory control complements (c), the subject or controller NPs of the embedded predicates are *sisters* to V and hence c-command these predicates, as required. In contrast, inside nominalizations these same NP need a case-marking P *of*, and being in PPs they fail to qualify as their predicates' c-commanding subjects (or controllers). This correctly excludes Kayne's paradigms in (1.21a-c). This explanation for (1.21b) is not specific to nominalizations; as is widely understood, objects of Ps, including in PP complements to Vs, are cross-linguistically *never* subjects of secondary predication. Paradigms (1.21a–c) thus do not count in favor of SC structures.

In English double object constructions, Barss and Lasnik (1986) show that a promoted indirect object must asymmetrically c-command a following direct object. But this necessary c-command again implies that a promoted object cannot receive case in a nominalization inside an *of*-headed PP, for it would then fail to c-command the direct object. This incompatibility accounts for paradigm (1.21d), again obviating any need to group two objects into an SC.[12]

Finally, Kayne's discussion sometimes misleadingly conflates properties that distinguish result nominals from complex event nominals (Grimshaw,

1991; Emonds, 2000a: Ch. 4). His ungrammatical nominalizations containing two NPs in (1.21e) are systematically event nominals whose Goal phrases are introduced by *of*. But independently of double complements, even single *of*-phrases in event nominals cannot express Goal phrases (Emonds, 1991b):[13]

(1.22) *The horse's jump of the fence was amazing (cf. jump the fence)
 *Your obedience of the law was long overdue. (cf. obey the law)
 *I don't like the boss's threat of strikers. (cf. threaten strikers)
 *Their robbery of Mary took 15 minutes.(cf. rob Mary of money)

An SC explanation of the paradigms (1.21e) is thus redundant.

Acceptable *of*-phrases in nominalizations with two NP complements must express Themes, as in fact attested in several of Kayne's paradigms. In these grammatical configurations, "on our reasoning, (91)–(93) evidently cannot be instances of the structure 'N [$_S$ NP PP]', ... Therefore, the PP [a Goal phrase, JE] must be exterior to the constituent containing N and NP '[[N NP] PP]." (Kayne, 1981a: 172) He thus admits that arguments for systematically replacing double complements with SCs here reach their limits.[14]

My case here against SCs in nominalizations might seem to require different explanations for different paradigms, in contrast to Kayne's unified account. However, his account is "unified" only because it depends on an ad hoc restriction applying to all the nominalizations under discussion:

(1.23) " ... the category N has the property that it, unlike the category V, can never govern across a sentence boundary." (Kayne, 1981a: 158).

It is actually this ad hoc restriction that guarantees that his SCs never occur inside NPs, not the SC hypothesis itself. In contrast, the approach here without small clauses accounts for the paradigms in (1.21) by general statements such as the definition of subject and an analysis of promoted indirect objects. It does indeed need a lexical restriction for complex event nominals (in which the item *of* can never introduce a true Goal), but one which is valid also for the single complement structures as in (1.22).

Kayne's "non-government of N across SC" (1.23) actually reflects a specific consequence of a more general principle of this volume's theory of complementation. Chapter 3 here develops a dichotomy between Direct and Indirect Θ-role Assignment, whereby complement XP inside NPs and APs can receive Θ-roles only "indirectly," which means they must occur inside PPs or CPs. This pattern generalizes to (1.24):

(1.24) *Deep Structure Case Filter. An argument projection* α^k other than PP must, prior to Spell Out, be a sister to a non-maximal projection β^j of V, P, I or D.

That is, no argument phrase α^k other than a PP can survive as a simple sister to N or A.[15] In most cases, Economy of Representation chooses P for β in (1.24), including inside NPs (Emonds, 2000a: Ch. 7). In this way, *both* NP complements and predicate attributes of an N are housed in PPs, unmarked *of*-phrases and *as*-phrases respectively. By the same reasoning, Exceptional Case Marked IPs must also be in CPs, a special case of PP; these intervening CPs between N and any ECM-type IP then *explain* why "the category N has the property that it, unlike the category V, can never govern across a sentence boundary."

The PP structures of underlying *of*-phrases remain unchanged if the NPs they dominate happen to move to possessive position.[16] Therefore, the same factors invoked above for excluding the untransformed paradigms listed in (1.21) also exclude the transformationally derived "objective possessive PPs" in Kayne's (1981a) paradigms (52), (62), (66) and (69).

In sum, however ingenious Kayne's system for explaining the lack of SCs in nominalizations, it is simply not needed. SCs don't occur in nominalizations because, more generally, they don't occur anywhere.

1.4 An Aristotelian legacy

As just seen, the syntactic arguments in favor of small clauses, which seemed to win over a majority of Chomskyan syntacticians, do not hold up under scrutiny. Both SC-based binary branching structures and those based on sisterhood equally well express subjecthood, binding domains for anaphors, and case-marking. Beyond these factors, expressing double complements through sisterhood and ternary branching is superior to small clauses in terms of categorial parsimony, computational simplicity and freedom from complex and ad hoc auxiliary hypotheses. Consequently, the burden of defending the SC proposals rests on the validity of independent syntactic arguments in their favor -- and as shown, these arguments just don't work.

Since so many Chomskyan syntacticians have not seen things this way, is it simply that they dispassionately evaluate the above arguments for SCs more favorably? I suspect rather that some deeper linguistic prejudice has made small clauses impervious to disconfirmation. If we can unearth some other plausible rationale for SC popularity, perhaps readers will better appreciate well motivated alternatives without feeling uneasy about the absence of small clauses.

As section 1.2 emphasized, the banner under which the small clause contingent has marched is that of "binary branching." The tactic has been to put forward as many SC analyses as possible for double complement structures. At stake are two kinds of double complements and a different strategy for each:

(1.25) Double complements which can't plausibly be analyzed in some kind of subject-predicate relation, e.g. those with *look, prevent, promise, require, rob, speak, strike, suggest* (section 2.2.1 below).
Strategy: Avoid discussion.

(1.26) Double complements XP-YP which, with the help of loose paraphrase and abstract linking formatives (akin to *be, have, become*, etc.), can be plausibly related to a predication [XP – YP].
Strategy: Present the properties of these sequences as support for yet another type of SC.

According to this battle plan, the real enthusiasm and effort of the linguist has been directed toward supporting the following:

(1.27) Every semantic proposition ω, defined as a grouping of subject and predicate *and nothing else*, is represented in natural language by a syntactic category.

This notion of a binary proposition as a basic *unit* of (compositional) semantics is of course from Aristotelian logic. I claim that a priori adherence to the semantically motivated (1.27) is what won the initial battle for the small clause. For supporters, even though the SC may be the most elusive variant of ω, it is still (and perhaps therefore) its most cherished embodiment.

Among researchers currently interested in formal semantic analyses of natural language, Fregean dissenters from the Aristotelian paradigm generally embrace some model of formal semantics with little regard for tenets of Chomskyan syntax. Chomskyans on the other hand remain convinced of the importance of the subject-predicate dichotomy in analyzing and interpreting sentences. It is no accident that for many years, Chomsky's (1957) original rule S → NP – VP was almost heraldic of the transformational approach, even though the main point of *Syntactic Structures* was to demonstraate the inadequacy of such rules.

That is, Chomskyan syntacticians including myself have continuously supported at least (1.28):

(1.28) Many semantic propositions ω, defined as groupings of subject and predicate and nothing else, are represented in natural language by a syntactic category σ. Moreover, σ is the privileged initial symbol and recursive category of computational syntax.

From this perspective, it is clear that small clause advocacy (1.27) is an *overextension* of (1.28). It is an intrusion of logical semantic intuition into syntax, a legacy of unexamined assumptions. But the facts of syntax actually provide *no justifications* for the too general (1.27). As a result, SC analyses are by now at cross-purposes with further development of empirically justified syntactic theory. So the postulation of small clauses as default analyses for multiple complements should be abandoned.

Notes

* This introduction to the category system used here throughout is a somewhat shortened version of Emonds (2000a: section 1.2).
1. An exact inventory of the categories in a theory cannot be required a priori, since otherwise the theory would be fully specified before investigation begins. No scientist can demand that an exact inventory of all distinctive features precede research in formal phonology, that a full inventory of chemical elements precede experimentation based on the periodic table, or that a complete inventory of elementary particles precede work in atomic physics. In fact, one rationale for pursuing a science is to arrive at such inventories.
2. It is not obvious that expletives such as *there* in the supposedly phrasal position SPEC(IP) or unmodifiable markers such as *whether*, *why*, French *dont* 'of which' in SPEC(CP) are phrasal, other than by assumption.
   On the other hand, certain finer analyses of extended projections of A (Corver, 1997) and P (van Riemsdijk, 1998b) argue that head and phrasal positions can be kept distinct, in line with suggestions in Chomsky (1986).
3. These include (i) coordinate conjunctions, (ii) the discourse particles or "delimiters" of several languages *even, only, also*, etc. which attach to any XP (Kuroda, 1965), and (iii) the emphatic particles *too, so, either* which appear only with finite verbs. (ii) and (iii) seem to escape classification as specifiers pre-

cisely because they can occur with them. The category of emphatic particles is also uncertain; perhaps, as argued in Laka (1990), they constitute a separate class of functional heads.

4. I do not identify all the features which traditional grammar associates with a lexical category as its features in UG; e.g. analyses of English, Kru languages (Koopman, 1984) and Chinese (Huang, 1990) have shown that TENSE is not a V feature but rather a separate category. But neither do I assume a priori that every syntactic feature projects as a separate head.

5. The feature +N unifying nouns and adjectives was historically adopted without regard to this issue of whether plus values of features can always correspond to marked values. A little reflection, however, shows that -N (V and P) is a marked value. N is certainly the unmarked word class, while P is the least numerous and hence plausibly the most marked.

6. Studies of types of aphasia invariably show that forms of the English copula group with closed class elements. But since such research is not examining any proposal to group morphemes except as members or non-members of the four lexical classes, it does not systematically investigate whether grammatical members of these classes differ from open class items.

7. The essays constituting Chapters 2, 3 and 4 here argue that no single verb may assign theta roles to *both* NP and XP. To account for this and for other paradigms, these chapters propose a simple "Revised Theta Criterion.," whereby "theta relatedness is anti-transitive." Since a subject/ predicate pair { NP, XP } are in a theta relation, they cannot then both be theta-related to the same V. Further implications are investigated in e.g. section 2.2.3.

8. Indeed, arguments in their defense grow more bold; small clauses are endowed with unique properties to insulate them from disconfirmation. Consider for example Kayne's (1983a, X) "small clause transparency": "Taking small clauses to be maximal projections ..., transparent to government only when the governor and the maximal projections are sisters ..." Thus, if in its base position an SC is a sister to a (governing) V or P, it acts as though it isn't there (it is transparent). Anywhere else (either base-generated in a non-case position or moved), an SC is ill-formed because its subject languishes without case, unavailable in these positions. Thus, SCs are finally either ill-formed or invisible, so that every failure to exhibit a syntactic property ends up a "confirmation" of small clause theory.

9. If use of argument information in lexical entries was not constrained by Economy arguments could occur anywhere–not even near their head.

10. Koster (1978b) briefly mentions some facts of P stranding in Dutch and then formulates a Nesting Hypothesis in terms of forbidding certain material on both the left and right of empty categories. His hypothesis can be better compared to Kayne's system by abstracting away from the stranding facts and limiting it to what is forbidden on the *right* of empty categories.

11. As noted in Emonds (1972), where this paradigm was first discussed, idiolects differ with respect to the status of the patterns in (1.18c) and (1.20c). Judgments here are the author's, and the problem with Kayne's analysis concerns properly describing this system.
12. Here the (cross-linguistic) motivation for c-command holds for applicative constructions in a range of languages, as demonstrated in the analysis of promoted oblique objects in Chapter 5. Although the reason for c-command is different than "subjecthood," the result is the same (no counterparts with *of*-phrases in nominalizations).
13. Kayne's nominalizations with *of*-phrases expressing Goals strike me as result nominals when embedded in full sentences:
??Mary's persuasion of John took a long time.
??The judge's acquittal of John took five minutes.
14. These limits lead to at least a highly ad hoc proviso. Kayne holds that the Source/ Goal PPs outside [X^0 YP] (*John's theft of the money from Mary; John's presentation of a medal to Mary*) receive Θ-roles from X^0, but above in paragraph (iv), he claims an NP could not receive a Θ-role in the same configuration.
15. The more complete treatment in Emonds (2000a, Ch. 7) explains *why* a PP always satisfies (1.24).
16. If NP objects of the Ps that provide "deep case" move to A-positions (e.g, a possessive or a promoted indirect object position), the Ps are licensed to remain empty according to a co-indexing convention discussed in section 5.1 of this volume.

Chapter 2
The restricted complement space of lexical frames*

2.1 The range of single phrase complements to verbs

In defending subcategorization as the sole lexical device for stating co-occurrence restrictions, Emonds (2000a, Chapter 2) argues that Chomsky's original conceptions need revision. Under certain conditions non-phrasal categories and sometimes non-sister categories satisfy frames of the form X, +___Y. Justifying these extensions and the constraints on them is a principal focus of that book.

Yet it should be kept in mind that these extensions concern only unstipulated universal representational *interpretations* of the lexical formulae employed. The actual lexical formalisms imputed to the ideal speaker-hearer (i.e. the formal grammar) are far more restricted than in any earlier framework – they are reduced to the ultra-simple format in (2.1) below. Even with the extensions on interpreting X, +___Y, the range of complement types and combinations does not much exceed those listed in Chomsky (1965, Ch. 2).[1]

These complement types, plus a few familiar additions such as English double objects, are common currency in syntactic analyses. This does not mean, however, that generative grammar has been operating with a model of why these types and combinations exist and not others. In fact, since embracing "s-selection" around 1980 it has not in practice even included a device to formally describe them – running on empty, so to speak. Precisely for this reason, formal modeling would have been better served by at least maintaining classical subcategorization. This work not only maintains subcategorization but I hope has significantly expanded the areas where it provides descriptive generalizations and explanations.

The sole subcategorization device needed for stating lexical combinations of a lexical item α with material exterior to any Z^0 which dominates it is the canonical frame in (2.1):

(2.1) Canonical lexical item: α, X, F_i, f_j, +___F_k

X is the category of α, the F_i are its inherent cognitive syntactic features, the f_j its inherent purely semantic features and the F_k are features in the subcategorization frame. An order-free notation replacing ___F_k with <F_k> is justified in Emonds (2000a, Chapter 3), but since this chapter will not discuss any Z^0-internal frames (for which the symbol ___F_k is more appropriate), I often use here the older, familiar notation in (2.1). That is, in this chapter ___F_k and <F_k> are entirely equivalent.

It is frames of this form that formally describe head complement combinations according to Generalized Subcategorization (2.2).

(2.2) *Generalized Subcategorization.* α, X, +<F> *is satisfied if and only if F is a syntactic feature of a sister β of X^0* = α *or of β's lexical head.*

We will investigate in this first section the range of possible sets of F_k for *single* complements and in Section 2.2 any combinations of *multiple complements* which (2.1) can generate. The goal is to propose a hypothesis for characterizing the notion "possible lexical entry" and *hence set limits on what kinds of frames a child can learn* – i.e. not to shift implications of the poverty of the stimulus argument for universal grammar to some other component such as conceptual semantics, but instread to directly constrain and thereby explain them.

2.1.1 *Variations on the frames* ___D, ___A *and* ___P

The widest range of complement types occurs with verbs, so in setting an upper limit on lexical frames, I concentrate on when X is V in (2.1) and (2.2).[2] The most prosaic frames are +___D for simple transitivity and +___A for predicate adjectives (*seem, become, get, remain,* etc.). Subclasses of these complement types are chosen by frames such as +___[D, ANIMATE] (*frighten*), +___[D, PLURAL] (*disperse*), and +___[A, INHERENT] (Spanish *ser* 'be').[3]

The frame ___P calls for more comment. Verbs such as *glance* and *reside* (from the list of prototypical frames in Chomsky, 1965, Ch. 2) and *go* plausibly have entries as in (2.3). For such entries, I assume there are some "underspecification" principles of lexical form which permit not stipulating (i) certain unmarked values of features and (ii) certain features with less specificity in the presence of those with more. Exactly how many features can be deduced rather than stipulated is not a central concern here.

(2.3) a. glance, V, +___[P, SPACE, PATH]
   b. reside, V, STATIVE, +___[P, SPACE, PLACE]
   c. go, V, (STATIVE), +___[P, LOCATION]⁴

The feature value -STATIVE (= ACTIVITY) with V is unmarked, and LOCATION is less specific than PATH or PLACE, so these features need not appear in (2.3a-b).

The broad distribution of *go* is exemplified in (2.4):

(2.4) a. This ugly machine goes {into the trunk, near the others, by the door, downstairs, outside, at the entrance, to the foreman, *of the director, *for another firm, *about the sale, *instead of that}.
   b. The meeting {will go until six/ has been going since six/ goes on}.
   c. This suitcase goes {without postage/ with your hat/ by train/ off (soon)}.

Of course, verbs irrespective of their class can appear with PP *adjuncts* of static location; these unselected PPs are not at issue here.

There are still redundancies in (2.3); stative verbs (*reside*) have PP complements of static location (PLACE) while activity verbs (*glance*) take complements of direction toward (PATH) or of source ([PATH, SOURCE]). It is thus likely that item-particular contextual specifications for PATH vs. PLACE complements are unnecessary. The few optionally stative verbs like *go*, illustrated in (2.4), can be listed as (STATIVE); hence their PP complements can be *either* of static location or of direction toward.

Another question for refining the lexical formalism is whether the frames +___P and +___[P, LOCATION] are distinct. At first glance no verb would seem to have a subcategorization that can be satisfied by *any* PP (headed by say *toward, at, for, by, of, without, despite,* etc.) irrespective of its cognitive content, so perhaps the simpler frame +___P should always be interpreted as +___[P, LOCATION].⁵ However this question is resolved, predicted frames of the form +___[P, F] are attested and remain well within the limits on lexical entries set by (2.1).

30 *Structures in lexical projections*

2.1.2 *The predicate nominal frame +___N*

The present framework using the canonical notation (2.1) predicts the existence of lexical entries of the form V, +<N> (i.e. V, +___N). The conjuncture of this frame with Abney's (1987) DP Hypothesis makes some novel but I think correct predictions. According to a theory of extended lexical projections (see Emonds, 2000a, Ch. 1, or Chapter 9 of this volume for one version), any NP complement selected by V, +___N must further project to DP. But at the same time, the N must remain the lexical head of this DP, in accord with the definition of lexical head of Emonds (2000a: Ch. 4).[6] Thus at the point of lexical insertion of V, the selected complement has an internal structure with an empty D as in (2.5).

(2.5) Complement generated by V, +___N at the point of inserting V:

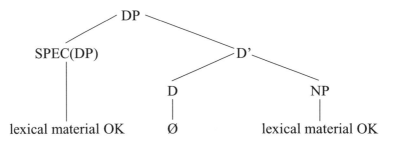

So the question is, does some complement type systematically exclude morphemes of a category D, with the possible exception of members of D that are inserted late at PF? Such complements are expected to be generated by the frame +___N.[7]

Abney (1987) does not actually establish any argued link between his D category and some specific class of English modifiers. But Lobeck (1995, Ch. 3) carefully integrates previous research on noun-modifying paradigms, and concludes that the head D is best identified with Jackendoff's (1977, Ch. 4) leftmost pre-nominal morpheme class SPEC(N''): *some, any, no, every, each, which, what*, etc. Her evidence based on NP-ellipsis then further confirms this choice. Lobeck thus establishes independently of our present concerns that D is precisely the category name of demonstratives, WH-determiners, and Jackendoff's non-adjectival quantifiers.

It is therefore of interest that a certain type of verbal complement, namely predicate nominals, excludes these Determiners. As seen in (2.6a-b), they do not tolerate non-adjectival quantifiers. Moreover, predicate nominals do not freely permit demonstratives (2.6c) or WH-determiners (2.6d).

(2.6) a. *Mary's sons {became/ looked/ remained/ seemed/ will be} {every local teacher/ each town clerk/ no successes/ some other friends}.
b. *{I don't consider his son/ Nobody could judge him/ We hired you as} {any friend/ each teacher/ some expert}.
c. *Mary's daughter became this famous success.
*Her son looked that available bachelor.
*Her children still remain these friends of mine.
*I don't consider his sons those good teachers.
*We hired you as this expert.
d. *{What/ Which} expert did Sam seem?
*Which expert did she expect to {become/ feel/ remain}?
*{What/ which} teacher did they judge you?

The elements excluded in selected predicate nominals are thus of Lobeck's category D. But since subcategorization theory predicts that a complement selected by +___N should exhibit exactly this restriction, as illustrated in (2.5), one naturally concludes that predicate nominals result from the frames V, +___N (for intransitives) and V, +___D, N (for transitives).

One could be led astray by focusing only on the form of the most frequently studied predicate nominals, those with the copula *be*. These latter can indeed include demonstratives and WH-modifiers, particularly in those predicate nominals with a specificational rather than a predicational sense (cf. Heycock and Kroch, 1999), as well as somewhat contrived uses of quantifiers:[8]

(2.7) Mary's daughter is that famous actress.
His cousins are those good teachers.
Which expert could that person have been?
What teacher are you, the chemistry teacher?
His children were all the friends I had.
John has never been any help.

But *be* is the otherwise unmarked stative verb inserted in PF via the very general frame +___X (= +<X>). This implies that *be* can have either a predicate nominal complement (2.5) like other linking verbs *or* a full DP complement as in (2.7). Hence the contrast between (2.6) and (2.7) is fully expected and in fact predicted by the differing subcategorizations of *be* and other linking verbs.

If one tried to simply generate English predicate nominals using Abney's phrase structure and a classical subcategorization frame +___NP, their internal possessive phrases and articles as in (2.8) would falsify the proposal.

(2.8) a. Mary's son {became/ looked/ remained/ seemed} {the dutiful teacher/ a (young woman's) manly ideal}.
She wanted to {become/ feel/ remain} {the/ a/ its} tobacco expert.
b. {I don't consider his son/ Nobody could judge you/ We hired you as} {the best speaker/ a good speaker/ his equal/ the town's hope}.

In contrast, these data actually *confirm* the present framework, because the theory of extended lexical projections requires that an NP appear *within a DP shell*. Consequently, predicate nominals generated by +___N should tolerate both possessive DPs, which are under SPEC(DP), and definite articles, which are inserted in PF and hence not present under D when a verb selects a phrase with the structure (2.5).

Finally, it is well-known that cross-linguistically verbs do not assign accusative case to predicate nominals; predicate nominals either agree with the DP they modify, receive some oblique case, or are morphologically caseless. Generating predicate nominals via the frame +___N can explain why the verb which selects them fails to mark them for case. To this end I replace the usual simple list of potential case assigners with the more accurate (2.9).

(2.9) *Case Indices. The case assigners are I, D and any V or P whose lexical realizations satisfy +___Y, where Y = I or D.*

Case itself consists of these very assigners appearing as features on nominal projections, which we can then call "case indices."[9]

The condition on V and P in (2.9) directly links case-assignment with subcategorization frames. A DP above a predicate nominal as in (2.5) results not from +___D, but rather from the theory of extended projections applying to an NP generated by a frame α, +___N or +___X, where α = *be, become*, etc. Therefore, α does not assign case to such a DP. This general restriction on case assigners thus blocks case on predicate nominals.

This restriction affects not only linking verbs but also certain grammatical P. As discussed in Emonds (1985, Ch. 6), a DP complement of the "copular P," non-comparative *as*, shares all predicate nominal properties, such as the exclusion of lexical choices for D seen in (2.6). Its frame is therefore +___N rather than +___D, and as predicted by (2.9), its counterparts in for example Czech *jako* 'as' and German *als* 'as' fail to assign a morphological case. Case Indices (2.9) thus eliminates stipulative features by which individual V or P "fail to assign case," replacing this with a mechanism that expresses a general and eminently predictable cross-linguistic pattern.

Another function of Case Indices is to guarantee that any V or P whose IP complements are subcategorized for obligatory control via the feature +___V, such as French *à* or *de* or possibly English *whether*, will fail to assign case within this IP. Since (2.9) requires Y to be I or D, no X^0 whose complement satisfies rather +___V can assign case. Thus, whether a given IP "blocks" or "allows" case to be assigned across it is predictable on the basis of the frame it satisfies; if IP results from V, +___I, the V can assign case, but if IP results from V, +___V, case cannot be assigned.[10]

2.1.3 Variations on the frames ___V and ___I

Perhaps the central conceptual difference between subcategorization in this work and Chomsky's classic proposals is that there is no longer a one-to-one (i.e. redundant) relation between the notations in the lexical frames +<Y^0> and the tree structures which they license: (i) The canonical lexical frames of (2.1) do not mention phrases, even though they generally do license them. (ii) A frame such as +<D> projects not only to a DP but in many cases to a higher PP as well (Emonds, 2000a, Ch. 7). (iii) An entry such as X^0, +<N> can generate either a flat structure if X = N (e.g., the pseudo-partitive or numeric classifier constructions in Chapter 6 of this volume), as well as predicate nominal NP phrases, which are themselves further embedded in DPs required by the extended lexical projection theory of Chapter 9.

These sorts of complex interactions between simple lexical frames and general category-independent principles are nowhere more evident than in the area of clausal complement selection by +___V and +___I.

(i) Selection by the frame +___V: obligatory control. I only briefly summarize general properties which are uniformly associated with +___V.[11] First I review default cases where the selected V projects to *at least a phrase XP*, namely a VP or NP. In such situations, the theory of extended projections (Chapter 9, this volume) immediately requires an extended projection ZP above XP. Then Generalized Subcategorization (2.2) requires that any such higher projected phrase (such as an infinitival IP or a gerundive DP) have an empty head, because the selected V must remain the lexical head of ZP (cf. the definition of "lexical head" in note 6.). Assuming now that empty functional heads don't assign case, any subject DP inside ZP can pass the Case Filter only if it is null, i.e., any higher ZP projected to satisfy +___V will exhibit obligatory control.[12] Moreover, at least for English, it seems that +___*V is the principal and perhaps only source of obligatory control.*[13]

A second type of realization of +___V as a *flat structure* results from a conjuncture of two conditions: occurring both (i) in a lexical entry of a closed class verb and (ii) in a language which freely allows co-indexing of a post-verbal subject with the position SPEC(IP). Standard Italian and Spanish are two such languages, and so grammatical verbs in their Syntacticons with the frames +<V> (restructuring verbs) or +<V, D> (causative and perception verbs) may appear *as sisters to V* as well as to V-headed phrasal structures. These structures are justified in detail in Chapters 6 and 7 of this volume.

(ii) Selection by the frame +___I: epistemic verbs. Let us turn next to how two variants of the lexical frame +___I generate certain finite clausal complements and certain types of English infinitives as well. Two familiar classes of verbs exemplify such complements and are thus specified as +___I: so-called epistemic verbs such as *assume, believe, consider, declare, imagine, judge, suppose,* etc. (2.10) and verbs of the *(dis)like* type: *dislike, hate, like, love, prefer,* etc. (2.11). *Expect* apparently belongs to both classes.[14]

(2.10) a. Jim imagines that {this city/ he} is more important than his school.
b. Jim imagines {this city/ himself} to be more important than his school.

(2.11) a. Most men (dis)like (it) {that/ if} a woman drives fast.
b. Most men (dis)like a woman to drive fast.

Consider first the standard case where I is *finite* in the (a) examples of (2.10)–(2.11). As with all embedded English finite clauses, an I with lexical content requires a lexical subject. For both these verb classes, a finite clause IP satisfies their frame +___I.

A finite IP selected by +___I may well be further embedded in a CP, whose head is necessarily empty (i.e. inserted in PF) in accord with the definition of lexical head (see note 6). This unmarked C with no intrinsic features is spelled out as *that* by late insertion in PF. With or without this CP, a finite clause in this kind of CP structure can thus satisfy +___I.

(iii) Selection by the frame +___SUBJUN: exceptional case marking.
The *infinitives* in (2.10b) and (2.11b) exemplify so-called "exceptional case marking" (ECM) complements, which these two classes of English verbs (but no others) permit. Besides their case property, they have three other co-inciding properties:

(a) Unlike finite clauses, ECM infinitives do not express tense.

(b) ECM infinitives must be a marked configuration, since a language such as French with syntax not so different from English excludes them.

(c) ECM infinitives do not freely occur with all verbs of similar semantics, as seen in (2.12). They thus seem syntactically selected on an item-particular basis.

(2.12)   *Jim {concluded/ confirmed/ denied/ feared/ hoped/ recalled} {this city/ himself} to be more important than his school.

The key to understanding the ECM infinitives requires appeal, I think, to a cross-linguistic feature on I, namely SUBJUN ("subjunctive"). Two salient facts about this feature in Romance languages, where it is morphologically overt, are relevant. First, SUBJUN appears to be an *absence of content feature* on I (cf. Ch. 1). As argued in Picallo (1984), although Catalan subjunctive morphemes realize finite agreements in PF, they are *not* tense morphemes with LF content. Therefore, using SUBJUN for English ECM complements can explain why their temporal sense is more neutral, less "realis," than their finite counterparts.

Second, the very fact that individual verbs in Romance languages vary as to whether they select a subjunctive complement demonstrates that +___SUBJUN is a marked lexical frame.[15] My proposal is then simply to extend this frame to only those English verbs which permit ECM infinitives as in (2.10b) and (2.11b), even though no morphemes in the current English Syntacticon express only this feature.[16] Precisely because of this latter fact, [I, SUBJUN] is empty in English at Spell Out and hence fails to assign nominative case. Consequently, the "next closest" case-assigner, the verb which selects I, assigns accusative case to the embedded subject.

Selecting ECM infinitives by the frame +___[I, SUBJUN] or +___[I, (SUBJUN)] thus explains their case property and all of (i)–(iii) above.

If this analysis of ECM is correct, the cross-linguistic role of the frame +___SUBJUN must be to allow an interpretation for an otherwise contentless, syntactically empty I in LF. Nonetheless, legitimizing a contentless form in LF does not suffice to license an empty I in PF; this requires phonological realization, provided in English by the all purpose infinitival marker *to*.

A striking property of ECM infinitives is that their subjects receive case precisely from the verbs which select them. I have accounted for this by formulating the list of Case Assigners (2.9) not only to cover standard assignment of accusative (case index V) and dative (case index P) but by extending them to V and P which select IPs. Thus, when nominative and/or genitive are for any reason not available to lower subjects in an IP or DP, an adjacent case assigner *exterior to* IP or DP can provide the subject with case.

(2.13) *Case Assignment Condition. A case assigner β becomes a case index on DP if among DP's potential case assigners some βʲ is the lowest non-maximal projection which c-commands DP.*[17]

(iv) Optional control. We have now covered obligatory control infinitives generated by +___V and ECM infinitives generated by +___[I, SUBJUN]. It remains to discuss *for-to* infinitives of optional control, which occur with the *(dis)like* class but not epistemic verbs.

(a) In some configurations, *for-to* infinitives are *not selected as complements*. For example, they simply exemplify freely generated IPs as adjunct purpose clauses or as topicalized DPs in root declaratives.[18] These IPs must then be sisters to a higher empty head P (= C), by virtue of the Deep Case Filter of Emonds (2000a, Ch. 7), reproduced below as (2.44).

(2.14)

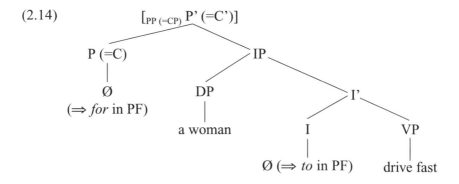

Like ECM verbs, the P *for* can have an IP complement selected by +___SUBJUN. The subject DP of this infinitive also receives case from P in accord with (2.13). As is widely recognized, the IP in *for-to* clauses resembles ECM clauses in having an irrealis sense; it typically paraphrases a finite IP with a modal. The unified lexical entry (2.15) expresses these properties of *for*:

(2.15) for, P, (LOC'), {+___D / +___[I, SUBJUN]}

LOC' is some cognitive syntactic content feature which minimally distinguishes *for* from the PATH preposition *to*.[19] Since clauses (P+IP) don't express space/ time and thus lack PATH, the feature LOC' is apparently uninterpretable, so in these cases *for* must be inserted in PF. The use of SUBJUN in (2.15) expresses the formal parallel with ECM constructions.

(b) In other contexts, *for-to* clauses are *selected complements*, and *for* itself often seems to carry meaning in LF. A wide range of predicates which select PP complements headed by *for* also select *for-to* clauses: *arrange, beg, hope, plan, prepare, pray, wait, anxious, eager, ready, chance, reason, time,* many manner of speaking verbs, etc. These predicates can be analyzed as having an eminently simple lexical frame +___LOC'; the fact that they accept alternately both *for* + DP and and *for* + IP then simply follows from the entry (2.15). That is, these predicates do not themselves have the frame +___I (unless they are additionally in the ECM class), but they select *for*, which in turn crucially uses the frame in (2.15).[20]

This then completes the review of a full range of finite and infinitival complements of the epistemic and *(dis)like* classes of verbs. Either directly or indirectly these complement structures involve the simple lexical frame +___[I, F_i], for some cognitive syntactic feature F such as SUBJUN.

Let's now review all the basic frames available for single complements of predicates. The restrictive syntactic category theory of Chapters 1 and 9 provides six head categories X: N, V, A, P, D, and I. The theory of subcategorization developed in Emonds (2000a) then expects different classes of predicates to realize all six frames of the form V, +___X, and indeed we have seen that familiar and much studied classes of complements correspond to all the predicted classes. For English, (2.16) then constitutes a rough table of equivalents between the frames available in the category system and the structures they project.

(2.16) Frame: Some instantiating complement structures:
V, +<D> Direct objects of transitive verbs
V, +<A> Predicate adjectives
V, +<P> Path PPs with activity verbs and Place PPs with statives
V, +<N> Predicate nominals
V, +<V> Participles, gerunds and infinitives of obligatory control
V, +<I> Complements of epistemic and *(dis)like* class verbs

2.1.4 Extrinsic features in single frames

We have seen scattered instances of subcategorization frames which require intermediate heads which are empty in the syntax, but are nonetheless specified for certain feature values. For example, marked indirect objects introduced by *of* rather than *to* require some kind of lexical stipulation.

(2.17) She {asked/ demanded/ required} {of/ *to} Bill that he be early.

Similarly, while verbs such as *wonder* and *inquire* whose only clausal complements are indirect questions can be listed with the frame +___WH, other predicates (*explain, know*, etc.) which take either a *that*-clause or an indirect question require a slightly more complex frame, which can be notated as (WH)^IP. However, our general subcategorization formalism (2.1) has eliminated the ad hoc concatenation sign from lexical frames, except perhaps to express truly idiomatic sequences.

We therefore need some notation to express marked features required on empty intermediate heads (i.e., those inserted in PF), for which I propose the following:

(2.18) *Subcategorized Features Convention. A feature complex in a lexical frame can be written in an ordered sequence +___[F$_1$, ..., F$_i$, ...], where at least F$_1$ is in its interpretable canonical position.*

The canonical position of a feature is that determined by Canonical Realization, as discussed with respect to (1.5) in Chapter 1. Any other F$_i$ whose canonical position is not that of F$_1$ must be interpreted as a feature on some intermediate empty head permitted by Generalized Subcategorization (2.2) and Economy of Representation.[21] The formulation (2.18) has the probably correct consequence that subcategorization cannot select morphemes expressing *only* alternatively realized features, because no such feature satisfies the condition on F$_1$.

The restricted complement space of lexical frames 39

With this clarification, we can now list in (2.19a) the extra features needed for the (optional) marked indirect objects of source in (2.17), and in (2.19b) the (optional) indirect question feature for verbs like *explain*. These entries are partial, as I put aside alternative frames not exemplifying (2.18).

(2.19) a. ask, V, +< D, ([ANIMATE, SOURCE]), ... >, ...
      b. explain, V, +< [I, (WH)], ... >, ...

In (2.19a), F_1 is ANIMATE, which must therefore be realized in its canonical position on the head of a DP. Since the canonical position of F_2 = SOURCE is not that of F_1 (that is, in this case, D), SOURCE must be a feature of a higher empty head, namely the PP required for assigning case to the second DP complement of *ask*.

Similarly, the node I is the F_1 for the complement of *explain* in (2.19b), which must be in its canonical position as head of an IP. If the optional WH is not chosen, a simple *that*-clause results, as explained in the previous subsection. But if WH is chosen (i.e. when *explain* takes an indirect question), since its canonical position is not I, it must be a feature of an intermediate empty head, namely a C sister of IP.

We have already seen other constructions which require the Subcategorized Features Convention (2.18). Two have been mentioned in discussions of subcategorized clausal complements:

(i) Note 20 evokes the possibility of an English verb such as *intend* that is subcategorized for a *for-to* clause but not for *for*+DP: such a verb would have the frame +___[I, LOC'], parallel to [I, (WH)].

(ii) The lexical entries for certain obligatory control verbs can be refined to reflect the fact that their infinitival complements have more of an irrealis sense than participles or gerunds. E.g., *He should manage to leave* vs. *He should manage leaving*. In the entries (2.20), adding the feature MODAL to the obligatory control subcategorization frame +<V> leads to a projection up to IP, whereby MODAL can furnish the irrealis part of the interpretation. If MODAL is obligatory (*decide*), this forces the presence of an infinitival IP in place of a verb phrase introduced by *-ing*.

(2.20) manage, V, +< [V, (MODAL)] >, ...
      try, V, +< [ACTIVITY, (MODAL)] >, ...
      decide, V, +< [ACTIVITY, MODAL] >, ...

These entries conform to the Subcategorized Features Convention (2.18).

2.2 Limitations on multiple complements

2.2.1 The puzzling descriptive generalizations

From the previous section, we can conclude that all subcategorization frames X, +<Y> for single complements are robustly exemplified in the English lexicon, for all expected values of Y. The question now arises, what combinations of complements can appear in a single frame? That is, how many lexical entries do we find of the form X, <Y, Z ...> where Y, Z, ... each take on all the same potential values as earlier: N, A, V, P, D, I?

Throughout this section, I will use the table (2.16) of typical complement types to exemplify various possible combinations.

(i) Direct objects with a second complement. There do indeed occur many structures containing two complements. To start with, *direct objects combine with all six values of Z*, instantiating the frames +<D, Z> and surveyed below in (2.21)–(2.26). As allowed by Generalized Subcategorization (2.2), a canonical cognitive syntactic feature of Z sometimes appears instead of Z, e.g., ANIMATE can replace D, PATH can replace P, etc. So as to satisfy the Deep Case Filter, given below in this chapter as (2.44), any second subcategorized DP must be generated inside a PP in order to receive a case from a grammatical P.

(2.21) The second complement Z is D or P, yielding indirect objects or PPs:[22]
give, V, +<D, D>   recommend, V, +<D, (ANIM)>
ask, V, +<D, ([ANIM, SOURCE])>   hand, V, +<D, {ANIM/ PATH}>
put, V, +<D, PATH>   situate, V, +<D, (PLACE)>

(2.22) The second complement Z is A or N, yielding secondary predication on a direct object:
render a poison harmless   name an unknown person the winner
consider John stupid   consider John a nuisance
paint the house red   call his friends copies of each other
declare any addiction illegal   declare any addiction a capital crime
describe Mary as paranoid   describe Mary as an artist

(2.23) The second complement Z is V, I or C, yielding a clausal complement:
catch Mary studying in the library
see Mary study(ing) in the library
persuade John {that it is raining/ to look for a job}
remind John when {he has an appointment/ to leave the meeting}

A second complement generated by the obligatory control frame +<V> can be specified for an additional feature, as in (2.24).

(2.24) prevent, V, +<D, [V, SOURCE]>
discourage, V, +<D, ([V, SOURCE])>

The Subcategorized Features Convention (2.18) requires that the non-verbal feature SOURCE in (2.24) be realized on an intermediate empty head P. In this way, a DP-gerund can be forced to appear as a second complement (2.25a) even when such a DP is not itself lexically selected (2.25b):

(2.25) a. That will {prevent/ discourage} us from studying in the library:
b. *Your reaction prevented Mary from serious work.
*Let's not discourage Mary from a vacation.

This contrast illustrates that DP gerunds can occur where lexically selected DPs cannot. It is furthermore well-known that not every DP position which alternates with clauses accepts a gerund: *John believed the box being open. This latter fact, in conjunction with the frames in (2.24), consequently demonstrates the full independence of the two subcategorization features +<D> and +<V>.

Most possibilities for the frame V, +<D, Z> are realized with the single verb *find*, whose lexical entry is (2.26a). Its direct object can accept secondary predication with all four lexical categories X (= N, A, V, P) as in (2.26b), and it also accepts indirect objects (2.26c) and clausal complements (2.26d).

(2.26) a. find, V, +<{D, (X) / [I, (SUBJUN)]}>, where X is not I:
b. secondary predication, where X = N, A, V, P:[23]
John found Mary {a pest/ very ill/ studying in a library/ in the garden}.
*I find my children$_i$ {some pests$_i$ / those clowns$_i$ / that it's tiring}.

c. indirect objects, where X = D:
John found good schools for his son.
John found his son good schools.
d. clausal complements, where I includes ECM complements:
John found that the lesson would be difficult.
John found the lesson to be difficult.

Earlier or competing lexical frameworks using semantic selection, theta grids or conceptual structures, etc. would be hard pressed to succinctly express the complement range of this versatile verb.

(ii) Indirect objects with a second complement. The next examples in (2.27)–(2.28) show that secondary predicates can also occur with *indirect* objects. Since in configurations without a direct object the Case Filter does not force oblique case, the lexical frame itself must be responsible for some feature such as LOC that induces a minimal case-assigning PP structure for the indirect object. In a frame +<Y, Z> indicating two such complements then, the indirect object Y is specified by as e.g., [D, LOC] or [ANIMATE, LOC], in accord with the Subcategorized Features Convention (2.18).

For example, since the (italicized) predicate adjectives and nominals in (2.27) do not themselves license *to*-phrase complements, the linking verbs themselves must be selecting the indirect objects.

(2.27) The second complement Z is A or N, yielding indirect object plus predicate attribute:
Sue seems *quite confident* to me.
That cod tasted *too salty* to Mary.
Sam has always been *a brother* to me.
The horse Doctor Syntax appeared *the winner* to some of them.

In contrast to secondary predications with direct objects, predicate attributes generated in the double complement constructions like (2.27) modify the *subject* rather than the indirect object, a point to which we return in section 2.3.

(2.28) The second complement Z is V, I or C, yielding indirect object plus clausal complement.
promise (to) your parents to paint their house
whisper to that student {that it's late/ (for someone) to close the door}
suggest to Mary where {she should live/ to look for an apartment}
require of the students that they be more punctual

Finally, indirect objects can combine with other PPs whose heads are specified in lexical frames for individual Vs, as in (2.29).

(2.29) Some students spoke to her {about/ of} each other.
Mary has heard from her friends about the protests.
People argued with the salespeople over the new prices.

Surprisingly, however, apparent combinations of indirect objects with [PP, PATH] complements of *motion verbs*, as in (2.30), do not seem to contain separate complements of V despite the apparent semantic independence of the two PP.

(2.30) The child ran *into the house to his mother*.
The tenants dashed *out of the house from the fire*.

The above italicized sequences are rather *single* constituents, as shown by their fixed order in (2.31a) and by two classic diagnostics for PP constituency in (2.31b-c) (cf. Jackendoff, 1973).

(2.31) a. *The child ran to his mother into the house.
 *The tenants dashed from the fire out of the house.
 b. Pseudo-cleft focus test:
 *Where the child ran to his mother was into the house.
 *Where the child ran into the house was to his mother.
 *Where the tenants dashed from the fire was out of the house.
 Where the child ran was into the house to his mother.
 Where the tenants dashed was out of the house from the fire.
 c. Cleft focus test:
 *It was to his mother that the child ran into the house.
 *It was from the fire that the tenants dashed out of the house.
 *It was out of the house that the tenants dashed from the fire.
 It was into the house to his mother that the child ran.
 It was out of the house from the fire that the tenants dashed.

These three diagnostics force the conclusion that a *single* complex PP of the form [$_P$ P – DP [{*to/ from*} – DP]] is the appropriate structure for the italicized sequences in (2.30). We are not used to thinking of a PP with internal structure analogous to that of a transitive VP containing both a direct and indirect object. But apparently one cannot have two separate PP complements of a V both of whose heads are +PATH.

In fact, a puzzling restricted pattern of combined complements has begun to emerge. Internal subcategorized complements of a selecting head V may include: *a single direct object* typically marked accusative; *a single "oblique" object* introduced by a grammatical P or morphologically marked as non-accusative; *and precisely one other phrase* chosen from among PPs with lexical heads, clausal structures and predicate attributes. Now the fact that predicate attributes don't receive case from the V which governs them (section 2.1.2) suggests that at some level they have no case at all. The observed pattern thus translates into what will be the main proposal of section 2.2.2; at some level of grammar other than PF:

(2.32) *The Complement Space. Subcategorized complements can specify at most one (abstract) accusative DP, one (abstract) oblique DP and one phrasal complement without abstract case.*

(iii) Excluded combinations of complements. In spite of all the double complements in (2.21)–(2.29), one needn't search too far to find that the many logically possible combinations of complements outside (2.32) simply don't occur. Moreover, the oddity of these constructs suggests that it is not a question of rarity but rather of some principled exclusion at work.

(a) *No verbs combine two predicate attributes* (+<A,A> (2.33a), +<N,A> (2.33b) or +<N,N> (2.33c). In classical notation, while +___DP^DP is possible and frequent, frames such as +___AP^AP are impossible.

(2.33) a. Exclusion of +___AP^AP:
   *They consider less expensive very chic.
   *John appeared sickly worrisome.
   *The guests changed irritated to cheerful.

   b. Exclusion of +___NP^AP:
   *Bill grew up [$_{DP}$ a Catholic] devout.
   *That university became [$_{DP}$ another Oxford] very famous.
   *He remains [$_{DP}$ the math teacher] stubborn.

c. Exclusion of +___NP^NP:
   *Bill grew up [_DP_ a Catholic] a small town boy.
   *That university became [_DP_ another Oxford] my dream.
   *He remains [_DP_ the math teacher] an example to youth.

Keep in mind that subject-modifying AP adjuncts *exterior to V'* or perhaps I' as in (2.34) are not structural complements and hence do not challenge the claim that no verbs take double predicate attributes.

(2.34) John [_V'_ appeared sickly] drunk.
       Mary [_V'_ felt mathematics too difficult] young.
       Sue [_V'_ became a math teacher] young.

(b) *No verbs combine two clausal complements unless at least one of them is a case-marked DP object of V or some P.* Since gerunds and indirect questions are the only English clausal complements which appear freely in DP object positions (Emonds, 1976, Ch. 4), a non-DP clausal complement may combine with these (2.35a) but not others (2.35b).

(2.35) a. The strike forced [_DP_ visiting Brooklyn] [_IP_ to be postponed].
          The man compared [_DP_ how he fixed it] with [_DP_ digging a tunnel].
          We limit [_DP_ drinking a lot] to [_DP_ how often I can afford it].
       b. *We preferred [_CP_ to visit New York] [_CP_ that you travel to Paris].
          *They prefer [_IP_ Sue to be here] [_CP_ to visit New York].
          *That prevented [_CP_ that you were ill] [_CP_ for us to be unhappy].

At the same time, since the direct object position is unique, two gerunds or a gerund and an indirect question together, without an additional P to assign case, are excluded (2.36).

(2.36) *The workman compared [how he fixed it] [his digging a tunnel].
       *I couldn't prevent [selling used cars] [depressing me].

Again, participial adjuncts which modify the subject outside V' do not constitute counterexamples to the restrictive pattern of complement combinations:

(2.37) John [_V'_ came running into the room] whistling Dixie.
       They [_V'_ preferred to visit Manhatten] driving with locked doors.

46 *Structures in lexical projections*

(c) *Predicate attributes and clausal complements never combine.* In the examples (2.38), no verbs can be found which can select two such separate complements:

(2.38) *We judged [that our kids visited New York] [too expensive].
 *The guests changed [to be irritated] [to cheerful].
 *Many people declare [for children to travel a lot] [an extravagance].
 *That book seemed [expensive] [to be in short supply].
 *Our friends felt [chilly] [that we couldn't afford more fuel].
 *Bill remained [a staunch Communist] [that he needed a philosophy].

(d) With one (only apparent) exceptional pattern analyzed below in section 2.2.3, *PP complements of direction or location cannot combine with either predicate attributes or clausal complements.*

(2.39) *Mary sounded proud onto the stage.
 *Sam became a salesman into the Prairie States.
 *The books looked very old {that/ like} they had been often resold.
 *The child got ill what food to feed her.

With respect to the excluded patterns in (2.33), (2.35)–(2.36) and (2.38)–(2.39), I stress that the issue is not whether particular predicates appear in the exemplified frames. Rather, *such multiple frames are simply not available for any verbs,* in spite of the fact that many of the combinations are semantically plausible and often made acceptable with small morphological changes such as changing infinitival *to* to *-ing*, inserting a purely grammatical P, etc.

We therefore need a grammatical principle to explain why internal complements of verbs are restricted to three types: unique direct object DPs, unique oblique object DPs of grammatical prepositions (including those realized with an oblique morphological case on their object), and non-DP arguments. Among the non-DP types of arguments (predicate attributes, finite and infinitival clauses, and PPs headed by lexical P), a given verb seems to take at most one. The proposal in the next section will attribute this pattern (2.32) to a general principle of case theory.

Before formulating this proposal, one might ask whether a restriction to binary branching could correctly exclude some complement combinations. But purely formal restatements in terms of binary branching must then allow for multiple complements at different hierarchical levels, and the restrictions on combinations remain exactly as puzzling as before. Another binary branching alternative is to group any sequence of multiple complements into small clauses without any motivation based on predication. But then the italicized pairs of complements in (2.40), which lack any subject-predicate relation, can be so analyzed only at the cost of "constituent" becoming a non-predictive theory-internal notion postulated to save constructs such as binary branching or Larson's (1988) "Sole Complement Condition."

(2.40) promise *Sam to shave myself*   require *higher fees of the students*
        rob *Bill of money*   speak *to a doctor about symptoms*
        strike *her as critical of each other* suggest *to him how Mary did it*
        look *ill to {her/ herself}*   prevent *Sue from getting angry*

If the italicized sequences in (2.40) are small clauses (SC), then this term is just a name for "unexplained combinations of multiple complements," with an added stipulation that an extra constituent with this name but no otherwise attested phrasal or interpretive properties be added to the set of syntactic categories.[24] Under this conception, the successful case-based restriction on combining complements of the next subsection would have to be adopted as a constitutive principle for small clauses or sole complements, replacing its definition in terms of subject and predicate (and hence any motivation for its name). The many analyses that move in this direction simply strike me as unfruitful. A priori commitments to binary branching at best just displace the problem of multiple complements, which as we will now see can be understood much better in terms of case theory.

2.2.2 The role of Abstract Case in Logical Form

Syntactic derivations can perhaps be best conceived of as mediating between three interfaces, an interface with linguistic memory (e.g. the open class lexicon), LF and PF. In my view, two basic conditions operate at each interface, one of economy and one of case. Before developing case conditions for each interface, I first review the economy principles.

In various parts of Emonds (2000a), each economy condition is formulated in terms of interface constructs. Perhaps the unity of the three conceptions can best be grasped in terms of some aphorisms:[25]

48 *Structures in lexical projections*

(2.41) Economy of Representation at the lexical interface: begin a derivation with the fewest possible maximal syntactic units, or *"start with as few phrases as possible."*

(2.42) Economy of Derivation at PF: arrive at PF by inserting the fewest possible maximal PF units, or *"insert as few words as possible."*

(2.43) Economy of Reference at LF: arrive at LF with the fewest possible units of reference, that is, *"minimize separate references to a universe of discourse."*[26]

It seems to me that a similarly pleasing three-way symmetry emerges in terms of Case Theory. According to an intuitive notion which I believe was first suggested by J. Aoun, case may be understood as a means by which constituents are made "visible" for interpretation. Continuing the metaphor, objects are visible only if we can distinguish them from their surroundings, and objects are visibly different from each other only if some visible aspect *distinguishes them from each other.*

Extending this metaphor, a syntactic derivation makes visible the lexical interface units (phrases) by marking them with case. I call this the Deep Case Filter; it essentially guarantees that phrases must occur in defined and distinct structural positions, which is what "visibility" in syntax amounts to.

(2.44) *The Deep Case Filter. Extended and maximal projections of α (= N, V, A) must, prior to Spell Out, be a sister to a non-maximal projection β^j of V, P, I or D.*

For full justification of (2.44), see Emonds (1985, Ch. 1, or 2000a, Ch. 7).

Precisely because this visibility marking is not fully achieved at one given "level" (e.g., in a bottom-up derivation, a direct object can either be accusative or remain caseless until it moves to subject position), a "check" at the end of the derivation must ensure that case has actually been assigned. This is the function of the classical Case Filter, properly formulated as in the Government and Binding framework as a condition on PF. The reason it fails to apply to empty items such as PRO is then clear: for a PF condition, entirely covert units are simply not available for inspection.[27]

(2.45) *Phonological Form Case Filter. At Phonological Form, any phonological nominal projection (D^j, N^j and A^j)* **must have** *Abstract Case.*

Any case framework requires some version of Stowell's (1981) adjacency condition on case-assignment. The following somewhat less restrictive condition will simplify an account of predicate attribute case in section 2.3.

(2.46) *Proximity Condition on Case Assignment. A category X can be assigned as case index to α only if the largest constituents separating X and α are not maximal YP.*[28]

Bearing in mind that the main function of Abstract Case is to distinguish phrases (i.e. the interpreted units at LF) from each other, it makes sense that a central aspect of case theory must involve an LF condition requiring case *distinctions*. Now such a condition apparently focuses on internal arguments, since the previous section concluded: subcategorized complements include at most one accusative DP, one oblique DP and one phrasal complement without Abstract Case – where the latter perhaps surprisingly include predicate attributes.

(2.32) *The Complement Space. Subcategorized complements can specify at most one (abstract) accusative DP, one (abstract) oblique DP and one phrasal complement without abstract case.*

Since V furnishes a case-index to a direct object, and a P realized by an empty item inserted at PF furnishes a case-index to a second object, the empirically justified overarching pattern (2.32) can be succinctly expressed as in (2.47).

(2.47) *Logical Form Case Filter. At Logical Form, internal arguments YP of X^0 are each specified differently for Abstract Case, where "no case" is one of the Case values.*[29]

The consequence of (2.47) is that internal arguments of an X^0 at LF may include a single AP, DP, PP, CP or IP unspecified for case. This is correct, provided that *predicate attributes count as unmarked for case in LF*, since they readily co-occur as complements with both direct (2.22) and indirect objects (2.27) and yet do *not* occur with the other caseless types of complements.

Nonetheless, predicate attributes are marked with morphological case in many Indo-European languages, indeed frequently with the same case as the DP they modify. Thus, translations of secondary predications as in (2.22) in several languages would reveal that both structural complements of the V often *agree in case*; cf. the Czech examples of (2.50) below. It is therefore crucial that a condition imposing distinct cases (2.47) holds at LF and not at PF, and equally important that the very same predicate attributes be forced to have PF case to satisfy (2.45).

There is no contradiction here, but only a proper and interesting theoretical tension that Chomsky and Lasnik's (1977) three-interface or "T model" of derivations is quite able to handle. If some process between Spell Out and PF assigns case to predicate attribute APs and nominals (which are selected by +___N but realized as DPs), then such YPs correctly count as "unspecified for case" for the LF side of the Case Filter (2.47), while at the same time complying with the PF side (2.45). I return to PF mechanism of case-marking predicate attributes in section 2.3.

Under this view of case, the complement space of lexical predicates (2.32) realizes *all and only combinations of two complements predicted to exist* by a "Two-sided" Case Filter – or perhaps better, the Three Interface Case Filter. This is the import of the grammatical patterns which the previous subsection extracted from the combinations of complements collected in (2.21)–(2.29) and the impossible combinations exemplified in (2.33)–(2.39).

2.2.3 Confirmation of the LF Case Filter from triple complement structures

Since an internal argument of a verb can be specified for abstract case at Spell Out in three ways, the LF Case Filter (2.47) should also tolerate lexical frames which combine up to three complements of a V, although such frames may be more marked and hence less frequent. At the same time, (2.47) sets a limit on what kinds of constituents may make up the "triple complementation" allowed in the Complement Space (2.32).To repeat, any such VPs must contain a direct object, an obliquely case-marked indirect object introduced by a purely grammatical P (inserted in PF or empty), and one other XP which lacks case at Spell Out: either a predicate attribute, a clausal complement, or a locational PP whose head is filled prior to PF (or perhaps alternatively realized by morphological case).

In fact, triple combinations with all and only the possible choices for the "caseless XP" are found in the English data. This finding strongly confirms not only the possibility of multiple complements but also the role of the LF Case Filter (2.47). It further undermines any "hope" that all complement combinations reduce to small clauses or Sole Complements.

(i) Double objects with predicate attributes

(2.48) Entries of the form V, +<D, D, {N/ A}> or V, +<D, [D, LOC'], {N/ A}>:
The staff keeps bringing the patients their meals cold.
Many students handed examination books to the teacher blank.

In some combinations, the grammatical copular preposition *as* obligatorily introduces the predicate attributes:

(2.49) a. *She described Clinton (to her friends) {a genius/ intolerant}.
*She bought *War and Peace* (for John) a present.
b. She described Clinton to her friends as {a genius/ intolerant}.
She bought *War and Peace* for John as a present.

Similar constructions in languages with morphological case, such as Czech or German, indicate that a copular preposition, e.g. Czech *jako* 'as', does not assign a particular case (Cf. also Emonds, 1985, Ch. 6). Rather, it introduces a predicate nominal (italicized) whose case agrees with that of the DP it modifies.[30]

(2.50) a. Cortéz   přijel do Ameriky jako *dobyvatel*.
Cortez-NOM arrived to America as conqueror-NOM
'Cortez arrived in America as a conqueror'

b. Domorodci sledovali Cortéze (dlouhou dobu) jako *přítele*.
Locals-NOM observed Cortez-ACC (long time) as friend-ACC
'The locals observed Cortez (for a long time) as a friend'

c. Cortéz   byl sledován (dlouhou dobu) jako *přítel*.
Cortez-NOM was observed (long time)   as friend-NOM
'Cortez was observed (for a long time) as a friend'

d. Král   poslal guvernéra   kolonistům   jako *poddaným*.
King-NOM sent governor-ACC colonists-DAT as subjects-DAT
'The king sent a governor to the colonists as royal subjects'

e. Cortéz   se neobešel bez   indiánů   jako *přátel*.
Cortez-NOM refl. not-do   without Indians-GEN as friends-GEN
'Cortez could not do without Indians for friends'

52 *Structures in lexical projections*

The role of both *jako* in Czech and *as* in English is thus not to assign case, but rather to circumvent potential violations of the Revised Theta Criterion of Emonds (1985, Ch. 2); for independent justifications of this principle, see Chapters 3 and 4 of this volume.

(2.51) a. *Theta Relatedness. X^0 and Y^0 are theta-related if and only if one assigns a theta role to a lexical projection of the other.*
b. *Revised Theta Criterion. Theta-relatedness is anti-transitive.*

Returning now to the English examples (2.49), it appears that the two verbs *describe* and *buy* assign theta roles to *each* of their complements, since the predicate attributes are integrally connected to the describing and the buying. At the same time, the predicate attributes assign a theta role to their own subjects (that is, the direct objects of the main verbs). Consequently in the examples without *as* (2.49a), the main verb, the direct object and the secondary predicate are all pair-wise theta-related, which violates (2.51b). On the other hand, when *as* heads its own PP as in (2.49b), this P rather than its XP complement can be theta-related to the verb, and thus the examples are consistent with the Revised Theta Criterion (2.51b). In contrast, the secondary predicates in (2.48) are irrelevant to the action of the main verb, and so *as* is not necessary.

In any case, the triple combination of direct object – indirect object – predicate attribute in (2.48) and (2.49b) occurs in the Complement Space, as the Logical Form Case Filter predicts.

(ii) Double objects with clausal complements

So-called "lower purpose clauses" introduced by empty operators O exemplify triple complementation in which the third element is a clause:

(2.52) We brought Hamlet to John to read on the train.
We bought John Hamlet to read on the train.

The appropriate lexical frames are +<D, D, [V, MODAL]> or possibly +<D, [D, LOC'], [V, MODAL]>. These structures are also predicted by the Complement Space (2.32) and the Logical Form Case Filter (2.47).

(iii) Double objects with PPs

A third type of triple complementation includes a PP whose head has lexical content.

(2.53) We pushed the salesman our form {through the slot/ over the counter}.
John painted Mary The Last Supper on rice paper.
That incident spoke volumes to me about their relationship.
Sue traded her bicycle to Ann for a fur coat.[31]

This construction thus further confirms the correctness of (2.32) and (2.47)
   There remains one combination of three complements which at first seems to undermine the LF Case Filter, because it includes both directional (PATH) PPs, italicized in (2.54), and either secondary predicates or additional PPs of PLACE in bold, none of which qualify prima facie as an indirect object.

(2.54) Many students brought some books *behind the counter* **dirty**.
The staff keeps putting main dishes *onto the tables* **cold**.
She sprinkled sage *over the soup* as **a seasoning**.
Sue handed the purse *into the police* {**for a reward/ through the slot**}.
The teacher brought a novel *to class* as **an experiment**.

Nonetheless, the feel of these examples is that the directional PPs are *alternating* with indirect objects. The key to an analysis therefore lies in isolating what PATH PPs and indirect objects have formally in common. Now on grounds independent of this issue, the Revised Theta Criterion (2.51b) requires that italicized directional PPs in (2.54) actually consist of an empty grammatical P of PATH whose internal complement is a PP of PLACE, as in (2.55a). This same structure is overt in (2.55b), where a morpheme *from* signals [P, PATH, SOURCE].

(2.55) a. $[_{V'}\ [_V\ \text{brought}]\ [_{DP}\ \text{some books}]$
$[_{PP}\ [_{P,\ PATH}\ \emptyset]\ [_{PP,\ PLACE}\ \text{behind the counter}]]\ [_{AP}\ \text{dirty}]]$[32]
b. We had to remove the cats from behind the barn.
c. French: Mets les chats en dehors de la maison.
        Put   the cats to outside of the house

In some other languages such as French (2.55c), the goal morpheme *en* 'to' with features [PATH, -SOURCE] is obligatorily overt. For more detail, consult Emonds (1996), which is Chapter 4 in this volume.

The only reason that (2.54) poses an apparent problem for the LF Case Filter (2.47) is that we have not yet fully specified what counts as an "indirect object" for the Filter or in fact for the LF component. The need to assimilate the structures in (2.54) to that of ordinary indirect objects suggests somewhat extending the usual limitation of "indirect object" to obliquely case-marked DPs.

(2.56) *"Oblique Case" for the LF Case Filter. An XP in the LF structure [PATH – XP] counts as obliquely case-marked in LF.*[33]

The PATH prepositions which introduce indirect objects can be (a) PF-inserted free morphemes (e.g. *to* and *for*), (b) alternatively realized either as oblique case on the DP or as applicative morphemes on V, or (c) licensed as empty by dative clitics or indirect object movement (Emonds, 1993, reproduced as Chaoter 5 in this volume). All these PF realizations of indirect objects correspond to a locational P of PATH on the LF side, as required in (2.56). This definition now makes clear that the PPs of PLACE in (2.54) count as marked for oblique case for purposes of the LF Case Filter (2.47) and hence satisfy it.

The formulation (2.56) also correctly entails that CPs, which never have an interpreted PATH feature, other non-locational PPs and even simple PPs of PLACE with interpretable lexical content all continue to count as having "no case" for the LF Case Filter, as throughout the preceding discussion.[34]

Although the definition of indirect object (2.56) is considerably broader than any envisaged in traditional grammar, it turns out that three paradigms additionally confirm this formulation. If directional PPs count as indirect objects for the LF Case Filter, they should be compatible with frames which also select a clausal complement. And in fact paradigms involving intransitive (manner of speaking) verbs (2.57a) and transitive verbs (2.57b) satisfy such frames:

(2.57) a. Harry shouted [into the microphone] [(for everyone) to dance].
            Sue whispered [over my shoulder] [that Sam was watching].
        b. Mary brought John [into the aerobics class] [to exercise with].
            Take those magazines [up to your office] [to get ideas from].

In addition, the definition (2.56) now explains why the strings *into the house to his mother* and *out of the house from the fire* in (2.30) must be united into single PPs rather than being two separate PP sisters to a selecting verb. If both were sisters, each would contain obliquely marked complements introduced by PF-inserted directional P, and this would violate the LF Case Filter.

To my knowledge, the combinations in (2.48)–(2.54) exhaust the possibilities for triple complementation in English. On the basis of exhaustively examining the complementation patterns in this language, we have thus arrived at a rather surprising and very strong hypothesis about the membership of the lexicon, in terms of the subcategorization frames of its predicates:

(2.58) *Lexical Density.* Predicates utilize all and only the subcategorization frames constructible by syntactic category theory and the LF Case Filter.

In light of (2.58), the lexicon seems to be much less the barely charted wilderness than studies which either abstract away from it or alternatively focus on semantics and conceptual structures would lead us to believe. In fact, the syntactic part of the lexical entries, which are the interface instructions for drawing out concepts from memory for use, now seems more understandable and transparent than either of their more "concrete" components, articulation and understanding.

2.3 The Case of predicate attributes

The combined implication of the PF part (2.45) and the LF part (2.47) of the Case Filter is that predicate attribute DPs and APs, italicized in (2.59), should all receive Abstract Case between Spell Out, where they are caseless, and PF, where at least all DPs must have case.

(2.59) a. Mary became *a chiropractor.*
Sam has always been *a brother* to me.
Mary has become *obsessed* in recent months.
Sam always seemed *angry* to me.
b. The florid judge declared the future mother *a criminal.*
Some call the economic reforms *a return to the jungle.*
Nobody wants to declare the elections *fraudulent.*
Many voters considered the system *undemocratic.*

In addition, assuming that the PF Case Filter is general, predicate attribute adjuncts exterior to X' which modify a subject as in (2.60) also need case at PF.

(2.60) a. Mary left the party *my friend*.
John worked in New York as *a clown*.
John's work in New York as *a clown* bothered his parents.
b. Mary left the party *thirsty*.
I found that book tedious *young*.
You will find the test a breeze *drunk*.

It should be kept in mind that no aspect of the "Three Interface Case Filter" has been motivated on the basis of morphology. The LF Case Filter is designed to account for the range of observed complement types in VPs, and the original Case Filter (at PF) has long been motivated at least for DPs in languages like English on syntactic rather than morphological grounds; for example, it plays an important role in the analysis of adjectival passives in Chapter 8 in this volume.

It comes then as a massive independent confirmation of the Case Theory developed here that in Indo-European languages with rich morphological case-marking, both DP and AP predicate attributes overtly and robustly display exactly the case properties required by the split between the LF and PF aspects of the Case Filter. That is, predicate attributes in these languages are overtly and obligatorily case-marked in PF, and yet this case-marking appears to play no role at LF.

The Czech agreements in (2.61) exemplify this point. As in many similar case systems, the (italicized) predicate attribute agrees in case with its DP subject. (for space reasons, NO = nominative; AC = accusative; DA = dative; MS = masculine singular.)[35]

(2.61)

a. Kanibal snědl turistu *{syrového/ *-vý}*.
cannibal-MS-NO ate tourist-MS-AC {raw-MS-AC/ *NO}
'The cannibal ate the tourist raw'

b. Turista$_i$ byl sněden t$_i$ *{syrový/ *-vého}*.
tourist-MS-NO was eaten-MS {raw-MS-NO/ *AC}
'The tourist was eaten raw'

c. Únosci   vrátili   chlapce   rodičům   *{živého/*-vý}*.
   kidnappers returned boy-MS-AC parents-DA {alive-MS-AC/ *NO}
   'The kidnappers returned the boy to his parents alive'

d. Chlapec$_i$ byl vrácen   t$_i$ rodičům   *{živý/ *-vého}*.
   boy-MS-NO was return-en-MS parents-DA {alive-MS-NO/*AC}
   'The boy was returned to his parents alive'

As determined by a generalized definition of structural subjects (justified in detail in for example Chapters 6 and 9 of this volume), the subject of *raw* in (2.61a) is the accusative DP *the tourist*, while its subject in (2.61b) is the nominative chain consisting of *the tourist* and its trace in object position. As predicted, the PF case of the AP *raw* varies with no effect at or contribution to LF. (2.62c-d) are similar, with the added factor that the predicate adjective is separated from the object it modifies, possibly due to Czech free word order.

More generally, both sorts of predicate attributes, DPs and APs, typically receive the abstract case of the DP they modify, often reflected in morphological agreement as in (2.61). Thus, the immediate source of abstract accusative case for secondary predicates modifying a direct object as in (2.22) and (2.59b) is not the governing verb, but the object DP itself. This "second chance" for receiving abstract and morphological case occurs after Spell Out but before PF.

The idea that case may be assigned at two levels conforms to a recurrent theme of this study: interpreted grammatical items are inserted prior to Spell Out, while those which don't contribute to meaning are inserted in PF. In particular, *the same elements can often be inserted in different components under essentially the same co-occurrence conditions*; cf. the study of *-en* in Emonds (2000a, Chapter 5) and of *-ing* in Chapter 3 here. Following this line of thought, abstract case indices whose only role is to satisfy the PF Case Filter (2.45) should be inserted subsequent to Spell Out under (nearly) the same conditions as are those case indices which satisfy the LF Case Filter (2.47).

In particular, the categories of the case assigners/ indices (2.9) are the same before and after Spell Out (I, D and those V and P which select I or D), and Case Assignment, at least in languages without free word order, is again subject to the Proximity Condition (2.46):

(2.46) *Proximity Condition on Case Assignment. A category X can be assigned as case index to α only if the largest constituents separating X and α are not maximal YP.*

58 *Structures in lexical projections*

Keeping in mind the goal of assigning case similarly in both syntax and PF, a near optimal solution for PF Case Assignment to predicate attributes is (2.62):

(2.62) *PF Case Assignment. Apply the Case-assignment Condition (2.13) again in PF to all nominal XP.*[36]

Even though PF Case Assignment is formally like case assignment in syntax, its actual effects on predicate attributes are superficially dissimilar. To see its effects, let us inspect two structures (2.63)–(2.64) which each contain a predicate nominal and a predicate adjective in italics. Although these attributes obviously lack overt morphological case in English, the following discussion should clarify the mechanics of how I assign case to attribute phrases, which "agree" with the DPs they modify.[37] The DPs which already have case indices in syntax, prior to PF Case Assignment, are in bold, while attributes still needing PF case are marked "??". For clarity, these structures include prepositions and articles which are actually not inserted until PF.[38]

(2.63) [$_{DP, I}$ **You**] [$_I$ will] [$_{V'}$ find [$_{DP, V}$ **the test**] [$_{DP, ??}$ *a breeze*]] [$_{AP, ??}$ *drunk*].

(2.64) [$_{DP, I}$ [$_{DP, D}$ **John**] [$_D$'s] [$_{N'}$ work in N.Y.] as [$_{DP, ??}$ *a clown*]]
      [$_I$ may] [$_{V'}$ seem [$_{AP, ??}$ *foolish*] to [$_{DP, P}$ **you**]].

Let us examine in turn (i) the predicate nominal *a breeze* in (2.63), (ii) the predicate attribute adjuncts *drunk* and *a clown* in (2.63)–(2.64), and (iii) the predicate adjective complement *foolish* in (2.64).

(i) The predicate attribute *a breeze* in (2.63) needs case. The category V has been transferred as a case index to the direct object *the test* as a result of case assignment in the syntax, so this case index on the object itself becomes a potential case-assigner. Since this V is moreover adjacent to the predicate nominal needing case, it can become the latter's case-index by PF Case Assignment (2.62). Accordingly, this type of predicate nominal in active clauses with secondary predication is morphologically accusative in many Indo-European case systems.

(ii) Predicate attributes in adjunct position, such as *drunk* in (2.63) and *a clown* in (2.64), also need case. The case-assigning categories I and D and also the corresponding case-indices I in (2.63) and D in (2.64) are respectively available for assigning them case according to the Proximity Condition (2.46), *because the intervening V' and N' are not maximal projections.*[39] Therefore, either instance of I and D may be available for assigning case to the predicate attributes they c-command.

(iii) In (2.64) the intransitive linking verb *seem* cannot assign case to anything, since it does not enter the tree by satisfying a subcategorization +___D or +___I, the requirement imposed by Case Indices (2.9). However, both the node I and the case index I on the subject DP are again, by the Proximity Condition (2.46), "close enough" to assign as a case index to *foolish*; the largest constituents separating them are not maximal projections.

The empirical prediction that predicate attributes have case in PF is strongly confirmed by Indo-European morphological case systems. They in fact assign actual morphological case to predicate attributes along the lines of the above English examples with "abstract case." The Czech system briefly exemplified in (2.61) is of this type. Moreover, the mechanism for assigning PF case (2.62) nicely mimics syntactic case assignment.

Finally, the dual level Case Assignment system here provides accounts for several additional recalcitrant grammatical puzzles (a-f) below. These solutions in turn further strengthen the case for this model.

(a) Accusative case on secondary predicates. PF Case Assignment and the proposal in Emonds (1985, Ch. 1) that case assigning categories are actually themselves the case indices together explain how *secondary predicates not assigned case directly by V^0 are nonetheless accusative only when this V^0 assigns some accusative*, as seen in the Czech paradigm (2.61).[40] It is the V assigned to the direct objects in syntax which serves a second time in PF as a case-assigner under adjacency. Such a unification of case assignment is impossible in frameworks which cling to the traditional case names as ad hoc categories distinct from the assigners.

(b) Adjacency of direct objects and secondary predicates. Contrasts such as the following are sometimes taken to support the existence of a small clause constituent uniting a direct object and a secondary predicate.

(2.65) The judge (rashly) declared the future mother (*rashly) a criminal (rashly).
Some (prematurely) called the reforms (*prematurely) frauds (prematurely).
The manager (unfairly) judged the applicant (*unfairly) too short (unfairly).

As in (2.65), when an English direct object and a predicate attribute are sisters, the object cannot be separated by any XP from its VP-initial V case-assigner. Thus, the predicate attribute XP, like an adverb, must follow a direct object. But then, again by the Proximity Condition (2.46), an adverbial AP cannot intervene either between this same object DP (marked with the case index V) and the secondary predicate to be marked for case in PF. Thus, the Proximity Condition accounts for the paradigm in (2.65) with no need for invoking small clause constituency.

(c) Absence of secondary predicates on indirect objects. When an English predicate attribute and an indirect object are sisters, the latter is in a PP and hence does not c-command the attribute. Consequently, *an indirect object cannot be the subject of a predicate attribute.*

(2.66) *A country drive appealed to Bill fatigued.
*He spoke to Mary pregnant.
*We demanded some action of them irresponsible.

This restriction has been reported in the literature as an ad hoc limitation on small clause distribution, i.e., small clauses cannot occur with obliquely case-marked subjects. In the framework developed here, the paradigm in (2.66) follows without stipulation.

(d) Word order of indirect objects and predicate nominals. The Proximity Condition (2.46) on case assignment prohibits an indirect object XP from intervening between the verb and a predicate attribute which must receive nominative case from I. Thus, the system here also correctly predicts, on the basis of case assignment, that *a predicate attribute typically precedes an indirect object*:[41]

(2.67) John became {a brother to us/ *to us a brother}.
Mary appears {unstable to Sam/ *to Sam unstable}.

(e) Simplification of the Binding Theory. It appears that principles of disjoint reference such as Principles B and C of Chomsky's (1981, Ch. 3) Binding Theory *should apply only to DPs which are case-marked at LF*; that is, to DP arguments with case prior to Spell Out.

If both predication and co-reference are parsimoniously represented with indices of the same formal nature, and if moreover there were no difference in level between case-marking of predicate nominals and argument DPs, then predicate nominals would need to be specially exempted from disjoint reference.[42] If not, the italicized predicate nominals in simple examples such as (2.68a-b) would violate Principles B and C respectively.

(2.68) a. The best singer seemed to be *you*.
       b. His parents were *an ideal couple*.

Clearly, the Binding Theory Principles have no effect on predicate nominal DPs. The case system of this section, which distinguishes Case Assignment in the syntax and PF, easily avoids this complication; these LF Principles affect only case-marked DPs.

(f) Parameters of morphological realization. A final advantage to the split between PF and LF Case concerns succinct descriptions of morphological types of languages. It is well-known that some languages exhibit morphological case *neither* on DPs nor in PF agreements (Chinese and outside of pronouns, English), while many other languages (Classical Greek, Latin, most Slavic languages, etc.) exhibit *both* types of case morphology.

Certain other languages such as French and Spanish have no morphological case on DPs; case distinctions appear only among their clitics, which are bound morphemes on verbs. Thus, we might say that their phrasal morphology fails to exhibit syntactic (i.e. LF) case. At the same time, these Romance languages have robust morphological gender and number agreement for predicative (and attributive) adjectives, which is operative exactly in the contexts where PF Case Assignment (2.62) imposes case agreement on adjectives. If number and gender agreement on adjectives reflects PF case agreement (Mateos, 1996), then overall, Romance morphologies exhibit PF case but LF case only marginally (among their clitics).

These three typological configurations suggest that some languages could have morphology that exhibits syntactic case on DPs robustly but PF or agreement case only sparingly. And indeed Japanese and Korean morphologically mark syntactic case on DP arguments, but their predicate attributes

62 Structures in lexical projections

exhibit very little morphological case and no agreement at all. The latter surface with either no case-marker (as with the Japanese copula) or in some non-agreeing oblique case. This latter point is not surprising, since some predicate attributes can surface with oblique case even in languages with predicate attribute agreement.

It appears then that languages vary independently as to whether they house ample syntactic (LF) or PF realizations of morphological case. English and Chinese have neither; Romance languages exhibit PF case; Japanese and Korean exhibit syntactic case; and the Classical and Slavic Indo-European languages exhibit both. *The symmetry of these four contrasting systems provides further conceptual support for a dual level model of case assignment.*

These accounts (a)–(f) all result from a system of assigning syntactic and PF case according to the same principles but at two derivational levels. Together, they further support the "Three Interface" conception of the Case Filter. This particular Case Theory in turn played a key role earlier in this chapter in showing that the notion of "possible lexical entry" developed in this work dovetails exceedingly well with the observed range of lexical complementation.

2.4 The restrictive Syntactic Lexicon confronts open-ended Conceptual Space

We have seen in this chapter that the system of lexical subcategorization reviewed in its introductory paragraphs provides exactly the right range of formal, simple subcategorization features for selecting complements to verbs, the category which exhibits the widest diversity of complement types. All six single frames provided by the extended projection category system, reviewed in this volume in Chapter 9, are realized as in fact long familiar sub-classes of predicates, as summarized in (2.16). Moreover, there are no construction types unaccounted for or "left over," which might testify to some deficiency in the system.

Perhaps even more surprisingly, with the aid of a plausible LF Case Filter (2.47) which states how complements must differ from each other at LF, the subcategorization framework formally predicts the existence of *all and only the combinations* of English complements which actually seem to exist. That is, the subcategorization formalism defines a "Complement Space" of possible lexical entries (2.32), and this space is densely but evenly populated, a property which I have called Lexical Density (2.58).

From the perspective of having completed this study, it appears that the old shibboleths about the irregularity of the lexicon, about how its entries shade off into unformalizable conditions of every sort, are just paraphrases of a lack of knowledge about its structure. I hope that this study constitutes a major step away from this attitude and toward achieving the goal announced in Emonds (2000a, Ch. 1), "of working out some type of formalized lexicon to actually generate the syntactic structures which then undergo the carefully studied derivations." Finally, the proposals here for developing syntactic theory also go a good part of the way toward explaining how such minimally specified lexical frames manage to generate a complex variety of structures.

The principal device of the lexicon is a streamlined and yet more syntactically "active" version of the subcategorization mechanisms introduced in Chomsky (1965). But instead of being an incomplete set of statements drawn from a disparate inventory of categories, this work's subcategorization frames classify morphemes by means of a reduced and highly structured set of cognitive categories developed in the intervening decades, utilizing all of the combinations available. Moreover, lexical entries here never mention phrases,[43] and possibly except for idioms (not investigated here), the syntactic frames stipulate neither concatenation nor any grammatical morphemes. The presence of specific morphemes such as English *to, as, that, if, for*, etc. and of many bound morphemes is predictable from the effects of case theory and the Economy Principles of Representation and Derivation. Nor do the syntactic frames mention linear order, although such frames do combine with Lieber's (1980, 1983) ordered morphological subcategorizations. In fact the subcategorization framework is finally the key that facilitates the merging of these two long segregated grammatical domains, phrasal syntax and morphology (Emonds, 2000a, Chapters 3 and 4).

Designing a simplified and predictive system of lexical frames has inevitably gone hand in hand with modifying various conceptions internal to syntax. The principal innovations, summarized and in part further developed in this chapter, concern case theory ("visibility theory") and the principles of economy. Both sub-theories operate in terms appropriate to the functions of the three interfaces with syntax: the lexical interface, LF, and PF.

It is true that this study and Emonds (2000a) have offered almost nothing in the way of semantics of individual lexical items – except to incorporate what is not individual into general interpretive principles. The remaining linkages of *particular lexical items* to conceptual space (= the psychological world which language tries to report on and modify) are, I feel, neither very amenable to formalization nor even particularly related to syntactic well-formedness.

I do not deny that particular meanings of open class morphemes are ultimately formalizable, but I do judge that we presently have no method for *reliably* accessing any aspects of those meanings. In practice, current linguistic semantics is either disguised syntax (i.e. using mnemonic terms which are actually justified solely on the basis of well-formedness, clear ambiguities, and intuitions of grammatical relatedness) or, especially when it treats concepts in isolation, without implications for natural language structure. Any approaches to lexical specifications recognizably labeled today as semantic seem to consist mainly of combining results from (non-verbal) psychology with "thinking hard" about how to represent meaning, and then trying to formalize these intuitions – usually by some analogy to syntactic structure, perhaps mediated by a dose of predicate calculus.

Although this intuitive method has produced a wealth of intelligent observations about what kinds of objects, events, situations or mental states words or classes of words can refer to, I fail to see an emerging systematic import for how words combine; the vast literature on presupposition, opacity, and factivity is just one example. The problem is that there is no systematic "data check" on intuitions about concepts and relatedness of concepts other than whatever is afforded by syntax. But if at bottom syntax provides the only reliable data for checking on conceptual representations of words, then in fact the conceptual constructs are essentially guesses, usually question-begging guesses, about what governs syntactic well-formedness. They cannot be expected to be more successful than other attempts at informed philosophical speculation, clever as many of these have been.

In practice, no formal limits have been set on the lexical conceptual structures of individual words which are (pre)supposed to determine how they can combine. The representations that have been proposed, analogous to logical representations to be sure, are taxonomic but otherwise open-ended. Restrictive systems of categories, either for separate concepts or systems of concepts, are entirely lacking. Moreover, couching shrewd intuitions in logical formulae only obscures the fact that modern logic itself, whose inventors were not even among the grammarians of the time, was just an early twentieth century guess about how to factor out what is "essential for proofs" from real language.

Even something as elegantly simple as L. Talmy's Figure-Ground dichotomy, certainly a central perceptual principle, seems to have import and predictive implications only when it interfaces with syntax and determines theta roles. Any conceptual semantic statements truly independent of syntax (we can't see colors at night, animate objects self-propel, we know the difference between up and down, etc.) come across as unrevealing truisms – unless we unexpectedly find syntactic verifications. But thinking hard about and reformulating truisms is a much slower road to syntactic confirmation than simply doing syntax. And the bonus of the syntactic method is its often interesting by-products for understanding semantics.[44]

I conclude that with methods and insights presently available, there is not nor can there be any reliable method for specifying lexical meanings in terms of concepts or conceptual space; the enterprise is too vague and too unsystematic. A fortiori, thinking about (classes of) concepts has not and doesn't show promise of shedding insight on the combinatory possibilities of language. The latter study, of syntax, is best undertaken autonomously: reference to meaning does not help us construct grammars. Rather, constructing grammars, which I take to be based on constructing a syntax of lexical combinations, sometimes – but not always – helps us understand meaning. This essential point of Chomsky (1957) remains as true as it was then.

This study has revealed a new and important justification for basing semantics on syntax. The fact that the range of subcategorization frames provided by syntactic theory seems to fit perfectly the range of actually occurring grammatical patterns suggests that whatever the semantics of head-complement combinations, this latter factor is not determining how the linguistic system works – or it if is, the semantic system is nearly isomorphic to its syntactic basis. That is, the logical system of language is precisely the subcategorization system. Humans can say, not what they want to say, but what the syntactic frames of the lexicon allow them to say. The combinatorial aspects of the lexicon are fundamentally syntactic.

One might object that it is easy to turn this formulation around. I have even maintained that all the grammatical features and categories, which organize syntax (N, V, ACTIVITY, ANIMATE, INHERENT, NEGATIVE, PAST, PATH, etc.) and are notated F_i, are the *most central* cognitive features both in LF and in the open class dictionary. In fact, I have found no use whatever for purely formal or diacritic syntactic categories or features. We can well say that the only features available for syntax are the most central features of man's conceptual structures and open class Dictionary; in this sense syntax is entirely dependent on conceptual structure. That is, the syntactic feature inventory is a "perfect system" in the sense of Chomsky (1995): it is derived entirely from the LF interface with understanding and cognition.

But what remains constant in both formulations is *the method by which we arrive at this feature inventory* (the set of cognitive syntactic $\{F_i\}$) and the roles in grammar played by these features. The only *reliable* guide leading to specification of the feature inventory is syntactic behavior, and once a feature is in the inventory, we expect it to behave according to the principles of syntax; it becomes irrelevant whether it then conforms to any essentially intuitive semantic categories which might or might not conflict with syntax. And in fact, whether researchers use a syntactic or semantic method, they seem to agree on labeling as syntactic any theory which privileges grammatical investigations as the high road to discovering the inventory of mental categories, whatever its ultimate claims are about semantics. In this sense, this book develops an almost exclusively syntactic theory of the lexicon.

Notes

* This chapter is a slightly abridged version of Emonds (2000a, Ch. 8), presenting the main results of its theory of complementation, which is based on subcategorization principles and a new "Logical Form Case Filter." As shown here, this theory turns out to permit and predict all and only the subcategorization frames that correspond to the traditionally discussed English complement types.

    I have reworded several passages, and omitted or relegated to footnotes some peripheral discussions and cross-references to other parts of Emonds (2000a). Because some of the changes involve footnotes and numbered examples, their numbers in the original and here do not always correspond. I have also left the analyses of the less transparent complement structures of English, such as non-finite clauses, post-verbal particles and double objects, to the following three chapters, which treat them in more depth.

1. According to Emonds (2000a), later accretions in the generative lexicon (theta-grids, linking devices, item-particular event structures, argument structures, etc.) can be entirely eliminated.
2. Since this chapter concerns upper limits on the kinds and combinations of complement types, it is not concerned with optionality (parenthesis notation) or choices among single alternatives (the brace notation {F/ G}) in lexical frames.
3. Thus, **ser muerto* 'be dead,' **ser inebriado* 'be drunk,' etc. The counterpart to *ser* with -INHERENT complements is *estar* 'be': *estar muerto, estar inebriado.*
4. There are some intransitive idioms with *go* not of concern here: *This {car/ watch} still goes. Since we are cleaning, this junk should go. It's time to go.*
5. Nonetheless, the discussion of the *spray/ load/ drain* classes of predicates in Emonds (2000a, section 2.4) concludes that the best treatment of the second complement generalizes across the variation in ±LOCATION; i.e. the proposed frames are based on +___D, (P) where P is *not* limited to +LOCATION.

6. In this framework only a *lexically filled* head can satisfy subcategorization; see e.g. Chapters 3, 5 and 6 of this volume. Higher empty heads such as the D in (2.5) are then irrelevant. The crucial definition from Emonds (2000a, Ch. 4) is: *Lexical Head/Projection. Let X^0 be the highest lexically filled head in Z^j. Then X^0 is the lexical head of Z^j, and Z^j is a lexical projection of X^0.*
7. Kallulli's (1999) convincingly analyzes non-specific "bare NP" objects in Albanian and Mainland Scandinavian, which alternate with both definite and indefinite DPs, as NPs which *don't* project to DP. If her analysis is correct, whether NP *must* project to DP or not is language-particular, requiring modifying the theory of extended projections. A reviewer points out that base-generated bare NPs would furnish a natural source for the transformationally derived N-incorporation structures of Baker (1988).
8. The linking verb *become* also marginally tolerates demonstratives in its predicate nominal complement; the marginality suggests to me that they are interpretable but not grammatical.
?I'd like to become that famous actor.
?Will they become those good teachers?
9. As is well-known, I can assign so-called nominative case (i.e., become a case index) only if I is "finite." This may be due to the fact that non-finite I (e.g., English *to*) is present or visible only in PF.
10. In earlier government and binding accounts, obligatory control IPs and "raising" infinitival IPs also result from different subcategorizations. But the present account requires no further theory of government beyond (2.9) for differentiating structures containing PRO from exceptionally case marked lower subject DPs.
11. For a full justification of my conclusions, consult Emonds (1985, Ch. 2) and Chapters 3 and 6 of this volume.
12. I will not review here how UG chooses among the three types of obligatory control phrasal projections above V in English (participles, gerunds, and infinitives). See Chapter 3 of this volume.
13. Hence, the easiest way for (C. Fillmore's) "working grammarian" and perhaps the language learner to associate +___V with structures is to link it with non-finite complements of obligatory control. But the same working grammarian *should not* then imagine that my +___V is simply shorthand for the notoriously debated "bare VP complements" (VPs not immediately dominated by IP).

In fact, precisely because of the theory of extended phrase structure of Chapter 9, *neither +___V nor any other frame can ever give rise to a "bare VP."* Rather, this frame "looks for" the most economic realization available among several structures that are everything but a bare VP.
14. We return below to infinitives of *optional* control, which are another kind of clausal complement available for the *(dis)like* class but not for the class of epistemics like *believe*.

15. French *espérer* 'hope', whose complement must be indicative, vs. Spanish *esperar* 'hope', whose complement is subjunctive, demonstrate such selection.
16. Jespersen (1940) already considers the English past subjunctive (*Were John here, ...*) an archaism. The "present subjunctive" in American English (*suggest that she be on time*) simply acts like a null allomorph of British English *should* and is not SUBJUN.
17. The Case Assignment Condition accounts for why a finite I rather than C case-marks a DP in SPEC(IP): I' is lower than C; thus, I case-marks a subject whenever it can. That is, a C or V with the frame +___I can assign case to SPEC(IP) only if I is non-finite and hence not a potential case assigner; cf. note 9.
18. A traditional idea based on examining only main clauses is that unselected sentence-initial *that* clauses and *for-to* clauses are in *subject* position. Many paradigms in Emonds (1976, Ch. 4) and Koster (1978b) show this conception is inadequate. E.g:

    *Could {for John to buy a ticket now/ that it snowed} be possible?
    *My friends considered {for Sam to be late/ that we are cold} to be unlikely.
    Such sentence-initial clauses pattern rather like *topicalized* subject PPs (Emonds, 1985, Ch. 7), in the sense that they are a root phenomenon.
    In the garden would be a bit warmer.
    *Could in the garden be a bit warmer?
    *My friends considered in the garden to be warmer.
19. As an approximation, I parenthesize LOC' in (2.15) to express the fact that *for* can lack any specific sense as in e.g. (2.14) and in many uses with DPs as well *(This sells for $3; I mistook him for a woman; we have nothing for dessert)*.
20. If a predicate (e.g., *intend*) selecting *for-to* clauses actually excludes *for* + DP, it can be listed with a more marked frame ___[I, LOC']; the next subsection makes precise a formalism for this (2.18).
21. See the longer discussion in Emonds (2000a, Ch. 7) for how Economy of Representation precludes superfluous structure with "too many" intermediate empty heads.
22. Throughout this chapter, I assume that English prepositionless double object structures *(You {ask/ give/ hand} the contestant the answer)* do not reflect a basic lexical frame but rather derive from an underlying sequence where the objects are in reverse order and the indirect object is in a PP. Several arguments for this early transformationalist position, independent of various updated executions, are provided in Emonds (1993, sections 1 and 2), which is Chapter 5 of this volume. That essay's particular version of indirect object movement is based on a structure-preserving interchange of DPs.
23. Recall from section 2.1.2 that predicate nominals are generated by +___N (not +___D). The next chapter in this volume shows that the most economical English realization of +___V is a present participle.

24. Koster (1978a) was perhaps the first to observe that extraction from within the *first DP of two complements* is excluded. This pattern can easily be illustrated with the complement combinations in (2.40), whose italicized first complements are not subjects of the second:
    *Who did Mary promise *some friends of* {to buy wine/ a free dinner}?
    This is the cafe that they robbed *the manager of* (*of the payroll).
    This is the room that you should strip *the door to* (*of its hardware).
    Which councilman did your remarks impress *the wife of* (*as absurd)?
    *Who did you suggest *to friends of* when to travel?
    Cf. Who did you suggest that schedule to friends of?
    The reader can construct more examples on this pattern so as to be convinced that this restriction has nothing to do with extracting from "subjects," counter to what Kayne (1982) and others have argued in works on binary branching and extending the range of constructions construed as small clauses. E.g., the contrast *a man we looked over the finances of* vs. **a man we looked the finances of over* is taken to motivate a constituent such as *[$_{SC}$ the finances over]*.
25. These formulations reflect the influence of some central ideas in Chomsky (1995). My executions of these ideas do not use covert movement but are not incompatible with it.
26. For justification and examples, consult Emonds (2000a, section 1.5).
27. The treatment here removes a conceptual anomaly in the Government and Binding framework: that a condition on visibility for *interpretation* should apply at PF.
28. The Deep Case Filter (2.45) and the Proximity Condition (2.46) together predict that a *non-adjacent DP sister* of a case assigner β can satisfy the former but fail to receive syntactic case because of the latter. Secondary predicates following a non-case-marked complement inside V' have this status.
29. Actually, (2.47) must hold at Spell Out as well as at LF, since no case is assigned between these two levels.
30. I appreciate the efforts of L. Veselovská in constructing these and other Czech examples in this study so that the appropriate morphological contrasts are overt.
31. It is sometimes unclear whether a given PP is a complement or an adjunct.
32. The head *brought* in (2.55a) is theta-related to the heads of both of its complements DP and PP, and *this same DP* is also the subject noun for the PP of location *behind the counter*. So by (2.51b), *brought* cannot be theta-related to *behind*. It must instead be theta-related to the head of a PP that is *not* related to the object DP, namely the head PATH.
33. The formulation in (2.56) deliberately omits a label for the outer brackets, as I don't exclude the possibility that languages with serial verbs have bare VPs which can house an indirect object if headed by a grammatical V with the feature PATH.

34. The feature LOC', which has been defined as distinguishing *for* from *to,* is a value of PATH in constructions with a *for* dative. As the LF Case Filter (2.47) predicts, two distinct indirect objects introcued by PATH, a *to* dative and a *for* dative, cannot co-exist: **She brought Jim a card to Bill.* (Adjunct *for*-phrases are of course irrelevant.)
35. Andrews (1971) provides Classical Greek paradigms with similar properties.
36. (2.62) applies to APs as well. This extends Syntactic Case Assignment (2.13), which does not affect APs.
37. Along with Mateos (1996), I take the pervasive number and gender agreement of Romance APs to reflect their abstract case. This study does not examine *DP-internal* agreement, including in case, among N, D and numerals.
38. I continue to conflate traditional case names (e.g. accusative) with the category that assigns them (V). Only the latter have any status in linguistic theory, as argued in Emonds (1985, Ch. 1). If for some reason one granted terms like "accusative" a status different than V, then the generalizations of this section, which unite case assignment with case agreement, would go unexpressed.
39. The non-maximal nature of any projection which has an adjunct as a sister is one of the consequences of the bare phrase structure theory justified in Speas (1990, section 2.2).
40. Among other things, the direct object DP would block any assignment of verbal case to a secondary predicate, by the Proximity Condition on Case Assignment (2.46).
41. Unsurprisingly, a complex or "heavy" predicate attribute can shift rightwards over a PP: *John became {to/for} us the brother we always wanted.*
42. This exemption is proposed in Safir (1985).
43. This conclusion is supported by various works reviewed in Emonds (2000a, Ch. 2), where the overall result is termed the Lexical Interface Principle.
44. The most interesting things we know about the semantic dichotomy between activity and stative predicates are by-products of early diagnostics which tried to make precise what verbs "took manner adverbials freely" (Lakoff and Ross, 1966). They involve compatibilities with imperatives, *do so* anaphora and progressive aspect.

Chapter 3
The autonomy of the (syntactic) lexicon and syntax: Insertion conditions for derivational and inflectional morphemes*

3.1 The problem of "neutralized" phrases

A central concern of western grammar has always been the proper characterization of what can be called non-finite verbal constructions: the infinitive, the gerund, and the participle. Under the aegis of generative grammar, progress toward this goal has been swift, in comparison to what went before; the principal clarifications will be outlined just below.

Nonetheless, we still lack a complete and fomalized understanding of what a "verbal noun" (gerund) or a "verbal adjective" (participle) is. We cannot be content with describing them loosely as "neutralized" categories, precisely because an English gerund phrase, for example, appears only in noun phrase positions (Emonds, 1976, Ch. 4) but has the internal structure of a verb phrase (Chomsky, 1970).[1] The pre-theoretical term "neutralization" sheds no light on why the opposite properties don't hold: why not internal noun phrase structure and external verb phrase distribution?

We can ask further questions: why are the modals and tense endings not available in "verbal nouns" and "verbal adjectives"? What determines the choices among infinitives, participles, and gerunds, especially in cases where all three have understood, rather than lexically overt, NP subjects? How is it that Modern English uses the same ending *ing* for participles and gerunds, which is furthermore a suffix of derivational morphology for turning verbs into both adjectives and nouns (*very intriguing buildings, a thought-provoking reading*)? Many more questions can be posed, questions whose import can't be understood, however, without entering into more detail about what we already know about these constructions.

In what follows then, I will first show, in section 2, how the four principal uses of *ing* in English form a balanced and quite abstract syntactic paradigm, which is centrally based on the property that *ing* is an N or A (and not a V). These findings are then formally expressed, in section 3, by a unified lexical representation which crucially uses the two levels of lexical insertion for grammatical formatives provided for in Emonds (1985).[2]

72 *Structures in lexical projections*

To fully exploit the predictive power of this framework, the notion lexical head must be refined, so that a bar notation head X^0 empty at deep structure yields its selectional predominance to a filled Y^0 sister (section 4). Once the appropriate modifications are in place, section 5 is devoted to, if I may cite a reviewer, "the order that the framework reveals and accounts for in what the GPSG authors have called 'the unruly and idiosyncratic syntactic facts of subcategorization' ... Most of the regularities discussed are not even observed in other approaches, let alone given a theoretical account."

If the analyses of English gerunds, infinitives, and present participles given here are satisfactory, a logical next step would extend the approach to passive and perfect participles, which are basically identical in several western languages, even though they differ both in their syntax and in their morphological (agreement) properties. In Chapter 8 of this volume and Emonds (2000a: Ch. 5), I argue that the passive/perfect participial ending (e.g., English *en*) is an A (but unlike *ing*, is never an N). The agreeing adjectival passive *en*, like the derived adjectival *ing*, is present in syntax, while the verbal passive *en* and the perfective *en*, like participial *ing*, are inserted only at Spell Out. The differences between the passive and the perfective all result from whether or not the A position into which a surface *en* is inserted agrees with its subject.

3.2 The uses of *ing*

3.2.1 Derived Nominals

Papers by Fraser (1970), Chomsky (1970) and Ross (1973) have shown that the italicized forms in (3.1) are nouns, even though the selection restrictions that these nouns enter into with surrounding argument phrases are determined by the verb to which *ing* is attached.

(3.1) your thought-provoking *reading* of that text to a large audience
       the *shooting* of the lions by the hunters

In fact, Walinska de Hackbeil (1984) shows that such "action nominalizations" are far from having all the properties of nouns. She proposes that the suffix *ing* is the "categorial head" of the NP, while the verb is the "lexical head" of the phrase. Roughly speaking, we may say that semantic selection proceeds as with verbs and that syntactic selection (i.e., the choice of phrasal categories in which arguments are represented) proceeds as with nouns. We return to this distinction later.

These derived nominals are incompatible with stative verb roots.

(3.2) *Your knowing of algebra surprised me.
*The possessing of a few art objects makes a good impression.
*Susan criticized such constant owing of money.
*Mary's preferring of (for) Cuban cigars got her in trouble.
*They warned me about television's boring of Sam.
*A lot of daily amusing of children is fatiguing.

The righthand head rule of English morphology of Lieber (1980) and Williams (1981), to the effect that the affixes of derived morphology are lexical category heads, squares well with general constraints on word order in the bar notation (e.g., only phrases follow the head; Emonds, 1985, Ch. 2). Under this approach, the *ing* of (3.1) is lexically represented as in (3.3).

(3.3) *ing*, N, + V___; V = +ACTIVITY

The subcategorization feature indicates that *ing* combines with an X⁰ of the bar notation, namely V. Combinations of an X⁰ (here, the N *ing*) with non-maximal phrases give rise to another X⁰, whose head, according to Williams and Lieber, is, in English and other suffixing languages, its righthand member, as in (3.4).

(3.4)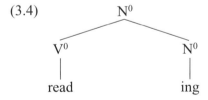

3.2.2 Derived Adjectives

Chomsky (1957) points out the fact that a class of verbs denoting psychological states and requiring animate direct objects can be systematically made into adjectives by the addition of *ing*. The possible realizations of

SPEC for adjectives, given in (3.5), can freely combine with the forms in (3.6a) but not with those in (3.6b).

(3.5) very, rather, so, too, more, less, how, etc.

(3.6) a. amazing, amusing, boring, exciting, fatiguing, frightening, irritating, pleasing, revolting, soothing, surprising, tempting, etc.
b. reading, shooting, barking, describing, destroying, completing

Like the derived nominals in *ing*, the forms in (3.6a) retain selectional properties of the stem verbs, while choosing the syntactic form of their complements like adjectives. For example, verbs but not adjectives can take direct object NP's:

(3.7) The political manipulations frightened my friends.
The manipulations were very frightening *(to/for) my friends.

Further, English adjectives with non-animate subjects cannot appear in the progressive:

(3.8) The manipulations were frightening my friends.
*The manipulations were being very frightening for them.

As pointed out in a careful study by Brekke (1988), certain other classes of verbs (in his terms, of "disposition", "manner" and "impact") form adjectives in *ing*. He further notes that, in order to form a true adjective in *ing*, the "psychological" feature "is only a necessary but not a sufficient condition, since the (overt or covert) *position* of the Experiencer argument appears to be crucial: psychological predicates with a β-Experiencer [i.e., in object position, J.E.] produce-*ing* adjectives, whereas those with an α-Experiencer do not" (172).

In Emonds (1991b), I argue that the direct object position of the Experiencer (the psychological Location, in thematic role terms) results from an intrinsic feature on the verbal head, +LOCATION. Thus, parallel to the earlier entry for derived nominals (3.3), we can represent the *ing* for the derived adjectives of (3.6) as follows:

(3.9) *ing*, A, +V___; V = +PSYCH, +LOCATION; V = "disposition," etc.

Throughout, I abbreviate the condition in (3.9) as V = +PSYCHOLOGICAL.

To express the similarity between (3.3) and (3.9), we can use the "archicategory" [+N] introduced in Chomsky (1970).[3] This archicategory is typically used to account for the many common properties of adjectives and nouns.

(3.10) $\quad ing,\ [+N],\ +V\underline{\quad},\quad \begin{Bmatrix} \text{N: V} = +\text{ACTIVITY} \\ \text{A: V} = +\text{PSYCHOLOGICAL} \end{Bmatrix}$

The lexical entry (3.10) maximally factors out the common properties of English *ing* in derivational morphology.

3.2.3 Gerunds

One of the principle clarifications achieved by early generative grammar in the study of non-finite clauses was the characterization of English "NP-gerunds," two examples of which are italicized in (3.11).

(3.11) We preferred *John's having been awarded the prize* to *your obtaining it fraudulently.*

Chomsky (1970) showed that this construction is entirely separate from derived nominals ending in *ing* in that inside its maximal projection, it has all the structural properties of verb phrases, including the requirement that a subject NP be structurally present (even if "understood"; Wasow and Roeper, 1972). Emonds (1976, Ch. 4) showed that, in contrast to infinitives and finite clauses, the NP-gerund has the external distribution of NP's with respect to both its deep structure positions and its behavior under movements in passives, clefts, etc. We can informally summarize these results in a quasi-lexical entry for gerundive *ing* as in (3.12):

(3.12) *ing*, [+N], +V___, N: V+[ing] selects like V inside its maximal projection, but its maximal projection is syntactically an NP.

3.2.4 Present Participles

Emonds (1985, Ch. 2), is a study of the properties of another set of maximal projections whose head is V+*ing*, the "present participles" of traditional English grammar. As with NP gerunds, these heads select inside their maximal projection like a V, but unlike NP gerunds, they do not appear in positions characterized by deep and transformational syntax as NP positions. Some examples of participles are italicized in (3.13).

(3.13)   We {found the students/went on} *studying French.*
    The students *conversing quietly* were waiting in the lobby.
    He made the children sandwiches (while) *describing Albania.*
    With John *having obtained his degree*, we can leave for Guadeloupe.

Participles never have an overt NP subject within these maximal projections. In addition, they do not exhibit overt COMP's, elements of INFL, or gaps characteristic of non-overt movements into COMP: **the, books sending on to John are expensive.*[4] I concluded that these "non-NP" forms are VP's immediately dominated neither by IP nor by NP – i.e., that these are "bare VP's." This analysis led to a couple of puzzling questions, however, within the framework I developed there.

(3.14)   What is the nature of the participial *ing*, since there is no morpheme category within which it can be associated?
    Might it be preferable to restrict complements to extended maximal projections, allowing VP to appear only as a sister to INFL?

In fact, I came to be aware of a generalization about the syntactic distribution of present participles, but did not really see how to express it naturally in my system. Terming such participles "bare VP's":

> Bare VP have turned out to have the deep structure distributional characteristics of AP's, which is to be expected if bare VP are V^2, and if V and A are considered to share a cross-classifying feature [+V], as in Chomsky (1970). Like AP's, bare VP's can be sisters to V (aspectual and object-controlled gerunds), sisters to N^1 and NP (reduced relatives), and sisters to V^1 and VP (adverbial gerunds; here an AP would have adverbial form). Also like AP's, [bare] VP's can be sisters to P, under restrictive choices of P. Lastly, [bare] VP's can occur in absolutive constructions, as can AP's (*With John sick*, ...). (Emonds, 1985, 97)

On other grounds, I am not convinced that the feature ±V plays a role in syntax, and yet the above passage crucially relies on the archicategory +V. Moreover, the passage leaves the questions in (3.14) unanswered.

The basis of an answer to these problems lies, I believe, in the empirical generalization in the citation; with respect to principles of phrasal distribution, participial VP's have the properties of AP's. If participial clauses are AP's, the lack of overt internal NP subjects for the participles is immediately explained. Moreover, this explains why participles do not combine directly with modals and tense endings (English AP's never do), and the category of participial *ing* is identified with that of derived adjectives.

Besides sharing the deep distribution of AP, present participles also share the following surface properties with AP.

(i) English pre-nominal AP's and participles must end in their head:[5]

(3.15) A few very unhappy (*about the exams) students were in the lobby.
A few conversing (*about the exams) students were in the lobby.

(ii) AP's and participles are incompatible with cleft focus position:

(3.16) *It was guilty about the exams that the students felt.
*It was talking about the exams that the students finished.

As indicated by a reviewer, this argument is strengthened by the observation that in dialects of English in which AP *may* appear in the focus position of a cleft, present participle phrases may also appear there. In some varieties of Irish English, examples like (3.17 a–b) are grammatical. In these dialects, (3.17 c–d) are also grammatical:

(3.17) a. It's cold and wet we are.
b. It's too full of spite they are.
c. Is it going home you are already?
d. It is trying to milk the poor you are.

If the phrases projected from present participles are simply VP, there is no explanation for this correlation.

(iii) Present participles in Spanisch, which indicate actions and not states, can be complements to the verb *estar* 'be', which is compatible only with those AP's which indicate non-inherent states.

78 *Structures in lexical projections*

Thus, the best approximate generalization about present participles is *not*, as in Emonds (1985, Ch. 2), that they are VP's which are not immediately dominated by NP or by IP. It is rather that their maximal projections have the external distribution of AP's, while inside the maximal projection, the participle selects complements like a verb.[6] Thus, we arrive at a preliminary statement for participles (3.18), analogous to the one for gerunds (3.12).

(3.18) *ing*, [+N], +V___, A: V+[ing] selects like V inside its maximal projection, but its maximal projection is syntactically an AP.

Before continuing, it may be appropriate to return again to the possibility of whether the behavior of a participle as in (3.18) can be explained by appeal to the notion of a category which is "neutralized" between A and V. The problem with such a notion is that we can perfectly well imagine a syntactic category which selects like an A inside its own maximal projection, but whose maximal projection distributes syntactically like a VP. The adjective in Japanese and Korean, which case-marks its closest complement differently than does a verb and also takes adjectival specifiers, is exactly a category of this type (Jo, 1986). In external distribution, the maximal projection of A can combine with INFL (tense and mood), like an English VP: Recourse to a "neutralized category" can't explain any of these asymmetries. We could as well say, with no better success in making specific predictions, that an ordinary English verb phrase is "neutralized" between the Japanese AP and the English participial phrase.

3.3 A generalized and autonomous lexical entry for *ing*

3.3.1 From Midde to Modern English

The similarity between the quasi-formalizations for gerundive and participial *ing*, (3.12) and (3.18), allows us to understand a development from Middle to Modern English. The Old English participial suffix *-end-* develops to *-ing(e)* in Chaucer's Middle English (late fourteenth century). In Emonds (1971), I show that Chaucer does *not* have a native gerund, a view reinforced by the more detailed study of Donner (1986). Thus, Chaucer's English represents *ing(e)* as follows:

(3.19) $ing(e)$, [+N], +V___, $\begin{Bmatrix} \text{N: V = +ACTIVITY} \\ \text{A: V = +PSYCHOLOGICAL} \\ \text{A: V +[ing] selects like V inside its maxi-} \\ \text{mal projection, but its maximal projec-} \\ \text{tion is syntactically a [+N]-phrase.} \end{Bmatrix}$

Even before formalizing the property in the third part of (3.19), it is easy to see why the falling together of OE *-ung-* (a derived nominal suffix) and *-end-* in Chaucer's time led to a further development, namely, a generalization. The symbol A (that is [+V]; see note 3) in the third line of (3.19) was eliminated, giving rise to the NP gerund in Modern English; e.g., Spenser (late sixteenth century) has a fully developed gerund. No explanation of the introduction of the NP gerund in Modern English could be simpler.

Unlike the English *-ing*, the Spanish suffix *-ndo* on verbs, whose lexical entry is (3.20), does not double as a derived nominal affix (Emonds 1985, Ch. 2).

(3.20) *ndo*, A, +V___, V+[ndo] selects like V inside its maximal projection, but is syntactically an AP.

Exactly as expected, given the above reasoning, there is no pressure on the Spanish participle to develop a gerundive usage. Such a verbal noun phrase in Spanish is expressed rather by the infinitive (*el* + V) (cf. Plann, 1981).

Let us now partly formalize the lexical specification "selects like V inside its maximal projection, but its maximal projection is syntactically a [+N]-phrase." One possibility is to derive participles and gerunds transformationally, as in (3.21).

(3.21)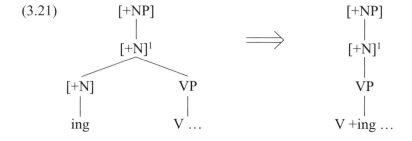

80 *Structures in lexical projections*

This approach fails to answer the second question in (3.14): it necessitates an *ad hoc* extension of affix movement beyond the well-established linking of I and V, and, worse, it fails to unify the syntactic and derivational morphology uses of *ing*.[7]

Another problem with (3.21) concerns a general property of gerunds and participles that I have not previously brought out. Not only does the head *V+ing* of these constructions select complements and specifiers inside its maximal projection like a V, it also *is lexically selected by exterior heads like a V,* and not like an NP with a lexical N, an AP with a lexical A, or an IP. That is, when the maximal projection of *V+ing* is in complement position and subject to lexical selection by a governing Y^0, it does not appear automatically as a possible complement to all (and only) the Y^0s which are subcategorized for NP's or AP's.

For example, intransitive verbs of temporal aspect and transitive perception verbs take present participle complements, but not necessarily AP's.

(3.22) John {kept, resumed, ceased} {criticizing me, *mad at Bill}.
John heard Mary {scolding Sam, *mad at Sam}.

Conversly, verbs which take AP's do not necessarily take participles:

(3.23) John {felt, looked, became} {sick, *taking medicine}.

A parallel distinction can be noted for NP-gerunds in object position.

(3.24) Mary {believed, repeated} {my account, *visiting Canada}.[8]

Thus, the distributional characteristics of gerunds and participles, roughly expressed in (3.12) and (3.18), can be rendered more adequately as follows:

(3.25) With respect to deep lexical selection, participles and gerunds select and are selected like V's.

(3.26) With respect to deep structure and transformational syntactic principles, participles act like AP's and gerunds act like NP's.

The syntactic principles referred to include the composition rules of the bar notation, the requirement that V's and A's must have subject NP's (Chromsky's Extended Projection Principle), the definition of subject, structure-preservation or some counterpart, case theory, binding theory, c-command, and word order parameters.

Given that a participle is now seen to be truly an AP as far as syntax is concerned, we can rewrite the Middle English (3.19) as (3.27).

(3.27) *ing(e)*, [+N], +V___, $\begin{cases} \text{N: V = +ACTIVITY} \\ \text{A: V = +PSYCHOLOGICAL} \\ \text{A: V +[ing] selection like a head of a VP} \end{cases}$

It is now even clearer how Modern English gerunds develop from (3.27): the category A in the third line simply disappears in Modern English.

3.3.2 Selection through lexical heads

It is hardly surprising that lexical selection should be sensitive to morpheme categories such as V (3.25), and that syntax should be sensitive to phrasal labels (3.26). The lexicon is, after all, the repository of properties of morphemes (not of phrases), and syntax has largely been elaborated on the basis of the properties and distribution of phrases. (3.25) and (3.26) are merely reflections of a more general autonomy between syntax and the lexicon; the lexicon expresses relations between categories of morphemes, and syntax expresses relations between phrases and other categories (phrasal or non-phrasal).

To better reflect the centrality of morpheme categories (in contrast to phrasal categories) in lexical selection, I now replace subcategorization frames such as +___NP and +___PP with +___N and +___P. The contextual feature +___X requires the selection of *the largest phrase of which X is the head*. For extensive justification of this move, see Baltin (1989).[9]

The feature +___V now specifies deep structure selection of a phrase whose head, or at least whose selectionally dominant element, is a V. Since the principles of syntax I use here do not permit a bare, the feature +___V in fact requires some other maximal projection, at first glance IP, which accommodates all the head properties of V. What I wish to show, however, is that the principles of syntax can conspire with morphology to produce situations in which a "non-head" V of Y^{max} can act as the selectionally dominant (head-like) member of Y^{max}. In particular, an AP or NP can in fact contain such non-head selectionally dominant V^0.

In order to represent this seemingly incongruous dichotomy, I turn to a proposal made in Emonds (1985, Ch. 5) for introducing inflectional morphology. In contrast to open class items inserted at deep structure, the morphemes of inflectional morphology, among which participial and gerundive *ing* certainly belong, are introduced into syntactic contexts defined in the structures of the phonological component, or "PF". In the cases considered there, the inflectional morphemes (e.g., the finite tense and adjectival comparison endings) are inserted under categories positioned by virtue of transformational movements such as "affix movement." However, there is no reason to exclude such PF insertion of inflectional morphemes into *base* positions of categories. In fact, as will now be explained, surface insertion of a head X^0 into a base configuration $[_x V^0\text{-}X^0]$ will have just the "incongruous effect" of making V^0 selectively dominant – the puzzling factor in (3.12), (3.18), and (3.19).

I thus propose to formally express the Middle English (3.27) by (3.28a). By the historical generalization which introduces the NP-gerund, (3.28a) becomes the Modern English (3.28b).

(3.28) a.

$ing(e)$, [+N], +V___, $\begin{Bmatrix} \text{N: V} = +\text{ACTIVITY; deep insertion} \\ \text{A: V} = +\text{PSYCHOLOGICAL: deep insertion} \\ \text{A: PF insertion} \end{Bmatrix}$

b.

ing, [+N], +V___, $\begin{Bmatrix} \text{N: V} = +\text{ACTIVITY; deep insertion} \\ \text{A: V} = +\text{PSYCHOLOGICAL: deep insertion} \\ \text{PF insertion} \end{Bmatrix}$

A final simplification is possible. In this model utilizing both deep and PF insertion, *deep structure insertion is restricted to inserting elements associated with* (either conditioned by or inducing) *the presence of a purely semantic (non-syntactic) feature.* Thus, since the two uses of *ing* as heads for derived nominals and derived adjectives are conditioned by the presence of semantic features (ACTIVITY, PSYCHOLOGICAL), their insertion in deep structure is fully predictable.[10] In this model, then, most of what is termed "derivational morphology" is the insertion of morphemes as deep structure N, A, and V heads, using the "righthand head" rule within words.

Members of closed classes, therefore, can be inserted in deep structures or PF. It is to be expected that the level of insertion can be predicted from other properties; for example, a proposal that determines which closed class verbs are inserted at deep structure is contained in Emonds (1985, Ch. 4), while

The autonomy of the (syntactic) lexicon and syntax 83

unresolved questions remain about insertion level for various SPEC. But for bound inflectional morphemes, it can be proposed that, *when no semantic features are associated with insertion, PF is always the level of insertion.* Thus, (3.28a–b) can be revised to their final versions:

(3.29) a. Middle English (Revised):

$$ing(e), [+N], +V\_\_\_, \begin{Bmatrix} N: V = +ACTIVITY \\ A: (V = +PSYCHOLOGICAL) \end{Bmatrix}$$

b. Modern English (Revised):

$$ing, [+N], +V\_\_\_, (\begin{Bmatrix} N: V = +ACTIVITY \\ A: V = +PSYCHOLOGICAL \end{Bmatrix})$$

Historically, the development from Chaucer's Middle English participle to Spenser's Modern English gerund consisted in simply moving the parentheses in (3.29) from inside to outside the braces.

The revised (3.29) gives the final simplified form of the lexical entry for *ing* in Modern English; it is completely general, and expresses, as no other competing theory, the related nature of derivational and inflectional *ing*. That is, *ing* is a morpheme added to V to yield forms of category [+N], at either possible level of lexical insertion. When the insertion is conditioned by a semantic feature, the level is deep structure.[11] When the insertion is unconditioned by any semantic factor, the level is PF.

We must now see how surface insertion of *ing* automatically predicts (3.25) and (3.26). We will be working with the representations of English present participles and NP-gerunds (3.30) and (3.31), respectively. These trees are both inputs to logical form. They provide the context for PF insertions; after the insertion of *ing*, the trees are representations in phonological form (PF).

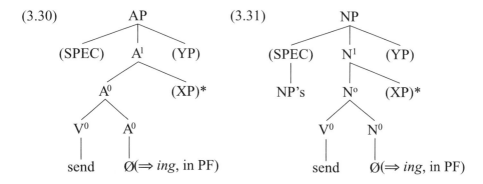

84 *Structures in lexical projections*

It is clear that such phrases will have the syntactic distribution and behavior of AP's and NP's, respectively, and hence conform to (3.26). However, it is not yet obvious how, in line with (3.25), the "non-head" V will select complements (XP), adjuncts (YP), and specifiers in (3.30) and (3.31). And it is even less clear why a higher governing predicate lexically specified as +___V would choose (3.30) or (3.31) instead of, say, an IP whose lexical head is V. Nonetheless, these properties follow from plausible generalizations of independently motivated principles of lexical selection, as will now be seen.

3.4 Defining the lexical head

We first discuss how and why the V in (3.30) and (3.31) acts as an "internal head." The basis of the explanation is a revision of the "righthand head" rule of Lieber (1980), Williams (1981), and Selkirk (1982). Following the lead of Walinska de Hackbeil (1986, Ch. 3), I recast Lieber's definition of head (of an immediately dominating node) so that certain Z^0 are defined as heads of entire maximal projections.

(3.32) *The "lexical head" of W^2 is the rightmost lexically filled Z^0 dominated by W^2 (and by no other maximal projection under W^2).*

In addition, a prohibition on empty deep structure complements is motivated in part by the need to prevent "accidental violations" of subjacency. The prohibition is as follows:[12]

(3.33) A subcategorization relation Z^0, +___X of a morpheme α is satisfied only by a lexical head Z^0 and a complement X^k which both dominate terminal elements after the operation inserting α, unless X is further stipulated as (possibly) empty by the feature in question.

Thus, in order for subcategorization to be satisfied, the selected head category must dominate a terminal element.

We now have the desired basis for explaining (3.25); namely, V^0 in (3.30) and (3.31) is the selected lexical head of AP and NP, due to the late (PF) insertion of *ing* into the bar notation head position of A/N.[13] This late insertion, in both Middle and Modern English, is effected by ignoring the parenthesized material in (3.29).

We now turn our attention to what is outside the first projection in (3.30) and (3.31). The interplay of syntactic principles and lexical selection with respect to the presence of the subject NP node under SPEC makes interesting predictions. We know that the English SPEC(N) may be expanded as an overt NP subject, while the SPEC(A) may not be.

(3.34) SPEC(N) → NP

The definition of subject and the requirement that verbs must have subjects are stated in (3.35)–(3.36).

(3.35) *The subject of a lexical head of W^1 is the closest maximal N^j which minimally c-commands W^1 and is in all the same NP and IP as W^1.*

(3.36) *Extended Projection Principle. Lexical heads which are V or case-marked A must have unique subjects at deep structure, s-structure, and logical form.*[14]

It follows from (3.35) and (3.36) that the optional expansion of SPEC(N) in (3.34) becomes obligatory in NP-gerunds (3.31). This NP may of course be "understood," i.e., an empty category, but the subject of gerunds is invariably structurally present (cf. Wasow and Roeper, 1972). In contrast, (3.35) and (3.36) have no effect in participles, because SPEC(A) does not permit overt NP subjects; consequently, English participles are indistinguishable from verb phrases as far as their relations to subjects go. Thus, principles of syntax correctly predict the existence of separate subjects for gerunds (3.31) and no separate subjects for participles (3.30).

It remains to discuss the selection of specifiers and adjuncts in (3.30) and (3.31). Since lexical selection is in general a relation between pairs of morpheme categories, it is natural to assume that the lexical classes SPEC(N) and SPEC(A), as well as numerals, are licensed by the category of the selectionally dominant lexical head of a phrase. In participles and gerunds, the lexical head (at the level of deep lexical insertion) is a V, and so only modifiers which are SPEC(V) can be chosen for the SPEC position (perhaps certain adverbs such as *already, yet, never, always,* etc.).[15] Similarly, since there are well-known selectional restrictions between nouns and modifying adjectives, it is plausible that in the absence of a lexical head N, no adjective can be chosen.

The particular kinds of adjunct allowed are determined by particular choices of SPEC; this is most evident in the AP system, where each specifier imposes a limitation on adjunct types (*so* with a *that*-clause: *more/less* with a *than*-clause; *as* with an *as*-clause; *too/enough* with an infinitive; *very* with no clause, etc.). Significantly, possessive NP's in SPEC(N) are incompatible with restrictive relative clauses (*John's friend that I saw*); since possessive NP's are always structurally present in NP-gerunds, this suffices to correctly exclude restrictive relative modifiers in this construction. In any case, the choice of adjuncts is dependent on the choice of SPEC, and the latter in turn depends on the category of the lexical head. It follows that gerunds and participles will contain only adjunct phrases compatible with the lexical head V, and none that are selected by lexical choices for SPEC(N) or SPEC(A).

In summary, the definition of a "lexical head" in (3.32) has allowed us to construct a thorough account of how and why NP-gerunds and present participles act internally like VP's. The simple fact that the bar notation heads N or A remain unfilled until after Spell Out provides the key for explaining the "dual nature" of these constituents.

3.5 Lexical selection of non-finite clause types

In the previous section, we have seen that a V whose deep structure sister is $_N[\emptyset]$ or $_A[\emptyset]$ satisfies the definition of "lexical head of a phrase," and thus induces "VP-internal structure" inside gerunds (NPs) and participles (APs). I have claimed that this same lexical head (V) is also selected by higher predicates subcategorized as +___V, with variations as discussed below. More precisely, general principles of grammar, and not *ad hoc* lexical selection for "participles," "gerunds," and "infinitives," determine when +___V leads to choosing one or another of these complement structures.

For example, I claim that verbs such as *keep, avoid, hope* and *decide* share the subcategorization feature +___V, even though they take, respectively, participle, gerund, infinitive and indirect question complement structures.

(3.37) a. John kept mowing the lawn.
      *John kept (when) to mow the lawn.

Participial (AP) complements do not move like NP's:

   b. *Mowing the lawn was kept by John.
      *It was mowing the lawn that John kept.

(3.38) a. John avoided mowing the lawn.
       *John avoided (when) to mow the lawn.

Gerund (NP) complements move like NP's:

   b. Mowing the lawn was avoided by John.
      It was mowing the lawn that John avoided.

(3.39) a. *John (hoped/decided) mowing the lawn.
       John (hoped/decided) to mow the lawn.
   b. *John hoped when to mow the lawn.
      John decided when to mow the lawn.

For discussion of tests which differentiate participles (3.37) from gerunds (3.38), see Milsark (1972), Emonds (1973) and Pullum (1974).

To explain such distribution, I utilize the theory of subcategorization and θ-role assignment developed in Emonds (1985, Ch. 1). The central principles are an uncontroversial condition for θ-role assignment (3.40) and an extension (3.41). Z is a lexical head subcategorized for a complement phrase α to which Z may assign a θ-role.

(3.40) *Direct θ-role Assignment. If Z = V or P, then Z and α may be sisters. A given lexical Z may assign only one θ-role directly.*

(3.41) *Indirect θ-role Assignment. If principles of syntax block (3.40), then α must dominate the only lexical material under a sister of Z.*

Unless otherwise licensed by (3.40), all phrasal sisters to an X^0 or X^1 in the bar notation are of the form PP or CP (cf. Emonds, 1985, Ch. 7, for arguments that CP is a subcase of PP).

In a phrasal subcategorization frame +___α, α can just be an X^0 (in our notation), or, as in Chomsky (1965), α may consist of a grammatical formative category linked to a phrase; e.g., α = of ^ N with the verb *think*. For typographical convenience, I introduce a caret ^ in subcategorization features for linking grammatical formatives and phrases to replace the arch "⌒" of Chomsky (1965) and Emonds (1985).

Let us start by simply illustrating indirect θ-role assignment in (3.42)–(3.44). In the first case, a verb and its associated derived nominal (*promise*) share the subcategorization +___NP^NP (+___N^N in our newer notation),

88 *Structures in lexical projections*

but the prohibition on direct θ-role assignment by N and A makes indirect θ-role assignment in the derived nominal (3.42) the only option. That is, since the only lexical material under sisters of X^0 must be under NP's, the P's in (3.42) are necessarily empty when *promise* is inserted.

(3.42)   promise of a book to John

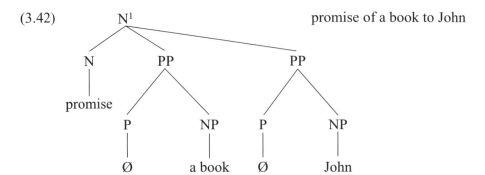

In (3.43), the deep structure for *decide when to mow the lawn* results from the frame for *decide +___(WH)^V*; the V determines that *decide* takes a complement phrase with a V head (a VP) which, prior to WH-movement, dominates the only lexical material under a sister (CP) of *decide*. The same frame for the related derived nominal *decision* gives rise to (3.44). Like many other grammatical morphemes, *to* under I is inserted only after Spell Out.[16]

(3.43)

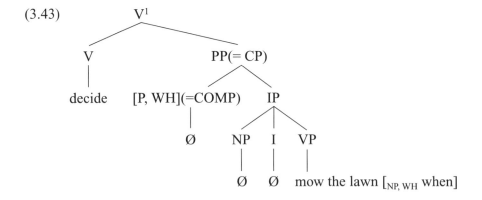

(3.44)

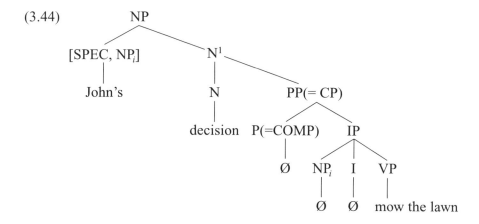

3.5.1 The choice between Participles and Gerunds

According to (3.41), direct θ-role assignment has priority over indirect θ-role assignment. We can factor this stipulation out of (3.41) and generalize it:

(3.45) *Minimal Structure: Co-occurrence restrictions are satisfied by deep structure trees which contain the fewest number of phrasal nodes consistent with the principles of syntax.*

Hence, verbs cannot take the "unnecessary" indirect θ-role assignment which would parallel the devived nominal (3.42):

(3.46) *Bill promised of a book to John.

Minimal Structure can be taken as a special case of a Principle of Economy of Representation in Chomsky (1988, 128): "The analogous principle for representations would stipulate that, just as there can be no superfluous steps in derivations, so there can be no superfluous symbols in representations."

Let us now turn to the selection of non-finite complements. The definition of lexical head (3.32) and Minimal Structure together now interact to make a series of correct predictions about the distribution of non-finite clausal structures in English. Since English PF insertion of *ing* de facto licenses [V-[Ø]] at Spell Out, the node which is both maximal with respect to V being its head and minimal in the sense of (3.45) *is in fact AP*. An NP with a lexical head V (a gerund) would contain an extra subject NP phrase, and a VP, not being an extended projection, would entail the presende of both an IP and a subject NP. Thus, the "preferred" non-finite structure, other principles of syntax permitting, will be a participle (AP).

In non-subcategorized positions (e.g., those of restrictive relative and of adverbial clauses), the non-finite English structures without overt subject NP's are in fact participles, as predicted. In subcategorized positions, the frames +___V of temporal aspect verbs (e.g., *keep*) and +___N^V of perception verbs (e.g., *hear*) are also satisfied by participles (cf. 3.37a).[17]

Nonetheless, it is only by virtue of an exceptional lexical property that the two classes of verbs just mentioned do not run afoul of a principle of syntax. Temporal aspect verbs assign no independent θ-role to their subject, nor do perception verbs to their object. In other words, *keep* and *hear* assign θ-roles following the downward solid arrows in (3.47 a–b), respectively, but not following the broken arrows. The θ-roles assigned by the embedded verbs to their NP subjects, as defined in (3.35), are indicated by upward solid arrows.

(3.47) a.

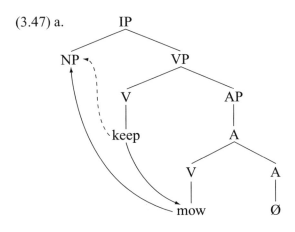

(3.47) b.

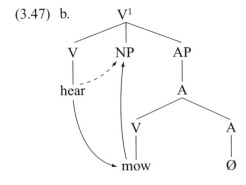

If θ-roles were assigned along the broken arrows in (3.47), this would violate a principle of syntax, the "θ-criterion," which under certain circumstances prevents a single NP from being assigned two θ-roles.[18]

Most verbs with the feature +___V do in fact assign θ-roles along the broken lines in (3.47a); e.g., *avoid, attempt, complete, describe, explain*, etc. In these case, Minimal Structure (3.45) allows a phrasal structure to be generated if it contains an additional NP that permits the θ-criterion to be respected, with θ-roles assigned as in (3.48).

(3.48)

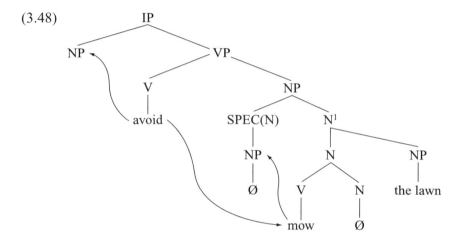

After *ing* is inserted according to (3.29) in PF, NP-gerunds as in (3.38) correctly result.

If a transitive verb, e.g. *tell, remind*, subcategorized as +___N^V assigns θ-roles to both complements, the θ-criterion could be respected via either (3.49a) or (3.49b).

(3.49) a.

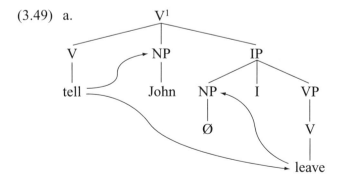

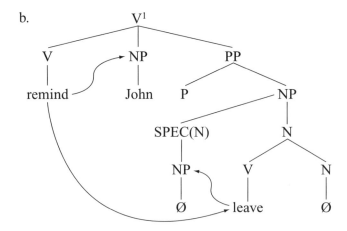

By inspection, we see that Minimal Structure allows either choice, if single bar projections are ignored. This seems correct, given possibilities as in (3.50).[19]

(3.50) They {reminded/told} John {to leave/of leaving}.

We have seen that the minimal structure induced by +___V in English (thanks to PF-inserted *ing*) is preferably a participial AP and then, *pace* the θ-Criterion, an NP-gerund. However, since gerunds are NPs, they cannot immediately follow direct objects, nor can they be sisters to N or A, because then there is no category to assign them Case. When a second complement to a V (or a first complement to N or A) is specified by +___V, and when the governing head assigns all its complements θ-roles, then +___V conforms to Minimal Structure (3.45) either via an NP-gerund embedded in a PP structure, as in (3.51), or via infinitives of obligatory control, as in (3.52).

(3.51) Bill accused John of working slowly.
       Bill limited John to working nights.
       His preference for eating fish is understandable.

(3.52) Bill forced John to work fast.
       Bill urged John to work nights.
       His tendency to eat fish is understandable.

3.5.2 Why Infinitives and not Gerunds?

Certain verbs do not accept a gerund or a participle as a first complement, yet are not subcategorized for a sentence (they are not listed as +___I). Such verbs take infinitives with obligatorily understood subjects (obligatory control), sometimes with the added possibility for fronted WH-constituents.

(3.53) John hoped (*when) {to mow/*mowing} the lawn.

(3.54) John will decide (when) {to mow/*mowing} the lawn.

Unless an indirect question is involved, some additional factor beyond +___V must force a verb like *hope* or *decide* to take an IP, rather than appear with gerunds. As discussed in more detail in Emonds (1985, Ch. 2), I claim that the complements of such verbs express an "unrealized" or future/potential modality, which is syntactically translated as the obligatory presence of the category modal M on the head I of IP. Thus, verbs like *hope* and *decide* have the subcategorization feature +___M^V, and verbs which take an indirect question appear with the similar lexical frame +___WH^V.

Consider now a verb like *hope*, which does not accept an indirect question. In the system used here, either the feature +___M^V or the feature +___GOAL^V (where GOAL characterizes the complementizer/preposition *for*) will induce an IP complement with obligatory control. In order for M or GOAL to be present, the sister of *hope* in Indirect θ-role Assignment (3.41) must include IP or CP. Either way, VP is the largest phrase for which *hope* is subcategorized (i.e., of which V is the head), so that at deep structure, all of COMP, its subject NP, and its I must be empty, by (3.41). The surface realization of unmarked COMP with an empty subject is Ø, and that of empty I is *to* (cf. Emonds, 1985, Ch. 7, and Lobeck, 1986, respectively). In this manner, infinitives of obligatory control arise from the frame +___F^V, without invoking any feature specific to infinitives; MODAL and GOAL are features which have independent justifications in any analysis of finite clauses and indirect object PPs.

It is a simple matter to specify other occurring subcategorizations of English verbs. For example, a range of verbs like *arrange, beg, pray, watch, wait*, etc. take either *for* + NP, *for* + IP, or an infinitive of obligatory control:

(3.55) John was waiting for the train.
John was waiting for the train to leave.
John was waiting to leave.

A verb like *wait* can be assigned the unified frame +___([P, GOAL]). The subject of an IP complement to P(=COMP) will be lexical or empty, giving rise to a *for-to* clause or a bare infinitive.

A verb like *decide* does not accept an *ing* complement clause (3.39). It might be listed as +___(WH)M^V. However, this frame would employ two pre-head features. The same complement types can be generated via the frame +___{WH, GOAL}^V. In fact, since the only complementizers (P) which are even compatible with an empty I (an infinitive) are WH (*whether*) and GOAL, the desired frame for *decide* might reduce to +___P^V. Indirect θ-role Assignment (3.41) will still insure that the subject NP is empty (obligatorily controlled).

If +___F^V (F = GOAL, WH, MODAL) are possible subcategorizations, then the features +___(F)^V should also exist. The value of F = M or GOAL is realized by several temporal aspect verbs whose complements are optionally realized as participles or as infinitives of "modal force": *begin, start, continue* (but not *finish* or *resume*). Such distributions can be elegantly captured by the feature +___(M)^V. Without M, Minimal Structure (3.45) will favor a participial (AP) complement structure for these verbs, made possible by the English PF insertion of *ing*. With M, an IP-complement containing [I.M] must be generated, yielding infinitives.

When the same frames +___(M)^V or +___(GOAL)^V occur with a non-aspectual verb, the choice of V without M leads, as expected, to an NP gerund complement. Consequently, there can be verbs which take either NP-gerunds, without modal force, or infinitives, with modal force.

(3.56) John has tried to climb the mountain.
John has tried climbing the mountain.

The fact that *try* can also occur with NP or *for* +NP suggests that its most general frame is +___(GOAL)^{N, V}, which correctly provides four different options.

Another example of the insertion frame +___V optionally accompanied by an introductory feature is provided by +___(WH)^V. This feature gives rise to a type of complement paradigm which is not uncommon in English, but which has not previously been naturally expressible in terms of even *ad hoc* features for gerunds and infinitives.

(3.57)

The lawyer discussed { buying some clothes in Rome.
*what clothes buying in Rome.
*to buy some clothes in Rome.
what clothes to buy in Rome. }

(3.58)

I don't recall { using these dishes for lunch.
*which dishes using for lunch.
*to use these dishes for lunch.
which dishes to use for lunch. }

That is, our system expresses very naturally the "changeover" from gerundive to infinitival structure with those factive verbs which can take indirect questions. No competing system which differentiates infinitives and *ing* forms on the basis of features internal to V, rather than on the basis of explanatory principles, can make this non-stipulative prediction.

To summarize, all classes of clausal complements not selected by +___I can be selected by +___(±F)^V, where F is WH, GOAL, or M. When F is present, some type of infinitive of obligatory control results. For gerunds and participles F is not present, the choice between the two being determined by Minimal Structure and the θ-Criterion. The features N or NP are not involved in choosing gerunds; lexical selection of participles and gerunds results entirely from their lexical head being V, and not from their empty structural head A/N. Thus, all "verbal" properties of participles and gerunds in fact result from deep lexical selection, in which verbs are both the selecting and selected verbal head. In other respects, these two constructions are unambiguously AP and NP (respectively) throughout their syntactic derivations.

3.6 Conclusion: all uses of *ing* result from a single entry

The crucial step in this unified analysis of derived nominals, derived adjectives, participles and gerunds is that the single "substantivizing" English verbal affix *ing*, associated with one general lexical entry (3.29), is inserted at both the deep and PF levels. When the insertion is "semantically conditioned," it occurs at deep structure, and selection proceeds as with nouns and adjectives. On the other hand, the "unconditioned" insertion of *ing* occurs, as predicted, at PF, giving rise to the well-known verbal properties of gerunds and participles, but in no way neutralizing their syntactic status as NPs and APs.

The verbal properties of gerunds and participles are in fact nothing other than what results from their having lexical V heads at deep structure. Entirely general principles of θ-role assignment and a newly isolated principle of "Minimal Structure" (3.45) determine when the feature +___V gives rise to participles, gerunds or infinitives.

Notes

* It is a pleasure to dedicate this study to my esteemed colleague, S.-Y. Kuroda. This work fits into our shared research program of rendering unto syntax what is syntactic (namely, most of what is linguistically interesting), and of rendering unto the lexicon very little.

   I am grateful to Professot José Deulofeu for providing teaching condictions under which research could be simultaneously undertaken. The stimulating paper presented by Professor Abdelkader Fassi Fehri at the 1987 International Conference of the Moroccan Linguistic Society on the related Arabic *masdar* construction was crucial in refocusing my interest on this topic.

   This essay here is a somewhat shortened version of Emonds (1991a). Some terms that have become unfamiliar have been changed: S is now IP and $\bar{\text{S}}$ is now CP. More centrally, what I called there "s-structure insertion" is here PF insertion or Spell Out, and my earlier "functional head" is here bar notation head.

1. Other languages have gerund phrases of this sort; cf. George and Kornfilt (1981) for Turkish and Fassi Fehri (1986) for Arabic.
2. Milsark (1988) also argues for a unified lexical entry for *ing*. His main proposal is that *ing* is "unique among derivational affixes, at least in English" (as well as among inflectional affixes) in lacking a category specification. (Uncontroversially, as here, *ing* suffixes to V.) The many problems with his proposal to my mind undercut severely his idea that (only) *ing* lacks a category.

   As one result, for example, Milsark is empirically "forced to predict that *ing* should be available to form lexical items of the class V in addition to the N, P, and A items exemplified above" (615). However, no examples of lexically derived V are provided, since none exist: **The article convincings me*; *she helpinged us, etc. For another example, Milsark ends up stipulating how "different instances of *-ing*-affixed lexical items acquire their various categorial identities in the absence of any specification thereof by either their stems or the *-ing* affix itself." Thus, such an item can become N or V by "the provisions of Case theory, predication, θ-theory, and so on"), P ("listed lexically under their appropriate categorial feature specifications"), or A ("a semantically motivated bifurcation of the class of verbs with respect to their ability to accept *-ing* affixation") (616).

Indeed, Milsark's sections 2 and 3 read as a catalog of problems that arise when *ing* is accorded unique categoryless status.
3. The N and A in (3.10) may be viewed as easy-to-read representations of [–V] and [+V] respectively, where, using Chomsky (1970), N = [+N, –V] and A = [+N, +V].
4. Some of them can contain parasitic gaps: *the papers he read without sending on to John*. An analysis of these gaps, which involves an operator in subject position but not a separate COMP, is given in Emonds (1985, section 2.5) and developed here in Chapter 10.
5. Borer (1990) claims that the pre-head participles as in (3.15) are AP's, and that their heads are A's; if Borer is right (i.e., *conversing* in (3.15) is a lexical adjective), the framework of the present study is unaffected; such forms are simply derived adjectives rather than present participles, and then cannot be used to further confirm that participles have the syntactic distribution of AP. However, since I contest some of her empirical paradigms, I continue to maintain that premodification by SPEC(A) = *very, rather, how, as, more, less, too*, etc. is necessary for the deep A status of V+*ing*, though, as Borer points out, it is only a sufficient condition for V+*en* (**very unoccupied*).
6. We have now seen that clauses headed by V+*ing* appear structurally in NP and AP positions, but not in VP, IP, or PP positions. In contrast, Milsark (1988) "would thus expect to find nominal, verbal, adjectival, and even prepositional 'gerundives,' ... It is the major contention of this article that essentially this state of affairs obtains in English ..." (618). Yet later, he observes: "Of prepositional gerundives there is not a trace" (631). His subsequent denial that the problem exists (section 5.3) is unconvincing; I see nothing in his system that excludes, for example, **They put us crossing the street*, analogous to *They put us across the street*. Moreover, there is no natural way for him to exclude gerundives in typical VP or IP positions; although for him present participles are "verbal gerundives", we have just surveyed the evidence that they have rather the distribution of AP.
7. The approach of Reuland (1983), who derives *ing* from INFL, provides no explanation for the NP and AP distributions of gerunds and participles, respectively, except through appeals to "neutralization".
8. Not all NP-gerund objects alternate with regular NP-objects with lexical head N's: *discourge/preyent friends from {taking pills/*a long vacation/*frequent visits}*.
9. Writing the selected category to the right of the blank (Y, +___X) requires selecting a phrase as a complement to Y, whereas Y, +X___ indicates selection of an X^0 underneath Y^0. Alternatively, we could define Y, +___X and Y, +X___ as directly representing left-to-right order, with a general word order parameter of English determining that all and only the complements to the right of a head Y are maximal in deep structure.

10. Similarly, insertion of open class N, A, and V can only take place at deep structure, since the members of N, A, and V (except for small closed subsets of grammatical N, A, and V) are differentiated only by purely semantic features.
11. I argue in Emonds (1985, Chs. 2 and 3) that "deep structure insertion" is actually insertion into the head of a given domain D at the beginning of the cycle on D. As long as insertion of all elements in D occurs during the transformational cycle on D (even at the end of this cycle), the head of D will be filled during subsequent cycles, which is all that is required for what I called "deep structure insertion."
12. For languages which allow empty "small pro" complements (English does not), (3.33) must be modified appropriately. This extension is not of concern here.
13. In recent grammatical discussion, one hears of insertion "at a level," as if an element (e.g., abstract case) could be simultaneously absent and present. This type of illogic is avoided here. S-structure defines the context for *ing*-insertion, but *ing*-insertion itself derives a post s-structure representation.
14. I make no effort to reconcile my proposals with "small clause" analyses of English AP's. Cf. Williams (1983) and the Appendix of Ch. 1 of this volume for critiques.
15. In derived nominals and adjectives, the head throughout the syntactic derivation is the N or A *ing*, so this filled head, like any other N or A, permits selection of SPEC(N) or SPEC(A) and appropriate corresponding adjunct phrases.
16. The explication of licensing conditions for zeroed infinitives after *to* in Lobeck (1986) utilizes this analysis of *to*, and thus provides independent support for it.
17. Milsark (1972) establishes that the domain of the "double *ing* filter" does not apply across an NP boundary, which seems like a plausible restriction on all such filters. However, Milsark (1988) recasts this filter to apply to "any sentence containing contiguous -*ing*-affixed words". I don't believe this succeeds, given examples such as *his amazing findings*, etc.
18. In Emonds (1985, Ch. 2), arguments are presented that the θ-Criterion of Chomsky (1981) must be modified as follows, where X^0 and Y^0 are "θ-related" if and only if one assigns a θ-role to the maximal projection of the other.

    Revised θ-Criterion, θ-relatedness is anti-transitive.
19. By Indirect θ-role Assignment, where α = VP in (3.49a) and NP in (3.49b), the lower NP in (3.49a) and the P in (3.49b) must be empty in deep structure. As discussed in detail in Emonds (1985, Ch. 2), "obligatory control" in infinitives is thus predicted by independently justified principles of θ-role assignment. Of course, as in competing accounts, the antecedent of the controlled NP must be determined by the binding theory or a special control rule.

Chapter 4
Secondary predication, stationary particles, and silent prepositions

Generative grammar has progressed to the stage where an interplay of simple theoretical statements, each formulated in exceptionless terms, should provide the only acceptable accounts of apparently skewed and highly language-specific configurations. Even "lexical residues" should express descriptive generalisations and conform to justifiable cross-linguistic properties of lexicons. In the best case, the contributions of lexical entries should be simple, if highly specific, since these entries must after all be learned, in the context of precisely the same incomplete poverty of the stimulus that is used to justify universal grammar.[1]

4.1 Lexical representations of Intransitive Prepositions

One lexical difference between English and French concerns the so-called adverbial post-verbal particles of English: *in, out, up, down, back, away, on, off, together, apart, through, over, by, around*. The verbs *go* and *come* and their combinations with certain of these particles are the best translations for a small set of non-transitive motional verbs in French with special syntactic properties.

(4.1) aller 'go'   venir 'come'
       entrer 'go/come in'   sortir 'go/come out'
       partir 'go away'   descendre 'go/come down'
       arriver 'come, arrive'   paraître 'come out, appear'

       revenir 'come back'
       rentrer 'go/come back'
       monter 'go/come up'
       rester 'stay, not go'

These motional verbs in French have at least the following two syntactic characteristics:

(4.2) i. Only these motional verbs form their composed past with *être* 'be' rather than *avoir* 'have'. Verbs for running, swimming, driving, moving, walking, flying, etc., like the vast majority of French verbs, are composed with *avoir*.
ii. Their infinitival complements (not adjuncts) of purpose, unlike other infinitives of purpose or other infinitives of obligatory control, cannot have independent aspect or negation nor be introduced by COMP elements, etc.[2]

The English adverbial particles which serve so well to translate these special French verbs, including many apparently idiomatic usages shared by the two languages, themselves have several well-studied grammatical characteristics. Semantically, these particles seem to express basic dichotomies of spatial orientation which children acquire very early. Both semantically and according to syntactic tests (discussed below), these particles contrast with other place adverbials which express more complex and/or culture-specific concepts, such as *downtown, indoors, nearby, outside, overboard, overhead, underneath, upstairs, backwards, crosswise, sideways*.

Plausibly, the post-verbal particles (and any corresponding grammatical prepositions) are characterised by a set of basic universal cognitive features of spatial orientation F_i. These F_i are then supplemented by more specified semantic features f_j in the lexical entries of adverbs of the *outside* type.

Both these adverbial classes should be analysed as intransitive P (Emonds, 1986:Ch. 6), since they satisfy the subcategorisation +___PP, may be modified by the P-specifier *right*, and occur in the root construction [PP, PATH] + *with* DP: *In (side) (the house) with that cat!* Consequently, the English lexicon contains entries as follows:

(4.3) a. out, P, +___(PP), F_n
back, P, +___(PP), F_m
b. outside, P, +___({PP, DP}), F_n, f_k
backwards, P, +___, F_m, f_l

We may ask if the universal cognitive features of spatial orientation F_i have any special status in grammar. It is immediately obvious they do; we have in fact divided the adverbial particles between "basic" and "derived" spatial concepts (e.g., between *out* and *outside*) precisely because one class has a range of characteristic syntactic behaviour. For example, the basic intransitive particles are ill-formed as the focus constituent in a cleft or pseudo-cleft sentence, while other PPs are well-formed.

(4.4) It was {in(side) the box / back in the shed / upstairs / outdoors / sideways / overhead / in there / with the lawn chairs} that she laid the tools.
*It was {out / back / down / together / around} that she laid the tools.
Where she laid the tools was {in(side) the box / back in the shed / upstairs / inside / overhead / in there / with the lawn chairs}.
*Where she laid the tools was {out / back / down / together / around}.

From (4.4) we can conclude that either a stipulation or a consequence of some general principle must have the following effect.

(4.5) PP is ill-formed as a (pseudo-)cleft focus if PP is intransitive and exhaustively dominates only F_i.

Chomsky (1965: Ch. 2) proposes that a feature is syntactic if and only if it appears in a syntactic rule or principle. To express (4.5), some syntactic statement must distinguish between the "basic" features F_i and the "more specific" semantic features f_j. It is furthermore hard to see how such a rule or principle might be stated or entailed in terms of a heterogeneous grouping of f_j and transitive PP lacking f_j (e.g., *in there*); therefore, some syntactic rule or principle must rather involve only F_i. Chomsky's proposal then suggests that it is the F_i which are syntactic, while the f_j are semantic. That is, the English post-verbal particles are fully specified by syntactic features (4.3a), while the other intransitive adverbials are further specified with what Chomsky (1965) calls purely semantic features (4.3b). We call items such as (4.3a) closed class or grammatical items, and those like (4.3b) open class or dictionary items.

(4.6) *Grammatical Heads. A grammatical N, V, A, or P is defined as one whose lexical entry contains no purely semantic feature.*

Returning briefly to French, the syntactic features F_i serve to define a closed class of (grammatical) verbs with entries as in (4.7), where MOTION is also a syntactic feature.

(4.7) sortir, V,+___(PP), MOTION, F_n, where F_n is as in (4.3).

Analyses of the constructions in (4.2) should crucially utilise the fact that the lexical entries of these French verbs contain no semantic features.

4.2 Case Transparency and Word Order of Intransitive Prepositions

Earlier work on post-verbal particles (e.g., Emonds, 1985:Ch. 6) demonstrates that both their literal (spatial) and idiomatic variants should be generated in deep structure in the same position as other directional PPs. Therefore, they occur without stipulation at least in the position *to the right* of object DPs.[3]

In order to generalise, let us follow the idea of Stowell (1981) that phrasal sisters to the English verb are ordered freely, and that direct object DPs are adjacent to the head V becaise only in this position can they receive abstract accusative case. Then intransitive as well as all other PPs should not intervene between V and DP, and they generally do not. Still, as is well-known, the post-verbal particles as in (4.3a) are the sole PP which may intervene between a V and a following case-marked DP.

(4.8) The lawyer took {down / away / *downtown / *outside} some papers.
They carried {up / out / *upstairs / *sideways} a chair.
The force pushed {over / back / *overboard / *backwards} John.

Early transformational grammar postulated a particle movement rule to account for the grammatical order allowed in (4.8). We can eliminate this ad hoc rule if we can find an unstipulated theory-based answer to the following question.[4]

(4.9) Why are intransitive grammatical (as opposed to lexical) Ps transparent for Stowell's adjacency condition on case assignment?

Three possible reasons, all to be rejected, come to mind.
 (i) The movement of particles (toward the verb) could occur only in the PF component, subsequent to case assignment at the s-structure level. But such a rule is ad hoc, and in general the PF component does not contain highly specific movement rules, if indeed it allows for any movement at all.
 (ii) These particles could transformationally "incorporate" into V, so that V-DP adjacency is not impaired. Several arguments against this view are

given in Emonds (1993: note 27). For example, the resulting [$_V$V-P] structures would violate the English Righthand Head rule, and are pronounced neither as compounds nor as inflections. Besides these problems, why should incorporation be limited to precisely the subset of grammatical Ps which lack purely semantic features?

(iii) Assuming particle movement (toward the verb), case assignment could take place at deep structure. Besides the accumulated evidence that accusative case is assigned at s-structure, why then could not all, say, intransitive Ps freely occur in V___DP, counter to the contrast in (4.8)?

In several works, I have argued for a dichotomy in how items undergo lexical insertion:

(4.10) *Deep Lexicalization. Items associated with non-syntactic, purely semantic features f satisfy lexical insertion conditions before any transformations apply to domains containing them.*

(4.11) *Late Lexicalization. Items specified by syntactic features alone can satisfy insertion conditions subsequent to when transformations apply to domains containing them.*

A much better answer to (4.9) is now provided by (4.12).

(4.12) *Case Adjacency. In Case Assignment, the case-assigning category and the DP cannot be separated by material in the terminal string.*

If DP and PP sisters to V are freely ordered, Case Adjacency (4.12) requires that only those PPs which dominate *no terminal element* may precede the object DP.[5] According to the proposed lexical entries for grammatical prepositions as specified in (4.3), their Late Lexicalisation guarantees that the intransitive post-verbal particles of English are precisely the only PPs which don't dominate terminal elements in syntax. Hence, (4.6) and (4.11) together predict that (only) these particles are transparent for accusative case assignment by the verb.

The hypothesis of Late Lexicalisation (4.11) also sheds light on the preliminary formulation (4.5) of a restriction on (pseudo-)cleft focus constituents. Under the late insertion of grammatical morphemes, (4.5) can now be generalised to the more plausible and perspicuous (4.13):

104 *Structures in lexical projections*

(4.13) The focus position in a (pseudo-)cleft must dominate a terminal element prior to Late Lexicalization.

Taken together, our hypotheses have eliminated the ad hoc local rule of English particle movement, have permitted us to maintain an exceptionless statement of case assignment, and have brought us closer to a general characterisation of the focus positions in pseudo-cleft and cleft sentences.

4.3 Stationary Particles and Secondary Predication[6]

In a series of studies involving prepositions, Jackendoff (esp. 1987, 1990) has developed a distinction between PATH (or directional) and PLACE (or static locational) prepositions. The post-verbal particles as in (4.3a) are of the PATH type, and thus PATH is included among the syntactic features F_i.

There are also instances of post-verbal particle morphemes occurring in PLACE rather than PATH contexts. In such instances, exemplified in (4.14), these morphemes usually take on a more specific meaning; e.g., *in* means 'in a house or office', *away* or *out* means 'not in a house or office', *over* means 'completed', *down* means 'not functioning properly', *on* means 'connected' or 'scheduled', *off* means 'disconnected' or 'not scheduled', etc.

(4.14) The salesman found John in.
The couple wanted their dog out at night.
We saw the computer down when we left.
She likes her parents together in their retirement.
The guests judged the dinner over soon afterwards.
The management always stores appliances off.

This added semantic specificity suggests two differences between the lexical entries of the usual post-verbal particles as in (4.3a) and these almost idiomatic extensions of them. Post-verbal particles of PLACE as in (4.14) (i) lack the feature PATH, and (ii) are characterised instead with some purely semantic feature(s) f_j.

An interesting difference between PATH and PLACE particles is that the latter systematically relate to direct objects as secondary predicates, as the paraphrases (4.15) show. When a similar exercise is carried out with the familiar post-verbal PATH particles, only sporadic and often inexact paraphrases (4.16) are found.

(4.15) The salesman found John in; that is, John was in
The couple wanted their dog out; that is, the dog was to be out.
We saw the computer down; that is, the computer was down.
She likes her parents together; that is, her parents are together.
The guests judged the dinner over; that is, the dinner was over.
The management stores appliances off; that is, applicances are off.

(4.16) *The salesman took John in; that is, John was in.
The couple let their dog out; that is, the dog was out.
*We set the computer down; that is, the computer was down.
She keeps her parents together; that is, her parents are together.
*The guests talked the dinner over; that is, the dinner was over.
*The management sells appliances off; that is, appliances are off.

Thus, the relation between the object DP and the post-verbal particle in (4.15) is systematic secondary predication, of the form V-DP-XP, where XP is a predicate.[7] We return to the "inexact" predications of (4.16) in section 4.

Our hypotheses (4.10) and (4.11) make an interesting prediction about the [PLACE, -PATH] post-verbal particles. Since they are lexically specified with some purely semantic feature(s) f_j, they must be inserted in deep structure, and will consequently block accusative case assignment under adjacency. Hence, PLACE particles should not "undergo particle movement" (i.e., they shouldn't occur in the V___DP). PLACE particles must rather be generated to right of the object and appear "stationary". Although this paradigm has largely escaped detection, it manifestly holds and confirms our approach.[8]

(4.17) The salesman {took / *found} in John.
The couple {let / *wanted} out their dog at night.
We {set / *saw} down the computer when we left.
She {keeps / *likes} together her parents in their retirement.
The guests {talked / *judged} over the dinner soon afterwards.
The management always {sells / *stores} off appliances.

Although research has shown that particles which are adjuncts cannot appear before object DPs (*Mark ate out lunch), all the particles in (4.14) can be shown to be complements rather than adjuncts, by say the *do so* test, as in (4.18). Therefore, adjunct status cannot be the explanation for (4.17).[9]

106   *Structures in lexical projections*

(4.18)   *Yesterday the boss found John in, even though today she did so away.
*My housemate saw the computer functioning, but I did so down.
*Other guests judged the dinner still in progress, but Mary did so over.

Finally, let us return to the partial characterisation (4.13) of focus positions in (pseudo-)cleft constructions. By (4.10) – (4.11), since PLACE particles are inserted prior to transformational movement and PATH particles subsequent to it, the acceptability contrasts of (4.17) should be reversed in focus contexts. This prediction of a contrast is borne out, though other factors seem to influence the absolute judgments.

(4.19)   It was in that the salesman {found / *took} John.
It was out that the couple {wanted / ?let} their dog.
It was down that we {?saw / *set} the computer.
It was over that the guests {?judged / *talked} the dinner.

(4.20)   {Where / How} the salesman {?found / *took} John was in.
Where the couple {?wanted / *let} their dog at night was out.
Where she {?likes / *keeps} her parents in retirement is together.
How the management {stores / *sells} the appliances is off.

This concludes the justification for analysing directional or PATH post-verbal particles as late-inserted grammatical P, in contrast to the open classes of intransitive adverbial P (4.3b) and stationary intransitive P of PLACE (this section). One puzzle however remains: is there some kind of secondary predication relation hidden within some PPs of PATH which follow direct objects, as the mixed judgments (4.16) might suggest?

4.4 Stacked PPs, Silent Ps, and the Revised Theta Criterion

The relation of directional or PATH PPs to secondary predication is best revealed in *from-to* constructions and in the unusual construction where *to* introduces an AP.

(4.21)   Ann took the kittens from inside the house to behind the barn.
News of the job transformed her from gloomy to optimistic.
They moved from west of Chicago to north of Miami.
A drink ought to change your mood to happy.

In these examples, the basic P of PATH *to* introduces an AP or a PP of PLACE which is secondarily predicated of the direct object DP. That is, a P of PATH is not a predication, but may rather introduce one, which may in turn be a PP. The structure [P, PATH *to*] plays a role similar to a copular verb, or more exactly to an inchoative verb expressing a change of state, as in *The kittens got behind the bar* or *She became optimistic*.

The same structure is reflected by the compound prepositions *into* and *onto*, where the optional *to* is a kind of "inflection" which expresses a higher governing empty [P, PATH], analogous to a verbal inflection expressing a higher empty governing I (cf. Emonds (1987), for a more general theory of such "alternative realisation" via inflection). Thus, in sentences like *They lifted Sam on(to) the chair*, the predication is not *Sam is onto the chair*, but rather, mediated by a P of PATH, *Sam is on the chair*.

Summarising, the constructions discussed here all point to the conclusion that PP predications are *uniformly* expressed by PPs of PLACE, not of PATH.[10] Four trees in (4.22) exemplify parallel PATH structures introducing English predication constituents.

(4.22) a.

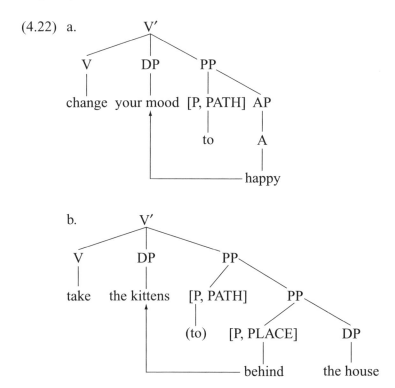

108 *Structures in lexical projections*

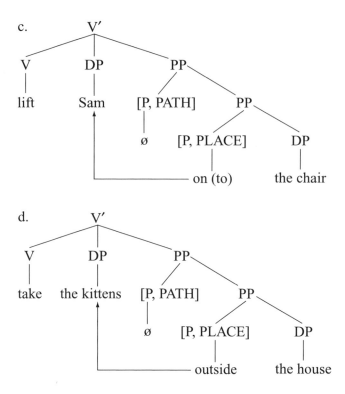

The arrows in (4.22) point from the heads of the constituents of secondary predication toward their subject DPs.

In languages other than English, overt morphology is more often required to express the tree structure for P of PATH seen in (4.22).

(4.23) Japanese translation of (4.22d):

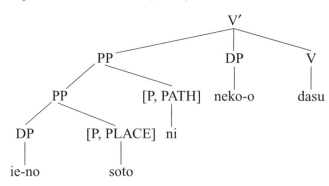

Secondary predication, stationary particles, and silent prepositions   109

French translation of (4.22d):

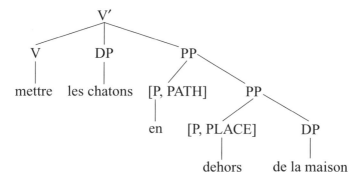

The structures (4.22) with silent prepositions raise an important theoretical question:

(4.24) What in the theory of grammar can require the presence of the phrases in (4.22) with empty heads?

Let us compare verbs whose complement structures consist of clear secondary predications in (4.14) (*find, want, see, like, judge, store*) with transitive verbs which take PATH complements as in (4.21). The former have essentially one semantic or theta role to assign to a complement, either to the object DP (e.g., *store appliances*) or to the predication constituent in other instances (e.g., *like* and *want*, as argued in Stowell (1981)). On the other hand, transitive verbs with PATH complements seem to assign roles to *both* the object DP and to the oblique complement, as seen in (4.25). As a result some verbs of this type can obligatorily require two complements and/or choose the introductory P of the directional PP idiosyncratically.

(4.25)

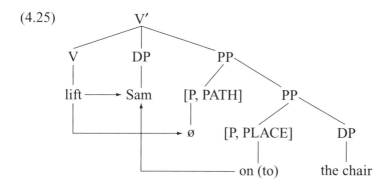

110 *Structures in lexical projections*

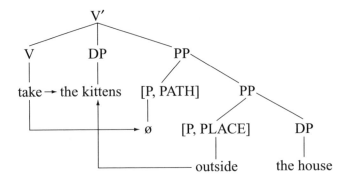

If these observations are accurate, then question (4.24) can be rephrased. (I here identify predication with theta-role assignment to an external argument.) What favours structures with theta-role assignments and predications as indicated by the arrows in (4.25) and (4.26), while the "simpler" or more economical representations of (4.27) are apparently illegitimate?

(4.26)

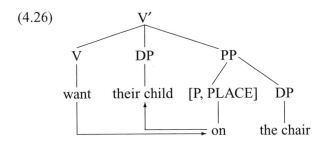

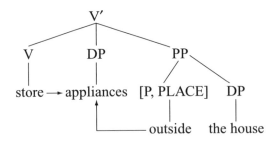

Secondary predication, stationary particles, and silent prepositions 111

(4.27)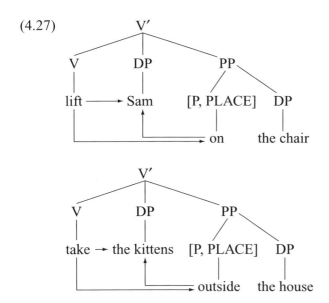

Earlier work (Emonds, 1985: Ch. 2 and 1991a, which is Ch. 3 of this volume) extensively argues in favour of a succinct and yet far from obvious principle of theta role assignment (4.28); its restrictiveness falls between Chomsky's (1981: 36, 335) two Theta Criteria, whose empirical imports greatly differ. The work cited shows how the formulation (4.28) predicts, for example, when and how simple undifferentiated subcategorisation for non-finite complements yields the varying distributions of infinitives, gerunds, and participles, with no lexical reference to their internal structure.

(4.28) *Revised Theta Criterion. Theta-relatedness is anti-transitive.*[11]

At the time I devised (4.28), I took the structures in (4.27) to be obvious representations for directional PATH PP complements.[12] Nonetheless, I was aware that they were (the only) potentially embarassing counterexamples to (4.28), as illustrated by the arrows in (4.27). In their place, the structures of (4.22) have been motivated here on independent grounds (i.e., PATH constituents *introduce* rather than correspond to secondary predications on direct objects). Happily the theta-role assignments in structures (4.25) and (4.26) are precisely those allowed by the Revised Theta Criterion while those in (4.27) are correctly excluded.

Turning around the conceptualisation, (4.28) in fact explains *why* an *obligatory* layer of PATH structure is superimposed on certain PP complements of PLACE. Generally, subcategorisation frames are realised with a minimum of phrasal projection, pace Chomsky's (1991) Economy of Representation. The secondary predications (4.26) reflect this directly. It is only when the Revised Theta Criterion prohibits otherwise economical realisations such as (4.27) – or participles in the case of non-finite complements – that "second-best" structures such as the empty-headed PATH PPs in (4.25) – or infinitival IPs of obligatory control – serve to express a verb's complements.

This account of English post-verbal particles and other PATH complements has required only simple theoretical statements, each formulated in exceptionless terms. A general statement distinguishes deep (4.10) from phonological or late lexicalisation (4.11); an uncomplicated adjacency condition (4.12) determines structural case assignment; a plausible restriction (4.13) limits focus constituents in (pseudo-)clefts; PATH complements introduce but are not themselves predications; and the widely predictive Revised Theta Criterion (4.28) is now completely general. The lexical residue of English is that its post-verbal particles of PATH appear in entries (4.3a) with no purely semantic features.

Notes

1. The progress of generative grammar toward these goals owes much to a widely influential essay on the passive (Hasegawa, 1968), which proposes and motivates decomposing transformations into simple operations affecting single constituents. This landmark pointed the way toward deriving all complex constructions from the interplay of simple theoretical statements.
2. Lamiroy (1983) makes a detailed study of these infinitives and their Spanish counterparts introduced by *a*, which are both something like "bare VP complements." She contrasts this type of infinitive with purpose clauses introduced by French *pour* and Spanish *para* 'for', which have rather the properties of adjuncts and of full IP infinitivals.
3. Discussions of English post-verbal particles, especially in linguistics textbooks, almost invariably describe them as deriving from some kind of deep verbal compounds (i.e., "phrasal verbs"), as far as I can tell for no reason whatever. All linguistic justifications I have heard for this source (beyond considerations such as "students don't understand a theoretical approach" or "that's what the constructions mean") were refuted in my earliest work on particles, amplified in Emonds (1985: Ch. 6).

    In a later variant, Keyser and Roeper (1992) first establish an interesting incompatibility of the verbal prefix *re-* with intransitive particles and indirect object DPs. I agree that they have established complementary distribution, and that this suggests the same source for *re-* as for intransitive particle PPs and indirect objects. But this source should then be whatever independent arguments show is the deep structure of particles and indirect objects. Emonds (1985, Ch. 6) argues that particles are deep PPs, and Emonds (1993) that indirect objects also derive from a base PP position.

4. Emonds (1993) maintains that particle movement is a local, non-structure-preserving subcase of Move Alpha, which I now believe is unnecessary.
5. The domains for transformational and other "bottom-up" processes are plausibly maximal phrases. I assume that after such a domain is transformationally processed, then Phonological Lexicalisation proceeds in all phrases properly contained in that domain. Therefore, during operations on the IP domain when accusative case is assigned, any phonologically overt DP within a PP is present in the terminal string; thus, any [$_{PP}$ P-DP] interferes with Case Adjacency (4.12).
6. Material in the last two sections was first presented on Tilburg University's Dies Grammaticalis in the Spring of 1992. I am grateful to H. van Riemsdijk for organising this occasion for much grammatical reflection.
7. Nothing in this suggests a small clause must be present, except an a priori stipulation that predication can occur only between sisters that have no third sister X^0. In any case, if (4.15) is evidence that the post-verbal particles of PLACE head small clauses, then the irregularities of (4.16) are evidence that those of PATH do not.
8. The clear contrasts in (4.17) present a serious problem for hypotheses which link "particle movement" with predication, small clauses, and any general theory of movement. (4.17) shows that the particles which are clearly predications are just those which are stationary and *immune* to movement.
9. In the present framework, since particle "movement" just reflects the free order of phrasal sisters to V (i.e., complements of V), it follows that adjuncts are necessarily exterior to the complements, except when "heavy" complements shift rightward: *Mark chose to eat out the birthday lunch we promised to provide*.
10. The reason for the quasi-paraphrases of predications that directional particles sometimes seem to allow, as in (4.16), is that the more specific lexical meanings of PLACE particles extend meanings of the more basic PATH particles, usually by sharing their syntactic "orientation" features F_j. Thus, the sense of *in* 'in a house or office' further particularises the PATH particle *in* but still shares the latter's features. Therefore, the more general PATH usage of a particle (*he urged Bill on*) only sporadically gives rise to a corresponding predication of PLACE (**so Bill was consequently on*).
11. In these terms, X and Y are "theta-related" if and only if a head X assigns a theta role to YP.
12. The arguments and observations here are equally valid for intransitive verbs with directional PATH complements. The only difference is that the subject DP in those structures replaces the object DP in the discussion here.

Chapter 5
Projecting indirect objects[1]

Introduction: a path not followed

Indirect objects take on a bewildering variety of surface forms in languages. In pre-theoretical terms, they may appear as (i) NPs marked with a productive morphological dative Case (e.g., Classical Greek, German, Latin), (ii) NPs which agree with an appropriately inflected verb (Basque, Georgian), (iii) PPs with an overt P, and (iv) object NPs without overt Case but positionally identified in fixed word order patterns. The patterns (iii) and (iv) are exemplified by pairs in English such as (5.1).

(5.1) a. The paper that I wrote a letter **to John** on was old.
I showed a photograph **to every friend of mine**.
Jim bought a drink **for Margaret**.
b. The paper that I wrote **John** a letter on was old.
I showed **every friend of mine** a photograph.
Jim bought **Margaret** a drink.

In such sentences, the bold indirect objects in (a) with prepositions will be called P datives, and those in (b) without prepositions will be called P-less datives. Many intensively studied "fixed word order" languages with V-initial verb phrases, including Chicheŵa, Chinese, English, and Indonesian, exhibit essentially optional alternations between P datives (5.1a) and P-less datives (5.1b), in which the V in the P-less pattern often occurs with a "(benefactive) applicative" suffix. These alternations, with or without a suffix, will be referred to as "indirect object movement", and are the focus of this study.

In general terms, I have found that closely examining a wide range of these and other indirect object phenomena invariably suggests the plausibility of postulating NP–PP sequences as the basis for direct/indirect object combinations. Especially in languages exhibiting indirect object movement in types (iii) and (iv), the grounds for such an approach are especially strong, because this hypothesis leads to unexpected and striking confirmations of other principles of syntactic and lexical theory. In this study, I say relatively little about languages whose indirect objects are expressed as (i), (ii), or only (iii), concentrating my remarks on them in section 2.²

My analysis derives (iv) from (iii) via a structure-preserving interchange of two arguments, somewhat as in Emonds (1972). The earlier analysis requires reformulation in the light of more recently proposed principles, and this study shows how subsequent studies, particularly those with a strong empirical basis, strengthen the case for it. Construction-specific *ad hoc* aspects of my earlier analysis will be subsumed under principles governing empty categories and transformational operations. There remains, of course, a lexical residue, but reduced to an absolute minimum. In particular, the Projection Principle, widely felt to be inconsistent with a structure-preserving interchange, is shown, when carefully formulated, to allow such an operation under highly particular conditions, exactly those fulfilled in dative constructions. Indeed, one central result of this paper is this sharpened conception of a completely formalized Projection Principle.

In a neutral formulation, this principle claims that lexical properties are preserved at several levels of a transformational derivation. But lexical properties are widely thought of as highly variable within and across languages, free of syntactic constraints, and defined in terms of imprecise semantic and idiosyncratic concepts with no real promise of being formalizable. Mysteriously, the Projection then plays the role of a sort of midwife which transforms such informal lexical properties into formalized syntactic structures. A contrary interpretation, defended in section 3, treats this Principle as a universal and meaning-free device of syntax which severely restricts lexical, semantic, and dialectal variation. As will be shown, the many advantages of structure-preserving indirect object movement support the latter interpretation of the Projection Principle, not only philosophically, but empirically. At the same time, the locality of indirect object movement, as well as the lack of traces, will follow from, and not contravene the Projection Principle.

This picture of the debate surrounding English and similar indirect object movements might be summarized as follows. Just when a structure-preserving analysis of this rule was justified, an otherwise productive research strategy (trace theory and subsequently the Projection Principle) developed, but only imperfectly. As a result, the most principled version of transformational syntax seemed unable to explain indirect object movement phenomena and relegated them to the lexicon. Therefore, the research program of formal grammar required some appropriate clarification to again become compatible with a descriptively adequate and comprehensive treatment of indirect objects. The needed sharpening is the formalization of the Projection Principle undertaken in this study.

Not surprisingly, this intellectual scenario is a bit too simple; it neither puts into perspective a score of published papers on the subject, nor explains how their authors' positions are related to mine. The fact is, the inability of general transformatinal theory during a twenty-year period to fruitfully address an issue of traditional syntax as central as indirect object alternations invited competitors into the breach. The energetic candidates with alternative approaches to indirect object movement are of three inspirations: (i) relational grammar, (ii) lexicalism, and (iii) formal semantics.

A favorite theme of the relational grammar literature has been *3-to-2-advancement* (i.e., the counterpart to transformational movements from oblique object to direct object position). Below, I discuss one example of this approach, including its argument against transformational grammar, Chung's (1976) analysis of Indonesian indirect object movement. Sections 1.2 and 5.1 conclude that the rich array of Indonesian paradigms adduced by Chung turn out to confirm the structure-preserving approach.

The second current opposed to transformational indirect object movement is the lexicalist approach, first fleshed out in Green (1974) and Oerhle (1976), with a recent advocate in Jackendoff (1990). Under this view, devices of subcategorization, predicate–argument structures, or theta-grids in lexical entries of verbs license alternative deep structures for P datives and P-less datives. Lexicalist authors underscore the complexity of the indirect object alternations, but typically stop short of a comprehensive solution; they concentrate rather on inadequacies of transformational accounts. Nonetheless, they assume that a frame +___NP NP for a P-less dative is available at deep structure and "lexically relatable" to a frame with P. In contrast, my conception of the lexicon and of lexical rules (section 5) prohibits both the notion that the types of available phrasal frames vary on a language-particular basis and any lexical means of relating one frame to another. In addition, each V can assign a theta-role to at most one NP sister (Emonds 1985: Ch. 1). Thus, in such a framework, lexical alternatives to transformational relationships are excluded in principle, and my purpose here is to show that descriptive adequacy can be fully achieved under this stricture.

A third alternative approach to indirect object movement is represented by Larsons's (1988, 1990) influential account. Even though it is elaborated in syntactic terminology, I maintain that his approach can be characterized as of (non-lexicalist) formal semantic inspiration. In Emonds (1985: Ch. 1, 1987, 1991b), I suggest that a trademark of formal semantic or analytic philosophical influence in grammatical studies is a *de facto* downplaying or elimination of any central role for PP structures, especially covert PPs. The hidden logic behind this assumption is simple: the superficial equivalences between logic and language are NP~argument; VP and S~proposition; V and A~predicate; N~variable or name. P and PP do not appear, because in human cognition, these structures represent linguistically (Kant's) innate space–time grids; for discussion, see Emonds (1986b: conclusion). When a researcher approaches language from a "logical" point of view, space and time and the structures that represent them are extraneous intrusions. Because linguistics has not fully shaken off its logical positivist inheritance, these "PP-free" or "formal semantic" analyses have a perennial appeal, that of making linguistics like the *a priori* systems of logic.

From this admittedly special perspective, Larson's approach can indeed be considered a formal semantic one, since neither the hierarchial structure introduced by PP nor the structural effects of an empty P play any but a peripheral role in his proposals.

Ultimately, only criteria of empirical adequacy, formal explicitness, and generality of the devices employed can decide among competing accounts. The transformational account of indirect object movement here attempts to satisfy these criteria with exceptionless syntactic principles and a central role for PP structure. The argument is organized around the traditional pillars in transformational accounts of any constructions which exhibit numerous peculiarities. Using the peculiarities, we try to determine (i) the surface structure of the construction; (ii) its deep structure; (iii) a theoretically sanctioned derivational history linking (i) and (ii); (iv) how universal principles determine these structures and act upon them to license empty categories; and (v) how language-particular variation interacts with (i) through (iv) to yield observed linguistic differences. In this study, these topics will be treated in the above order, in sections with these numbers.

5.1 The surface structure of the prepositionless dative

5.1.1 English double objects

Since the theoretical status of prepositionless indirect objects has been so uncertain, it is not surprising that the paradigms available shed light principally on their surface structure. For example, Barss and Lasnik (1986) give six arguments based on Chomsky's (1981) binding theory, quantifier-bound pronoun pairs, weak crossover, *wh*-extraction restricted by superiority, reciprocal constructions, and negative polarity, which show that a P-less dative as in (5.1b) asymmetrically c-commands a direct object in s-structure. As pointed out in Larson (1988), their arguments equally well show that the direct object in the (5.1a) sentences above asymmetrically c-commands the P dative NP. Barss and Lasnik go on to point out the empirical inadequacy or theoretical undesirability of almost every previous generative analysis in the light of these facts: they thus refute (i) Oehrle's (1976) proposal that a P-less dative and the direct object are both sisters to the V;[3] (ii) Kayne's (1981a) "Unambiguous Paths" proposal; (iii) the "small VP" of Chomsky and Lasnik (1977); and (iv) Stowell's (1981) "phrasal cliticization". They further observe the *ad hoc* character of introducing discontinuous constituents or unrealized heads for Kayne's small clauses as possible routes for accommodating their arguments. Barss and Lasnik (1986: 350) then summarize their findings as follows: "The problem now is to determine how it is that the first NP in a double-object VP asymmetrically c-commands the second NP, and this requires discussion of the phrase structure of these VPs."

Then, in a footnoe otherwise devoted to critically appraising unrealized heads of small clauses, the authors introduce a second tree, unaccompanied by verbal comment. However, it is logically implicit in their presentation that this second tree (5.2), in contrast to the other proposals they discuss, adequately represents the elusive asymmetric c-command needed for explaining all their paradigms involving the English double-objects.

(5.2)

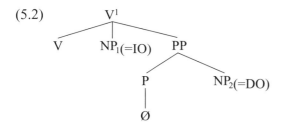

This tree is the derived structure for the structure-preserving indirect object movement of Emonds (1972). Its essential property is that the indirect object is in the direct object position (3-to-2-advancement, in relational grammar terms), and that the direct object appears in a PP with an empty P (a *chômeur*, in relational grammar). I repeat my original argument for this, which corroborates the six others by Barss and Lasnik.

Intransitive directional prepositions in English cannot follow PPs which contain maximal phrases:

(5.3) *The secretary sent a schedule to the stockholders out.
*Some cigars were brought for Dad down at the party.
*I tried to scrape the paper with a knife off.
*They took Sam in the van away already.

Additionally, intransitive directional P can precede or follow the direct object; (5.4) exemplifies only the latter pattern:

(5.4) The secretary sent a schedule out to the stockholders.
They brought some cigars down for Dad at the party.
I tried to scrape the paper off with a knife.
They took Sam away in the van already.

In the light of this clear contrast between (5.3) and (5.4), the following paradigm confirms the hypothesis embodied in (5.2), that the direct object in a P-less dative is in a PP-like rather than an NP-position:

(5.5) *The secretary sent the stockholders a schedule out.
The secretary sent the stockholders out a schedule.
*They brought Dad some cigars down at the party.
They brought Dad down some cigars at the party.
*Bill fixed John a drink up.
Bill fixed John up a drink.

The above argument involves neither simple precedence nor c-command, but rather a distributional distinction between NP and PP. The identical exclusion of the sequence *[$_{PP}$ P-XP][$_{PP}$ P] explains the starred examples in both (5.3) and (5.5), *provided the latter are analyzed as in (5.2)*.[4] Thus, with no circular appeal to c-command, an actual asymmetric c-command relation using a PP has been established for the surface of P-less datives, which in turn accounts for the Barss and Lasnik paradigms. They do not take this possibility into account, but finally opt, without providing any independent support, for re-introducing precedence into the binding theory and other principles of universal grammar.

Nonetheless, at least some Barss and Lasnik paradigms require asymmetric c-command in addition to linear order. Consider for example the contrasts in (5.6)–(5.7) partly provided by Jackendoff.[5]

(5.6) Mary described Bill and John to each other/themselves.
Did she tell Bill and John about each other/themselves?
The company reimburses my brothers for each other's expenses.

(5.7) *Mary talked about Bill and John to each other/themselves.
*Did he argue about John and Mary with each other/themselves?
*Did he argue with John and Mary about each other/themselves?
*Mary spoke of Bill and John to each other/themselves.
*The company relies on my brothers for each other's expenses.

Contrary to Jackendoff's (1990: 435) conclusion about such paradigms ("An account appealing to linear order generalizes with the greatest of ease"), in these sentences, an object of a P to the left of an anaphor doesn't qualify as an antecedent, presumably because c-command is a necessary condition on an antecedent, and by parsimony, a sufficient one. Moreover, the c-command must be asymmetric, for otherwise P-less indirect object antecedents of direct object reflexives would be bound by the latter, and violate Chomsky's Principle C.[6] Therefore, we indeed seem to need asymmetric c-command in P-less datives, exactly as Larson claims.

A different dominance-based account of the Barss and Lasnik paradigms, which neutralizes any pivotal role for PP-structure, is offered in Larson (1988: 339), who asks: "if complement asymmetry in standard datives is simply a matter of the structure introduced by PP, then why, in double object constructions, where such structure is absent, do we not find symmetric behavior?" This question arises only because it crucially presupposes that the absence of an overt P means the absence of PP structure; this is then his point of departure for analyzing P-less datives. However, this presupposition has been challenged in Emonds (1987: sections 3 and 4), which advances a detailed alternative to Larson's (1985) account of a different construction, the superficially P-less "bare-NP" adverbials.

Rather than providing any reason to doubt a role for PP in these paradigms, Larson bootstraps a PP-less but dominance-based account of direct/indirect object asymmetry with two pre-theoretical and entirely inconclusive considerations.

I. Indirect objects and verbs form purported deep (V′) constituents which exclude direct objects on the semantic basis that "giving an object to the world has a rather different character from giving an object to an individual ... The exact semantic role assigned to the direct object thus depends on the nature of the recipient appearing in the goal phrase" (Larson 1988: 340). But consider in turn the different senses of the direct objects in *give {roast mutton, the cold shoulder, a cold, more time, good reasons, whatever it takes} to your children*. *Mutatis mutandis*, giving an object to an individual has a rather different character from giving an attitude, a disease, time, propositions, or activities to an individual. For instance, from these examples we can conclude that the children have respectively roast mutton, a cold, and good reasons, but not that they have the cold shoulder, more time, or whatever it takes. As a result, "the exact semantic role assigned to the [indirect] object thus depends on the nature of the [concept] appearing in the [theme] phrase." By Larson's reasoning, one can now conclude that a V and its direct object theme form a deep constituent V', which excludes goal indirect objects, contradicting his conclusion. But clearly, this kind of impressionistic bootstrapping can lead anywhere, and hence nowhere; it cannot count as scientific discourse.

II. Larson's equally inconclusive second motivation for assigning deep V'-status to V+indirect object (without direct objects) is the existence of "discontinuous idioms" such as *take ... to task*. He himself cites enough counterexamples in his (11) and note 4 to undercut any argument for an asymmetry between direct and indirect objects (a few more: *give the cold shoulder to NP, sell a bill of goods to NP, read the riot act to NP*). But even if one granted the putative deep constituency of idioms (with its contradictory consequences for the inner or outer status of indirect objects), no light is shed on any related semantic or lexical issue. Moreover, the resulting syntactic analyses verge on the incoherent, as they would then sanction lowering of NPs from various, one imagines, adjunct positions into a V' such as *pull X's leg* or into an IP such as *the cat has X's tongue*. A more promising analysis is that idioms may consist of constituents with one internal open variable (NP) slot, and are thus irrelevant for determining the deep order of arguments.

In summary, Larson's two motivations for a lower deep position for indirect objects with "inner" complement status evaporate. Lacking these motivations, his analysis becomes a purely deductive exercise on how to construct a dominance-based account of indirect object movement without recourse to PP-structure. It simply leaves us back at the point of departure, which is Larson's own summary of his first section: "The facts are accommodated smoothly, it seems, by appealing to the structure introduced by PP" (Larson 1988: 338). In this subsection for English and in the next for non-

Indo-European languages, I am justifying that an s-structure like (5.2) containing a PP is indeed just as appropriate for a P-less dative as for one with an overt P; subsequent sections mainly concentrate on how such structures are generated and related to each other.

5.1.2 Some non-Indo-European prepositionless datives

5.1.2.1 *Indonesian.* Research in both the relational and transformational frameworks has shown that the P-less datives are productive in many languages and show remarkable similarities to the English version. For example, the thorough and enlightening study of Chung (1976) on the P-less dative in Indonesian, a typical head-initial language,[7] reveals a construction with essentially the properties of its English counterpart:

> The optional rule that I refer to as Dative applies to sentences with a direct object (DO) and an indirect object or benefactive (IO). Indirect objects in Bahasa Indonesia occur with the preposition *kepada* 'to'; benefactives with the preposition *untuk* 'for': ... Dative removes these prepositions and places the indirect object/benefactive between the underlying direct object and the verb, so that the word order is S V IO DO ... (Chung 1976: 54).

An important difference between Indonesian and English P-less datives, which sheds light on how empty P with indirect objects is licensed (or not licensed, as in the Romance languages), is that the Indonesian P-less dative is productive and with non-exceptional verbs occurs only with a benefactive suffix on the verb: "In addition, some form of the benefactive suffix must be attached to the verb. The suffix is normally realized as *-kan* (5.46), but it has the form *-i* or Ø for a handful of verbs whose indirect objects have undergone Dative." (Chung 1976: 55)

With this difference, the otherwise similar behavior of the indirect object constructions in the two languages is truly impressive:

> Two general properties of Dative can be immediately established. First, a direct object, as well as an indirect object/benefactive is required in order for Dative to apply: [cf., typically, *John read my father *(the letter), John built his children *(some toys)*, J. E.] ... Second, ... The preposition cannot be omitted unless the IO is moved between the DO and the verb: ... Under normal circumstances, moreover, the IO cannot be moved between the DO and the verb unless its preposition is omitted. (Chung 1976: 56)[8]

Chung aims to establish that Indonesian P-less datives are derived by advancement from a deep indirect object position to a direct object position. The logic, the empirical force, and the variety of grammatical demonstrations in her argument for this claim seem incontrovertible. Particularly telling are her numerous arguments that the P-less dative is in surface direct object position while the logical direct object is not. Moreover, she also shows that the deep position of the P-less dative is in a PP. Thus, her conclusions taken together motivate an NP movement from within PP to direct object position, with simultaneous vacating of the latter position by the deep direct object. What remains at issue, however, is the theoretical framework that her arguments actually support.

Chung's summary of her refutations and her introduction of a structure-preserving "Restatement of Dative" directly reflect these points:

> The failure of the proposals sketched above [the transformational solutions, J. E.] makes it unlikely that any additional syntactic device could save the transformational solution for Dative. There is, however, another kind of alternative for accounting for the facts of sections 3.2 and 3.3. The essence of this alternative is that, in addition to permuting DO and IO, *dative has the effect of turning the DO into a prepositional phrase*: [my emphasis, J. E.]

The preceding quote clearly shows that Chung's extensive comparisons of alternative structures, her sections 3.2 through 3.7, straightforwardly support the surface structure (5.2) for P-less datives. They thus establish on the basis of Indonesian (against her intent) exactly the same conclusion that Barss and Lasnik (against their intent) establish a decade later on the basis of English: the surface structure of a P-less dative is the same, *modulo* different realizations of P, as that of a P dative.

5.1.2.2 *Chinese*. Research on other languages with P-less datives converges to the same conclusion. In a study of Chinese double object constructions, Huang (1991) compares three structures (i) V-NP_{DO}-*gei*-NP_{IO}, (ii) V-NP_{IO}-NP_{DO}, and (iii) V-*gei*-NP_{IO}-NP_{DO}. While Chinese has a main verb *gei* 'give' that appears in (ii), Huang argues that *gei* in (i) is rather a P to be glossed as 'to', that the structure to be associated with the productive pattern (i) is exactly as in English/Indonesian (V-NP-P-NP), and that the less productive structures (ii) and (iii) are both derived instances of V-NP_{IO}-$_P[\emptyset]$-NP_{DO}. Thus in the main, her analysis of Chinese accords with the structures proposed in this paper for English, Indonesian, etc. In addition, Huang focuses on the status of *gei* in pattern (iii), which we return to in section 5.1, but the potential controversy as to whether this *gei* is a V or an incorporated P in no way undermines her argument that double object constructions in Chinese are structurally parallel to those in English and Indonesian.

5.1.2.3 *Bantu*. In a commentary on rules interchanging arguments, which he presupposes are "lexical rules",[9] Poser (1982: 97) shows "that at least two languages have morphological rules whose effect is to exchange internal arguments, rules directly comparable to English Dative shift." After summarizing Chung's work, he discusses Kinyarwanda:

> ... the object of the deleted preposition does indeed advance to direct object status. We have already seen two ways in which this NP behaves like a direct object: ...
> In addition to the absence of the preposition, Kimenyi (1980) lists no less than ten properties that distinguish direct objects from oblique objects. Direct objects, but not oblique objects, are potential targets for Passive, Stativization, Object-Subject Reversal, Pronoun Incorporation, Reflexivization, Clefting, Pseudo-Clefting, Exclusive Insertion, and Existential Insertion. By all of these criteria the prepositionless oblique object of the (b) sentences is a direct object. ...
> These cases refute the claim that lexical rules can be restricted to internalization and externalization of arguments. It is necessary to permit rules to interchange internal arguments. (Poser 1982: 98–99)

Finally, the work of Baker (1988b) on Chicheŵa also supports the claim that P-less applicative benefactives have a surface structure that mirrors that of transitive counterparts with an overt benefactive PP.[10] Of the two object NPs in Chicheŵa's goal and benefactive applicative constructions, only the derived direct object (=the underlying indirect object): (i) must be adjacent to the VP-initial verb (Baker 1988b: 370); (ii) undergoes passivization (386), as in American English; (iii) "can be expressed by the object prefix on the verb" (354); and (iv) *cannot* be relativized (355), exactly as in English; see note 26 for a theoretical explanation of this fact.

These properties are precisely those predicted by a structure-preserving interchange, provided that object prefixation is based on the s-structure object. In addition, Chicheŵa's derived goal and benefactive applicative objects do not undergo noun incorporation into the verb (363), a property reserved for deep objects. While these facts are used by Baker to support his Case assignment analysis, all are consistent with the structure-preserving account that takes (5.2) to be the derived structure for goal/benefactive applicatives. Baker's Case theory is implausibly ad hoc (Emonds, 1993: note 28), but even if it were not, the structure he proposes for benefactive applicatives (359, 375) is refuted by the Barss and Lasnik arguments, unless the binding theory facts for Chicheŵa, nowhere discussed by Baker, are entirely different than those for English.[11] Such difficulties do not arise in the alternative structure-preserving account.

All this work converges on a clear conclusion: the sense of the decade 1975–1985 that P-less datives are some sort of peripheral lexical phenomenon was a delusion. No construction has a better claim on the attention of universal grammarians, since the same theory-determined particularities of this construction crop up in diverse and unrelated languages. The simplest way to represent most of these properties, established by many independent arguments, is to recognize that a P-less dative (in a head-initial language without overt productive morphological dative Case) and a P dative have the same surface structures, namely (5.2), repeated here with no value specified for P.[12]

(5.2)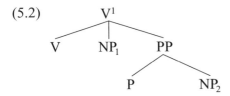

5.2 The deep structure of indirect object constructions

The review of the literature has made it clear that the surface structure of both indirect object constructions in Chicheŵa, English, Indonesian, and no doubt many languages is (5.2). We next determine whether there are independent reasons for considering this to also be their deep structure.

P dative clauses and P-less dative clauses, as in (5.8a) for example, are cognitively synonymous, sharing truth values. They contrast with alternating transitive pairs as in (5.8b), which are not cognitively synonymous:

(5.8) a. Although Mary sent Herb candy, he never got it.
Although Mary sent candy to Herb, he never got it.
Anomalous: Although Mary gave Herb candy, he has never had any.
Anomalous: Although Mary gave candy to Herb, he has never had any.

b. Anomalous: Although Mary loaded the truck with the books, it was still almost empty.
Felicitous: Although Mary loaded the books into the truck, it was still almost empty.

This contrast between pairs of P and P-less datives as in (5.8a) and other alternating transitive pairs as in (5.8b) is convincingly established in Anderson (1971). Although Green (1974) and Oerhle (1976) have argued that indirect object movement doesn't preserve truth values, to me their examples all do. Such cognitive synonymy of productive syntactic paradigms, as exemplified in say (5.9), is generally taken to justify deriving them from identical or similar deep structures.

(5.9) a. We know when Harry bought which fish.
We know which fish Harry bought when.
b. Beth seems to be in a revolutionary mood.
It seems that Beth is in a revolutionary mood.

We capture cognitive synonymy of dative pairs as in (5.1) by assigning them identical deep structures and identical grammatical relations, and relating them transformationally, in accord with earlier generative practice and also with critical evaluations of the lexicalist approach (Czepluch 1982, and Larson 1988).

If P and P-less datives are to be transformationally derived from (nearly) the same deep structure, there are strong reasons for identifying this structure with the P-dative (i.e., V-DO-P-IO). For despite the many surface realizations of indirect objects in the world's languages, there is [almost always] a productive form of indirect objects for which a PP-structure is arguably a preferable analysis.

For example, the advantages of a PP representation for a productive morphological dative (oblique) Case on lexical NPs (e.g., in languages such as Classical Greek, German, and Latin) are given in Emonds (1985: Ch. 5). An *Invisible Category Principle*, defended there and in Emonds (1987), explains why the P in such datives remains empty even in Phonological Form. These issues are not our focus here, but are clearly part of an argument for universally associating indirect objects with deep PPs. Consequently, my general hypothesis is that the universal deep structure of indirect objects is a PP, where P has the particular form outlined below in (5.11) and (5.12).

The same conclusion holds for languages lacking a productive morphologically marked dative Case, such as Chinese, English, Indonesian, Modern Standard Arabic and Spanish. While P datives are productive in such languages, in some like Spanish and French, P-less datives don't appear at all (except under pronominal cliticization). In others including English, productively many verbs (which ones we will return to) forbid P-less datives. The following descriptive generalization seems to hold:

(5.10) Languages with neither productive morphological dative Case nor productive indirect object agreement on the verb productively allow P datives, but often fail to allow productive P-less datives.

We can conclude from (5.10) that the P datives of such languages, in which indirect objects are in PPs, are the best candidate for reflecting generally valid deep grammatical relations.[13]

If linguistic principles need stipulate only marked features, the best candidate for a universal representation of an indirect object is therefore (5.11):

(5.11) *Universal Indirect Object: [+PATH^NP, X¹]*

This notation for grammatical relations adapted from Chomsky (1965) means that the first term of the pair, here +PATH^NP, forms a constituent immediately dominated by the second, here the lowest projection in the bar notation. (Thus, the definition of direct object of a verb is [NP,V¹].)

For all head-initial languages discussed here, a deep indirect object should thus be represented as the PP in (5.12). For ease of reference, I add a direct object NP.

(5.12)
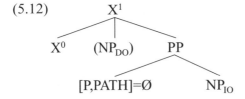

Some universal definition for indirect objects as in (5.11) is also envisaged in Czepluch (1982).[14]

The idea that indirect objects are PPs in deep structure can hardly strike the generativist as revolutionary. Nonetheless, many analyses of indirect objects to highlight properties which at first glance distinguish indirect objects from PPs, rather than assimilate them, even for languages whose indirect object NPs in traditional terms always exhibit Ps, such as the Romance languages. For example, Strozer (1976) presents several paradigms which distinguish Spanish indirect objects from other PPs and concludes that the former are NPs introduced by a non-P Case marker *a* 'to'. Similarly, studies of Japanese which clearly presuppose a difference between NPs with Case markers and full PPs often classify *ni* 'to' as a Case marker rather than a P.

Such analyses of languages like Spanish and Japanese are failing, however, to exploit a central theoretical construct of generative grammar, the empty category. In several studies, beginning with Emonds (1985: Ch. 4 and 5), I have argued that certain morphemes which spell out X^0 with purely grammatical features are absent at syntactic levels (deep and s-structure), and are present in trees only at Phonological Form (PF). Thus, the deep indirect object configuration (5.12) contains P=Ø, in contrast to typical PPs whose heads are filled at both deep and s-structure.

In these terms, it is trivial to express the many ways (often downplayed) that indirect objects pattern with other PPs in contrast to subject and object NPs. For example, the English P specifier *right* can occur with *to* as well as with a lexical P, and neither type of PP can be the subject of a passive or of secondary predication. In French, the relative/interrogative *qui* 'who' is animate in PPs, including after *à* 'to' (brought to my attention by C. Piera). Kayne's (1984) classic argumentation concerning subjacency and the clitic *en* crucially requires that an indirect object be a PP. Further similarities between Romance indirect objects and PPs with semantically specified heads are studied in Comrovski (1989). In Japanese, neither an indirect object marker *ni* 'to' nor a PP with a lexical P allows floating quantifiers (Takezawa 1987) while NPs do allow them. Both types of Ps appear with the particles *wa* 'topic' or *mo* 'too', while these particles necessarily suppress simple nominative and accusative Case markers (Kuroda 1965). Thus, Romance and Japanese indirect objects are best analyzed as PPs.

Besides the positive advantages of characterizing indirect objects by (5.11), it is instructive that two analyses of English P-less datives which do not postulate PP structures, namely in Hornstein and Weinberg (1981) and Chomsky (1981), are subject to a number of telling criticisms in Czepluch (1982). In addition, these analyses both fail to explain the Barss and Lasnik paradigms.

Nothing in the above determination that a deep indirect object is a specific type of PP has indicated which projection of V this PP should be a sister of.

At the end of section 1.1, I discussed why Larson's (1988) proposed justifications for a deep structure in which indirect objects are lower than direct objects must be rejected.

If one assumed that a deep indirect object were higher than a direct object, that is, in adjunct position, this would pointlessly conflict with V¹ constituency tests (for example, *do so*, PP-preposing, selection by the head, etc.). In addition, indirect object movement would then be movement between NP positions not in a c-command relation. In fact, the simplest assumption is that a deep direct object NP and deep indirect object PP are sisters to V; see note 12 regarding ternary branching. These considerations conclusively establish (5.12) as the representation for deep indirect objects.[15]

5.3 Prepositionless datives: theoretical issues

5.3.1 Structure-preserving derivations and the Projection Principle

Both the similarity and the exact nature of the difference between the empirically justified deep structure (5.12) and surface structure (5.2) of the P-less datives can hardly be overlooked. The structures are identical, except that the two NPs are interchanged. The putative structure-preserving derivation is distinguished by the fact (still to be explained) that P is empty when the arguments are interchanged, while it is filled in P datives. In sum, it appears that dative movement preserves structure in the strongest sense: it doesn't change structure, but rather just interchanges arguments.

This structure-preserving version of Move α is indeed supported by the fact that only this constraint, over all competing proposals for restricting movement, predicts on completely general grounds the exact derived structure (5.2) for P-less datives, amply supported in the literature reviewed here.

Nonetheless, the literature review in section 1 also suggested that generativists have not, since the inception of trace theory, accepted a structure-preserving analysis of dative movement.[16] In part, this is attributable to lexicalist emphasis on its seeming imperfect productivity, but subsequent detailed government and binding analyses by Hornstein and Weinberg, Czepluch, Whitney, Baker, and Larson demonstrate that the lexicalist point of view is now far from hegemonic. Given the many paradigms that support structure-preserving dative movement, the remaining objections must be theoretical, in that no empty NPs co-indexed with the two moved NPs (no traces) are left behind in the derived structure (5.2), and that straightforward argument interchanges seen not otherwise observed in language.

In terms of GB, structure-preserving dative movement is considered to violate a possible theoretical successor to the Structure-Preserving Constraint, Chomsky's Projection Principle (1981), which supposedly excludes all argument interchanges and infallibly guarantees the presence of NP traces in derived structures. Chomsky's (1981: 29) first version of the Projection Principle, stated in terms of subcategorization, is fully formal:

(5.18) *Projection Principle. Representations at each syntactic level (that is, LF and d- and s-structure) are projected from the lexicon, in that they observe the subcategorization properties of lexical items.*

Obviously, a structure-preserving derivation of the dative does not violate (5.18). In fact, the Projection Principle as given above follows from structure-preservation, since (5.18) simply restricts the latter to X^1 domains (or more generally, to argument positions including subjects). In one sense, however, (5.18) goes beyond structure-preservation; it is intended to guarantee that movement of a constituent C out of an X^1 domain cannot be "total" – C cannot disappear from within X^1. Notice that one could perfectly well construe (5.18) to mean that movement of various sorts occurs outside X^1 domains, but no movement occurs inside X^1. However, such has never been the intent of the Projection Principle. Rather, (5.18) is to mean that if C moves out of X^1, an empty C remains in C's original place.

Now, in the original definition of a structure-preserving operation (Emonds 1976: Ch. 3), movement of a category C can optionally leave an empty C in the original position of C, unless the operation itself otherwise fills in the original position. If we add co-indexation between the original and empty C, we obtain traces exactly in cases of a vacated position. In excess of structure-preservation, then, the Projection Principle need only guarantee (5.19).

(5.19) Subcategorization properties of lexical items must be observed at each level L_i; if and only if a position is vacated, the properties are observed by the generation of traces.

The discussion in Chomsky (1986b: 84) confirms this central function of the Projection Principle.

A moment's reflection shows that (5.19) still allows argument interchanges, because subcategorization is formulated in terms of types of constituents, rather than tokens. However, the reformulation of (5.18) in Chomsky (1981: 38) contains the following clause:

(5.20) If a lexical item @, an X, selects C in X^1 as a lexical property, then @ selects C in X^1 at each level L_i.[17]

If we interpret "C at a level" as meaning a token of C, complete with an index, then (5.20) excludes argument interchanges between subjects and objects and between arguments of different heads.

In this study, I retain Chomsky's Projection Principle, but I continue to interpret "select" as subcategorization, as in (5.18).[18] What therefore seems to be the proper and minimal revision of (5.18) incorporates only that aspect of (5.19) which requires that a subcategorization restriction be satisfied at each level by the "same" constituent. This is the amalgam of Chomsky's successive versions of the Projection Principle which I claim is correct.

(5.21) *Original Projection Principle. If a lexical item @, an X, selects C in X^1 as a lexical property (that is, given an item @, X, +___C), then a single C_k^j satisfies @, X, +___C at each level L_i.*[19]

We can see immediately that (5.21) forbids subject–object interchanges. Moreover, consider a variant of the underlying dative structure (5.12) in which P is filled with a lexical item at deep structure, say *toward*, P, +___NP. The deep object NP_k of *toward* is required by (5.21) to also be its s-structure object, which means that structure-preserving dative movement cannot occur. Akin to its more loosely conceived semantic descendants, the Original Projection Principle thus rules out dative movement in any language or derivations in which deep indirect object structures contain a lexical P.

In contrast to its descendants, however, the Original Projection Principle correctly permits structure-preserving dative movement if P=Ø in the underlying (5.12). To see why, we must first introduce the independently justified definition of what structures can satisfy a subcategorization, developed in Emonds (1985: 39).

(5.22) A phrase subcategorized by a member of a lexical category X, possibly together with an introductory grammatical formative, can be assigned a θ-role (satisfies the subcategorization) only if it constitutes a sister of X.

(5.23) *Definition. α constitutes a β if and only if α dominates any and all lexical material under β.*[20]

Combining (5.21) and (5.22) yields (5.24):

(5.24) *Theorem of the OPP. The subcategorization of a lexical category X for a complement YP is satisfied if and only if a single YP_k constitutes a sister of X at each level L_i.*

Recall that the levels L_i in the Projection Principle include s-structure but not the transparent structure (PF) in which grammatical formatives inserted in s-structure defined contexts are actually present.

In the light of (5.24), consider an English verb that can undergo structure-preserving dative movement; that is, which appears in a deep structure (5.12) with an empty P. Such a verb is subcategorized to take two NPs. Now, (5.24) – that is, subcategorization and the Original Projection Principle – is satisfied if there are two distinct NP which each constitute, in the sense defined in (5.23), a sister of V at both deep structure and s-structure (and also at Logical Form). But in structure-preserving dative movement, this is so; the IO constitutes a sister of V at both levels (even though it moves), and similarly for the DO. Moreover, as no lexical category head besides V is associated with a subcategorization in the deep structure (5.12) (that is, *P is empty*), the derivation of the desired s-structure (5.2) is allowed.

Since the derivation of (5.2) from (5.12) satisfies the Original Projection Principle, *there is no need for traces*. In fact, because the structure-preserving operation in dative movement is a mutual substitution (a permutation), traces cannot be generated in any event. More generally, the structure-preserving framework allows permutation, or traceless interchange, only if the two constituents are both subcategorized complements of the same head, with no intervening preposition, since then and only then is the Original Projection Principle satisfied. These are the 3-to-2-promotions that create chômeurs, much discussed in the relational grammar literature.[21]

5.3.2 The interpretation of indirect objects and further predictions

Let me now address the question of how the double object deep structures (5.12) are made available to semantic interpretation. A Ground (=Goal) θ-role of V must be associated with an NP object of the [P,PATH] in (5.12), which is

134 *Structures in lexical projections*

one of the interpretive principles justified in Emonds (1991b). A Figure (=Theme) θ-role, assigned to an NP necessarily distinct from the Ground, is then the only one available to interpret the direct object.

We now turn to two interesting consequences of a structure-preserving dative movement. An additional correct prediction of the Original Projection Principle (5.21) is that, while allowing traceless complement permutation, it forbids interchanging a complement and an adjunct. Some relevant contrasts are provided by Jackendoff (1990: 447–448).

(5.25) a. Enrico sang an aria for Luisa (for the audience).
I'll fix a sandwich for you.
The host cracked the walnuts for his guests.
b. Enrico sang Luisa an aria (for the audience).
I'll fix you a sandwich.
The host cracked his guests the walnuts.

(5.26) a. Susan ate an apple for Luisa (? for the audience).
I'll fix the radiator for you.
The host brushed the wall hangings for his guests.
b. *Susan ate Luisa an apple (for the audience).
*I'll fix you the radiator.
*The host brushed his guests the wall hangings.

Jackendoff suggests a possible solution, seconded by Larson (1990): a verb of creation or preparation has an optional indirect object in complement position, as in (5.27), whereas verbs without this feature do not, as in (5.28). Thus, the verbs of creation or preparation in (5.25a–b) are +___NP([F]^NP), while those in (5.26) are simply +___NP. We thus obtain the contrasting deep structures in (5.27)–(5.28).

(5.27)

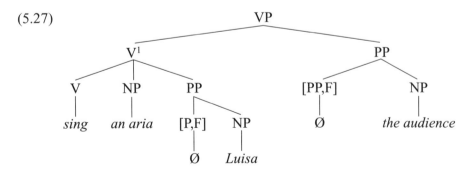

(5.28)

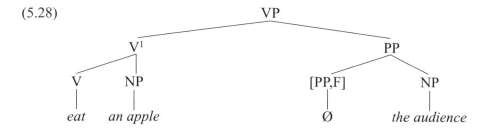

By the Original Projection Principle (5.21), the two NPs inside V^1 in (5.26a) can interchange since each NP still constitutes a sister of V at both deep and s-structure. If, however, the two NPs in (5.28) interchange, neither NP can constitute a sister of V at both levels, violating the Original Projection Principle; thus, the contrast (5.25)–(5.26) is explained without stipulation.

Larson (1990) notes that in (5.25) but not (5.26), "the theme is for the benefit of the beneficiary." That is, in (5.25a), the aria is for Luisa, while in (5.26a), the apple is not for Luisa. This follows from the fact that a subject relation defined as c-command by NP, holds equally well between the NP and the *for*-phrase in both (5.27) and in a copular sentence paraphrase, whereas this relation does *not* hold in (5.28).

A second consequence of the structure-preserving derivation of indirect object movement concerns intransitive verbs. A number of researchers have claimed that *both NPs must be present in order to productively generate a benefactive or dative applicative.* "It has been observed in the literature that in many languages one cannot form a benefactive applicative based on an intransitive verb (Chung 1976; Aissen 1983; Marantz 1984). This is generally true in Chicheŵa as well." (Baker 1988b: 386) This restriction on productive promotion of indirect objects is a theoretical consequence of the structure-preserving framework, for such a process would create a trace, by (5.19), yielding two NP_k for the same subcategorization requirement, and also would require a deep empty NP, without any interpretation, as a landing site for the promotion. All this violates (5.24). This prediction of the structure-preserving account is often a stipulation in other accounts.

We have seen how the Structure-Preserving Constraint and the Original Projection Principle together provide an explanatory account of how the deep structure (5.12) may be transformed into (5.2) without at the same time licensing argument interchanges in general. A crucial step in the reasoning claims that indirect objects contain no lexical P at the levels subject to the Projection Principle. In this way, the variable distribution of P-less datives within and across languages without productive morphological dative Cases is reducible to the following questions: (i) which languages permit an empty P in (5.12) to be licensed after structure-preserving dative movement (and with which verb classes), and (ii) how?

The second question (ii), like all questions about empty categories, involves universal grammar (cf. section 4.1). But the first question (i) leads into the realm of the language-particular and into the problem of how verbs and grammatical morphemes are differently specified in different lexicons (section 5). The fact that structure-preserving dative movement leads us to locate the language-particular not in differing syntactic rules but rather in minimally divergent lexical specifications is entirely consonant with Borer's research program, [1983: 29] of assigning cross-linguistic variation to the lexicon. And, as is typical in research programs, when the success of the individual analysis agrees with the overall aims of the program, this constitutes confirmation of both.

5.3.3 The passivizability and abstract Case of NPs in P-less datives

To complete the specification of the underlying structure of both P and P-less datives, the deep sequence V-DO-P-IO must be related to a system for abstract Case and to NP traces. In general Case is assigned to a movement chain as follows:

(5.29) Case is assigned at Spell Out to a chain of a moved NP at the highest position where a Case assigner is available.

As van Riemsdijk and Williams (1981) point out, the advantage of assigning Case before *wh*-movement is that the clumsy "inheritance" of Case by NPs moved into non-argument positions can be eliminated.

In line with my arguments in Emonds (1985: section 5.7), abstract Case is best considered as an indexation of NPs by their Case assigning category; for example, NP_V is an accusative, AP_P is an adjective phrase in the oblique Case, etc. Since Case cannot be assigned non-adjacently over an intervening phrase (Stowell 1981), and since there are no traces in structure-preserving dative movement, the principle (5.29) determines that the following extension of (5.2) given in (5.30) is the appropriate surface Case representation of P-less dative structures in languages with verb-initial VPs.[22]

(5.30)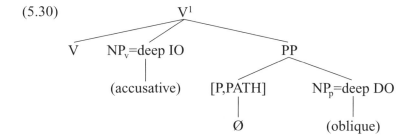

The Case theory that I use has one general principle of (structural) Case assignment. As argued in Emonds (1985: Ch. 5; 1987), "inherent" or "semantic" Case is a superfluous intrusion of traditional grammar into the generative model. (Inherent, semantic Case is not to be confused with lexical "quirky Cases" idiosyncratically assigned by heads to complements.) Unfortunately, structurally unmotivated concepts such as "inherent Case" are often the basis of elaborate quasi-formal systems which seem to be empirically based, but upon examination dissolve into terminology.[23]

5.4 Accounting for P-less datives

5.4.1 The licensing of the empty P in P-less datives

In section 1, we established on the basis of English and several non-Indo-European languages that the surface DO of a P-less dative is preceded by an empty P. Then, section 2 established that the deep structure of a P-less dative (5.12) contains [P,+PATH] and is identical to its s-structure, except that the deep order of object NPs is that found in P datives. Finally, in section 3, we saw that the Original Projection Principle permits DO-IO interchange only if [P,+PATH] is Ø. (We defer until section 5 determining the language-particular lexical factors which *allow* this P to be empty.)

This section will show why a P-less dative, in the language type being considered, *can* and *must* surface with IO-DO order. In other words, this section shows why the P must be null if the DO and IO permute (structure-preserving dative movement implies a null P), and also why the DO and IO must permute if the P is null (a null P implies structure-preserving dative movement). To this end, I add a crucial but entirely plausible co-indexing requirement in the definition (5.22) of *satisfying subcategorization*.

(5.31) A phrase subcategorized by a member of a lexical category X, together with an optional introductory grammatical formative, can be assigned a semantic role (satisfies the subcategorization) only if it constitutes *and has the index of* a sister of X.

Ordinarily, complement phrases cannot be co-indexed with a head, but (5.31) implies that purely structural head-complement co-indexation arises when a subcategorization feature for X is satisfied not by a sister ZP of X, but by a YP contained in ZP. In this situation, since YP and ZP share an index, by transitivity of co-indexing Z° and YP end up co-indexed.[24]

To illustrate, I reproduce the deep structure (5.12) of P-less datives as (5.32), adding indices which reflect the normal sharing of features by a head and its maximal projection, and in addition incorporate requirement (5.31).

(5.32)
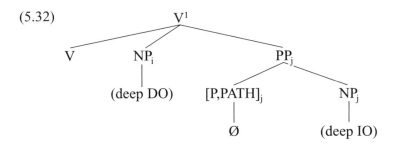

The reason this structure cannot surface unchanged is simple; an empty category (here P) cannot remain antecedentless throughout a derivation. Throughout, morphemes which only spell out purely syntactic features are inserted in Phonological Form according to s-structure contextual frames. Thus, a filled P in an untransformed (5.32) results from insertion after s-structure of a lexical P expressing +PATH, which yields a P dative.

A permissible alternative derivation from (5.32) results from the structure-preserving permutation that yields (5.33):

(5.33)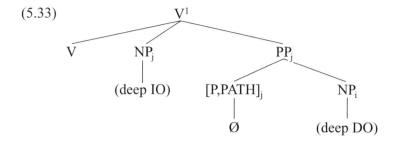

Apparently, the empty P_j in (5.33) is sanctioned at least in part because it has a co-indexed antecedent NP_j which is sufficiently local to license it (that is, to antecedent-govern it, whatever the exact definition of this concept). It is not difficult to discern a crucial difference in the relation between NP_j and P_j in (5.32) and (5.33), but the notion of antecedent must be sharpened to reflect this distinction. The appropriate clarification (5.34) is entirely plausible on its own grounds:

(5.34) A phrasal antecedent of an X^k must be exterior to X^{max}.[25]

We see immediately why (5.33) is an acceptable (P-less) surface structure: NP_j is exterior to P_j^{max}, and no matter how strict a locality condition is imposed by antecedent government, the pair $\{NP_j, P_j\}$ will satisfy it. Thus, P may be empty in the sequence V-IO-P-DO. In (5.32), by contrast, NP_j is not a possible antecedent of P_j.[26]

In summary, the empty [P,+PATH] in a deep P-less dative structure is co-indexed with the following IO, but remains antecedentless if structure-preserving dative movement fails to occur, necessitating late insertion of *to* or *for* under P. Only if structure-preserving dative movement permutes the DO and IO can the moved IO serve as the antecedent required by (5.34) in order to license the empty P (that is, an empty P implies structure-preserving dative movement). [By Economy of Dervation (Emonds, 2000; Ch. 4), an empty P is more economical than any lexicalized variant], so late P-insertion is not then possible (structure-preserving dative movement implies empty P). These are the results we set out to obtain in this section.

5.4.2 Phrasal antecedents for empty heads

I have now claimed that object interchange is required in P-less datives because only in this way can the indirect object NP_i provide (as the sister of

140 *Structures in lexical projections*

PP$_j$) a proper antecedent for the empty category P$_i$. A legitimate concern would be to find other cases where moved phrases provide antecedents for an empty category (P) that would not be licensed without movement. Clearly, no *wh*-movement or movement into Comp ever allows an otherwise stranded P to be null. So phrasal antecedents that can identify empty heads must be limited to single IP domains. Within these limits, we can find instances of empty heads which are permitted only when their complements move.

A possible instance of such a situation is the English possessive NP. Emonds (1976: Ch. 3), proposes the derivations in (5.35)–(5.37) by means of Possessive Formation.

(5.35) The paper (of) yesterday   Yesterday's paper
       The legs of the chair   The chair's legs

(5.36) The move by Nicaragua   Nicaragua's move
       The screenplay by Faulkner Faulkner's screenplay

(5.37) The wanton destruction   Rome's wanton destruction of Carthage
       of Carthage by Rome   Carthage's wanton destruction by Rome

Inside NP, the prepositions *by* and *of* are purely grammatical formatives which are inserted in s-structure contexts under empty P. That is, the deep structures of the lefthand examples include the sequence N-[$_P$Ø]-NP as in (5.38). Assuming these to be the source for the righthand exmaples as well, the P can remain empty only if it is licensed by Possessive Formation.

(5.38)

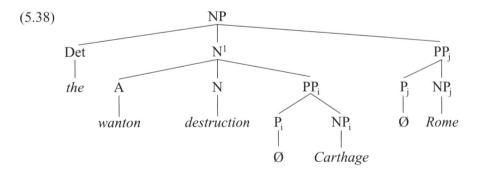

If there is no movement, the empty deep PS must be realized as late-inserted *of* and *by*.

This pattern of Possessive Formation (5.35)–(5.37) further justifies the dual effect of the co-indexing convention (5.31) and the general definition of antecedent (5.34), providing independent evidence for the earlier explanation of why the P in dative constructions can remain empty only if the two object NPs are interchanged. Thus, the analysis given here explains why, universally in head-initial languages with applicative datives and benefactives, the P-less dative is always outside of its base position; this occurs so that the P may become a well-formed trace. Thus, movement of the deep IO into DO position both preserves structure and allows the P to remain empty throughout the transformational derivation.

5.5 Accounting for crosslinguistic variation

5.5.1 Applicative suffixes

I have now provided a complete analysis of the transformational derivation and interpretation of P-less datives on the basis of the deep structure (5.12), claiming that P is null through s-structure in both P-less datives and the P datives that alternate with them. Subsequent to s-structure, a goal preposition *to* or *for* is inserted under P if and only if the following co-indexed NP (unmoved from deep structure) is marked with oblique Case. This analysis has explained why P must be empty if and only if the DO and IO undergo structure-preserving dative movement, and how P-less and P datives are similarly interpreted and assigned identical θ-roles. The surface structure (5.30) of the analysis accounts for all the syntactic and binding patterns observed by Baker, Barss and Lasnik, Chung, and others. I claim the analysis should be valid for at least head-initial languages such as English, Indonesian, etc.

The last topic to be addressed is how a P-less dative is allowed under such diverse conditions among head-initial languages. In Indonesian, P can be zero in the syntax (productively) only if the verb is suffixed with *-kan*; if we follow Huang (1991), the Chinese counterpart to *-kan* is a verbal suffix *-gei* homonymous with *gei* 'give'; in Standard American, almost all the "short" double object verbs allow P-less datives, but the "long" verbs (roughly, those borrowed from Romance) do not; and in French and Spanish, P cannot be empty in (non-pronominal) dative con-

142 *Structures in lexical projections*

structions. We need to account for this variation, and in addition understand the mechanism(s) by which a language tolerates even further irregularity; for example, some "short" English verbs forbid or require the P-less form (they exclude alternations), and Indonesian *-kan* is replaced by "*-i* or Ø for a handful of verbs whose indirect objects have undergone Dative." (Chung 1976: 55).

A clear, minimal contrast between Indonesian and Romance emerges if we say that Indonesian *-kan* licenses the empty P in (5.30), and that Romance lacks such a morpheme. A plausible entry for this suffix is (5.39).

(5.39) *kan*, category?, +F, +V___

An analysis as in Baker (1988a) would take *kan* as an incorporated P, but it seems more in conformity with other head-initial languages to take it as a regular righthand head of a morphologically complex applicative verb. In any case, my reasoning depends not on this label in (5.39) but rather turns on the feature F, once *-kan* is added to the s-structure (5.33).

(5.40)

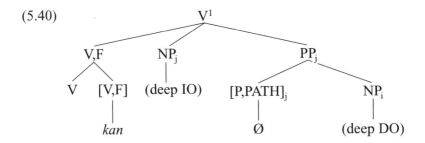

We inquire now as to the value of F which can license P=Ø in the syntax and hence force structure-preserving dative movement. We know that the P in (5.40) is a minimally specified preposition with a marked feature PATH, by virtue of the productive alternation of P-less datives with P datives. Now typically, an element can be empty in a surface structure only if its features can be found in its proximate syntactic environment. So, the most plausible candidate for the F which characterizes the Indonesian formative *kan* is PATH as well. That is, *kan* is: V,+PATH,+V___.

As discussed in section 2, grammatical morphemes with only PATH features are inserted not at deep structure, but rather at Phonological Form, into configurations defined at s-structure. Under this view, the feature matrix [P,+PATH,–SOURCE] is Ø at s-structure in all languages, and can remain so at PF in Indonesian (if -*kan* is present) but not in Romance. Why?

Emonds (1987) argues that closed categories can remain empty at Phonological Form if their features are spelled out "close by":

(5.41) *Invisible Category Principle (ICP). A closed category B with positively specified features C_j may remain empty (in PF) if the features C_j are all alternatively realized in the phrasal sister D^{max} of B.*[27]

Now, suppose that a (closed) category B can be subject to the Invisible Category Principle equally well when all B's features C_j, including B's index, are realized not only on phrasal sisters which B governs as in (5.41), *or alternatively* on nearby X^0 nodes which govern B. It is a simple matter to express this by generalizing the Invisible Category Principle, crucially using the percolation property by which heads and phrases in the bar notation share features.

(5.42) *Extended Invisible Category Principle. A (closed) category B with positively specified features C_j may remain empty (in PF) if the C_j are each alternatively realized on a sister of some projection of B.*

By (5.42), P (=B) can be null in the double object construction (5.40) precisely because its positively specified features, namely (i) the index of P and (ii) the feature PATH, are both realized on sisters of P^{max}, that is, on NP_j and V. We have already seen in section 4.1 that in languages which allow structure-preserving dative movement (Chicheŵa, Chinese, English, Indonesian), P is null if structure-preserving dative movement occurs because then and only then is the index of P realized on a promoted indirect object which can serve as P's antecedent, in conformity with (5.34). So (5.42) explains two things: why P can be null only if structure-preserving dative movement occurs (i.e., P's index is alternatively realized), and only if +PATH occurs on the head V which is a sister to PP (i.e., PATH is alternatively realized). That is, applicative suffixes such as Indonesian -*kan* in (5.40) are +PATH; this feature then percolates to the head V which is a sister to PP. This possibility is excluded in Romance, which has no lexical item with the features [V, +PATH] needed for P-less datives.[28]

The licensing of the empty P in Chinese appears similar to that in Indonesian. As discussed in Huang (1991), the counterpart to the Indonesian applicative verbal suffix *kan* is homonymous with the preposition *gei* 'to'. That is, most Chinese verbs which permit the derived order V-NP$_{IO}$-NP$_{DO}$ are of the form [$_V$ V-*gei*]. She provides a number of arguments for analyzing *gei* in this configuration as the V head of a verbal compound, in which case Chinese *gei* and Indonesian *kan* are analogous, both being of the form [V,+PATH] and licensing an empty s-structure [P,PATH] by virtue of the Extended Invisible Category Principle (5.42).

If arguments as to the verbal status of immediately post-verbal *gei* can be countered, an obvious alternative is that *gei* is an incorporated P, as in Baker (1988a). As indicated earlier, my argumentation on licensing empty P in the P-less dative does not depend on the category (P or V) of the applicative suffix, but only on the fact that V carries the feature PATH.[29] But a more likely candidate for full P incorporation is provided by languages in which a P-less dative (without morphological Case) is the *only* expression of an indirect object NP, and in which interchange with the direct object is forbidden. That is, the IO structure has the form [V-P]$_V$-NP$_{DO}$-[$_P$Ø]-NP$_{IO}$. This is the situation in Tzotzil (Aissen 1983; Baker 1988a: 231–232).

It does not seem that the P-less dative is ever truly lexically governed by indefinitely many verbs which have no applicative suffix and which cannot be independently characterized as a syntactic class. English is often thought to have such irregularity, but in fact exhibits a quite restricted lexical variation between P-less and P datives. As a result, the syntactic feature PATH should not appear randomly among lexical V. I exclude this possibility by claiming that syntactic features are primarily associated with a single bar notation host category (GENDER on N, PAST on I, PATH on P, ACTIVITY on V, etc.), and that the following restriction holds:

(5.43) *Alternative Realization. If F is a syntactic feature of a host category Q, a purely syntactic statement (a lexical entry or redundancy rule with no semantic feature) may realize F on some E≠Q provided some E^j is a sister to some projection of Q.*

Exactly because of this restriction on alternative realization of PATH, languages with structure-preserving dative movement such as Chinese and Indonesian require a lexical item of a closed class (=no semantic features) to express the feature PATH on V. Such affixes then permit the Extended Invisible Category Principle (5.42) to license P=Ø.[30]

5.5.2 Accounting for crosslinguistic variation: The English gambit

Turning now to English, it is well known that verbs which take indirect objects with *to* or *for* differ as to whether they accept the P-less order of V-IO-DO.[31] The most pervasive difference is that common verbs of "Anglo-Saxon form" (*bring, pay, scribble, send, take, teach, tell, write*, etc. with *to* and *butter, color, cook, fix, kindle, make, paint*, etc. with *for*) appear with P-less datives and those of "borrowed form" do not (*communicate, deliver, demonstrate, describe, dispatch, explain, introduce, recommend, suggest* with *to*, and *balance, classify, develop, devise, invent, organize, pronounce, provide, repair, review, submit* with *for*). This classification only indirectly reflects history.[32]

Emonds (1986a) argues that native form elements in a language, which I therm there *primary*, have several concomitant properties. For example, English primary verbs may not have Romance stress patterns (see note 32) and only primary verbs can be morphologically irregular; English primary vocabulary resists latinate morphology. Moreover, borrowing into the primary vocabulary in periods of intense language contact is claimed to be no more extensive than at other periods; extensive borrowing must go into the secondary vocabulary. Finally, all grammatical formatives are necessarily in the primary vocabulary.

In the terms developed here, primary or Anglo-Saxon form verbs may optionally have the feature PATH, thus allowing the [P,PATH] in (5.33) to remain empty by Principle (5.42), while boorowed form English verbs do not have this feature. Anglo-Saxon form verbs are thus like Indonesian *-kan* (when they occur in deep structure with the inherent feature PATH, they exclude the P dative), and borrowed form verbs, like all verbs in French and Spanish, lack the P feature PATH and are incompatible with a P-less derivation.

However, Alternative Realization (5.43) precludes listing the P feature PATH with any lexical entry for a verb with a semantic feature. Thus, in order to associate the feature PATH with Anglo-Saxon form verbs, we must use some device free of semantic features. For this, I propose a highly restricted type of purely syntactic lexical redundancy rule. In my view, lexical rules should be limited to inherent features and non-variable contextual features, as in phonology, and not usable, contrary to long practice, to create novel contextual frames for constructions that resist syntactic treatment. Thus, the optional lexical rule for English double object verbs which licenses the P-less s-structure (5.33) is simply the following:

(5.44) V, Anglo-Saxon or primary form, -LOCATION → +PATH

In Emonds (1991b), verbs have the syntactic feature +LOCATION if and only if their direct object is a "Ground," so they will be –LOCATION if their direct object is a Figure (=Theme). All double object verbs are of the latter type. By (5.44), *any* primary form verb whose deep object is not a Ground and which has a deep frame +___NP,PATH^NP, even if such a use is coined (e.g., *cry a river [of tears] for me*), is immediately available for a P-less dative (*cry me a river*).

Suppose one insists, against (5.44), that some feature which triggers the V-IO-DO pattern were distributed randomly among English verbs. In this case, this feature is PATH, in accord with the preceding section; of the principles in this analysis, only Alternative Realization (5.43), which restricts such a feature to appearing in purely syntactic statements, would need to be relaxed. However, any such insistence on irregularity is just disguised empiricism. There may be some individual variation as to what counts as an Anglo-Saxon or primary verb, but once an English speaker classifies a verb which is –LOCATION as primary, the P-less dative with the verb will be sanctioned. That is, (5.44), by virtue of (5.43), cannot have exceptions.

Residual questions are now easily disposed of. A few Anglo-Saxon form verbs, in particular *say* and *do*, do not accept P-less datives. These are to be lexically listed as -PATH, with this more specific restriction overcoming, by the Elsewhere Condition, the more general optional rule (5.44). Precisely in accord with Alterantive Realization, these verbs whith a lexical non-verbal, prepositional feature specification are arguably among the purely grammatical verbs (lacking purely semantic specificity) of Emonds (1985: Ch. 4).

The literature has unearthed a number of verbs which require the P-less dative construction (e.g., *allow, ask, bet, charge, cost, deny, envy, forgive*). Alternative Realization (5.43) does not allow us to list them as +PATH, since they are clearly not purely grammatical verbs. They may be listed as verbs whose second object is a quirky accusative via the feature+___NP_V, PATH^NP_V. As observed by Czepluch (1982: 16), "a verb that Case marks two objects must assign one Case structurally and the other lexically," where furthermore the accusative (structurally assigned) Case is verb-adjacent. With this deep frame, *to/for* insertion will be blocked (these prepositions, as noted earlier, require a following NP_P); structure-preserving dative movement will be the only derivation compatible with some device to license the empty deep P, namely, the principles (5.31) and (5.34) of section 4 will come into play. In this way, the only s-structure allowed for a double object verb such as *cost*, after structure-preserving dative movement, is as in (5.45a):

(5.45)

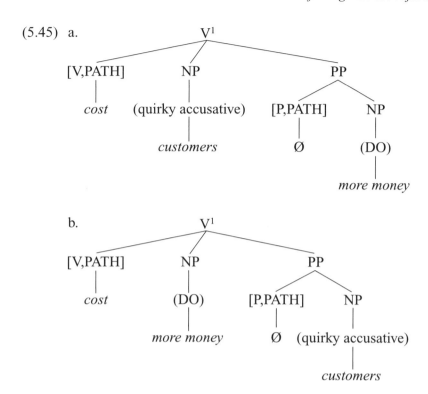

In the untransformed (5.45b), *to/for* cannot be inserted with quirky accusative objects, so the structure is ill-formed.

These accounts of the "exceptions" in both directions to productive, optional structure-preserving dative movement in English have little interest in themselves, but they show how a well-conceived syntactic account can accommodate lexical variation. Nothing, even in the exceptions, depends on diacritic or purely semantic features. The exceptions to the lexical rule (5.44) in one direction are irregularly marked –PATH (and these are limited to grammatical verbs), and those in the other direction are marked with a quirky accusative Case in the lexicon. Such simple devices open the way for accounting for cross-linguistic variation concerning dative movement with minimal lexical specifications. Indonesian has a dative applicative morpheme *-kan* marked +PATH licensing an empty [P,PATH], and Chinese has a similar morpheme *-gei*; Romance does not. English has a simple and entirely syntactic lexical redundancy rule (5.44) which makes its primary verbal vocabulary (of Anglo-Saxon form) behave like the Indonesian bound morpheme *-kan*. In contrast, its secondary vocabulary, borrowed from Romance for the most part, acts like Romance verbs in failing to license the empty P with (5.44), which would be needed to permit structure-preserving dative movement.

5.6 Conclusion: syntax rules OK

I have argued that almost every facet of the P-less dative/applicative benefactive construction that has been discussed in the generative literature is accounted for by dative movement, that is, the structure-preserving, traceless sub-case of Move α. Dative movement is triggered by the prepositional feature +PATH on a V-bound grammatical verb in Chinese, Indonesian, etc. and by a lexical redundancy rule's assignment of the same feature to the English primary verbs (= of Anglo-Saxon form). In both situations, this syntactic feature +PATH is not in its basic position with P, and therefore must be assigned under strictly syntactic conditions, as dictated by Alternative Realization (5.43). In this context, the concept of *lexical redundancy rule* is vastly more restrictive than in the previous grammatical literature; such rules here can depend on but cannot furnish contextual frames.

When the feature PATH is present on a head verb, a natural extension of the Invisible Category Principle (5.42) permits a purely syntactic node [P,PATH] to be empty at Phonological Form. In such cases, various devices of Universal Grammar insure that dative movement can apply to these and only these indirect objects, and the properties of indirect objects in several languages observed in the works cited here fall into place.

Certain aspects of and justifications for a structure-preserving dative movement analysis have been accruing for over twenty years. What is novel here is the account of the triggering mechanism (the deep empty P with the lexical feature PATH) and a syntactic formulation of the Projection Principle (the Original Projection Principle) that is compatible both with structure-preserving dative movement and with other transformational processes. Moreover, the Original Projection Principle has been counterposed and found superior to a vague but widespread version of the Projection Principle, whereby "nothing moves within X-bar." However, both the deep and derived structures of the P-less dative, from which the multiple empirical and theoretical advantages of dative movement follow, are not novel. They were not only in my initial study, but also, for example, in Chung's (1976) Restatement of Dative, extensively discussed in section 1.2.1. The explanatory character of these deep and derived structures has simply been sidestepped or overlooked. It is tempting to probe a bit deeper for an interpretation of why the research focusing on P-less datives has seemingly avoided an available satisfactory analysis.

To my mind, Chomsky's *Syntactic Structures* introduced an era when a syntactic interpretation of deep structure (and the Projection Principle) held a sociologically fragile sway, and for which the structure-preserving analysis of prepositionless datives and applicative benefactives is important support. Unfortunately, an extreme lexicalist interpretation of the Projection Principle has been used, often unconsciously, as a way to restrict the generative revolution to a drastically narrowed set of grammatical phenomena, those interacting in no interesting way with complement structures (=X-bar domains). For the moment, the generative focus on this narrower set of phenomena still addresses an interesting range of problems concerning coreference and long distance syntactic dependencies whose characterizations were not envisioned in traditional grammar.

Nonetheless, it is no doubt a comfort to skeptics that generative syntax presently tends to discuss only peripherally almost all the substantive issues of traditional grammar. (Baker 1985, 1988a, are refreshing exceptions.) Inflectional variation has often been excluded from the syntactic domain and relegated via "autonomy" (a return to American structuralism's "separation of levels") to a "morphological component"; complement structure is typically attributed to the lexicon, which is studied in a purely intuitional and introspective way, and for whose entries the issue of mathematical well-formedness is assumed to be premature. The lexicalist interpretation of the Projection Principle is then taken to suffice as a basis for discussing derivations, although the metamorphosis of informal lexical entries into formal phrase markers is unclear at best. This study has argued that such an approach to datives and benefactives does not stand up under scrutiny.

What emerges from studying datives and benefactives is that lexicon-independent and semantics-determining universal principles of syntax (e.g., the Original Projection Principle, structure-based abstract Case marking, the bar notation, the (Extended) Invisible Category Principle for empty X^0, and the structure-preserving constraint) completely and elegantly account for the grammatical variation and superficial irregularity noted in traditional grammar and in lexicalists' accounts. When potential success rather than failure seems to impel researchers to search for alternatives, one can only wonder whether the syntax-centered research program itself might be the cause of such discomfort.

Notes

1. I am greatly indebted to several readers, including Marcel den Dikken, Julia Herschensohn and Paul Postal, for suggestions. This abridged version of Emonds (1993) omits certain passages that served to situate this analysis with respect to competing views. Nonetheless, this version omits no paradigms or argumentation that directly concern indirect objects. Comments or phrasing not in Emonds (1993) are in square brackets.
2. Holmberg (1991) argues that the indirect objects of Icelandic, type (i), should be analyzed as PPs with an empty P, which is reflected by the overt morphological dative Case; cf. Emonds (1985: Ch. 5) for this view of dative Case. A few languages apparently have only pattern (iv), for example the Mayan language Tzotzil reported on in Aissen (1983); how this configuration may fit into the theory proposed here is sketched in section 5.1.
3. Barss and Lasnik argue against Oehrle's structure without mentioning its source. In addition to their arguments, we may also add the conclusions of Czepluch (1982: 5): "Oehrle's proposal faces at least three problems: It is not well suited for a grammar that incorporates a formal theory of syntactic functions [i.e., a universal theory of grammatical relations, J. E.]; it does not account for the passivity differential; and its solution to the ungrammatical UIO [= P-less dative, J. E.] interrogative seems to be questionable. All three deficiencies are crucially related to the assumption that UIO-DO structures are base-generated with two bare NPs as sisters to the verbal head."
4. The sequence [$_{PP}$ P-IP][$_{PP}$ P] is also thereby correctly excluded. Using the result of Emonds (1985: Ch. 7), CP=P+IP. Then (examples furnished by Paul Postal), *figure that 2+2=5 out, *work himself to attack the director up, *figure where to lecture out.
5. Jackendoff questions the acceptability of *showed John and Bill to each other* (fully acceptable to me), and we both accept *talk to John and Bill about each other*. As can be seen from (5.7), most Ps do not act like *to/from*. Perhaps the empty s-structure P underlying the PATH preposition *to* should be deleted in Logical Form when adjacent to the verb. Any such LF deletion cannot be linked to a reanalysis of *to* in PF, as shown in Postal (1986: Ch. 6).
6. Fassi-Fehri (1992: Ch. 1) argues that in Standard Arabic, both c-command and left-right considerations play a role in co-reference, but that for anaphora, only c-command is relevant.
7. For a more general study of this language's syntactic structure in a government and binding framework, see Salleh (1987).
8. In notes 9 and 10 keyed to this passage, Chung points out further parallels to English: "... Dative is not allowed for: (i) sentences with a deleted, generic direct object ...; (ii) sentences in which the direct object is deleted through the ordinary rules of pronominalization; and (iii) sentences in which either DO or IO

has undergone Topicalization, Question Movement, Scrambling, or Heavy NP Shift." "However, permutation of DO and IO is allowed [without P deletion, J. E.] if the DO is a heavy NP". These restrictions hold as well for English datives, except of course that English lacks null pronominal objects and scrambling. For an account of (iii), see Whitney (1982), and note 26.
9. Poser's letter does not itself attribute such rules to the lexicon; he is only responding to a claim about lexical rules in Williams (1981a). The terminology is understandable, however, since in the same issue Czepluch (1982: 1) observes: "Nowadays it is widely held that the alternation between the prepositional IO and the prepositionless IO represents a lexical rather than a transformational relationship."
10. As Baker acknowledges, the generalizations about Chicheŵa are drawn from works on object cliticization by Mchombo (1986) and Bresnan and Mchombo (1987).
11. That is, Baker's proposed structures require that all of Barss and Lasnik's binding theory arguments be reversed for Chicheŵa. Even in this unlikely eventuality, Baker's stipulative Case theory furnishes no explanation for the parallels between English and Chicheŵa benefactive applicatives enumerated just above.
12. An objection may be made that (5.2) violates a limitation to binary branching trees. The empirical argumentation for this limitation is simply invalid. [See the Appendix to Chapter 1 of this volume.]
13. The number of double object verbs in English which don't allow P-datives are few (*allow, ask, bet, charge, cost,* etc.). Moreover, the most natural method for accounting for these exceptional verbs, to which I return in section 5.2, crucially depends on their indirect objects appearing in deep structure within a PP. Thus, even these exceptional verbs do not undermine the descriptive generalization (5.10), the basis for claiming that the underlying structure of an indirect object is a PP.
14. However, Czepluch's analysis for the English P dative involves the base-generated structure V-[$_{PP}$[$_P$Ø]NP]-NP. This analysis leaves the Barss and Lasnik paradigms unaccounted for, makes the wrong predictions about English particle placement (as discussed in section 1.1), and requires that accusative Case be assigned across an intervening PP, in violation of Stowell's (1981) adjacency requirement. While rejecting Czepluch's analysis of the P-less dative, I certainly accept his proposal to associate indirect objects crosslinguistically with a fixed structure.
15. The distinctions maintained here between argument and adjunct positions are related to clear-cut differences in paradigmatic behavior of classic transformational vintage. The directions taken by Larson (1988) lead toward abandonment of a clear appreciation of this contrast. On the one hand, some NP arguments he characterizes as "adjuncts". On the other, Larson (1988: 346, 384) repeatedly endorses the view that adverbials are closer in deep structure to V than comple-

ments, which necessarily leads to abandoning long-standing accounts of various paradigms in terms of V' or VP constituency.
16. Larson's (1988, 1990) account of indirect object movement also involves the structure-preserving (passive) subcase of Move α. But it is not the argument interchange I argue for here. For the most part, Larson's comparisons of his analysis to passives are metaphorical, since passive movement has no special status within a Move α framework. When he attempts a closer parallel, problems emerge. For example, *to* remains in *John was spoken to by Mary* but not in what he claims are the parallel *They sent John Mary* or *John was sent a book*. Along the same lines, his own analysis (section 4) forces him to justify an alternative to the classic explanation of Fillmore (1965) that indirect object movement in English accounts for which deep indirect objects can be passivized.
17. In (5.20) I have spelled out the intended bar levels and conflated two *if-then* clauses into one. In his reformulation, Chomsky adds a further proviso to the Projection Principle prohibiting subcategorization of C by X without θ-marking of C by X.
18. [For extensive justification, see Emonds (2000, esp. Chs. 2 and 9).]
19. For a reason independent of dative movement, the bar level of a complement C is not stipulated in the subcategorization feature itself. Up to this point, we can take C and C^j to be NP for the complements discussed here.
20. To avoid misunderstanding, if α constitutes β but is dominated by (lower than) β, α does not c-command material outside β.
21. If a transitive verb takes a PP whose P is filled in deep structure, then the Original Projection Principle prevents application of structure-preserving dative movement. A range of such PP appear with verbs lexically specified as +___NP ([PP,+PATH]). But when P has only minimal grammatical features, P=Ø in the syntax (cf. section 2), and structure-preserving dative movement is possible: *Kick/throw Mary the ball*.

    Jackendoff (1990: 449) notes that indirect object movement is blocked with verbs like *drag, shove, move*, and *dribble*, which "... imply influence of the Agent continuing throughout the Theme's trajectory ..." In my terms, such verbs act as though the grammatical formative *to* is *present* in deep structure: **Drag/move Mary the ball*. A minimal extension of my proposal on insertion of grammatical formatives naturally accounts for this instance of Jackendoff's "picky restrictions on the meaning of the verb." Emonds (1985: Ch. 4) argues that grammatical formatives are inserted in deep structure only if they are *associated with* a purely semantic feature, either in their lexical entry (not the case with *to*), *or by virtue of the item's requiring a semantic rule that applies at deep structure*.

    Chomsky's (1972) Agent rule, namely animate subjects of activity verbs can be construed as Agents, is arguably a rule of this type, and it can be extended to include P of path as well as activity V. Thus, if a preposition under P(path) requires the Agent rule to apply (i.e., Jackendoff's "influence of the Agent continuing throughout the Theme's trajectory" with *drag* and *move*), its presence in deep structure blocks structure-preserving dative movement. But if a P(path) itself requires no Agent i.e. "the Agent applied force to the Theme just at the beginning of the Theme's trajectory of motion" (Jackendoff 1990: 449) as with *kick* and *throw*, then the P *to* is associated with no semantic rule and is inserted after s-structure; hence structure-preserving dative movement applies.

22. In support of this configuration, a reviewer notes: "In a language like Chamorro, a structure ... shows up with the supposedly dative NP [the deep IO, J. E.] in direct (=accusative) Case, while the supposedly accusative NP [the deep DO, JE] is in oblique Case."

23. For example, Baker's (1988b) analysis of Chicheŵa benefactive applicatives is developed in terms of a convoluted theory of inherent and structural Case, none of which is morphologically predictive, since Chicheŵa NPs exhibit no Case marking. The complexity of Larson's (1988) Case theory approaches that of Baker's, especially as it is based only on English, again a language without morphological Case (Emonds 1985: Ch. 5). For Larson, (i) V+NP sequences (reanalyzed as V, though no other rules treat the sequence as V) can assign Case (359); (ii) a single V assigns both inherent and structural Case, sometimes to the same NP and sometimes to two different NP (360); (iii) an accusative Case requires INFL (360), notwithstanding analyses whereby English V+*ing* participles and gerunds lack INFL (chapter 3 of this volume); and (iv) "Passive actually suppresses two Cases to maintain the familiar Government-Binding account of NP movement" (361).

24. I use a single type of co-indexation throughout, which is interpreted as co-reference when a co-indexed pronoun or anaphor is an NP, and as identity of sense in a range of other cases.

25. It might be objected that empty elements and their antecedents should be of the same category. However, it has long been appreciated (cf. Jackendoff 1972) that antecedents of overt pronouns need not be NPs.

26. It has been known since Fillmore (1965) that promoted IOs in P-less datives are at best marginal when further preposed into initial position:
    (i) ?Who did Mary bring a radio?
    ?His friend he found a nice coat.
    ?Not one friend did Sam bring a present.
    Cf. Mary brought who what?

    This restriction has been both generalized to other constructions and explained in terms of Chomsky's binding theory in Whitney (1982; 1983; the latter work must be consulted for a refinement). Essentially, when NP_j in (5.33) becomes an A-bar bound trace, it is then wrongly bound from inside the domain of its A-bar operator. For Whitney (1983: 317), the illicit binding is done by an NP_j trace of dative movement, while here it is by PP$_j$, but otherwise I concur with her argument. Curiously, this explanation in terms of the binding theory goes unmentioned in subsequent more stipulative accounts (e.g., Baker 1988b: 375–376).

Readers observe that Whitney's explanation of the mild unacceptability of A-bar traces of P-less indirect objects assimilates them to the stronger intuitions about strong crossover violations. But the latter are not strongly intuited as *ungrammatical*, but as having *other interpretations*. In Whitney's paradigm, no alternative interpretations can be constructed, so naturally these "strong intuitions" about meaning and co-reference fail.

27. No lexical statements achieving alternative realization can involve purely semantic features (i.e., alternative realization stipulated on open class lexical items is excluded.) Some typical triples of [B,C], D subject to the ICP discussed in Emonds (1987) are [I,PAST], V;[DET,PLURAL],N; and [P,DIRECTION],N, where here PATH and DIRECTION are equivalent.

28. Nothing prevents the applicative morpheme which is V,PATH,+V___ from realizing other features; that is, Bantu *-ir* is used in instrumental applicative constructions as well (Alsina and Mchombo 1990).

29. If the applicative dative suffix is an incorporated P, then it of course is co-indexed with and carries all the features of the P from its deep position. Thus, incorporation trivially satisfies the requirements of the Extended Invisible Category Principle (5.42); that is, head-to-head movement is a trivial subcase of it. But under this view, one must ask why the P-less dative in so many head-initial languages invariably involves DO-IO obligatory interchange. Section 4.1 argued that only this interchange provides a necessary antecedent for an empty P, but if incorporation is involved, this motivation disappears, leaving no account of the obligatory interchange in Chicheŵa, Chinese, Indonesian, etc.

30. This claim appears compatible with Chung's observation that only a "handful of verbs" have this property in Indonesian. Such verbs are presumably "grammatical verbs."

31. The variation is often exaggerated for empiricist purposes. For example, Allerton (1978) finds discrepancies in the grammaticality judgments accorded the P-less order for verbs which take *for* complements. However, the author doesn't distinguish between *for* phrase adjuncts (where *do X for Y* means *in Y's place*) and *for* dative complements. Therefore, it is not surprising that *phone me my wife* ("7% acceptable") differs from *phone me a doctor* ("82% acceptable"), since the former phoning is readily interpreted as acting in my stead (adjunct) and the latter as obtaining for me some service (complement). Similarly, the low acceptability of *open me the door* and *park me the car*, etc., are due to confusing adjuncts and complements. Such structures differ in meaning, long distance extractability and preposing with a comma, and thus can be distinguished independently.

32. For example, *promise* and *offer*, though borrowings from French, are of native form, have initial Anglo-Saxon stress, allow P-less datives, and exclude Latinate nominalizations (**promis[s]ion, *ofference*). *Provide, submit, refer* and *prefer*, from the same Latin roots, have non-initial stress, allow only P datives (**provide me this, *submit John this, *refer John this, *prefer me him*), and have Latinate nominalizations (*provision, submission, [p]reference*).

Part II
Minimal structures for functional categories

Chapter 6: "The flat structure economy of semi-lexical heads." Reprinted from *Semi-Lexical Categories: The Function of Content Words and the Content of Function Words*, edited by N. Corver and H. van Riemsdijk, Mouton de Gruyter, 23–66 (2001).

Chapter 6 presents a uniform treatment of 3 structures widely associated with "modification" or "higher functional categories": PRT + P (= P + P), DEG + A (= A + A) and quantify nouns (= N + N). A fourth structure (V + V), e.g, for **Romance restructuring and causative constructions**, has previously been treated as clausal complementation. Hence this chapter completes this volume's survey of traditional complement types and lays the basis for the main idea that organizes Chapter 7.

Chapter 7: "How clitics license null phrases: A theory of the lexical interface." Abridged and revised from *Empirical Approaches to Language Typology: Clitics in the Languages of Europe* edited by H. van Riemsdijk, Mouton de Gruyter, 291–367 (1999).

Chapter 7 uses the results at the end of Chapter 6 for establishing a simple **"phrase mate" condition for all Romance clitics** – they always remain within their lowest VP. This conclusion goes against almost all the previous literature on this topic in a Chomskyan framework. It fully exploits the principles of Alternative Realization and Late Lexical Insertion for bound morphology introduced in Emonds (2000: Ch. 3–4) and in Part I of this volume.

Chapter 8: "English indirect passives." Reprinted from *Facts and Explanations in Linguistic Theory: A Festschrift for Masaru Kajita*, edited by Shuji Chiba et al., Kaitakusha, 19–41 (2003). (permission obtained)

Chapter 8 develops and extends the theory of ordinary English passives from Emonds (2000a, Ch. 5) to a previously undelineated set of paradigms that are here presented for the first time as a new variant of "true mono-clausal verbal passives." The Syntacticon properties of verbs explain these new paradigms, called **English indirect passives**, and confirm several other hypotheses used in earlier chapters.

Chapter 6
The flat structure economy of semi-lexical heads*

6.1 Van Riemsdijk's Categorial Identity Thesis

This study starts out from an idea of H. van Riemsdijk (1998a), which can be paraphrased as follows: If parsimony would force us to assign closed class modifiers F(X) of some lexical category X (=N, V, A, P) to one of these four values of X, then the paradigms of language invariably and in fact overwhelmingly suggest that the best choice for F(X) is X itself.

For examples, closed class modifiers of N are decisively more like N than like V, A or P; closed class modifiers of P are decisively more like P than like N, V or A, etc. Since so many paradigms across languages conform to this, any theory of syntax that treats this tendency as accidental (i.e. any theory which fails to naturally relate "functional categories" to the lexical categories they modify) is defective, i.e. fails to capture empirical reality. The general tendency can be schematized as follows: if (6.1a), then (6.1b).

(6.1) a.

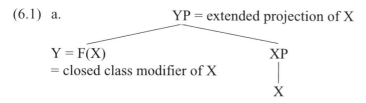

      b. If we must assign Y to one of N, V, A, P, then Y is an X.

To capture this tendency, van Riemsdijk (1998a) proposes (6.2).

(6.2) *Categorial Identity Thesis (CIT): In the unmarked case the lexical head and the corresponding functional head have the same categorial features.*

This paper elaborates on a version of the CIT. Nonetheless, it stops short of implementing one of van Riemsdijk's suggestions, that D might be assimilated to N and I to V. Rather, D here remains distinct from N and I distinct from V.[1] For all other closed class modifiers, including N modifiers other than D and V modifiers other than I, this study provides support for the CIT.

160   *Minimal structures for functional categories*

The main and I think richly supported conclusion of this study is that the CIT results from a particular conjunction of general phrase structure principles which gives rise to "flat structures." These structures contain what might be termed somewhat inaccurately "multiple heads," of which only one, the least peripheral, can be realized as an open class lexical item. Such structures do not conform to a widespread and to my mind a priori insistence on binary branching trees, but I perceive no adverse empirical or theoretical consequences of this.[2]

Flat structures are unstipulated consequences of a hypothesis that complements can be non-phrasal under highly specific conditions, one of which is satisfied when a functional head F(X) is an X^0 subcategorized for a complement with the same value of X (= N, V, A or P). Under these conditions, an X' can immediately dominate a series of X^0. The conclusion (6.2), that a functional head Y shares the same category features as the X it modifies, then follows from the bar notation.

6.2 Expected properties of phrasal XP complements

As a backdrop to determining an appropriate phrase structure for functional heads, let's consider first some empirical properties of open class or "full" lexical heads and their ordinary phrasal complements.

(6.3)   *Full lexical heads are X^0 whose lexical entries contain non-syntactic, purely semantic features (lower case "f") which play a role in selection/ interpretation but not in derivations.*

In all that follows, full lexical heads are inserted under the same conditions established in classical generative treatments (e.g., Chomsky 1965, 1973):

(6.4)   *Deep Insertion. Full lexical items of category X (with purely semantic features f) must be inserted prior to transformational computation on any corresponding domain XP.*

Such lexical entries constitute the open classes of N, V, A, and P (*sorrow, flee, soft, aboard*, etc.). No purely semantic features f at all appear on any categories other than N, V, A, P. In contrast, all the features which characterize members of other (closed class) categories are syntactic in that they all play a role in derivations.[3]

A reviewer asks why lexical insertion should take place prior to a derivational computation. The answer emerges when we realize that the fixed entries of the lexicon constitute quite a different mental faculty from our (ever changing) mental representations of the physical world (and its history, culture, etc.). "Using a sentence" consists of assembling open class items from one mental faculty, the lexicon, and processing the result so that it can be presented to another, the interface of real world understanding (LF). There would be no point in processing an empty set, which is what the function of syntax amounts to in theories of uniform lexical insertion at PF.

In terms of (6.3) and (6.4) then, a familiar tree such as (6.5) exemplifies a typical transitive open class verb whose object noun has in turn a PP complement; both are full lexical heads.[4]

(6.5)

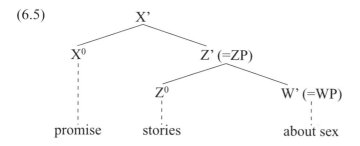

Nothing of course prevents sequences in which X selects Z and where both are full lexical heads of the same category, as can be seen in (6.6a) where X = Z = V and in (6.6b) where X = Z = N.

(6.6) a. [$_{V=X}$ promise] to [$_{VP=ZP}$ [$_{V=Z}$ sell] [$_{DP}$ these apartments]]
b. [$_{N=X}$ evidence] of [[$_{NP=ZP}$ [$_{N=Z}$ scandals] [$_{PP}$ about sex]]

It is of some importance for what follows to tease apart the principles of Universal Grammar which license typical phrasal complementation structures as in (6.5)–(6.6). Let X' be a phrasal projection of X^0, with XP simply a notation for those maximal X' which don't project to a larger X'. In a head-initial structure:

(6.7) *Bar Notation. An X^0 which is a maximal word is immediately dominated by an X'.*[5]

(6.8) *Head-initial Parameter. A head of category X^0 merges only with following phrases ZP.*[6]

I assume throughout that a necessary condition on qualifying as a head is that α *be associated with a morpheme from the lexicon*, and thus that a node α is the head of a larger constituent *at a level*. Thus, if a potential head is empty in underlying structure, it does not act like a head until it is lexically filled, i.e., affected by the operation Merge.

(6.9) *Merging X^0 with some Z^j "extends the projection," i.e. an X' then dominates X^0 and Z^j in the resulting structure.*

(6.10) *Extending the projection occurs (only) at the outset of a derivation on a domain, and immediately triggers transformational computation on that domain.*

It is widely assumed that the properties (6.7) and (6.8) are principally conditions on "underlying structure," i.e., on deep insertion or on extending projections. However, this study will claim that (6.7) and (6.8) are more general conditions on all syntactic structure. That is, the bar notation and the head-initial parameter also come into play for "late" lexical insertion which does *not* extend projections. Even so, this interesting eventuality is not the canonical case. Typical ZP complements, such as those in (6.5)–(6.6), satisfy all of (6.7)–(6.10).

They moreover participate in the familiar head-complement properties (i)–(vi) enumerated below. Almost all justifications for "phrase-hood" are subcases of these six criteria for phrasal status:

(i) In a structure $[_{X'}\ X^0 - [_{ZP}\ Z^0 - WP]]$, ZP can move as a unit.

Ross (1967) proposes this most classic of generative syntactic tests as a diagnostic for whether a sequence is a constituent or not. A VP is widely accepted as a constituent separate from IP precisely because it can undergo movements such as VP preposing in English or Italian focus movement (Rizzi, 1978).

(ii) ZP can under certain conditions be ellipted as a unit.

(6.11) Should I [$_{VP}$ speak of this]? I've already promised to [$_{VP}$ Ø].
We have evidence of [$_{NP}$ Ø] and strategies for [$_{NP}$ scandals about sex].

A reviewer observes that a proponent of larger inventories of functional heads FH might propose that if X = FH in (i), then ZP cannot move or ellipt, i.e., these FH would fail to "properly govern" empty categories. The proposal seems unconvincing in light of Lobeck's (1995) careful and extensively supported theory of ellipsis, which shows that the well motivated functional heads I, D, and C play a central role in ellipsis, even more central than their less inflected lexical counterparts. Consequently, the proposed larger set of FH divides into those which are well motivated and conform to (i) and (ii), and those which violate (i) and (ii) and have little independent motivation. Methodologically, it seems obvious that the proposed larger inventory is simply misguided.

(iii) ZP can block certain extractions.

The central role of phrasal categories in defining structures which resist extractions, such as those figuring in treatments of subjacency, is well-studied and widely accepted. But additionally, VP and NP can play such a role as well. Baltin (1982) argues that VP is a bound on rightward movements, and Rizzi (1978) shows that a VP can block several "clause bound" extractions in Italian:

(6.12) a. The enclitic *loro* can only attach to a V in its own VP:
Pensavo   di consegnar   loro   i   soldi.
'I thought to give   them the money.'

*Pensavo loro di consegnare i soldi.

   b. VP appear to block extractions of null operators:
Questo lavoro   è facile da finire per domani.
'That work   is easy to finish by tomorrow.'

*Quest lavoro   è facile da promettere di finir   per domani.
'That   work   is easy to promise   to finish by tomorrow.'

(iv) Only X^0 and not Z^0 enters into selection restrictions as head of X'.

(v) X^0 can have purely semantic features f, as defined in (6.3).

(vi) Complements of Z^0 cliticize onto Z^0 hosts but not X^0 hosts in e.g. Romance cliticization.

Note that if some sequence β fails to act as a unit under these criteria, to claim that β is a phrase would only weaken the explanatory force of the theoretical construct "phrase." In the rest of this study, we will see many examples of sequences, often assumed in previous work to be phrases, which nonetheless uniformly fail the tests (i)–(vi). Certain of these sequences will form an important empirical foundation for the postulation of "flat structures."

6.3 Defining semi-lexical heads

In (6.3) we have seen a definition of purely semantic features, i.e. those which play no role in grammatical derivations. Categories known as "functional heads" are precisely those lacking such features. That is, all their features are syntactic in the sense that they potentially play a role in accounting for some grammatical process:

(6.13) *Syntactic features (notated upper case "F") on all grammatical categories play central roles in syntactic derivations (as well as in lexical selection and interpretation).*

Most discussions contrasting lexical and functional heads give the impression that the categories N, V, A, and P cannot be thought of as "functional." But there is no reason to assume that all members of these classes must occur with some purely semantic f. In fact, a lot of evidence, some collected in Emonds (1985, Chs. 4 and 5), indicates rather that the most central items in these categories lack purely semantic features. These more "grammatical" heads encompass what many call semi-lexical heads, light verbs, etc.

(6.14) *Semi-lexical heads (= grammatical heads) are those N, V, A, and P which have no purely semantic features f.* (self, thing, do, get, much, so, by, of, etc.)

The lexicon thus has two kinds of entries, full (open class) items in the categories N, V, A, P with features F and f, and grammatical (closed class) items in all categories with only features F. In these terms, van Riemsdijk's CIT (6.2) claims that lexical heads, including open class items, are modified in at least unmarked cases by grammatical heads of the same category. What we need to determine now is the structural relation between these grammatical heads and lexical heads.[7]

6.4 Flat structures when X = Preposition

Jackendoff (1973) has observed some P-P combinations whose first elements, in bold in this section, appear to be closed class modifiers of second, lexical heads. In this study, I adopt and extend the hypothesis, perhaps argued for first in Baltin (1987), that phrasal categories should not appear in subcategorization frames and in fact can be eliminated from the lexicon altogether. Under this view, all Jackendoff's grammatical modifiers discussed here have lexical entries of the form: α, P, $+F_i$, $+\_\_\_[P, +F_j]$. Such entries do not in themselves determine whether the complement sister of a given α will be P or PP.

The first type of P-P combination to be examined concerns modifiers such as *over, down, back, out*. These modifiers are plausibly a set of grammatical formatives fully characterized by syntactic features F. They also serve as the post-verbal particles which can precede direct objects in English, (Cf. Ch. 4 of this volume.)

(6.15) He left a coat (right) **over** (*right) near the couch.
Put the linens (right) **up** (*right) behind the books.
Mary pushed her toys (right) **back** (*right) under the chair.
They ordered more agents (right) **out** (*right) into the Rockies.

The modifier *right*, which can ordinarily introduce English PPs of location, is excluded before the second P, which suggests that no PP dominates *only* the underlined sequences. Rather, these P-P combinations are internal to a single PP. Consequently, we expect the underlined sequences Y of (6.15) to *fail* to exhibit the phrasal properties of section 6.2, summarized in (6.16).

(6.16) (i) In a structure $[_{X'} X^0 - [_{ZP} Z^0 - WP]]$, ZP can move as a unit.
(ii) ZP can under certain conditions be ellipted as a unit.
(iii) ZP can block certain extractions.
(iv) Only X^0 and not Z^0 enters into selection as head of X'.
(v) X^0 can have purely semantic features f, as defined in (6.3).
(vi) Complements of Z^0 cliticize onto Z^0 but never onto X^0.

Non-constituent sequences inside $[_{X'} X^0_1 \ldots X^0_n \ldots WP]$, where Y is the sequence $X^0_n \ldots WP$, should exhibit rather the opposite *non-phrasal properties* in (6.17).

(6.17) (i') Y doesn't move as a unit.[8]
(ii') Y can't be ellipted as a unit.
(iii') Y fails to block extractions.
(iv') X^0_n has the main role in selection as head of X'.
(v') Among the X^0, only X^0_n has semantic features f.
(vi') Complements of X^0_i can cliticize onto X^0_1.

By (6.16i) the full PPs with two Ps in (6.15) can move to focus positions:

(6.18) Where he left a coat was [over near the couch].
It's [up behind the books] that the linens are usually put.
Where Mary pushed her toys was [back under the chair].
It was [out into the Rockies] that they ordered more agents.

However, as suggested by the exclusion of *right*, the second P heads no separate PP which can move, in accord with (6.17i'):

(6.19) *Where he left a coat over was near the couch.
*It's behind the books that the linens are usually put up.
*Where Mary pushed her toys back was under the chair.
*It was into the Rockies that they ordered more agents out.

We cannot ellipt the underlined sequences in (6.15), as expected under (6.17ii'):

(6.20) Some agents from Chicago have flown out to the Rockies.
*Should others from Salt Lake go over Ø?
*Put the boys down Ø and the girls up in the guest rooms.

Nor is there a PP within PP structure which could block extraction of DP (6.17iii'). Rather, we observe in this case the familiar English preposition stranding. The examples (6.21) may require a certain discourse context; e.g. the first example can be a response to: *He left the clothes over near something, but I don't know what.*

(6.21) What he left the clothes over near was the couch.
It's those books that the linens are usually put up behind.
What Mary pushed her toys back under was the bathtub.
It was the Rockies that they ordered more agents out into.

Finally, the verb selects and assigns a semantic role to the *second* P in (6.15), again suggesting the latter is the head (6.17iv'):

(6.22) Sam placed the books ({down/ back/ over})
{in/ ?into/ *to/ *from} the drawer.
Sam put the books ({down/ back/ over})
{in/ into/ *to/ *from} the drawer.
Sam moved the books ({down/ back/ over})
{in/ into/ to/ from} the drawer.

The fact that the underlined sequences in (6.15) fail all applicable XP tests is captured by assigning them the following flat structure:[9]

(6.23)

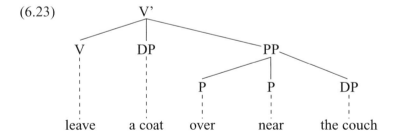

Assuming that a PP as in (6.23) projects when its lexical head merges into the tree, and that by the Head-initial Parameter (6.8) this merging head must be the leftmost lexical item in its phrase, the initial grammatical P in (6.23) must be Ø just after *near* is inserted:

(6.24)

```
              V'
         ┌────┼──────────┐
         V    DP         PP
                     ┌────┼────┐
                     P    P    DP
                     |    |    |
        leave  a coat Ø(=over in PF, LF) near the couch
```

It appears that later in the syntactic derivation, the Head-initial Parameter (6.8) can again have effect, so that a grammatical P can be inserted into the tree during the syntactic derivation. This configuration in turn suggests the following general characteristic of lexical insertion:

(6.25) *Claim 1. The merger of semi-lexical heads X need not extend a projection X'.*

Claim 1 follows from a theory of lexical insertion which integrates the two principles (6.4) and (6.10) of section 6.2 (repeated below) into a model which also crucially utilizes a *lexical version* (6.26) of Chomsky's "Procrastinate" principle.

(6.4) *Deep Insertion. Full lexical items of category X (with purely semantic features f) must be inserted prior to transformational computation on any corresponding domain XP.*

(6.10) *Extending the projection accompanies lexical insertion (only) at the outset of a derivation on a domain, and immediately triggers the transformational computation on that domain.*

(6.26) *Late Insertion. Lexical items are inserted into a derivation as late as possible.*

In view of (6.4), (6.26) has a non-vacuous effect only on a (subset of) grammatical or semi-lexical heads, as defined in (6.14). If an XP dominates a string of X^0, each must be lexicalized in a head-initial language when no lexicalized X are on its left, by (6.8); i.e. the X^0 are inserted right to left. Due to the effect of (6.10), only an *innermost* X^0 can be lexically filled prior to the transformational component; all others must be filled during a syntactic derivation. Grammatical morphemes interpreted in LF must of course be inserted prior to Spell Out, while only morphemes which have no LF role are inserted at PF.

These (I claim typical) effects are precisely those exemplified in (6.24). The P-modifying P discussed above (*over, back, down, off,* etc.) lack purely semantic +f and so are not subject to Deep Insertion (6.4). Consequently, they must be inserted as grammatical heads as late as possible before LF, i.e. late in the syntactic derivation.[10]

We have thus derived necessary (but not yet sufficient) conditions for the emergence of flat structures: The "multiple heads" immediately dominated by a single X' must be of the same category by the bar notation, and all but the rightmost must be semi-lexical (with no purely semantic +f) and subject to late insertion (6.26).[11]

In contrast to the P sequences in (6.15), a second class of Jackendoff's P-P combinations introduced by *to* and *from* do *not* qualify as flat structures. As we will see, they must be assigned his "PP over PP" structures as in (6.27).

(6.27) They moved a car [PP **from** [PP (right) near the barn]]
       ([PP **to** [PP by the fence]]).
       They took the cat [PP **Ø** [PP in(to) the house]].

(6.28) French counterpart:
       Nous avons mis le chat [PP **en** [PP dehors de la maison]].
       'We have put the cat to outside of the house.'

(6.29) Japanese (head-final counterpart):
       [[Ie no soto PP] **ni** PP] neko o dasu.
       house of outside at cat-acc. take-pres.
       'They take the cat to outside the house.'

As expected in a recursive PP, the highest P in an English PP complement can be stranded.

(6.30) Where they moved it from was near the barn.
       It's by the fence that they should move it (to).

However, in contrast to (6.21), the second P cannot be stranded:

(6.31) *What they moved it from near was the barn.
*It's the barn that they moved it from near.

Thus, (6.30) shows that the embedded PP can move, in accord with (6.16i), while (6.31) shows that this PP also blocks extractions (6.16iii). And again as expected under (6.16iv), the main verb selects and assigns a semantic role to the higher (directional) P in (6.27)–(6.29), not the second P. These contrasts with the behaviors in (6.19)–(6.22) are quite striking.

We thus see that Jackendoff's recursive PP structure is vindicated in this construction. This remains so even though the introductory P is an archetypal grammatical head (*to, from*) fully characterized by syntactic features. However, since this introductory P is a grammatical head subcategorized for +___P and hence at least a candidate for a flat structure, we naturally want to determine *why this construction excludes a flat structure.*

Observe first that the predication on the object DP in (6.27)–(6.29) is a static location expressed in the lower PP, bold in (6.32).[12]

(6.32)

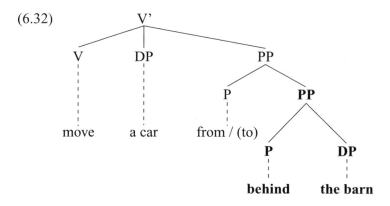

We might suspect in (6.27)–(6.29) and (6.32) that some principle of grammar is imposing the extra structure in the form of an intermediate "directional P.". I claim that the principle requiring an additional head is a "Revised Theta Criterion" (6.33), which prohibits a theta relation between two phrases that both stand in theta relations to a third element, here, the main verb. Chapters 3 and 4 in this volume (Emonds, 1991a and 1995) provide fuller justifications involving other constructions.

(6.33) *Revised Theta Criterion. Theta role assignment, defined as a relation between heads, is anti-transitive.*

For instance, the three heads A, B, C in (6.34) are each theta-related to the others, and the examples are excluded.

(6.34) *We [$_A${discouraged/ prevented}] [$_B$ Sue] [$_C$ taking] the job.
       *They [$_A$ described] [$_B$ him] [$_C${dysfunctional/ a bore}].

Grammaticality resurfaces when, following (6.33), an extra P head, bold in (6.35), introduces the second complements.

(6.35) We {discouraged/ prevented} Sue **from** taking the job.
       They described him **as** {dysfunctional/ a bore}.

Here V assigns theta roles to its object and to this mediating PP, while the predication on the object (also a theta relation) is expressed not by this intermediate P but by its object.

We can now answer an unanswered question about Claim 1 (6.25): when does the merger (insertion) of semi-lexical heads (= grammatical) heads extend projections and when not?

(6.36) *Claim 2. Semi-lexical heads extend a projection if and only if some principle of grammar requires the extension.*

Examples of such principles are the Revised Theta Criterion (6.33) or the Bar Notation (6.7), which requires that if some Y ($\neq$ X) satisfies a subcategorization for a semi-lexical head such as α, X, +F_i, +___Y, then Y must still be dominated by Y' $\neq$ X'. Thus in (6.37), even though X is semi-lexical, the Bar Notation requires that X and Y each head their own maximal projection and thus excludes a flat structure.[13]

(6.37) John may [$_{X=V}$ be] [$_{AP}$ [$_{Y=A}$ angry] at Ann].
       A nice [$_{X=N}$ one] [$_{PP}$ [$_{Y=P}$ for] Sue] might cost more.

In fact, a moment's reflection shows that Claim 2, a strengthening of Claim 1, follows from the requirement that structures used in satisfying subcategorization ought to be as sparse as possible, as measured in terms of phrases. That is, they follow from Economy of Representation.

6.5 Flat structures when X = Adjective/ Adverb

Throughout, this study is based on van Riemsdijk's (1998a) extensive observations to the effect that members of functional categories which modify a lexical category appear to share the structure, and often the morphological form, of the latter. The adjectival system reflects this tendency directly, in that "specifiers" or "degree words" which modify A are typically words which can be also be used alone as heads of AP:

(6.38) a. She seemed {real/ pretty/ awful/ damned} {upset/ happy}.
The book seemed {real/ pretty/ awful/ damned}.

b. French counterparts:
Cette histoire semble {fort/ bien} intéressante.
'That story seems {strong/ well} interesting.'
Votre ami semble {fort/ bien}.
'Your friend seems {strong/ well}.'

The specifiers of A *how, so* and *too* also have certain combinatorial properties of A. For example, they all satisfy +___A. Then *how* and *so* are specified as A, +F_i, +___(A) in certain contexts, while *too* is A, +F_i, +___A.

(6.39) How will this food {look/ seem/ be/ be judged}?

(6.40) Is that house still shabby$_j$? It {got/ seemed/ remained} so$_j$ last year.
Their living in it made it so$_j$. I found it so$_j$, I must say.

(6.41) Some party snacks are obviously cheap. Those choices may {look/ seem/ be/ be judged} too *(cheap).

We cannot be too quick to classify degree words as A, because we must account for why many of these putative A (e.g., *so, too, how, quite,* etc.) cannot themselves be modified by degree words:

(6.42) We were surprised at how (*so) sad she was.
Mary was very (*too) sad.

But in fact this marked lexical property of not occurring with degree words is shared with many open class adjectives, those which traditional grammar treats as inherently expressing a degree of comparison or as inherently incapable of comparison:

(6.43) Are those lakes (*very) exterior to our territory?
We examined the (*quite) lunar soil.
The animal skeletons seemed (*so) four-footed.
His logic was (*too) circular.

And on the other hand, the degree word *very* can be taken as an A unmarked for this same property; namely it can appear with other degree words:

(6.44) Mary seemed so very sad.
How very sad Mary was.
Mary seemed very, very sad.

It thus seems plausible to conclude that degree words are semi-lexical A (6.14) with the feature +___A, and by (6.26) are late-inserted.[14]

(6.45)

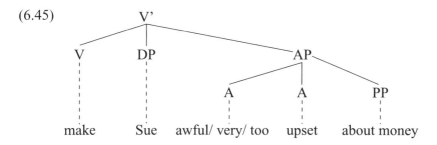

The empirical properties of non-phrasal sequences listed in (6.17) hold for sequences Y in (6.45), where Y = *upset about money*. Thus, the sequence Y doesn't move (6.17i'), nor does it ellipt (6.17ii'):

(6.46) *What Mary seemed {very/ awful} was upset about money.
*What you made Sue {too/ real} was upset about money.

(6.47) Is Sue upset about money now?
*She got {awful/ very/ so/quite/ pretty/ real/ too} last year.

It is moreover uncontroversial that an added degree word in an AP neither affects post-head extraction possibilities (6.17iii') nor plays any role in selection outside AP (6.17iv'). Finally, as we have been observing, the degree words in a flat structure don't have *purely semantic features* interpreted in LF (6.17v'). Even if some open class adjectives double as degree words (*pretty, real, damned, awful*), their interpretations in the latter usage are limited to expressing extreme degree, like *very* and *most*. Any purely semantic features lexically associated with them are apparently inaccessible in LF.

Finally, we can observe that in flat adjectival structures like (6.45), neither a degree word modified by a measure phrase nor sequences of degree words are constituents. Hence such sequences, bold in (6.48), cannot undergo movements, as shown in (6.49):

(6.48) John is **twenty IQ-points less** smart than Bill.
John is **so extremely** afraid of spiders that he won't go.

(6.49) *How many IQ-points less is John smart (than Bill)?
*So extremely is John afraid of spiders that he won't go.

These improper frontings cannot be attributed to some version of Ross's (1967) Left Branch Constraint, since measure phrases can be fronted in these contexts:

(6.50) [$_{DP}$ How many IQ-points] is John less smart (than Bill)?
[$_{DP}$ So much] is John afraid of spiders that he won't go.

These contrasts are from Corver (1997), who successfully argues against previous analyses of degree modification in which the fronted sequences would be constituents.[15]

It seems justified to conclude that APs as well as PPs exhibit flat structures introduced by a sequence $X^0 - X^0$ of "multiple heads," of which the rightmost is an open class full lexical head inserted in underlying structure in accord with (6.10). The other X^0 are closed class grammatical heads inserted later, during the syntactic derivation.

6.6 Flat structures when X = Noun

A central basis for Van Riemsdijk's CIT (6.2) is that quantity words which modify nouns cross-linguistically have nominal properties themselves. For example, English quantity words such as *bunch, couple, group, piece, pile,* etc. are clearly nouns, as argued in both Jackendoff (1977) and Selkirk (1977). Since they are typically followed by full lexical nouns, they must have the subcategorization N, +___N, as expected under the CIT. There is in fact ample evidence that cardinal numerals in many languages have a similar lexical status. Babby (1987) and Veselovská (2001) show that numerals beyond 4 in the highly inflected Slavic systems have nominal properties.

Combinations of these nominal quantity words and numerals with a following N which itself accepts a separate set of determiners are called "partitives." Jackendoff and Selkirk propose that the second N is the lexical head of a maximal projection (a DP in current terms) embedded in another (e.g. *[$_{DP}$ four of [$_{DP}$ them]]*). In such structures, the references of the larger and contained DP are always in principle distinct; the larger being a "part of" the smaller. It is presumably these two distinct references which require two Ds and hence two DPs, even when the head of the whole construction is a grammatical item.

The quantifying word, as head of the whole construction, determines agreement.

(6.51) [$_{DP}$ A pile of [$_{DP}$ his bills]] {was/ *were} found in the box.
[$_{DP}$ Four of [$_{DP}$ that family]] {were/ *was} quite a burden.

Jackendoff and Selkirk successfully use a number of the diagnostics of (6.16) to establish the "phrase within phrase" partitive structure for this sort of example.

Of particular interest here is a structure minimally different from the partitive that they call the "pseudo-partitive," in which the modified N does not exhibit a separate set of determiners. In such cases, interpretive judgments typically deny that separate references are involved. Moreover, sometimes the quantifying noun and sometimes the lexical noun seems to determine agreement.

(6.52) A pile of bills {was/ were} found in the box.
Four weeks {were too much/ was quite a long time}.

Such variation leads to some uncertainty in the literature over the best structure to assign to the pseudo-partitive. The most promising hypothesis appears to me to be in terms developed in this study:

176 *Minimal structures for functional categories*

(6.53) *Pseudo-partitives exhibit flat structure behavior if and only if any purely semantic feature +f of a quantity noun N_Q plays no role in syntax or LF.*

This hypothesis is graphically represented in (6.54)–(6.55):

(6.54)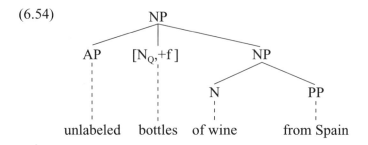

(6.55)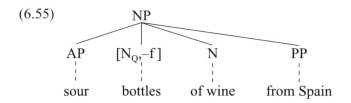

This hypothesis, if correct, is exactly what the framework of this paper predicts, since the presence of a semantically specific feature +f leads to Deep Insertion (6.4). Such deep insertion implies previous phrasal extension (6.10) of the complement selected by +___N, since only a grammatical head in a flat structure can be inserted late. On the other hand, absence of such a feature +f leads to Late Insertion (6.26) of N_Q and the flat structure consistent with Claim 2 (6.36).[16]

English subject-verb agreement seems determined by the noun which heads a DP at the *start* of a derivation of DP. Standard numerals and some quantity nouns N_Q like *a lot/ lots* never have +f; while others like *bouquet* always do. Hence the late inserted quantifiers *a lot/ lots*, absent at the start of a derivation in (6.56), never determine agreement, while a noun like *bouquet* invariably does:

(6.56) They say {a lot / lots} of milk {spoils/ *spoil} easily.
  They say {a lot / lots} of eggs {*spoils/ spoil} easily.
  Another bouquet of roses {has/ *have} greeted me.

Several quantity nouns N_Q can appear with or without +f, hence in either flat or articulated structures. In such cases, number agreement is predictably either with the N_Q or with the full lexical N, as in (6.52).

To test the hypothesis (6.53) more thoroughly, let's recall the contrasting sets of tests for hierarchical structures (6.16) vs. flat structures (6.17).

(6.16) (i) In a structure $[_{X'}X^0 - [_{ZP}Z^0 - WP]]$, ZP can move as a unit.
(ii) ZP can under certain conditions be ellipted as a unit.
(iii) ZP can block certain extractions.
(iv) Only X^0 and not Z^0 enters into selection as head of X'.
(v) X^0 can have purely semantic features +f, as defined in (6.3).

But in a flat structure $[_{X'}X^0{}_1 \dots X^0{}_n - WP]$, where Y is the sequence $X^0{}_n -$ WP:

(6.17) (i') Y doesn't move as a unit.
(ii') Y can't be ellipted as a unit.
(iii') Y fails to block extractions.
(iv') $X^0{}_n$ has the main role in selection as head of X'.
(v') Among the X^0, only $X^0{}_n$ has semantic features +f.

Hypothesis (6.53) directly reflects the contrast (6.16v) vs. (6.17v'), and the empirical confirmation of (6.53) then consists in verifying this contrast with the other properties (6.16i–iv) vs. (6.17i'–iv').

(i) Extraposition of pseudo-partitives (movement)

(6.57) a. A bouquet arrived of roses with stems.
b. *A lot was eaten of leftover turkey.   (Selkirk, 1977)
c. A load {was/ *were} discovered of counterfeit bills.
d. We saw a bunch in the kitchen of {radishes/ *money}.

As expected according to (6.53), the pseudo-partitive sequence Y introduced by *of* can extrapose if and only if the quantity N_Q retains semantic specificity as in (6.54), e.g., in (6.57c) *load* must be literal, and in (6.57d), *bunch* is naturally literal with *radishes* but not with *money*.

178   *Minimal structures for functional categories*

(ii) Ellipsis of pseudo-partitives

Similarly, quantity N_Q which have a purely semantic feature +f permit a pseudo-partitive NP to ellipt *only if* they are interpreted as semantically specific. If the same N_Q are interpreted as purely syntactic (semi-lexical), then ellipsis is excluded.[17]

(6.58) *Bunch, couple, load* and *pile* must be literal:
   a. Roses with stems are hard to find, but we found a { **bunch/ load**} in the market.
   b. I don't like to invite lots of guests, but inviting a **couple** might be nice.
   c. Two dollar bills are rare, but there was a **pile** on that table.

(iii) Blocking extraction from pseudo-partitives

It is relatively difficult but not impossible to extract from within English subjects via WH-fronting. However, it is notably more acceptable to extract out of a flat structure (6.55) than out of an articulated structure (6.54):

(6.59) ?Which country are sweet bottles of wine from often so cheap?
   ?Which law was a bunch of letters about found in the attic?
   *Which country are unlabeled bottles of [$_{NP}$ wine from] often so cheap?
   *Which law was a boxful of [$_{NP}$ letters about] found in the attic?

This contrast is expected under the hypothesis (6.53).

(iv) Selection in pseudo-partitives by verbs and of adjectives

According to Late Insertion (6.26), a semi-lexical N_Q without semantic specificity is not present at the outset of a derivation and hence should play no role in selection (a head property) at that level. Therefore, (6.53) predicts that a full lexical head noun of a DP is able to select an adjective which precedes an intervening N_Q only in (6.55), where the latter is semi-lexical (without +f) rather than literal.

The verb selection in (6.60) indicates that the bold quantifying or container noun has an interpreted +f, and so it can select prenominal adjectives.

(6.60) a. We {broke/ *drank} a {green/ hand-blown} **bottle** of Spanish wine.
   b. That cracked **bottle** of wine from Spain has cut my finger.

In (6.61) the verb selection shows that the container noun is purely grammatical (lacking +f), so the bold full lexical noun governs selection of A.

(6.61) a. We {drank/ *broke} a {sour/ aromatic} bottle of Spanish **wine**
   b. *That cracked bottle of **wine** from Spain has stained my rug.

Moreover, since prenominal adjectives which modify a literal and hence selecting [N_Q, +f] signal "phrase within phrase" structure, they are compatible with ellipsis of a phrase ZP (6.16ii).

(6.62) Some local wine is cheap, but a corked bottle would impress them.
   Though tomatoes are hard to find, there is a heaping pile in that stall.

On the other hand, any quantifying or container noun which intervenes between an adjective and a full lexical head it modifies must be semi-lexical. Consequently, such a sequence is a flat structure and is correctly predicted to be incompatible with ellipsis of the sequence Y (6.17ii').

(6.63) *Some local wine is cheap, but a dry bottle would impress them.
   *Though croissants are hard to find, there is a stale pile in that stall.

Finally, another type of grammatical modifier of nouns, itself plausibly of category N, is observed in languages which count instances of nouns by combining numerals with closed classes of numeric classifiers (Loebel, 2001). Many of these classifiers are recognizable as a subset of less specific nouns.

Kubo (1996) proposes that Japanese numeric classifiers can be characterized precisely as grammatical (semi-lexical) N, i.e. as lacking purely semantic features f (6.3). She presents several arguments that in the Japanese pseudo-partitive construction, these grammatical classifiers N_{cl} are right hand heads with (flat) open class N^0 complements. Hence, her conclusions square well with Hypothesis (6.53), where numeric classifiers are a special type of N_Q. They thus provide another source of confirmation for both the CIT (6.2) and the claims about flat structures (6.25) and (6.36).

180   *Minimal structures for functional categories*

6.7 Flat structures when X = Verb

Sections 6.4 through 6.6 have investigated closed classes of grammatical P, A and N which modify open class elements of the same category. To complete a survey of constructions expected under the CIT, we must now identify some *verbal* constructions which seem both to lack canonical behavior of phrasal embedding and also (in head-initial languages) to consist of closed class semi-lexical verbs with open class verb complements.

Some thoroughly studied candidates for such V-V combinations are the "restructuring" and "casuative" constructions of Romance languages. The meanings of these small classes of verbs are among the most basic and their translations tend to serve as auxiliaries or "quasi-auxiliaries" in various languages.

6.7.1 Romance restructuring

Italian and Spanish restructuring has been studied in detail in Aissen and Perlmutter (1976), Rizzi (1978), Zagona (1982), and Burzio (1986). The restructuring verbs V_X are a small subset of so-called "like subject" (raising or control) verbs, whose overt surface subject is the same as the understood subject of their complement verb V_c. Burzio's (1986, 324) list of Italian restructuring verbs contains *andare* 'go', *venire* 'come', *sembrare* 'seem', *stare* 'stay', *continuare* 'go on', *cominciare* 'begin', *sapere* 'know', *volere* 'want', *dovere* 'should', and *potere* 'can'.[18]

Although variation exists among speakers as to exactly which verbs have restructuring behavior (Rizzi, 1978, note 6), the pattern is inevitably one of "semantically more impoverished verbs allowing restructuring more readily" (Burzio, 1986, 220). Hence, it appears likely that restructuring verbs are exactly those like subject verbs which are fully characterized by syntactic features, i.e. they are semi-lexical heads.

Previous accounts have treated the limitation of restructuring to "semantically impoverished verbs" as accidental or due to some elusive semantic factor. But in the present account, a *lack* of purely semantic features +f is precisely the formal property of the grammatical verbs defined in (6.14) which can license flat structures. And it is precisely the flat structures which can explain all the previously mysterious properties of the complements to restructuring verbs.

The focus of argumentation in earlier treatments of restructuring is that the very same V+V sequences exhibit a kind of dual syntactic behavior.

This situation differs somewhat from the similar but distinct sequences of X^0-X^0 which we have examined in previous sections. It appears that the same sequences, such as Italian *verro a parlare* 'come to speak' and *cominciare a discutere* 'begin to discuss' can be realized as *either* articulated structures containing a VP within VP as in (6.64) or flat structures as in (6.65).

(6.64)

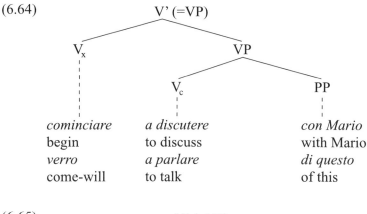

(6.65)

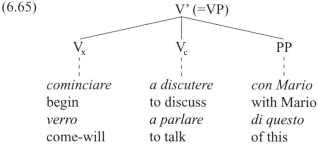

In the present framework, these structures are generated as derivations begin and remain unchanged throughout derivations.[19]

All the paradigms assembled in studies of Romance restructuring support a structural alternation such as (6.64)–(6.65). To justify these dual structures, one first chooses a diagnostic which unambiguously indicates one of these two structures, and then tests these structures for either phrase within phrase behavior (6.16) or for flat structure behavior (6.17). In accord with the contrast between expected properties of articulated VPs and flat structures, only the rightmost full lexical head in (6.65) can have a semantic feature +f. The Vs in (6.64) are subject to no such restriction.

182 *Minimal structures for functional categories*

Most research on these structures has at least begun with the diagnostic (6.16vi) vs. (6.17vi'): that the placement of (non-reflexive) clitics suggests the type of structure present.

(6.16vi) In a structure (6.64), $[_{X'} X^0 - [_{ZP} Z^0 - WP]]$, complements of Z^0 cliticize onto Z^0 but never onto X^0.

Rizzi's examples in (6.66) exemplify placement of the bold clitics -*ti* and -*ne* on Z^0, and hence the familiar articulated structure (6.64).

(6.66) Questi argomenti, dei quali verro   a parlar**ti** al piu presto, …
        These topics,   of which come-will-I to talk-you at most soon, …
        'These topics, about which I'll come to talk to you as soon as possible …'

        Ho cominciato a discuter**ne**   con Mario da Gianni.
        Have begun   to discuss-thereof with Mario at Gianni's
        'I have begun to discuss it with Mario at Gianni's house.'

The synonymous restructured alternatives in (6.67) exhibit these same clitics on the initial semi-lexical verbs in the verbal sequences:

(6.67) Questi argomenti,   dei quali **ti** verro   a parlare al piu presto …
        These topics, of which you-come-will-I to talk at most soon, …

        Ne ho cominciato   a discutere con Mario   da Gianni.
        Thereof-have begun   to discuss with Mario   at Gianni's

The examples in (6.67) follow the pattern expected of flat structures:

(6.17vi') In a flat structure (6.65), $[_{X'} X^0_1 \ldots X^0_n \ldots WP]$, complements of X^0_n can cliticize onto X^0_1.

When other syntactic behaviors are combined with clitics corresponding to WP complements or adjuncts, the empirical findings conform to the behavior expected under the other tests of (6.16) and (6.17). First, all complement and adjunct clitics must cluster on a single verb in the sequence.[20] Second, examples with clitics on the last verb test out according to the articulated structure (6.64). Third, those with clitics on the first verb act like the flat structure (6.65). As these rather complex contrasts have been thoroughly documented in the literature, I will only summarize results.

(i) Phrasal movement (6.16i) vs. (6.17i')

Rizzi (1978) shows that an Italian complement VP as in (6.64), but containing clitics, can move as a unit under focus fronting, right node raising, complex NP shift and WH-fronting in non-restrictive relatives. He shows that in contrast, a "restructured" V_c +WP in the flat (6.65) cannot so move.

(ii) Phrasal ellipsis (6.16ii) vs. (6.17ii')

This diagnostic appears to be irrelevant, as VPs in Romance do not seem to ellipt (Zagona, 1982).

(iii) VP role in blocking extraction (6.16iii) vs. (6.17iii')

Rizzi (1978) shows that embedded VPs as in (6.64), as evidenced by the presence of clitics on their head, play a central role in blocking Italian movements to subject. Two such processes are middle formation with reflexive *si*, which moves object DPs, and the counterpart to the *easy to please* construction. Again in contrast, when the first verb in a restructured sequence (6.65) hosts these same clitics, clause-mate movements to subject position are allowed.

(iv) Role as phrasal head in selection (6.16iv) vs. (6.17iv')

The choice between an initial Italian auxiliary *essere* 'be' or *avere* 'have' in a composed past depends on only the last V in a restructuring sequence (Rizzi, 1978).[21] Since the auxiliary is itself a restructured verb, as argued by Napoli (1981), then this choice is easily stated in terms of the trees (6.64) and (6.65): the auxiliary is uniformly selected by *the lexical head of the same VP in which the auxiliary appears,* V_x in (6.64) and the (final) V_c in (6.65).

We thus see that the same tests for phrasal vs. flat complementation utilized in previous sections establish that Romance restructuring exemplifies a nearly optional structural alternation. Both options are apparently generated by a single subcategorization frame as in (6.68), where the lack of a purely semantic feature +f is the by now expected characteristic of a grammatical head of a flat structure. (Lack of +f corresponds to Burzio's "semantic impoverishment.")

(6.68) cominciare, V, +F_i, +___V, 'begin'

The existing literature on restructuring and causatives contains no convincing proposal for what if any non-random factor determines use of a flat or an articulated structure, and I have no arguments to help settle this question. In any case, a theory of grammatical relations and theta-role assignment must treat the two variants as equivalent, since from this perspective they are synonymous.

It should be kept in mind that a restructuring verb bears the same LF relation to its non-finite complement in both structures (6.64) and (6.65). Since the explanatory adequacy of the Revised Theta Criterion (6.33) suggests that theta role assignment is a relation between heads, it is not surprising that these structures are semantically identical, except possibly for discourse interpretation.

A second concern is to determine how both verbs in restructuring sequences relate to their subjects. A grammatical verb in restructuring superficially shares its surface subject with a following non-finite open class verb, as in Rizzi's examples in (6.66) and (6.67).[22] We can ask how this squares with the Revised Theta Criterion introduced earlier.

(6.33) *Revised Theta Criterion. Theta role assignment, defined as a relation between heads, is anti-transitive.*

Several restructuring verbs assign no theta role to their subject DP, as seen in the list of restructuring verbs in the first paragraph of this subsection. On the other hand, some obligatory control restructuring verbs V_x such as Italian *sapere* 'know' and *volere* 'want' assign theta roles both to their subject and to their complement V_c. By (6.33), these complement V_c can assign theta roles to their own subject only if *that subject is distinct from the subject of* V_x. The question then is, where can this distinct structural position of a null subject of V_c be?

A generalized definition of subject that sheds light on this question is (6.69).

(6.69) *Generalized Subjects. Outside of complement DPs, the lowest DP c-commanding some projection of [+V] is its LF subject.*

(6.70) *Projection. If X^0 heads an X' in LF, then all such X' are its projections. An X^0 inside some other Y^0 has no projection. Otherwise X^0 is its own projection.*

According to (6.70), the lexical head V_c in a flat structure is *its own projection* in LF. Hence, a DP sister to any projection of V in (6.71) is actually a potential structural location for this verb's null subject, since such a DP c-commands V_c.

(6.71)

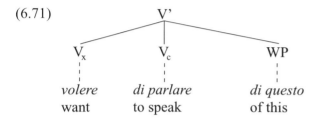

Since restructuring V_x are "like subject" verbs, their subject DP_i must be co-indexed with any null subject ß of their complement V_c. But if ß were structurally a complement inside V' in (6.71), Principle B of the Binding Theory (Chomsky, 1981: Ch. 3) would force ß to be disjoint in reference from DP_i, a contradictory requirement. Thus, the subject ß of V_c must be *outside the V'* in (6.71), as it indeed is in (6.72).

(6.72)

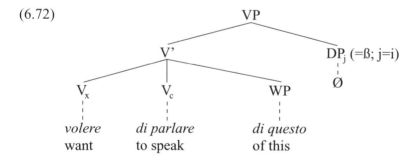

In this position DP_j satisfies (6.69) as the subject of V_c, as well as the Revised Theta Criterion (6.33). At the same time, the subject DP_i external to the whole VP in (6.72) can satisfy the definition of subject of V_x.

The structure (6.72) for restructuring now provides an answer for a hitherto mysterious fact: Modern French excludes restructuring – i.e. the flat

186   *Minimal structures for functional categories*

structure properties (6.17) are not exhibited with any of its raising or control verbs. As is well known, Italian and Spanish freely allow overt postposed DPs inside VP to be co-indexed with the subject in SPEC(IP). Such co-indexing of subject positions is a necessary prerequisite for a flat structure whose semi-lexical heads have the like subject property. Now, Modern French (and English) must forbid this co-indexing of subject positions, since neither tolerates freely postposed subjects. Thus, Modern French and English lack restructuring because they do not tolerate freely postposed subjects.

6.7.2 *Romance causative structures*

In addition to restructuring, Romance languages exhibit another construction in which small classes of causative and perception verbs are followed by a bare infinitival complement (one lacking any preposition-like complementizer). The subjects of these V complements, whether overt or understood, (i) can *follow the dependent verb* when overt and (ii) are always *disjoint in reference* from the higher subjects of the causative/ perception verbs:

(6.73) a. French causative verb *laisser* 'let':
    Marie **les** a laissés   laver trop vite   {à Anne/ Ø}.
    Marie them-has let   wash too fast   to Anne
    'Marie has let {Anne/ someone/ *herself} wash them too fast.'

  b. Italian causative verb *fare* 'make':
      La ho   fatta   riparare   {a Giovanni/ Ø}.
      It[FEM]-I've made[FEM] repair   to John
      'I have made {John/ someone/ *myself} repair it.'

  c. Spanish perception verb *ver* 'see':
      Los hermanos **la** han   visto preparar {a Ana/ Ø}.
      The brothers   it [FEM]-have seen prepare to Ana
      'The brothers have seen {Ana/ one/ *themselves} prepare it.'

In these examples, the bold clitics on the initial verbs correspond to complements or adjuncts of the complement verbs. This link between "clitic climbing" and a closed subclass of semantically less specific verbs again suggests, by criterion (6.17vi'), a flat structure hypothesis.

Throughout this section, the term "causative construction" is reserved for infinitival constructions in which overt subject DPs of the complement verbs *follow* that infinitive, as in (6.73).[23] When on the other hand these subjects *precede* an infinitival complement, as in corresponding examples in (6.74), the syntax differs little from standard infinitives after open class transitive verbs. For example, the same clitics (in bold) in these cases must appear on the complement verb. For such cases I assume a familiar, articulated "VP within VP" structure, consistent with criterion (6.16vi).

(6.74) a. Marie [$_{VP}$ a laissé Anne [$_{VP}$ **les** laver trop vite]]. (French)
       Marie has let Anne them-wash too fast
       'Marie has let Anne wash them too fast.'

b. [$_{VP}$ Ho fatto Giovanni [$_{VP}$ ripararla]]. (Italian)
   'I've made John repair it.'

c. Los hermanos [$_{VP}$ han visto Ana [$_{VP}$ prepararla]]. (Spanish)
   'The brothers have seen Ana prepare it.'

Like restructuring verbs, causative construction verbs (i.e. in which a complement verb's subject follows both verbs) are few in number and plausibly lack purely semantic features +f. Typically, they translate only a few words like *make, let, send, see, hear, feel*. In Burzio's phrase for restructuring verbs, causative verbs are also "semantically more impoverished." Hence, causative and perception verbs also satisfy criterion (6.17v') for flat structures introduced by a class of semi-lexical (grammatical) heads.[24]

Two typical lexical entries for French semi-lexical verbs are given in (6.75). The configurations that are relevant for the causative construction are the frames containing V, namely +___V and +___V (D).[25]

(6.75) laisser, V, +F$_i$, +___{D, V}(D), 'let'
       voir, V, +F$_i$, +___{D, V}, 'see'

We will next see how these frames generate typical causative (French) examples such as (6.76):

(6.76) Marie veut {laisser/ voir} danser Pierre avec les convives.
       Mary wants {let/ see} dance Peter with the guests.
       'Mary wants to {let/ see} Peter dance with the guests.'

188 *Minimal structures for functional categories*

Marie veut {laissser/ voir} lave toute la vaisselle par Pierre.
Mary wants {let/ see} wash all the dishes by Peter
'Mary wants to {let/ see} Peter wash all the dishes.'

Marie veut {laisser/ *voir} laver toute la vaisselle à Pierre.
Mary wants {let/ see} wash all the dishes to Peter
'Mary want to {let/ see} Peter wash all the dishes.'

Convincing and detailed studies of causatives in Spanish (Zagona, 1982), Italian (Burzio, 1986) and French (Miller, 1992) have argued that causative construction complements are not maximal projections in surface structure, i.e. they have properties which can be explained by the flat structure hypothesis. Thus, Burzio observes that (6.74b) but not (6.73b) contains an embedded VP headed by *riparare* which can move to focus position, as predicted by the contrasting movement property of articulated structures (6.16i) vs. flat structures (6.17i'); Zagona observes that complements as in (6.74c) accept independent negation and freer co-occurrence with adverbs in contrast to those in (6.73c).

Interestingly, Zagona and Burzio conclude that *all* syntactic differences between restructuring verbs (as summarized in section 6.7.1) and causative/ perception verbs are due to whether a complement verb's postposed subject is co-indexed with a higher subject and hence empty (as in restructuring), or disjoint in reference with that subject (as in causatives). The consequence of this reasoning is that the V frames in (6.75) for Romance semi-lexical causative and perception verbs can be optionally realized in a flat structure (6.77), which is structurally parallel to the restructuring tree (6.72):

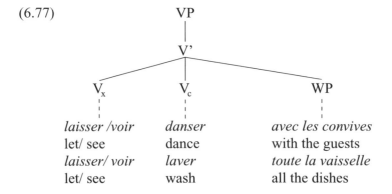

Recall that following the definition of Projection in (6.70), a full lexical head V_c in a flat structure is *its own projection* in Logical Form. Hence by the definition of Generalized Subjects (6.69), a sister to *any V projection* in (6.77) is a potential structural location for the DP subject of the complement of the causative verb.[26] Thus, the trees (6.78)–(6.80) below all provide acceptable positionings for the subject DPs of these dependent predicates, with extra Ps required for assigning case to some of them.

faire par. In (6.78) the subject DP_j of V_c in a flat structure is realized as a sister to V', i.e., *in an adjunct position*. As such it conforms to the simple structural definition of subject (6.69).[27] Moreover, the choices of case-marking Ps as *par* in French, *da* in Italian and *por* in Spanish are not surprising, since precisely these P mark postposed subjects in these languages' verbal passives. As in (6.72), the index i is that of the external subject DP of the highest VP.

(6.78)

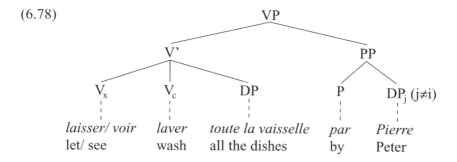

Kayne (1975, Ch. 3) studies this "*faire par* construction" (6.78) in detail. Among other things, he demonstrates several properties which its agent phrase shares with its homonymous, similarly structured passive counterpart. He observes that (non-reflexive) clitics corresponding to complements and adjuncts of V_c invariably appear on V_x, exactly as we expect under the flat structure hypothesis.[28] The sequence *laisser danser avec les convives par Pierre* is excluded, presumably because the extra PP is a less economic representation than the semantically equivalent (6.79) below (*laisser danser Pierre avec les convives*).

faire à. In (6.79)–(6.80) the bold subject DPs of V_c in flat structures are realized as sisters to V^0, i.e., *in complement positions*. These DP also conform to the structural definition of Generalized Subjects (6.69), because V_c in a flat structure is its *only* own projection, by (6.70).

(6.79)

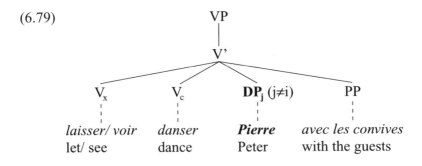

(6.80)

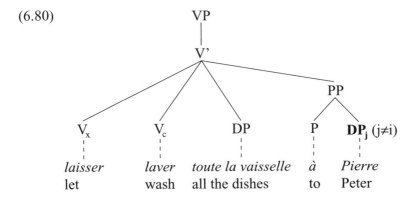

These two possibilities correspond to the *faire* ... *à* construction of Kayne (1975, Ch. 3). A sister DP of a non-initial V in flat structures as in (6.79)–(6.80) can thus actually be that V's subject in LF. In such structures, the definition of Generalized Subjects (6.69) correctly specifies that the subject verb pairings are exactly the same as in the synonymous articulated VP within VP structures (6.74).[29]

The literature on the causative construction has brought out a number of additional properties which can be easily explained by the flat structures hypotheses in (6.78)–(6.80). I do not enter into the details of these arguments already presented by other authors, but simply indicate their main point.

(i) Word orders. The observed word orders in complex French causative constructions (with post-infinitival subjects) correspond precisely to those predicted by treating the latter as constituting a single underlying VP (Miller, 1992). For example, as Kayne (1975) himself points out, (6.81) is inconsistent with his embedded clause sources for causatives, unless one postulates an otherwise unmotivated rule for moving non-constituent sequences.

(6.81) Jean a fait   faire sauter   le pont   à son fils.
John has made make explode the bridge to his son
'John has made his son make the bridge explode.'

This word order is exactly as expected in the pattern (6.80).

(ii) Abstract Accusative Case. As predicted by the flat structures (6.78)–(6.80), only one accusative case is available for DPs in the causative construction (Burzio, 1986). When V_c is transitive, the subject of the complement verb must then receive case from a grammatical P as in (6.80). This restriction contrasts with the articulated VP over VP structures (6.74), where each V can assign an accusative case in its own VP.

(iii) Participle Agreement with objects. If a causative construction contains a past participle which satisfies the structural conditions in Italian for agreeing with a direct object DP, a participial V_x will agree with this object in flat structures such as (6.78)–(6.80), but not in the VP over VP structures appropriate for the examples in (6.74). This suggests that a DP object of V_c is structurally an object of V_x as seen in (6.79) (Burzio, 1986).

(iv) Causative subjects satisfy subcategorizations for dative DPs. Overt lower subjects in a flat structure (6.80) can appear in dative PPs only if V_x is subcategorized to take a second DP (Herschensohn 1981; Milner 1982). Hence this type of *faire à* causative occurs with French *faire* 'make' and *laisser* 'let', but not with *entendre* 'hear' or *voir* 'see':

(6.82) J'ai laissé {mes biens/ gaspiller mes biens} (à mes enfants).
I've left/ let {my wealth/ waste my wealth} to my children

(6.83) J'ai entendu {la porte/ ouvrir la porte} (*à mes enfants).
I've heard {the door/ open the door} (to my children)

The contrast again shows that the "lover subjects" must be structurally complements of V_x.

(v) Incompatibility of causative subjects with Subject Raising. Kayne (1975) establishes that lower post-verbal subject DPs in a causative construction, bold in (6.84), never serve as landing sites for "NP movement."

(6.84) *Son expression peinée fait sembler **Jean** souffrir.
His expression pained made seem John suffer

*Son expression peinée fait paraître **Jean** en colère.
His expression pained made appear John in anger

Kayne's discussion makes clear that this paradigm does not involve any semantic restriction involving stative verbs; it rather involves the narrower class of subject raising predicates.

Yet the landing site of subject raising is generally agreed to be a subject position external to a VP. Consequently, Kayne's observation that the subject of the complement verb in a causative construction is never such a landing site strongly suggests that it is internal to a VP, in accord with the flat structure analysis. Ironically, Kayne's sophisticated empirical argument undermines the assumption in the rest of his work that all causative constructions contain full embedded clauses.

6.7.3 Concluding remarks on flat V-V structures

We have found two robust instantiations in Romance of flat V-V structures, whose existence is predicted by the principle of Late Insertion (6.26) of semi-lexical heads (items lacking purely semantic features) and the broad claim that certain late insertions do not extend projections (6.10).

(6.10) *Extending the projection accompanies lexical insertion (only) at the outset of a derivation on a domain, and immediately triggers the transformational computation.*

(6.26) *Late Insertion. Lexical items are inserted into a derivation as late as possible.*

The flat verbal structures of this section thus take their place among the other same category combinations of modifiers and lexical heads (P-P, A-A and N-N), the focus of earlier sections. Throughout, I have argued that such combinations are *all* best analyzed as flat structures in which a series of lexical category heads X^0 are daughters of the same X'. Moreover, by the Head-initial Parameter (6.8), all but the least peripheral positions of such flat structures must exhibit semi-lexical (=grammatical) heads.

(6.14) *Semi-lexical heads (= grammatical heads) are those N, V, A, and P which have no purely semantic features f.*

While the principal hypotheses of this study thus seem confirmed, there remain some uncertainties. First, English does not seem to exhibit flat verbal sequences like those studied in this section; that is, there is an unexplained gap among English constructions (see again note 23).

Second, recall that flat structures whose left hand heads are semi-lexical are supposed to conform to (6.36):

(6.36) *Semi-lexical heads extend a projection if and only if some principle of grammar requires the extension.*

This restriction is no separate principle of grammar but rather simply a part of Economy of Representation, to the effect that the phrase structures of language should be as compact as possible. Since the flat structures justified for Romance restructuring and causative verbs have been claimed in the literature to be fully optional variants of articulated structures, it is not obvious what principle of grammar can require "VP within VP" structures instead of flat structures. Put another way, in the framework of this paper, flat structures are expected if possible.

The studies here of P^0-P^0, A^0-A^0 and N^0-N^0 structures in fact confirm and justify this expectation. What now becomes problematic is how flat V-V structures alternate with articulated "VP over VP" structures, in particular those introduced by the grammatical restructuring, causative and perception verbs of Romance. In terms of (6.36), it is hard to see what principle of grammar could "optionally" require extended projections.

My best guess at present is that *some optional feature F' playing a role in either discourse representation or aspectual structure of V requires the presence of maximal phrases in LF.* Such a feature co-occurring with a complement V_c of a restructuring, causataive or perception verb would fail to be well-formed in a flat structure. Hence [V_c, F'] could only be realized on the head of phrasal complement in articulated "VP over VP" structures, as for example in (6.74). From this point of view, flat verbal structures would not really be optional variants of the articulated structures.

And indeed, at least complements of the minimally specified French causative *faire* 'make' seem to be flat under conditions of economy; that is, *faire* takes the full VP complement structure when various discourse and modification potentials are exploited, but otherwise seems to require the "clause union" alternative (Abeillé, Godard and Miller, 1997). These types of conditions suggest that flat V-V structures may be obligatory if F' is absent, but excluded if some F' is present.

If the choice between flat and articulated Romance VPs is partly a speaker option – i.e., for choosing a feature F' on the lexical head V_c and thus forcing an articulated structure, this same F' might be used for discourse effect even when X ≠ V, in what are usually judged as ungrammatical collocations in neutral contexts.

(6.85) !!Mentally disturbed that friend of yours is very!
 !!Right in the toy box you put those toys back!
 !!A lot – way too much – was eaten of leftover turkey!

As a reviewer suggests, it might be that the flat structures preferred by Economy of Representation can be overruled exactly in cases like (6.85) when a speaker wishes to achieve some pragmatic effect.

Notes

* I wish to thank the organizers, Norbert Corver and Henk van Riemsdijk, of a very fruitful and collaborative conference on semi-lexical heads in 1998 at Tilburg University. The comments of the participants helped enormously in preparing this study. I am especially grateful to Lida Veselovská and an anonymous reviewer for many insightful suggestions. This chapter reproduces my contribution to the resulting volume, *Semi-Lexical Categories: The Function of Content Words and the Content of Function Words*. N. Corver and H. van Riemsdijk (eds.), 2001. A few sentences have been added or deleted for clarity.

1. The hypothesis that I and V share no syntactic behavior is justified in detail in Emonds (1976, Chapter 6), where the term AUX corresponds to what has been renamed INFL and I. Even though later studies suggest a return to the past, i.e. that Modern English modals in I are still verbs like their Middle English ancestors, the most convincing analyses of languages which have a class of free morphemes of the category I (Chinese, English, Indonesian, and certain Kru languages; cf. Koopman, 1984) still seem to me to indicate the separate category status of I and V.

2. A reader who recoils at the thought of ternary branching can, following a suggestion of Baker (1999), reconceptualize this study's constituents of the form $X^0 - X^0 - ZP$ as $X^0 - [_{X'} X^0 - ZP]$, where X' is *not* a maximal projection. Zagona (1982) has argued that such structures are appropriate for Spanish restructuring and causative verbs and their complements (i.e., when $X = V$).
Whatever one's a priori commitments, any theory of possible categories defines a restricted set of dominance relations, but does not, in the absence of added stipulation, guarantee the uniqueness of either a head or a phrasal complement. On complements and binary branching, see the Appendix of Chapter 1 here.
3. The stricture that purely semantic features do not appear outside N, V, A and P is a fully justified empirical claim. It implies that every feature used to characterize items in other categories is syntactic, in that they play a role in some syntactic process (Chomsky 1965, Ch. 4). Consequently, any two elements in any category outside N, V, A and P differ by at least one syntactic feature and are thus expected to differ in their syntactic behavior, i.e., each closed class item has unique syntactic behavior. I know of no counter-examples to this strong claim about grammatical morphemes. This idea is developed in Emonds (1985, Ch. 4).
4. In this study, I do not formally distinguish various phrasal projections of the same X^0, in line with argumentation in Stuurmann (1985) and Speas (1990, section 2.2); XP is only a familiar notation for an X' which does not further project.
5. That is, when X^0 is not a subpart of a compound word or a larger formation which includes bound morphemes.
6. With the exception of some mentions of Japanese, this paper treats only head-initial languages.
7. Probably every word in the following example is fully characterized by features which all play a role in syntax. That is, the sentence may contain no purely semantic features at all. Sequences of like category grammatical and lexical heads are in bold.
    (i) Two **hundred people** will **come be** with us and then go **down from** here.
8. Even if WP isn't present, (6.17i') can still be used to test for the presence of a phrase which includes X_n but not X_1, provided the movement being used as a diagnostic is independently known not to affect bare heads. Thus, topicalization in English declaratives affects phrases but cannot front heads alone; consequently, a single word can topicalize only if it is a maximal phrase:
    (i) [$_{DP}$ Three] Mary seemed to like, vs. *[$_{NUM}$ Three] Mary seemed to like those.
9. A reviewer suggests that modifiers of P such as *down, back* and *out* in (6.22) might be SPEC(PP) and that the sequences following them such as *near the couch* might be P', provided principles of syntax make P' invisible for movement and ellipsis. Such intermediate projections should nonetheless be available for coordination. But consideration of (i)–(ii) shows they are not:
    (i) John put the books he found back in the desk and on the stairs.
    (ii) Please arrange the laundry up on the shelves or in these boxes.

The sense of (i), that the books had previously been in the desk, does *not* carry over to them having been on the stairs. Similarly, there is no interpretation for (ii) whereby *these boxes* is modified by *up*. Thus, the putative P' fails to exhibit the one property we might expect it to have. These facts are predicted by flat structures as in (6.23).

10. The claim that a class of elements lacks purely semantic features +f should not be misread as implying that they "lack semantics." Syntactic features +F such as ANIMATE, COMPARATIVE, DUAL, PAST, PATH, PLURAL, POTENTIAL, PROXIMATE, WH, II PERSON, etc., all clearly function *centrally* in LF, as stated in their definition (6.13). The statement that P-modifiers lack purely semantic +f implies that their semantic specificity is limited to (syntactically relevant) cognitive primitives expressed by +F.

11. Theories of uniform "late lexical insertion" or "PF insertion" capture none of the linguistically significant generalizations expressed by a theory distinguishing Deep Insertion of open classes (6.4) from Late Insertion of closed classes (6.26).

12. The configurations in (6.27)–(6.29) and (6.32) are cross-linguistically standard: "Sometimes PLACE and PATH are conflated in the position of P^0, but when the two are separated, it is always PATH which is 'externalized' to a functional position." (van Riemsdijk and Huijbregts, 1998b).

13. For example, the Bar Notation requires that C, in my view a subclass of P (Emonds, 1985, Ch. 7), and its complement I each head their own maximal projection. However, IP doesn't freely move or elide, and C can host clitic forms of various constituents internal to IP. A reviewer wonders if these facts might suggest a flat structure relationship even between C and I.

   Nonetheless, IP does elide after [C, +WH] (in "sluicing"; cf. Lobeck, 1995: section 2.3.3), and Bresnan (1970) initially motivated IP by observing its rightward movement in so-called Right Node Raising. The constituency tests (6.16i) and (6.16ii) don't require that various ZP move and elide under every imaginable circumstance, prior to analysis. Furthermore, the fact that clitics typically found in an I position can appear on the C governing IP is analogous to the fact that clitics for D can appear on the P governing DP (van Riemsdijk, 1978). (This parallel also strengthens the hypothesis that C = P.)

14. Doetjes, Neeleman and van de Koot (1999) argue for phrasal status as ModP for degree words such as *more, less* and *enough*, which they distinguish from *too, as, very, how*, etc. Their conclusion is compatible with mine; only one of my patterns in the text mentions a property of comparative modifiers.

15. In Corver's system, the degree word DEG appears to be the head of an adjectival phrase for purposes of selection and possibly LF interpretation. This may be a wrong result, in light of co-occurrence restrictions between a subject and a full lexical A as in (i).

    (i) *The {day/ *girl/ *color/ *attitude} seemed [$_{AP}$ [$_A$so/ too/ pretty] {eventful/ long}].*

In a classical model of lexical insertion based on Chomsky (1965, Ch. 2), selection restrictions between heads have effect at the point of lexical insertion. I retain this characteristic here; modifying semi-lexical items such as *so, too, pretty* in (i) are not yet lexicalized when Merge combines a phrasal complement with a higher head.

16. Adjectives without complements can pre-modify the second N in a flat structure, as in *sour bottles of Spanish wine*. The issue is how A can come to precede full lexical heads (whether or not these are modified by N_Q): in these pre-theoretical terms this is independent of whether the sequence with N_Q is flat or not.
17. There are nonetheless syntactic quantifying modifiers with anaphoric uses. These are apparently limited to those N_Q which never occur with purely semantic features +f.
    (i) *Two dollar bills are rare, but there were {three/ a lot} on that table.*
18. Aissen (1974) and Aissen and Perlmutter (1976) analyze a similar Spanish phenomenon in terms of the "clause union" of Relational Grammar, providing a similar, slightly larger list of restructuring V_x for Spanish.
19. Although this renders Rizzi's term "restructuring" inaccurate, I retain it for familiarity.
20. Rizzi (1978) uses a superficial exception to this clustering in Italian to construct an additional independent argument for dual structures. The only multi-syllabic clitic *loro* 'them, DAT, PLUR' must be enclitic and can attach to any V in the VP where it replaces an indirect object. Hence, exactly as predicted by the dual structures (6.64) and (6.65), *loro* can attach only to the second V in (6.64) but to either V in the flat (6.65).
21. According to Burzio (1986), *essere* is selected when the head V in a restructured sequence immediately precedes an empty DP.
22. For an interesting reason discussed below, Modern French lacks a counterpart of this Italian and Spanish restructuring.
23. I do not know why English lacks a true causative construction:
    (i) **John {made/ let/ saw} dance Bill with the guests.*
    *John {made/ let/ saw} drive Bill to the museum by their host.
24. I claim that lack of semantically specific features +f is the *only* criterion which characterizes causative/ perception V as a natural class and distinguishes them from open classes of semantic causatives such as Romance translations of *cause, force, oblige, persuade, urge*, etc. which disallow postposed subjects of their infinitival complements:
    (i) **On a {forcé/ obligé/ persuadé} de partir tout de suite ({à/ de}) Jean.*
    One has {forced/ obliged/ persuaded} to leave right away ({to/ of}) John
25. The issue arises as to how the same frame +___V can give rise both to like subject restructuring with a verb such as Italian *volere* 'want' and an unlike subject construction with a causative such as *fare* 'make'. This difference can perhaps be satisfactorily expressed generalizing a proposal of Koster (1978) that certain

DP arguments, such as objects of English *promise*, are lexically annotated as ineligible for serving as "controllers" (i.e., understood subjects) of a complement verb. *Subjects* of grammatical causative or perception verbs may be lexically specified for this property.

26. An X^0 can be its own projection in LF only in those phrases where X^0 doesn't project to a distinct higher phrase. This happens only in flat structures. *Hence a sister of X^0 (i.e. its structural complement) can be its subject only when X^0 is a complement to a semi-lexical head.* This restriction has been a mystery in all previous accounts, and generative analyses have postulated any number of ad hoc configurations to avoid this consequence. But it is a natural prediction of the theory presented here.

27. Many overt subjects in causatives are case marked by a PF-inserted P (French *à, de* or *par*, Italian *a* or *da*, Spanish *a* or *por*). This case-marking PP structure must be *absent* at LF, thus allowing these DPs to c-command V or V', which makes them subjects by (6.69).

28. VP-internal subjects in a PP are a less economical representation than a subject external to VP, e.g, in SPEC(IP). They are used as a subject of V_c in a flat structure only when the external position is not available for V_C, as when the subject of a passive auxiliary V_x can't receive a theta role, or a causative V_x separately assigns an agent role to the external subject. This explains why VP-internal PP subjects occur only with semi-lexical heads.

29. Kayne's (1975) account of certain blocked cliticizations in the *faire ... à* construction uses Chomsky's (1973) Specified Subject Condition, which corresponds to Principle A of the Binding Theory in Chomsky (1981). We can still explain Kayne's paradigms in terms of blocking intervening subjects, but without mentioning some clause-like domain which putatively always immediately dominates subjects. As with the original Principle A, intervening subjects have no effect on binding pronouns and A-bar traces.

   (i) *Principle A Recast. In a c-commanding sequence X ... Y ... Z, X cannot bind Z if Y is an LF subject that asymmetrically c-commands Z.*

   As discussed in Emonds (2000a, Appendix to Ch. 6), such a revision eliminates certain problems in Kayne's original analysis brought out in Rouveret and Vergnaud (1980) and Aoun (1985). See the next chapter of this volume for details.

Chapter 7
How clitics license null phrases:
A theory of the lexical interface*

7.1 The apparent non-local character of clitic placement

7.1.1 Five contexts for long distance licensing

Ever since Kayne (1975: 201) first formulated a Clitic Placement transformation, a central question in studies of Romance clitics has been (7.1):

(7.1) What is the maximal "structural distance" between a clitic on a verb and the empty phrase licensed by the clitic?

Under very restrictive conditions, intervening heads and boundaries of phrases presumably projected by these heads separate clitics and their verbal hosts from the empty phrases that the clitics seem to replace. Such structures differ from the more typical situation in Romance in which clitics and the phrases they replace are "clause mates" (Rizzi 1978: 115). In the atypical cases, using the descriptive terminology of movement, Romance clitics originate as arguments or adjuncts *within* clausal or phrasal complements of higher hosts, and then "move up" or "climb" to these verbal hosts. The five Romance constructions which seemingly exhibit movement over intermediate heads involve verbs (cases i and ii), participles (case iii), adjectives (case iv), and determiners and/or nouns (case v).[1]

(i) Restructuring Verbs. Clitics skip over non-finite complement verbs with null subjects, apparently optionally, and attach to a closed subset of higher governing verbs. These verbs in Italian and Spanish are called "restructuring verbs" after the classic study of Rizzi (1978). Two of his Italian examples:

(7.2) a. *Questi argomenti,*   *dei quali*   *ti*   *verrò*
       these topics,   of which   you   come-will
       a parlare   *al piu*   *presto, ...*
       to talk   at most   soon, ...
       'These topics, about which I will come to talk to you as soon as possible ...'

b. *Ne   ho   cominciato a   discutere con   Mario da Gianni.*
   thereof have begun   to discuss   with Mario at Gianni's
   'I have begun at Gianni's house to discuss (of) it with Mario.'

A puzzling restriction on Modern Standard French is that such "clitic climbing" out of control and raising infinitives is systematically excluded e.g., in translations of (7.2):

(7.3) *Ces questions, dont je (*te) viendrai parler aussitôt que possible, ...
      J'(*en) ai commencé chez Gianni à parler avec Mario.*

As explained in Rizzi (1978: note 6), variation exists among speakers as to exactly which verbs with non-finite complements trigger restructuring. In general, a higher degree of semantic specification precludes restructuring, "with semantically more impoverished verbs allowing restructuring more readily" (Burzio 1986: 220).[2]

Restructuring produces strings as follows, where V_x (Rizzi's term) is a closed subset of "trigger" verbs, and V_c is a non-finite verb governed by V_x; WP and WP' are complement/ adjunct positions of V_c co-indexed with the clitics. If V_x is finite, then the clitics will be proclitics.

"restructured clitics" + V_x host - V_c ... WP ... WP' ...

(ii) Causative and Perception Verbs. In both restructuring languages and in French as well, clitics can skip over infinitival complements to a small set of causative and perception verbs V_x. Again, there is some variation as to which verbs allow climbing (Zagona 1982: 46). In this case, where the clitic (cluster) surfaces also depends on the location of an expressed subject of the lower complement verb V_c. All authors agree that if a lower subject intervenes between V_x and V_c, clitic climbing to V_x is excluded.

(7.4) *Los hermanos dejan a Ana prepararsela   algunas veces.* (Spanish)
      the brothers   let   to Ana prepare-them-it sometimes
      'The brothers let Ana prepare it for them sometimes.'
      *Los hermanos se la dejan a Ana preparar algunas veces.

(7.5) *Marie laisse Anne les   leur   distribuer.*   (French)
Marie lets   Anne them to-them distribute.
'Marie lets Anne distribute them to them.'
**Marie les leur laisse Anne distribuer.*

If a lower subject follows V_c, (non-reflexive) clitics must attach to the first verb V_x, or in certain cases cliticisation is blocked altogether.

(7.6) *Los hermanos (*se)   la han dejado preparar a Ana.* (Spanish)
the brothers (themselves) it have let   prepare to Ana
'The brothers have let Ana prepare it (for themselves).'
**Los hermanos han dejado prepararsela a Ana.*

(7.7) *Marie les   (*leur) a   laissé distribuer à Anne.*   (French)
Marie them to-them has let   distribute to Anne
'Marie has let Anne distribute them (to them).'
**Marie a laissé les (leur) distribuer à Anne.*

Spanish and Italian causative and perception verbs thus alternate as follows, where again V_x is the triggering verb, V_c the infinitival complement, and WP, WP′ complement and adjunct positions of V_c.

V_x - DP subject of V_c - V_c + clitics ... WP ... WP′ ...
clitics + V_x - V_c ... WP ... WP′ ..., where V_c precedes its DP subject.

In French, proclitics on V_c replace enclitics. In order to generate the well-formed sequences involving causative and perception verbs, authors advocating clitic movement postulate an additional, invariably ad hoc "causative formation" movement of some projection of V_c.

(iii) Auxiliary Verbs. In the Romance languages under discussion, clitics which replace complements or adjuncts of past or passive participles obligatorily move up to auxiliary verbs which govern these participles. The phenomenon is exemplified above in Italian (7.2b), Spanish (7.6), and French (7.7). One can think of it as obligatory restructuring, required in French as well as in the restructuring languages (cf. Napoli 1981; Abeillé and Godard 1994).

(iv) Complements to Adjectives. Clitics preferentially replace pronominal complements of certain adjectives. In the Romance languages, clitics necessarily attach to verbs and not to adjectives, so if cliticisation occurs at all, it is onto a higher verbal head. To my knowledge, the three languages differ little in this area, but Spanish lacks "PP clitics" such as French *en* and *y*.

(7.8) Intransitive linking verbs in French, cf. Kayne (1975: 71):
Jean leur restera fidèle (à toutes les deux).
Jean them stay-will faithful (to all two)
'Jean will stay faithful to them (both).'
Elle m'en paraît capable.
she me-thereof appear capable
'She appears to me capable of it.'
La situation y semble lieé.
the situation thereto seems related
'The situation seems related to that.'

(7.9) Intransitive linking verbs in Italian:
Gianni gli resterá fedele (a lei).
Gianni him stay-will faithful (to him)
'Gianni will stay faithful to him.'
Mario me ne sembra capace (di questo).
Mario me thereof seems capable (of that)
'Mario seems capable of that to me.'

(7.10) Transitive verbs with secondary predication in French; Kayne (1975: 306):
Tout le monde en croit Jean digne.
Everyone thereof thinks Jean worthy
'Everyone thinks Jean worthy of it.'
On y croit Jean fidèle.
one thereto believe Jean faithful
'People believe Jean faithful to it.'
Cet évènement y a finalement rendu Jean sensible.
that event thereto has finally made Jean sensitive
'That event has finally made Jean sensitive to it.'

Thus, we should explain why in the following paraphrases, where PP is a complement of A, a cliticised variant is both possible and, in some dialects (languages?), preferred.³

    V - (DP) -A ... [$_{PP}$ pronoun /adverb] ...
    clitic + V - (DP) - A ... [$_{PP}$ Ø] ...

(v) The "Genitive" Clitics. In the first four cases of putative clitic movement just discussed, the clitics are attached one head higher than the head which selects them. Moreover, whether clitics may so appear depends on the lexical class of these higher heads. A fifth distinct case of apparent clitic movement is independent of the verbal host and depends rather only on syntactic structure. French *en* and Italian *ne*, roughly translatable as 'of/from it/them/there', are clitics which can replace a DP or PP sister of a direct object Determiner or Noun, and appear on the V which governs this object. These clitics are consequently sometimes separated from the empty categories they license by two intervening heads, D and N, bold in these French examples taken from Kayne (1975: 109).⁴

(7.11)   ...bien   qu'elle n'en   ait lu   que   *la*   *première* **partie**
        ...although she   thereof has read only the first   part
        '...although she has only read the first part of it.'

        Il va en   repeindre **les portes**.
        he will thereof repaint   the doors
        'He will repaint the doors of it.'

Italian examples from Burzio (1986: 72, 222) are similar.

(7.12) *Ne   appreziamo   **la generosità***.
        of-him appreciate-we the generosity
        'We appreciate the generosity of him.'

        Ne   conosco ***l'autore***.
        thereof know-I   the author
        'I know the author of that.'

It is to be noted that a Spanish counterpart of *en/ne* is entirely lacking.

The earliest and most persistent analyses of the structural distance between Romance clitics and their gaps are in terms of movements of clitics and of some projection of V_c (Kayne 1975, Quicoli 1980, Rouveret and Vergnaud 1980, Haverkort 1989, 1993). A competing approach considers the clitic-verb combination as crucially satisfying some government-like condition which then licenses a corresponding phrasal gap: subcategorisation-government in Jaeggli (1981: 18) and a clitic-theta-role co-indexing convention in Borer (1984: 38–39). A potential critique of these alternatives to movement is that their licensing mechanisms for empty phrasal categories may not extend naturally beyond clitic systems. That is, a government-based theorisation may be ad hoc in the sense that it can apply only where clitics are bound morphemes on selecting heads.

The detailed re-examination of Romance paradigms in this paper takes the Kayne–Rizzi observation that clitics usually license clause mates as the basis of a fully accurate, exceptionless characterisation of these clitics. Concomitantly, movement of clitics out of their deep phrase and also any movement of V_c or its projections is superfluous. I argue that all the paradigms (i)–(v) have misled researchers into postulating interclausal movement, and claim rather that a clitic on a verbal host always reflects an empty (or doubled) phrase in that same verb's VP. I then account for this general property of clitics by a licensing system for empty categories with significant explanatory power outside clitic systems. This system of licensing thereby escapes the charge that clitic movement can answer (7.1) in more general terms than can its rivals. The features of the clitics are themselves generated "in situ" on their V host, but overtly realised only in Phonological Form.[5]

Preliminary to elaborating this system, section 7.1.2 outlines deficiencies of the movement approach. We then move in section 7.2 to "genitive cliticisation" with *en/ne* (v), whose proper understanding involves different considerations than do cases (i)–(iv) of clitic climbing. The proposed in situ licensing system for genitive clitics, which additionally provides a formal basis for treatment of other clitics, emerges in section 7.3. Section 7.4 treats the "clitic climbing" of restructuring and causative verbs, as in (i)–(iii). Section 7.5 is devoted to AP structure and clitics which represent complements of adjectives (iv). Section 7.6 surveys how this study's approach relates to several other issues in Romance clitic theory.[6]

7.1.2 Problems with the Movement approach

Put briefly, Romance clitic systems lack essentially every property expected in a construction derived by transformational movement. It is instructive to run through some typical aspects of convincing movement analyses to see how (badly) clitic movement fares by comparison. Of the points below, (b) and (c) are further elaborated in what follows.

(a) In well justified movement paradigms, all members of grammatical categories are affected (e.g., Wh-phrases, English I Inversion, German/Dutch V-Raising, etc.), whereas any such (small) category for clitic movement must be defined ad hoc. Further, Romance clitics which attach to a V are not a subcase of any independently justified category, since they include (only) the least marked members from a variety of syntactic categories, D, P, NEG, A, etc.[7]

(b) If clitics move to their surface positions, they should move either as heads or as phrases; but they do not. We return to this.

(c) We could expect similarities between forms in base positions (when clitic movement is blocked or optional) and those in derived positions; instead, the correspondences are highly, one might say systematically suppletive across languages.

(d) Movement should leave traces rather than full forms, but such complementary distribution is lacking. As is generally acknowledged, the full or "doubling" DPs and PPs in argument and adjunct positions which agree with clitics are a serious problem for the movement approach. If clitics are pro-forms (or empty categories later filled with pro-forms) which originate in phrasal positions, then they must somehow co-occur in these deep positions with full phrases (sometimes empty and sometimes not) which do not move. Such a situation does not arise in other analyses in which movement plays an explanatory role. The problem attendant upon doubling has been well characterised by Jaeggli (1981: 15–16), who notes in particular: "Rather, what would be needed in these cases in a rule which *leaves the entire constituent C in its place, and only moves a pronominal copy of C* – that is, the inverse of the 'trace-proposal'." [original italics]

(e) Well-justified constraints on transformational movement might predict restrictions on clitic movement. Nonetheless, classic attempts to do so (e.g., Kayne 1975: Ch. 4–6; Quicoli 1980, Rouveret and Vergnaud 1980) achieved a modicum of explanation only by crucially splitting clitic placement rules, ordering these rules differently in and after the cycle, postulating a construction-specific causative formation rule, and setting up constituent structure ad hoc (sometimes using "reanalysis"; cf. Kayne's treatment of *en* and *y* in his section 7.4.5).[8]

In any case, these attempts to predict restrictions on clitic placement were based on Chomsky's (1973) Specified Subject Condition ("SSC"), generally taken today to be part of Principle A of the Binding Theory in Chomsky (1981: Ch. 3). Cinque (1980) argues further that some restrictions on clitic placement mirror other Principle A effects. Since the Binding Theory is held to apply to outputs of Move α rather than to movement itself, any interaction between clitic placement and Principle A (i.e., any restriction on clitic-phrasal pairing by some condition involving intervening subjects) is simply irrelevant to deciding between movement and in situ approaches to Romance clitics. I recast Kayne's SSC as a restriction on Logical Form in Emonds (2000a, Appendix to Ch. 6), at the same time removing a stipulative auxiliary hypothesis. The reformulation reflects the fact that SSC paradigms furnish no rationale for clitic movement in causatives.

Return now to (b), the question of whether clitic placement should be head movement or phrasal movement. If head movement is involved, one expects analogies with other well-attested cases, say as in Dutch/German verb-raising (Evers 1975) or Incorporation (Baker 1988). In both these studies, head movement from an adjunct position is excluded, a point emphasised by Baker; for example, heads of adverbial clauses do not incorporate with main verbs. Yet locative pro-PP adjuncts (French *y* an Italian *ci*) easily cliticise, as do case-marked "affected datives", shown in Authier and Reed (1992: 297) to be adjuncts rather than internal arguments.

Outside the domain of cliticisation, heads of adjuncts do not transformationally incorporate, nor do D heads of direct and indirect objects (cf. note 4). No matter how one modifies notions such as c-command, government, lowering, raising, co-indexing, or whatever, Romance clitic movement cannot be explanatorily subsumed under head movement, since empirically the categories which cliticise on V are entirely different from those that incorporate into V.

In view of these and other difficulties, some authors (e.g. Sportiche, 1998: section 4) propose that clitic placement involves movement of empty, minimally specified phrases to abstract positions termed Specifiers. It is rather natural to consider that such phrasal movement of clitics is to an "A–bar position" (Aoun 1985: Ch. 4). Nonetheless, expectations that clitic movement should then uniformly license parasitic gaps and be more rather than less free than "A movement" are frustrated, as discussed in Burzio (1986: section 1.4) and Sportiche (1998: section 6.2). Consequently, clitics end up being arguments for some purposes (e.g., failing to license parasitic gaps) but not for others (e.g., non-reflexive clitics can locally bind non-anaphors). The convoluted nature and ad hoc mechanisms of these proposals testify to their lack of explanatory force.

Moreover, phrasal movement analyses additionally fail to express clitic properties easily expressed either by head-adjunction to V or by generation in situ within V: the presence of only φ-features on clitics, the impossibility of stress, a lack of phrasal boundary phenomena, absence of any internal constituent structure, no alternation with any overt "Specifiers", and various orderings of clitics as enclitics or proclitics. Summarising, approaching clitic placement as phrasal movement faces different but equally many objections as head movement.[9]

Finally, let us examine (c), the lack of similarity between the forms in the deep phrasal positions and the surface forms hosted by verbs. Romance clitics are architypical instances of Zwicky's "special clitics", whose forms characteristically differ from the full forms they replace. This discrepancy between pre-movement and post-movement forms sharply distinguishes clitic placement from other paradigms for which movement has provided satisfying analyses.

Traditional grammars distinguish between Romance clitics and "strong pronouns", which spell out the same feature sets in argument or adjunct positions. (Cf. Kayne 1975: 66–69.) Given the discrepancies, which further differ across languages (e.g., Spanish first and second plural clitics differ from its strong pronouns though the French ones do not), Romance lexicons must include "post-clitic-placement" insertion contexts for pronouns. The French entries (7.13)–(7.15) are typical.

(7.13) *me*, I singular, -nominative, +___V

(7.14) *moi*, I singular, { [free form]/ [–nominative, +V___] }

(7.15) *lui*, III singular, -reflexive, {[–feminine]/ [dative, +___V]}

Paraphrasing, *lui* is a third person singular non-reflexive, being either a masculine strong form for any case if not in clitic position, or as a clitic a dative of either gender.

Such distributional generalisations for special clitics require insertion contexts statable only in Phonological Form ("PF"). Since additionally only the least specified members of various syntactic classes appear as clitics,[10]

208 *Minimal structures for functional categories*

a natural conclusion would be that clitic placement, if a movement, moves only phonologically empty feature bundles, which are then realised in PF by statements as in (7.13)–(7.15).[11] Consequently, the best version of transformational clitic placement, one consistent with the most general statements of lexical insertion and with facts of clitic ordering, must apparently postulate a movement restricted to empty categories. This is a strange result; if a syntactic model postulates a category or operation but, to achieve descriptive adequacy, must stipulate that the category or operation is specially reserved for empty elements, an alternative seems called for. Such an alternative is provided here.

7.2 Right dislocation as the key to *en/ne*

7.2.1 Distribution of the genitive clitics

This section examines the source of French *en* and Italian *ne*, which replace phrases introduced by French *de* and Italian *di* 'of', 'from'. Traditional treatments distinguish four types of phrases which these clitics replace. In types (iii) and (iv), bold font indicates D and N heads over which *en* and *ne* are thought to move to reach their verbal hosts.

(i) Subcategorised PP complements, whether literal or idiomatic.

(7.16) French: cf. similar Italian example in (7.2).
      a. *Mon amie revient de Paris samedi prochain.*
         'My friend returns from Paris next Saturday.'
      b. *Mon amie en revient samedi prochain.*
      c. *Marie parlait de ça avec Paul.*
         'Marie spoke of that with Paul.'
      d. *Marie en parlait avec Paul.*

(ii) Direct object DPs of transitive or "unaccusative" verbs with indefinite partitive articles introduced by *de/di*.

(7.17) French:
      a. *Cette amie apporte des livres au patron.*
         'That friend brings (some) books to the boss.'
      b. *Cette amie en apporte au patron.*

(7.18) Italian:
   a. *Sono arrivati dei parenti a Giovanni.*
      '(There) have arrived (some) relatives of Giovanni.'
   b. *Ne sono arrivati.*

(iii) PP complements within direct object DPs.

(7.19) French: cf. similar Italian examples in (7.12).
   a. *Lise a lu* **la** *prémière* **partie** *de ça hier.*
      'Lise read the first part of that yesterday.'
   b. *Lise en a lu* **la** *prémière* **partie** *hier.*
   c. *Le concierge va repeindre* **les portes** *de l'immeuble bientôt.*
      'The doorman will repaint the doors of the apartment house soon.'
   d. *Le concierge va en repeindre* **les portes** *bientôt.*

(iv) NP sisters to direct object DPs headed by indefinite Ds. (NP = the N-bar of earlier work; cf. note 4.) French grammatical tradition often refers to this fourth usage as "*en*-quantitatif".[12]

(7.20) French:
   a. *Marie voit* **peu** *de clients le matin.*
      'Marie sees few customers mornings.'
   b. *Marie en voit* **peu** *le matin.*
   c. *Paul a acheté* **deux kilos** *de pommes de terre au marché.*
      'Paul bought two kilos of potatoes at the market.'
   d. *Paul en a acheté* **deux kilos** *au marché.*

(7.21) Italian:
   a. *Il governo inviterà* **molti** *esperti.*
      'The government will invite many experts.'
   b. *Il governo ne inviterà* **molti**.
   c. *L'artiglieria ha affondato* **due** *navi.*
      'The artillery has sunk two ships.'
   d. *L'artiglieria ne ha affondate* **due**.

Milner (1978: Ch. III) establishes that in addition to these "pronominal" uses, *en* can "double" overt right-dislocated *de*-phrases in counterparts to these same four constructions. Mutatis mutandis, the parallels hold for Italian.

(i) Doubled subcategorised PP complements:

(7.22) a. *Mon amie en revient samedi prochain, de Paris.*
b. *Marie en parlait avec Paul, de tout ça.*
c. *Ne ho cominciato a discutere con Mario, del film.*
d. *Maria ne discute ogni giorno, di questo.*

(ii) Doubled partitive direct objects:

(7.23) a. *Cette amie en apporte au patron, des livres.*
b. *Ne sono arrivati ieri, dei parenti a Giovanni.*

(iii) Doubled PP complements within direct objects:

(7.24) a. *Lise en a lu la première partie hier, de ce livre.*
b. *Le concierge va en repeindre les portes bientôt, de l'immeuble.*
c. *Lisa ne ha letta la prima parte ieri, di questo libro.*
d. *Ne abbiamo dimostrato il talento al direttore, di Gianni.*

(iv) Doubled NP sisters of indefinite direct object Ds:

(7.25) a. *Marie en voit peu le matin, de clients riches.*
b. *Paul en a acheté deux kilos au marché, de pommes de terre.*
c. *Maria ne vede pochi di mattina, di clienti ricchi.*
d. *Paolo ne ha comprati due al mercato, di patate.*
e. *Il governo ne inviterà molti, di esperti.*

One might be tempted to treat these right dislocations as some kind of stylistic options that reflect no real differences among grammatical systems. But this would be an error, because French and Italian speakers unhesitatingly accept a wider range of right dislocation constructions than do speakers of languages such as Spanish or English. Moreover, right dislocation is closely tied to *en*. Milner's detailed study of French dislocation concludes that "the possibility of having *en* presupposes that there is *de* + Pro", where *de* is "evidenced by right dislocation" (Milner 1978: 164). His examples below show that even quantitative *en*, usage (iv) which can occur superficially without *de*, does not escape this correlation.

(7.26) *J'ai en lu deux hier, de livres.* (3.36)

(7.27) *Elle en a publié deux, du théorème de Lagrange,
        de démonstrations.* (3.48)

(7.28) *Il en est paru plusieurs en 1974, de livres de Zola.* (3.56)

The cleavage between French and Italian on the one hand, and English and Spanish on the other, is brought out when phrases properly contained in direct objects are right dislocated in the latter languages. Dislocated PP complements from within these objects are weakly ungrammatical (7.29)–(7.30), and NPs dislocated from within object DPs are firmly excluded (7.31)–(7.32):

(7.29) ?*Lisa read the first part yesterday of the book.*
        ?*The doorman will paint the doors soon of the apartment house.*

(7.30) ?*Laura ha leido la primera parte ayer del libro.*
        ?*El portero va a pintar las puertas proximamente del edificio.*

(7.31) ?*Paul bought four pounds at the market, of potatoes.*[13]
        **Mary sees few mornings, (of) rich customers.*
        **I read two yesterday, (of) books by Calvino.*
        **She has published two of Lagrange's theorem, (of) proofs.*
        **There have appeared several in 1974, (of) Zola's books.*

(7.32) ?*Pablo ha comprado dos kilos en el mercado, de papas.*
        **Marìa ve pocos por la mañana, (de) clientes ricos.*
        **He leido dos ayer, (de) libros de Calvino.*
        **Ana ha publicado dos de uno artículo famoso, (de) versiones.*

Milner proposes that French right dislocation in (7.22)–(7.25) is movement and adjunction of DP or NP (in terms prior to the DP hypothesis, of NP or N-bar) to the right periphery of a cyclic domain (i.e., DP or IP in the system of Chomsky, 1986).[14] We thus obtain the following typical representations for usages (i)–(iv); these trees ignore verb-raising. I assume that right dislocation can adjoin a phrase as high as possible, but *always within the second cyclic domain, in accord with subjacency.*

212 *Minimal structures for functional categories*

(7.33) Right-dislocated subcategorized PP complements (i):

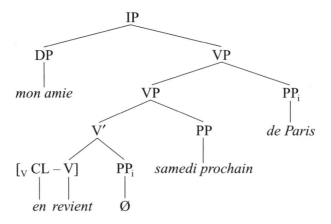

(7.34) Right-dislocated partitive direct objects (ii):

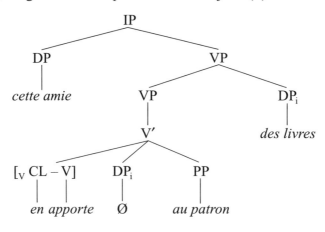

(7.35) Right-dislocated PP complements within direct objects (iii):

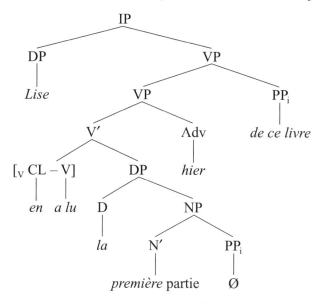

(7.36) Right-dislocated NP sisters of indefinite direct object Ds (iv):

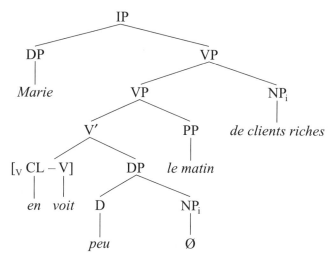

We are especially concerned with how the empty categories in counterparts of (7.33)–(7.36) which lack dislocation, namely those in the (b) and (d) examples of (7.19)–(7.21), can "move over" the italicised heads D and N within the direct objects, so as to be related to the clitic *en* on the verb.

214 *Minimal structures for functional categories*

Recall that Milner (1978) establishes that whenever *en* is possible in French, then so is a right dislocated phrase introduced by *de* (or the full partitive composed of *de* + definite article), which *en* can double. That is, in some languages with verbal clitics, some mechanism licenses right-dislocated DP, PP, and NP phrases. It is then natural enough to assume that these clitics co-occur not only with *overt* right dislocated phrases as in (7.33)–(7.36) but also with *empty* dislocated XP_i as well, just as clitics can co-occur with both doubled and null phrasal arguments. These null dislocated phrases are the needed representations for the (b) and (d) examples of (7.19)–(7.21). I therefore propose that dislocated configurations as in (7.33)–(7.36) are always available whenever *en* can appear:

(7.37) *Genitive Phrase Mate Hypothesis. The clitics en/ne on V_i are related only to (possibly dislocated and possibly empty) PP, DP or NP which are sisters to some V_i^k.*

It remains to formulate in the next section a general clitic-dependent licensing mechanism for empty phrases (dislocated or not). Beyond this, the trees (7.35)–(7.36) demonstrate why there is no longer any issue of how *en/ne* move over the italicised heads in (7.19)–(7.21). Milner's right dislocation of phrases, subject to subjacency rather than head movement, explains why these clitics appear to "skip over" D and N heads. The genitive clitics are themselves uniformly related to sisters of projections of their verbal host, and do not climb at all.[15] Moreover, since Spanish does not allow for right dislocation of phrases from within direct objects, (7.37) correctly predicts that Spanish can have no counterpart to *en/ne*, as desired.

7.2.2 The relation of en/ne *to subject position*

Apparently counter to (7.37), *en/ne* sometimes seem related to empty phrases within a subject DP (i) when the clause has a copular or linking verb, and (ii) when the clause contains certain intransitive verbs. However, Couquaux (1981), seconded by Burzio (1986: 73), has effectively argued that all such subject DPs of linking verbs have an underlying post-verbal source.[16] Gaps within such post-verbal DPs then reduce to the types seen in (7.16)–(7.21).

As for gaps corresponding to *en/ne* in surface intransitives, the widely accepted analysis of Burzio (1981, 1986: Ch. 1) holds that *en/ne* can correspond to gaps within apparent subject DPs of intransitive verbs only if these DPs are underlying (post-verbal) direct objects. Such gaps in deep objects can satisfy the Genitive Phrase Mate Hypothesis (7.37) via the type of structure discussed in note 16. [For more discussion, see Emonds (2002).]

7.2.3 Free right dislocations without en/ne

Kayne's (1975) argument that subjacency restricts movement of *en* from phrasal to pre-verbal position has become a classic in the clitic literature. I claim this follows from right dislocation being subject to subjacency as well, as argued in Milner (1978).[17]

Both Kayne (1975: 125) and Milner (1978: 142) find French examples of right dislocation from within PPs, as in (7.38a–b) respectively. In such cases, *en* can't appear.

(7.38) a. *Il (*en) est tombé sur la mienne, de voiture.*
  'He fell on mine, (of) car'
  *Marie se (*en) servira du tien alors, de stylo.*
  'Marie will use yours then, (of) pen'
 b. *Ça me (*en) fait penser au mien, de secret.*
  'That makes me think of mine, (of) secret'
  *Je préfère (*en) aller dans celle-là, de boutique.*
  'I prefer to go into that one, (of) shop'

Italian translations follow the same pattern:

(7.39) *(*Ne) è caduto sulla mia, di macchina.*
  *Maria si (*ne) servirá della tua, di penna.*
  *Questo mi (*ne) fa pensare al mio, di segreto.*
  *Io (*ne) preferiso andare in quello, di negozio.*

Kayne claims that right dislocation/detachment violates subjacency in (7.38), since the *de*-phrase has moved out of both a noun phrase and a PP, which he takes (and I concur) as bounds for subjacency. However, he assumes that the landing site for dislocation is outside such a PP rather than within it; crucially, this assumption is unwarranted.

Investigating this question, Milner (1978: 151–156) observes that material which cannot be construed as part of a PP prevents right dislocation from moving a constituent over it. That is, an element right-dislocated from within a PP must remain contiguous to the DP from which it is removed.[18]

(7.40) a. French:
Je me suis intéressé à [$_{DP}$ *la fin* t$_i$]
I got interested in the end
(*pour sa grande valeur), [*de ce livre*]$_i$.
(for its great value) of this book

(7.41) *J'ai vendu beaucoup de livres de* [$_{DP}$ *la mienne* t$_i$]
I've sold lots of books of mine
(*à Paul), [*de collection*]$_i$.
(to Paul) of collection

(7.42) *Je suis venu avec* [$_{DP}$ *la mienne* t$_i$] *(*hier),* [*de voiture*]$_i$.
I came with mine yesterday of car

(7.43) *Je préfère aller dans* [$_{DP}$ *celle-là* t$_i$] *(*avec toi),* [*de boutique*]$_i$.
I prefer to go into that one with you of shop

(7.44) *Ça me fait penser au* [$_{DP}$ *mien* t$_i$] *(*avec anxiété),* [*de secret*]$_i$.
that makes-me think of mine with anxiety of secret

(7.45) Italian:
Io ho venduto molti libri della mia (*a Paolo), di collezione.
Io preferiso andare in quello (*con te), di negozio.
Questo mi fa pensare al mio (*con ansia), di segreto.

Right dislocation indeed occurs in these examples, because the characteristic *de/di* would otherwise be absent. But its landing site must conform to subjacency, and hence, as indicated in Milner's tree (156, note 2), must be within the PP itself. (7.46) reproduces his tree in terms of DPs, with subjacency bounds italicised.

(7.46)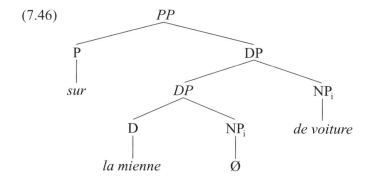

I conclude then that Kayne has correctly identified cases of French right dislocation from within PP, but has wrongly diagnosed the landing site for this dislocation as violating subjacency. Milner's extension of Kayne's paradigm shows that subjacency is observed. Moreover, because the landing site for this dislocation paradigm as (7.46) is not a sister to a V projection, as required by the Genitive Phrase Mate Hypotheses (7.37), the clitic *en* cannot, as Kayne indeed observes, correspond to such dislocated phrases. Thus, the Kayne–Milner paradigm confirms not only subjacency but also the non-trivial restriction in (7.37) that *en* must relate to *sisters of its verbal host*, not to just any sentence-final dislocated *de*-phrase.[19]

The grammatical French and Italian right dislocations out of PPs evidenced in (7.38)–(7.45) are impossible in English, as shown by inspecting the glosses. Such dislocations are also firmly excluded in Spanish:

(7.47) *He vendido muchos libros de la mia (de) colección.*
     'I've sold many books of mine (of) collection'
   Vine en/el mio (de) coche.
     'I came in mine (of) car'
   Prefiero ir a esta (de) tienda.
     'I prefer to go into that one (of) store'
   Esto me hace pensar en el mio (de) secreto.
     'That makes me think about mine (of) secret'

Right dislocation from within PP is thus part and parcel of the freer dislocation that divides Spanish from French and Italian. Since this dislocation has just been shown to be independent of *en*-cliticisation, the latter cannot be the grammatical factor which licenses freer right dislocation. As is implicit in (7.37), the licensing goes in the other direction: provided a right dislocated phrase is adjoined to a V projection rather than some other node, it can give rise to the clitic *en*.

Kayne's and Milner's examples in (7.38) illustrate an additional property of French right dislocation again unrelated to *en* and again impossible in Spanish. French XP can dislocate from within definite as well as indefinite DPs, and in such cases *en* is decisively excluded. Milner (1978: 164) notes: "il y a des cas où *de* existe (explicite en surface ou attesté par la dislocation droite), sans que *en* puisse apparaître". In his examples, the adverbs *hier* 'yesterday' and *pour moi* 'for me' show moreover that the dislocated element is VP-final, and hence a "phrase mate" which might induce *en* by (7.37).

(7.48) *J' (*en) ai pris la tienne hier, de voiture.*
I (thereof) have taken yours yesterday, of car
Je n'(*en) ai pas vu ceului-là hier, de film
I (thereof) have not seen that one yesterday, of film
Je (*en) veux l'autre pour moi, de roman policier.
I (thereof) want the other for me, of detective story

Kayne (1975: 110, note 55) observes the same pattern: "The detached complements of (152) also occur with definites ... But here *en* is impossible."

(7.49) *Passe-moi (*en) le rouge, de crayon.*
pass me (thereof) the red one, of pencil
Tu peux (*en) prendre la mienne, de voiture.
you can (thereof) take mine, of car
Elle a envie d' (*en) acheter celui-là, de bouquin
she wants to (thereof) buy that one, of book

Precisely because of this "definiteness restriction," the Genitive Phrase Mate Hypothesis (7.37) states that a sister to V^k is necessary but not sufficient for the appearance of *en/ne*. The grammar of French and Italian (presumably the full lexical specification of *de/di*) must ultimately characterise all free right dislocation possibilities of both definite and indefinite DPs, both from within object DPs and from within PPs. Once this is provided, precise conditions can be sought for when *en/ne* double dislocated constituents and furthermore license them as null (just as definite clitics double certain argument DPs and also license them as null).

The defense of the Genitive Phrase Mate Hypothesis does not require us to find these fully sufficient conditions for dislocation or the appearance of *en/ne*. Nonetheless, we are close enough to this goal to give a descriptive generalisation (7.50) for the definiteness restriction in (7.48)–(7.49).

(7.50) *En/ne* are well-formed if co-indexed with a dislocated XP_i sister to V^k, if not also co-indexed with a definite DP_i within the clause.

An NP extracted from within a definite object DP as in (7.48)–(7.49) is plausibly co-indexed not only with its empty NP trace but also with the overt DP containing this trace. If *en/ne* also appeared, the dislocated constituent would be co-indexed with two overt elements in the same clause. On the other hand, a dislocated NP from an indefinite object DP has a different index than DP, so that *en/ne* coindexation with a dislocated NP is possible.[20]

In this section, I have argued that there is no basis for relating French and Italian *en/ne*, by movement or any other means, to any constituents other than sisters of some projection of their V host. This has been expressed as follows:

(7.37) *Genitive Phrase Mate Hypothesis. The clitics en/ne on V_i are related only to (possibly dislocated and possibly empty) PP, DP or NP which are sisters to some V_i^k.*

To be complete, this hypothesis must explain why a range of dislocated phrases adjoined to V^k may be empty if a clitic such as *en/ne* appears on V. Such an explanation should follow from a general principle for licensing empty phrasal sisters of V^k in any position, dislocated or not, in the presence of appropriate clitics. As indicated earlier, such a principle, the "Invisible Category Principle", is one focus of the next section (subsection 7.3.3). Section 7.4 then returns to other apparent cases of Romance clitic climbing, with restructuring verbs, auxiliary verbs, causative/ perception verbs, and linking verbs. In all these constructions a generalised Phrase Mate Hypothesis can be profitably brought to bear.

7.3 Alternative realisation: Minimising covert syntax

7.3.1 The host of clitic placement

We can properly formulate a licensing principle relating empty phrases and verbal clitics only if the host category of these clitics is known. A short preliminary thus consists of justifying why this host is V.

Kayne's (1975: Ch. 2) pioneering generative study of French clitics argues that clitic pronouns attach to V. Additionally, generative accounts widely accept the arguments of Emonds (1978) that finite verbs, and hence their clitics, are raised to the category I in French, a sister to VP. This seems to have led some researchers to assume that I rather than V is the basic locus of clitic attachment.

The original arguments for French finite verb raising to I are based on the fact that certain presumably VP-initial adverbs, including negative words, must follow finite verbs (V raised to I), but must precede infinitives (V within VP):

(7.51) *Paul ne donnerait {jamais, point} ces cigares aux enfants.*
Paul not give-would {ever, at all} these cigars to kids
'Paul wouldn't give these cigars to kids { ever, at all }.'

(7.52) *Dis à Paul de ne {jamais, point} donner ces cigares aux enfants.*
'Say to Paul to not {ever, at all} give these cigars to kids.'

In such contrasting patterns of finiteness, with V being in I vs. not being in I, French object and adverbial clitics obligatorily maintain the exact same proclitic positions on the V, as in (7.53)–(7.54):

(7.53) *Paul ne les leur donnerait {jamais, point}.*
Paul not them to-them give-would {ever, at all}
'Paul wouldn't {ever, at all} give them to them.'

(7.54) *Dis à Paul de ne {jamais, point} les leur donner.*
'Say to Paul to not {ever, at all} give them to them.'

In contrast to these clitics which are always with V, the negative clitic *ne* invariably occurs in the I position, to the left of VP-initial negative adverbs, as in (7.54). These clear paradigms lead to the conclusion that French object and adverbial clitics attach to V without exception, and that their presence in I is but an incidental side effect of finite V-raising.[21]

The same conclusion that clitics attach to V rather than to I can be reached via an entirely different route. Emonds (1985: Ch. 2) argues in detail that Spanish gerundives in *-ndo* are not IPs and contain no I. Nonetheless, these verbal forms host clitics exactly as do Spanish infinitives (presumably instances of Vs under IP), so it must be that here again, V and not I is the locus of clitic attachment.

7.3.2 *In situ representations of clitics in trees*

Consider now a tree-like generalisation of the Genitive Phrase Mate Hypothesis; the aim of this study is to extend it to all Romance clitics.

(7.55)

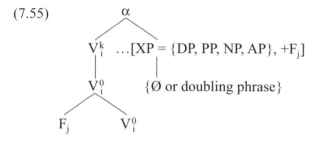

I propose to establish that this sub-tree properly represents a single proclitic characterised by some purely syntactic feature(s) F_j. For definite DPs, the F_j are the "φ-features" of Chomsky (1981); for PP (in French and Italian), F can be [P, ±GOAL]; for the invariant partitive clitic *en/ne*, F can be simply N; the invariant predicate attribute AP clitic can be represented just by A. As remarked in section 7.1.2(a), only the most minimally specified representatives of phrases cliticise, a mysterious property in the movement approach which an in situ framework makes sense of.

Some remarks on how (7.55) can represent dative clitics are in order. Kayne (1975) shows that two kinds of French *à* 'to' introduce DP complements; one heads a typical PP and is cliticised by the PP clitic *y*, while the other introduces phrases thought of as indirect object DPs, represented by dative clitics with φ-features. In Chapter 5 of this volume, I argue that indirect objects are universally represented as PP sisters to V whose head P is *empty in syntax*, prior to being filled in Phonological Form by morphemes such as French *à*.[22] Thus, if (7.55) is to encompass indirect object cliticisation, when PP = [[$_P$ Ø] DP], this DP must count as a sister to V_i^k.

Now, for many reasons having to do with selection mechanisms treated in e.g. Emonds (1991, 1993, 1994), the notion "sister" must be extended. Since precedence and dominance are the primitive relations in trees, we are free to define sisterhood recursively. First, daughters of the same node are sisters. Then:

(7.56) *Extended Sisterhood. If W and Z are sisters, W dominates X, and X dominates the only lexical material under W, then X and Z are "extended" sisters.* (The term "extended" is purely for exposition.)

It now follows that DP objects of Ps empty in the syntax (prior to PF) are sisters in this extended sense to a projection of V; they thus may cliticise onto V under a generalisation of the Genitive Phrase Mate Hypothesis (37):

(7.57) *Phrase Mate Hypothesis. Romance clitics on V_i are related only to XP sisters to some V_i^k, where XP = DP, IP, PP, NP, AP, VP.*[23]

A second kind of dative clitic is generally called an "affected dative". Kayne (1975: section 2.15) shows convincingly that such dative DPs do not originate within other complements, but are simply sisters to V. Authier and Reed (1992) argue further that affected datives are not arguments and thus are sisters rather to V^1.[24] In my view these dative sisters to V^k, like indirect objects, also have the syntactic form PP = [$[_P$ Ø] DP], and are cliticisable by virtue of extended sisterhood (7.56). Alternatively, if no P is involved with one or the other kind of dative, they are a fortiori cliticisable by (7.57).

The sisterhood condition in (7.57) accounts for many paradigms that have been taken for granted ever since Kayne's (1975) pioneering work; for example, that neither objects of lexical P nor complements to object nouns other than those discussed in section 7.2 cliticise. It also accounts for the ill-formedness of clitics as in (7.58); pronominal DPs in coordinate objects or within French *ne...[que – DP]* are not sisters of V.

(7.58) *Jean voit elle et sa soeur.*   vs.   **Jean (la) voit et sa soeur.*
       'Jean sees her and her sister.'   'Jean her-sees and her sister.'
       Marie ne parle que de ça.   vs.   **Marie n'en parle que (de ça).*
       'Marie speaks only of that.'   'Marie thereof-speaks only of that.'

Having seen in section 7.2 that genitive clitics conform to (7.57), it remains to show that paradigms involving restructuring, auxiliary, causative/perception verbs, and complements to adjectives do as well. The argumentation of sections 7.4 and 7.5 will indeed be that *all* Romance clitics obey the Phrase Mate Hypothesis.

7.3.3 Realising syntactic features in different positions

We now turn to mechanisms which allow XP sisters of V^k to be null in (7.55) and (7.57) in the presence of a clitic. In Emonds (1987), I argue that a variety of closed class elements and syntactic features which are realised "close to" but not in their "canonical" syntactic position can be nicely treated by a pair of related principles termed Alternative Realisation ("AR") and the Invisible Category Principle ("ICP"). These principles explain both clitic doubling and clitic licensing of empty phrases. However, their most restrictive formulations require a theory of categories that sharply distinguishes between open and closed classes. Since this theory is also central to explaining restructuring and related phenomena, it is summarised here.

Among its categories, language clearly distinguishes four "open" or "lexical" categories, whose members number in the hundreds or thousands.[25] In contrast, membership in each non-lexical, "closed", or "functional" category is limited to about twenty or so morphemes. Suppose we generalise as follows. Universal Grammar provides a set of bar notation categories {B}: heads, specifiers, and perhaps a few others. UG further matches a small range of cognitive/ syntactic feature complexes F with each category B such that these feature combinations characterise up to a maximum of say twenty or so members of B. Of course, these cognitive/syntactic features F contribute centrally to meaning. But many finer distinctions of meaning in four open lexical classes are made in terms of purely semantic features f which play no role in syntax (Chomsky 1965: Ch. 4). On the other hand, outside the lexical categories N, V, A, and P, syntactic features F (and the small sets of morphemes they generate) are the only ones allowed. Hence all non-lexical categories can be termed "closed" because they crucially lack purely semantic features f (they have few members, disallow coining, etc.).

As examples of how UG matches syntactic features F to categories B, tense and modal features are matched with I, quantifier features appear only in D, space-time coordinates characteristically appear in adpositions P, the features ACTIVITY and PERFECTIVE (aspect) occur just with V, comparisons and expressions of degree are matched with SPEC(A), ANIMATE and COUNT are properties limited to N, etc.

A central tenet in this approach to the lexicon is then (7.59).

(7.59) *Canonical Realisation.* UG canonically matches a few syntactic features F to each syntactic category B. These features F contribute to LF only in these "canonical positions" on B, and appear elsewhere *only via language-particular lexical stipulation.*

Although this property of natural language is implicitly respected in most generative work, the restrictions it can impose on grammatical description have not been formalised or exploited.

Now, there is no reason to specifically exclude the four lexical categories from this scheme. If these categories are like the others, each has a subset of say up to twenty or so elements, which spell out and are fully characterised by syntactic features F. In fact, certain subclasses of N, V, A, and P have properties characteristic of the non-lexical classes, such as post s-structure insertion and unique syntactic behaviour (cf. Emonds 1985: Ch. 4). These closed subsets of open categories can be appropriately called "grammatical" N, V, A, or P. For example, English grammatical verbs include *be, have, do, get, go, come, let, make*, etc. English grammatical nouns include *one, self, thing, stuff, other(s), place, time, way, reason* (Emonds 1987). The distinction between grammatical and lexical P is well-known, and this scheme naturally integrates it into a theory of categories. A closed grammatical class is then one whose members have no purely semantic features.[26]

Returning now to Romance clitics, their features of person, number, gender, case and ±GOAL match not with V but rather D, N and P. The features of Romance verbal clitics are thus not canonically positioned and by (7.59) must result from stipulated alternative positionings in the lexical entries for clitics (e.g., as in (7.13)–(7.15) of section 7.1.2); corresponding statements are entirely absent in say the English lexicon. Such syntactic features which appear elsewhere than on their UG-matched host category can be termed "alternatively realised". The following principle sets limits on stipulated deviations from the UG norm.

(7.60) *Alternative Realisation ("AR").* A syntactic feature F matched in UG with category B can be realised *in a grammatical morpheme under X^0*, provided X^k is a sister of [B, F].

It can be observed that all Romance clitics are grammatical morphemes (expressing only syntactic features F), and are under V^0, where V^k is a sister of an XP with the UG-matched features F. That is, even though Alternative Realisation has been developed without reference to clitics, it perfectly describes the Phrase Mate Hypothesis depicted in (7.55) and stated in (7.57).[27]

Among other syntactic features which are alternatively realised are (i) those involved in most inflectional morphology (verbal inflections spell out I features and nominal inflections spell out D features), (ii) grammatical features of an argument DP realised on I or V as agreement, (iii) features of adjunct P realised on certain N objects (so-called "bare NP adverbials") and (iv) features of complement P realised on governing V (in "applicative constructions").[28] Many extremely diverse, language-particular constructions thus fall under a single restrictive principle of AR, which permits much syntax to be expressed by lexical entries of simple and uniform format. It is striking that this same principle fully and easily subsumes Romance clitic distribution as well. If a principle of wide applicability successfully describes the complex patterns of Romance cliticisation, this nullifies any claim that a movement approach to clitics is more general (section 7.1.1).

AR (7.60) does not itself predict the circumstances under which verbal clitics will double or replace phrases inside the VP; it rather sets limits on what a language's closed class verbal affixes may correspond to. The lexical entries themselves determine which XPs can be cliticised, whether a verbal affix or clitic will double (= agree with) overt XPs, whether a doubled phrase must be specific or discourse-linked (as in Modern Greek; cf. Anagnostopoulou 1993), or whether a clitic can correspond only to empty XP, as do Romance accusative clitics.

Nonetheless, a further generalisation is possible. Previous study has indicated that when AR of the features F of some category B is "complete," then B can in fact be licensed as empty. This principle combined with AR constitutes the mechanism by which Romance clitics license empty complements, adjuncts and dislocated phrases, in accord with (7.57).

(7.61) *Invisible Category Principle. If all marked canonical features F on B are alternatively realised by (7.60), except perhaps B itself, then B may be empty.*

Again, the ICP does not require that a category B that may be empty must be. In my studies on these topics (see note 28 and section 7.6.6), the final step of obligatory zeroing is typically attributed to a version of Economy of Derivation (viz., "insert as few free morphemes in a derivation as possible"). In any case, the issue of when a potentially empty category must be empty is complex and is not the focus of this study.

A little reflection on how this AR or "in situ" framework treats almost all of what might be called traditional grammar (i.e., syntax with a morphological dimension) reveals an impulse different from much practice under the name of the minimalist program. The two approaches agree on much,[29] but differ on how they motivate morphologically-based syntactic processes. Both must describe (sometimes long-distance) phrasal movements subject to something like subjacency that are relatively free of morphology: topicalisations, extrapositions, and free word order. Moreover, both approaches must conform to empirical reality by postulating roughly equivalent lexical stipulations so as to describe the morphologically-related overt syntax of diverse languages.

The in situ framework here developed claims that language-particular morphology is a marked variation on UG structures driven by Economy of Derivation ("use as few free morphemes as possible") and of Representation ("use as little phrasal embedding as possible"); cf. section 7.4.3 and Emonds (2000a, Ch. 7). When closed class lexical entries fail to specify alternative realisations or mechanisms which avoid embedding, the assumption is that nothing happens; *there is no further covert syntax*. This study as well as my other works cited attempt to demonstrate how Alternative Realisation thus lays the basis for both a parsimonious UG and a theory of particular lexicons whose entries are formalised, simple, and learnable in terms of positive evidence (= deviation from canonically realised structures of UG; cf. 7.59).

7.4 The "absolute transparency" of phrases allowing clitic climbing

In this section, we return to the patterns of clitic climbing (i)–(iii) introduced in section 7.1.1, and show how a proper theory of lexical representation and the Phrase Mate Hypothesis (7.57) explain all these phenomena.

7.4.1 Rizzi's paradigms for restructuring verbs

Early generative treatments of the restructuring verbs of section 7.1.1, Aissen (1974) and Aissen and Perlmutter (1976), argue that Spanish clitics are paired with empty (or doubled) phrasal categories in the same surface structure clause. That is, in restructuring contexts, they claim that the Phrase

Mate Hypothesis holds in surface structure for all clitics. Monachesi (1993) proposes a similar analysis for Italian.

Extensive argumentation for this point of view is presented in Rizzi's (1978) classic treatise on Italian, although he hesitates about the exact position of the lower complement verb V_c in structures like (7.2a–b). But he demonstrates beyond doubt that phrases YP which are co-indexed with a "raised" clitic are themselves surface *daugthers* of some projection of the higher verb V_x. In other words, no projection of the complement V_c in surface structure contains YP but not V_x. Thus, while the non-restructured (7.62) contains a VP as indicated, there is no corresponding *VP in the restructured (7.63 = 7.2b). (e_i = empty YP).

(7.62) *Ho cominciato a [$_{VP}$ discuterene$_i$ con Mario e_i] da Gianni.*

(7.63) *Ne$_i$ ho cominciato a [$_{*VP}$ discutere con Mario e_i] da Gianni.*

A movement advocate might suggest that a "transparent" embedded *VP in a structural source for clitic raising would still allow adequate descriptions of Italian and Spanish (Strozer 1981). But such a hpyothesis fails to fully explain the clearly distinct behaviours enumerated by Rizzi. His tests distinguishing usual clausal complementation like (7.62) from restructured sentences like (7.63) are listed in (7.64)–(7.66); Strozer's hypothesis has difficulties especially with (7.65)–(7.66). In the face of these contrasts, the notion that a *VP might be present but transparent for clitic raising collapses.[30]

(7.64) a. Non-finite VP but not *VP may prepose in non-restrictive relatives.
b. Non-finite VP but not *VP can be the focus of a cleft sentence.
c. Heavy non-finite VP but not *VP can postpose over adjuncts linked to V_x.
d. Non-finite VP but not *VP may undergo "Right-Node Raising" in conjoined sentences.
e. Non-finite VP but not *VP blocks attachment of the Italian enclitic *loro* 'to them' to V_x. Consequently, both auxiliaries and main verbs can host *loro* in the structure (7.63).

Rizzi also shows cases where VP, but not VP*, can block movement:

(7.65) Italian NP-preposing of an object into an empty subject position over si + V is subject to a clause mate constraint. VP blocks this movement, but *VP does not; this process and clitic raising are compatible.[31]

(7.66) VP plays a role in blocking null operator constructions in Italian, but *VP has no such effect.

If one claimed that *VP is maintained in a derivation but is transparent, then optional lower positioning of clitics shouldn't interfere with that same transparency which permits the movements in (7.65)–(7.66). But the lower positioning of clitics indeed does block these movements. Similarly, one should expect that transparent *VPs in (7.64a–e) could move, but they do not.

In place of a "transparent" *VP, descriptive and explanatory adequacy require two alternative underlying structures for V_x–V_c sequences involving restructuring verbs. An unrestructured derivation should contain two clauses (i.e., at least one VP embedded in another) with the attendant effects in (7.64)–(7.66). As proposed in Monachesi (1993), a second "flat" structure should contain only one VP, since restructured derivations reveal no structural hint whatever of any VP embedding. For this reason Aissen's (1974) analysis of Spanish proposes a "pre-cyclic" rule and Aissen and Perlmutter (1976) advocate "clause union."

In both structures, clitics attach obligatorily to the left-hand head V of the lowest VP dominating the phrases they correspond to. Such an analysis with dual derivations immediately explains why, as often noted (Contreras 1979, Bok-Bennema 1981), all clitics corresponding to complements and adjuncts of one verb must surface on a single verbal host, though that host is not always the selecting verb. This "saturation" property is explained if a clitic's verbal host is uniquely determined by the structure the clitic appears in (Rizzi 1978: note 26).[32] That is, if the Phrase Mate Hypothesis is extended to restructuring verbs and auxiliary verbs, all of Rizzi's classic tests and also saturation fall out naturally.

We thus need an explanation for why (only) a certain closed class of restructuring verbs V_x, whose non-finite complement verbs V_c in turn select complements WP and permit adjuncts WP′, can be directly inserted either into structures like (7.67a) – Rizzi's (138) – or alternatively into structures properly containing a VP projection of V_c (7.67b).[33]

(7.67)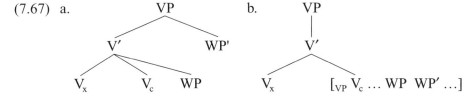

As argued by Rizzi (1978: 148–150), dual subcategorisation of V_x fails to adequately express the thoroughly optional restructuring alternation in (7.67). Rather, a single lexical specification of V_x must yield two distinct but synonymous structural configurations. Yet this is not possible in either (i) the unrevised subcategorisation framework of Chomsky (1965), or (ii) any existing or plausible semantic-based system of selection ("s-selection").

In contrast to these unpromising approaches, dual structures and derivations for certain closed class heads are characteristic and unstipulated consequences of revised principles of lexical insertion and subcategorisation justified in a series of studies (cf. Emonds 2000a: Ch. 2 and 4). With little modification, these principles explain all the subcas(es) of restructuring. Such relatively straightforward results indicate how recalcitrant syntactic problems can be solved by developing lexical insertion theory.

7.4.2 Lexical theory: Late insertion

Throughout the history of generative grammar, careful attention to the syntax of a given grammatical formative α has typically led to formulating a "late transformation" which centrally affects α. Such a transformation often specifies a unique insertion context for the formative in terms of outputs of Move α, i.e., in terms of s-structure. For example, Borer (1984: Ch. 4) focuses on nominal constructions containing Hebrew *šel* 'of', and her *šel*-insertion rule is specified as operating in the phonological component. English *of*-insertion, *do*-insertion, *for*-insertion, and *there*-insertion exemplify this same practice. The "doubly-filled COMP filter" and many conditions on specific morphemes ascribed to filters in earlier work are more late transformations of this sort.

These analyses taken together justify a hypothesis that the lexical entries of a wide range of closed class items, and in fact their entire contribution to grammar, are nothing other than these late or PF transformations reformulated as post s-structure (= PF) insertion contexts in a lexicon of closed class elements. Typical entries in the English Closed Class Lexicon inserted in PF have something like the following form:

(7.70) ed, PAST, -MODAL, +V ___
        do, V, +___ [I, -MODAL]
        of, P, -LOCATION, +[+N] ___ DP
        there, D, -REFERENCE, -DEFINITE, -___ NP[34]
        ing, [+N], +V ___ [35]
        that, P, -WH, + ___ [IP, FINITE]

It can be observed that the entries in (7.70) contain only syntactic features F (section 7.3.3). These features are moreover limited to the morpheme's bar notation category plus three sub-classes of features whose common property is that of playing no direct role in LF interpretation: (i) contextual features, (ii) feature values indicating a marked absence of semantic content (-LOCATION, -REFERENCE, -DEFINITE), and (iii) alternatively realised features not in their canonical UG positions and hence uninterpretable (cf. 7.59). Thus, late-inserted items are in some sense simply "place-holders" – they fill bar notation positions which may not be zero, but which have no features that are utilised in determining LF meaning.

In order to characterise this place-holding property of late-inserted items, recall the distinction drawn between closed and open classes in the lexicon in section 7.3.3. As indicated there, membership in non-lexical or closed categories is limited to about twenty or so. Moreover, we saw that closed subsets of open categories which lack semantic features can be appropriately called "grammatical" N, V, A, or P; e.g., English grammatical verbs include *be, have, do, get, go, come, let, make*, etc. As indicated in note 26, all and only closed class items lack purely semantic features f.

Let us now formalise two different modes of lexical insertion appropriate for the closed class lexicon (including the place-holding entries) and the open class lexicon respectively.

(7.71) *Phonological Lexicalisation (PL). Items specified solely in terms of contextual and other non-interpretable features are inserted subsequent to any operation contributing to Logical Form.*

The place-holding entries in (7.70) are tentative entries for typical closed class items subject to (7.71).[36]

(7.72) *Deep Lexicalisation (DL). Items associated with non-syntactic, purely semantic features f satisfy lexical insertion conditions (just) before transformations apply to domains containing them. Such f occur only on N, V, A, and P.*

As discussed in section 7.3.3, alternatively realised features F (7.60) do not, by (7.59), contribute to Logical Form. Rather, such F license phonetically null and/or doubled phrases with canonical features [XP, F], and these latter are interpreted. In particular, the D, N and P features F of verbal clitics are not interpretable. Consequently, Romance clitics fall under PL (7.71). AR and PL together thus predict that clitics are subject to syntactic and morphological distribution restrictions of a surface nature (cf. those of French clitics in section 7.1.2).

Moreover, clitics and inflections are the kind of elements for which phonologists such as Hayes (1990) and Nespor (1990, 1993) have found it necessary to postulate lexically "pre-compiled rules" in models where lexical insertion precedes syntax. When insertion of such elements is rather into contexts defined in PF under PL (7.71), these pre-compiled contexts lose their special status and simply revert back to contexts specified in terms of elements present at the level of insertion. Pre-compiled phonological rules are an artefact of an inadequate theory of lexical insertion.

In this perspective, the auxiliary verbs *avoir/être* (French), *avere/essere* (Italian), and *haber/ser* (Spanish) are also expected to be subject to Phonological Lexicalisation, as traditional and generative grammarians alike have recognised that they have no inherent content (idioms aside) and apparently differ only by contextual features. The 'have' verb lacks specific meaning beyond its ability to assign accusative case to a (DP) complement, and (perhaps thereby or perhaps through a stipulation) to appear in the composed past, while the copula is the elsewhere empty verb in the context +___XP. Both verbs are –ACTIVITY, in the marked class of stative verbs. The following simplified lexical entries for the French pair are then subject to Pl (7.71):

(7.73) a. avoir, V, - ACTIVITY, -INCHOATIVE, +___$XP_{[CASE]}$
   b. être, V, -ACTIVITY, -INCHOATIVE, +___$XP_{[-CASE]}$

Before demonstrating how PL (7.71) explains the "obligatory restructuring" with *have* and *be* auxiliaries, we must investigate further the nature of subcategorisation features themselves.[37]

7.4.3 Lexical theory: Satisfying subcategorisation

A classical subcategorisation frame of a lexical item, α, X, +___YP, means that YP is a sister of [$_x$ α] after lexical insertion occurs. Baltin (1987), Emonds (1991a, 1993), and Kubo (1992) provide arguments that such subcategorisation frames should be written not to select phrases but to select a category Y^0 which is *the head* of a maximal projection sister to X^0.

(7.74) *Extended Classical Subcategorisation (tentative).* α, X, +___Y *is satisfied if and only if Y^0 is the lexical head of a (maximal projection) sister to X^0.*[38]

Some reasons for this are the following:

(a) This notation eliminates all mention of phrases in the lexicon. Since lexical items are possibly the only learned aspect of natural language, to thus simplify the inventory of categories necessary for acquiring the lexicon is highly desirable.

(b) According to Kubo (1992), Japanese passives consist of two different constructions, a "gapped passive" involving a verbal suffix *(r)are* which induces DP movement from any base position and a "gapless passive" involving a main verb *(r)are* with both a subject and a VP complement. She argues that all properties of both passives follow from an entry which (i) contains a single subcategorisation frame, and (ii) optionally assigns a theta-role: *(r)are*, V, +V___, (+malefactive). The fact that, with no mention of different frames, a single entry accounts not only for similiarities but also for differences between two passives justifies interpreting +V___ as simultaneously permitting both VP and V sisters of *(r)are*.

(c) Chapter 3 of this volume (i.e. Emonds, 1991a) argues that English present participles and gerunds have respectively the forms [$_A$ V — [$_A$ Ø]] and [$_N$ V — [$_N$ Ø]] in the syntactic component; the *ing* suffix is inserted as head of the word only in Phonological Form. Through a syntactic derivation, the Vs act as heads of participles (APs) and gerunds (DPs); moreover, these non-finite clausal structures (AP and DP) are selected by governing predicates via the feature +___V.

This analysis of *ing* as a category-changing inflection in PF dissociates the category correspondence between head and maximal projection. Thus, the definition of lexical head and lexical projection should be generalised further; this last extension will play an important role in the treatment APs in section 7.5.

(7.75) *Lexical Head/Projection. Let Y^0 be the highest lexically filled head in Z^j, where $Y^0 = N, V, A, P$. Then Y^0 is the lexical head of Z^j, and Z^j is a lexical projection of Y^0.*

Let us return to Extended Classical Subcategorisation. Because of considerations involving (a)–(c) above, phrasal categories no longer figure in the selection formalism (7.74). Ordinarily, it is a bar notation requirement that any non-maximal Z^k not properly contained in a X^0 is immediately dominated by a Z^j ($j \geq k$). But now I drop any stipulation that such a Z^k must be unique, in favour of letting (7.75) serve as a uniqueness requirement on heads. Thus, I permit "flat structures" as in (7.77).

(7.77)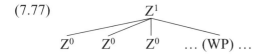

When a head is not contained in a larger word, then in head-initial languages such as those under discussion, the head is the leftmost of all filled nodes and to the left of any (possibly empty) phrases. Thus, when lexical insertion occurs under a given Z^0, any other Z^0 to its left must still be null at that point in the derivation.

Although the lexical head of a lexical projection is unique at a level, it may change after Spell Out if empty syntactic Z^0 are filled by late Phonological Lexicalisation (7.71).[39]

The strucure (7.77) now at our disposal is exactly the restructured (7.67a) deemed necessary by the examination of Rizzi's arguments in section 7.4.1. Using the extended subcategorisation notation of (7.74), (7.67a) can be generated by a V_c specified as +___W and a V_x which is specified as +___V and inserted by PL (7.71). When V_x is inserted by DL (7.72), the very same pair of lexical entries generate instead (7.67b).

(7.67)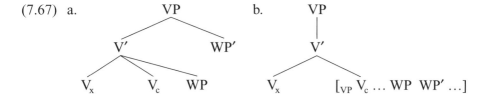

234 *Minimal structures for functional categories*

Moreover, as reflected in (7.77), the system developed here correctly permits "a priori unlimited sequences of Restructuring verbs" V_x (Rizzi 1978: 155).

The reader may have noticed parentheses inside (7.74). They guarantee that Y will have its own subcategorisation frames satisfied under a YP, which Deep Lexicalisation (7.72) seems to require. Yet inspecting the dual complement structures (7.67) needed for restructuring verbs, we see that the parenthesised condition would wrongly exclude (7.67a) as a realisation of V_x, +___V.

We can allow both trees in (7.67) by dropping the parenthesised material in (7.74) and simply using Deep Lexicalisation as already formulated.

(7.78) *Extended Classical Subcategorisation.* α, X, +___Y *is satisfied if and only if* Y^0 *is the lexical head of a sister to* X^0.

(7.72) *Deep Lexicalisation (DL). Items associated with non-syntactic, purely semantic features f satisfy lexical insertion conditions (just) before transformations apply to domains containing them. Such f occur only on N, V, A, and P.*

Immediately after a deep lexicalisation, the syntactic derivation of the inserted item's lexical projection begins. Thus, deep lexicalisation of V_c may occur in either (7.67a–b), but in (7.67a) V_x is unavailable for additional DL and must remain empty during the syntactic derivation. Therefore, from what has been said so far, α, V_x, +___V yields either (7.67a) or (7.67b) if V_x is inserted late, but only (7.67b) if V_x is inserted at deep structure.

A final device bearing on subcategorisation concerns choosing among such alternatives. Emonds (1991a) shows, on grounds quite different from those investigated here, that allowing subcategorisation frames to be satisfied in different ways requires a principle of "minimal structure" to guarantee, among other things, the same results as traditional subcategorisation where the latter is adequate. Chomsky (1991) also briefly refers to a principle of Economy of Representation, which I formulate as follows:

(7.79) *Economy of Representation. At a given level of lexical insertion, satisfy subcategorisation with as little phrasal embedding as possible.*

Clearly (7.67a) realises α, V_x, +___V more economically than (7.67b), if the frames of V_c are satisfied in both cases. Thus, revising what was just said, while Deep Lexicalisation of V_x, +___V yields only (7.67b), Phonological Lexicalisation yields only (7.67a).

Everything is finally in place for solving the restructuring problem, and for extending the Phrase Mate Hypothesis to Romance auxiliary, restructuring, causative and perception verbs.

7.4.4 Clitic climbing, dual insertion levels, and the Phrase Mate Hypothesis

As seen in section 7.4.1, restructured Romance clitics as in (7.80) are found with the distribution (7.81)–(7.83). (The proclisis in (7.80) requires V_x to be finite.)

(7.80) "restructured clitics" + V_x host - V_c ... WP ... WP' ...

(7.81) No restructuring: the vast majority of verbs in all three languages, and French counterparts to Italian and Spanish restructuring verbs.

(7.82) Obligatory restructuring: the auxiliaries *avoir/être* (French), *avere/essere* (Italian), and *haber/ser* (Spanish) with past/passive participles.

(7.83) Optional restructuring: a closed class of verbs with infinitival and gerundive complements in both Italian and Spanish.

I am proposing that the configuration of paradigms in (7.81)–(7.83) follows from the dual levels of lexical insertion (7.71) and (7.72), Extended Classical Subcategorisation (7.78), and the Generalised Phrase Mate Hypothesis (7.57).

(7.57) *Phrase Mate Hypothesis. Romance clitics on V_i are related only to XP sisters to some V_i^k, where XP = DP, IP, PP, NP, AP, VP.*

All restructuring paradigms concern verbs V_x which govern non-finite verbal complements termed V_c in (7.80). By the modified lexicalisation/subcategorisation theory summarised in section 7.4.3, the single lexical specification α, V_x, +___V can generate two different trees: (7.67a) if V_x is inserted at PF and (7.67b) if V_x is inserted pre-transformationally. I now use this frame and these trees to show how the restructuring paradigms (7.81)–(7.83) follow from inserting V_x at different levels.

(7.67) a.

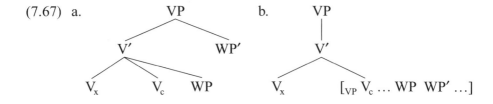

b.

a. The vast majority of verbs in all three languages (among those taking non-finite complements) have purely semantic features f in their lexical entries: counterparts of *decide, fear, force, hesitate, intend, persuade, plan, refuse, remember*, etc. Consequently, by DL (7.72), these V_x are inserted prior to a transformational derivation. This is incompatible with (7.67a). For of course, V_x selects V_c, so V_c must also be filled by DL. But then the syntactic derivation on V_c's lexical projection VP must be the next operation, so V_x in (7.67a) is thus unavailable for deep insertion. This problem doesn't arise with (7.67b), which is thus the only structure generable by α, V_x, +___V whenever V_x has purely semantic (open class) features.[40] Then, by the Generalised Phrase Mate Hypothesis (7.57), all clitics corresponding to WP and/or WP' in the non-finite complement to these verbs attach to V_c in (7.67b), as required in (7.81). No restructuring occurs for open class V_x.

b. The auxiliaries *avoir/être* (French), *avere/essere* (Italian), and *haber/ser* (Spanish) require restructuring. That is, the following participle and its complements don't act like a constituent, and clitics must occur on the auxiliaries. Since the lexical entries for these verbs (7.73) contain no contextual or otherwise interpretable features, these verbs are "place-holders," and so must be *inserted at PF*, by (7.71). Hence their subcategorisations, which include +___V as a special case, allow them to appear as V_x in (7.67a). As mentioned earlier, their appearance as V_x in (7.67b) is ruled out by Economy of Representation (7.79). The Phrase Mate Hypothesis (7.57) permits all clitics corresponding to WP and/or WP' in (7.67a) to appear on V_x, as required in (7.82). Restructuring is thus obligatory in both passive and "composed past" constuctions.

c. The verbs that allow restructuring are among those that tend to have unique syntactic behaviour; Burzio (1986: 324) lists Italian *andare* 'go', *venire* 'come', *sembrare* 'seem', *stare* 'stay', *continuare* 'go on', *cominciare* 'begin', *sapere* 'know', *volere* 'want', *dovere* 'should', *potere* 'can'. Aissen and Perlmutter (1976: 5) provide a similar, slightly larger list for Spanish. These verbs in (7.83) are among those with the most basic meanings and whose translations tend to serve as auxiliaries or "quasi-auxiliaries" in various languages. I propose that they are fully characterised in the lexicon by basic cognitive/syntactic features F that place them among the grammatical verbs defined in section 7.3.3.[41]

How are these grammatical verbs, specified for interpretable syntactic features F but for no purely semantic features f, lexically inserted? By inspecting DL (7.72) and PL (7.71), we see that they fall under neither principle. It can therefore follow without stipulation that grammatical verbs, whose features are interpretable at LF (unlike those of auxiliaries) may be inserted whereever lexical insertion is permitted, either at deep structure or in PF. Consequently, restructuring verbs, that is, grammatical verbs whose syntactic features are used at LF, may appear as V_x in both (7.67a) (via PF Lexicalisation) and (7.67b) (via Deep Lexicalisation). As is by now familiar, the Phrase Mate Hypothesis (7.57) determines that in (7.67a) clitics appear on V_x and in 7.(67b) on V_c, as required. Restructuring is thus optional for grammatical verbs with interpretable syntactic features, and results from exactly the same insertion frame +___V which generates the unrestructured (7.67b).[42]

In section 7.4.1, one restructuring paradigm of Rizzi (1978) was left aside, that of auxiliary choice in composed pasts. The above three way division now solves this problem. According to Burzio (1986: 55–56), the conditioning factor which leads to chossing the Italian auxiliary *essere* 'be' over *avere* 'have' is co-indexing between the subject DP and a post-verbal DP' in a sequence $DP_i...AUX...V...DP_i$'; the co-indexing can be due to passivisation, reflexives, or object to subject movement. Needless to say, outside restructured sentences, such co-indexing and attendant auxiliary choice are a clause bound phenomenon.

Thus, any verbs which superficially "lexically select" *essere* are those whose deep objects move to subject position; hence they immediately precede an object trace of the surface subject. From this perspective, lexical auxiliary choice is determined by that verb in a VP (not in any lower VP) which immediately precedes an empty DP direct object. Now, in the flat structures (7.77) which our analysis provides for restructuring verb sequences, only the last verb immediately precedes the object DP_i whose indexing determines auxiliary choice, and hence appears to itself "select *essere*". And indeed, "only the last verb of the verbal complex created by Restructuring can trigger *avere* → *essere* of the first Restructuring verb, no matter which other Restructuring verbs are in the middle. This point becomes more obvious with longer sequences of Restructuring verbs." (Rizzi 1978: 137). Thus, the last and most puzzling of Rizzi's paradigms is fully explained.[43]

7.4.5 Causative and perception verbs

As summarised in section 7.1.1, in the three Romance languages under discussion, non-finite complements of a small number of causative and perception verbs occur in two distinct patterns, each giving rise to different clitic configurations. Again, V_x is the triggering verb, V_c the non-finite complement, and WP and WP′ the complement and adjunct positions respectively of V_c. (7.84) shows the uniformly proclitic French patterns; when an Italian or Spanish host verb is non-finite, the pattern is always enclitic.

(7.84) a. Climbing: clitics + V_x - V_c ... WP ... WP′ ...
       b. Separate VPs: V_x -DP subject of V_c -clitics + V_c ... WP ... WP′ ...

In the clitic climbing pattern (7.84a), the DP interpreted as the subject of V_c follows V_c and is interspersed among its complements and adjuncts. The climbing pattern (7.84a) is exemplified in (7.6)–(7.7), repeated as (7.85)–(7.86).

(7.85) Spanish: *Los hermanos (*se)   la han dejado preparar a Ana.*
                The brothers (selves) it have let   prepare to Ana
                'The brothers have let Ana prepare it (for themselves).'
                *Los hermanos han dejado prepararsela a Ana.

(7.86) French: *Marie les (*leur) a   laissés distribuer à Anne.*
              Marie them to-them has let   distirbute to Anne
              'Marie has let Anne distribute them (to them).'
              *Marie a laissé les (leur) distribuer à Anne.

The lower clitic pattern (7.84b) is shown in (7.4)–(7.5), repeated as (7.87)–(7.88).

(7.87) Spanish: *Los hermanos dejan a Ana prepararsela   algunas veces.*
               the brothers   let   to Ana prepare-them-it sometimes
              'The brothers let Ana prepare it for them sometimes.'
              *Los hermanos se la dejan a Ana preparar algunas veces.

(7.88) French: *Marie laisse Anne les   leur   distribuer.*
              Marie   lets Anne them to-them distribute
              'Marie lets Anne distribute them to them.'
              *Marie les leur laisse Anne distribuer.

The dual pattern of causative cliticisation in (7.84) recalls that of restructuring and suggests a similar treatment. In this sense I follow Herschensohn (1981: esp. 221 and section 4.2), Zagona (1982: Chs. 1 and 2), and Burzio (1986: section 5.4), who demonstrate that those complements to causative/perception verbs (hereafter "c/p" verbs) and restructuring verbs which share clitic climbing share other properties as well. Burzio points out many similarities between causative and restructuring in Italian. For example, the "past participle agrees with the antecedent to the direct object of the embedded verb, from which we conclude that in both these constructions the dependents of the embedded verb are reanalyzed as dependents of the matrix verb as well, ..." (344). In another passage, his (68a–b) confirm that Rizzi's restructuring tests carry over to clitic climbing causatives, e.g. clefting is excluded.

(B68) a. *E proprio [andare a casa] che sarei voluto. (auxiliary change)
  'It is exactly to go home that I would have wanted.'
 b. *E proprio [leggere il libro] che gli faccio. (clitic climbing)
  'It is exactly read the book that I will make him.'

In a similar vein, Zagona (1982) observes that both types of "clitic climbing" constructions in Spanish lack independent negation and aspect on the complement verb V_c, and both exhibit a certain restriction on adverb placement. She analyses both restructuring and causative complements in which clitics climb as non-maximal verbal projections V′, a perspective which I adopt and take one step further – I analyse these non-finite complements as V^0 sisters to V_x, as already seen in the restructuring case.

In the present framework, treating c/p clitic-climbing verbs like restructuring verbs means that these c/p verbs are also lexically fully characterised by basic cognitive syntactic features F. Hence they are numbered among the grammatical verbs defined in section 7.3.3 and lack purely semantic features f. Therefore, like restructuring verbs, they may be inserted prior to Move α or in PF, where PF insertion gives rise to "flat" structures.

One irreducible lexical difference between restructuring and c/p verbs is that restructuring verbs take no overt DP object, while c/p verbs are at least optionally transitive.[44] Ignoring for exposition differences among c/p verbs and across Romance languages, let us examine a typical causative verb *laisser* (French), *lasciare* (Italian), *dejar* (Spanish) 'let'. Using Extended Classical Subcategorisation (7.78), the DP hypothesis, and the fact that it permits direct and/or indirect objects, the French verb's lexical frame is (7.89):

240 *Minimal structures for functional categories*

(7.89) laisser, V, +F, +___{ D, V } (D)

The subcases of (7.89) of interest here are +___V (D). As syntax rather than subcategorisation determines order among complements, this frame covers three cases: V_x — DP — V_c ..., V_x — V_c ... DP ..., and V_x — V_c ... Moreover, since by (7.78) either a bare V or a VP can satisfy +___V (D) for a grammatical verb like *laisser*, the single frame +___V (D) yields six structures. Adapting the dual structures of (7.67) to the transitivity expressed in (7.89), we obtain six trees for c/p verbs as in (7.90)–(7.92).[45] DP, WP and WP′ are respectively the interpreted subject, complements and adjuncts of V_c.

(7.90) V_x – DP – V_c ...

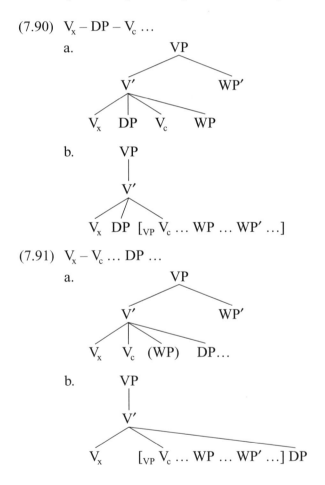

(7.91) V_x – V_c ... DP ...

(7.92) $V_x - V_c \ldots$

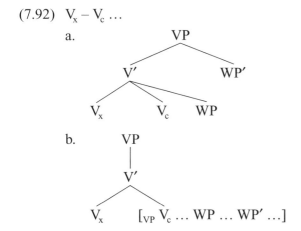

In turn, we examine (7.90)–(7.92).

In (7.90), (7.90a) is excluded, because a DP prevents V_c from being head-initial; V_c is hence unavailable for lexical insertion at any stage of a derivation. This leaves (7.90b). The Phrase Mate Hypothesis determines that in (7.90b) clitics for complements and adjuncts of V_c occur on V_c, while the clitics for the lower subject DP appear on V_x, independently of whether either verb is inserted at deep structure or in PF. (7.90b) is thus the well-known causative pattern without climbing (7.84b); that is, if the DP subject of an embedded infinitive precedes it, clitics corresponding to phrases in the lower VP may not climb (Kayne 1975: section 4.1).[46]

In (7.91), the lack of a case-assigner for DP excludes (7.91b). If a dummy PP were to provide case, (7.91b) would still be a less economical structure than (7.90b), so the structure cannot be salvaged.[47] The complex clitic climbing pattern with c/p verbs (7.84a), generated by the subcategorisation frame +___D^V, *must thus be realised as (7.91a)*, in which the DP subject of the causative is located among the internal arguments of V_c. This flat structure is then Kayne's (1975) *faire ... à* construction. Via a different route, we arrive at structures like those of Aissen (1974) and Miller (1992) and somewhat similar to those proposed in Zubizarreta (1987: section 3.2.2). For a full account of the exact role of the "internal argument subject" in blocking extraction, see Emonds (2000a, Appendix to Chapter 6).

As established in section 7.4.4 on restructuring, this flat structure (7.91a) arises only because V_x may be empty in the syntax and inserted in PF. The present framework thus explains why clitic climbing is invariably restricted to a small number of grammatical verbs V_x, and never genera-

242 *Minimal structures for functional categories*

lises to all non-finite complements. This cross-linguistic pattern, an apparent universal failure of speakers to generalise, is entirely mysterious in accounts which fail to crucially distinguish grammatical from lexical verbs.

Turning now to (7.92), either version can be well-formed if and only if V_c, like verbs in general, has a subject DP.[48] However, under certain circumstances, subjects of sentences (IPs) can be expressed in adjunct phrases, e.g., as PPs headed by (phonologically inserted) grammatical P such as French *par, de*, Italian *da*, and Spanish *por* or even as "arbitrary PRO".

In either version of (7.92), if V_x is filled by Deep Lexicalisation, V′ is not a lexical projection of V_c, so V_c lacks its required subject DP. On the other hand, if V_x is inserted rather in PF, V_c is the lexical head of V′ in syntax. A DP sister of V′ is then in principle available to serve as subject of V_c.

Crucially, in such cases (7.92a) will be preferred to (7.92b) by Economy of Representation (7.79). That is, provided a language's closed class lexicon contains appropriate grammatical P to case-mark a postposed subject DP, and provided that V_x is inserted in PF, the frame +___V gives rise to the tree (7.94), i.e., (7.92a) plus an optional adjunct phrase interpreted as subject of the second verb.

(7.94)

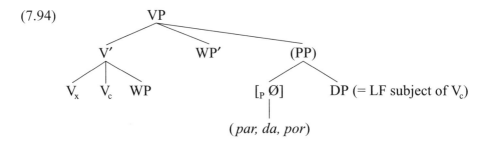

This structure corresponds to the French *faire...par* construction carefully investigated in Kayne (1975: sections 3.5 and 3.6). He establishes among other things that the construction is closely related to the passive construction. The relation couldn't be more transparent than in the present analysis, since (7.94) with the explicitly represented agent phrase replicates the structure (7.67a) attributed in section 7.4.4 to passive verb phrases with *être* 'be'. The only difference is that the grammatical verb V_x in the passive is marked as permitting an empty DP subject in SPEC(IP), while the c/p grammatical verbs V_x assigns an agent interpretation to their DP subject in SPEC(IP).

Kayne demonstrates the lack of structural or grammatical relation between the c/p verb V_x and the postposed subject DP of V in the *faire...par* construction; this non-relation is reflected in DP's adjunct status, which satisfies Full Interpretation only by virtue of its relation to V_c established by LF subjecthood.

Kayne (1975: 327–329) and Herschensohn (1981: 238–240) both observe that, except for reflexives,[49] the verbal host for clitics corresponding to complements WP or adjuncts WP′ in the *faire...par* construction is always V_x, as the Phrase Mate Hypothesis (7.57) applied to (7.94) predicts. That is, the present framework correctly predicts clitic climbing to V_x when the subject of an infinitival complement to a c/p verb is passive-like. The only difference between (7.94) (*faire...par*) and Italian/Spanish restructuring is that an overt or null subject DP of V_c in (7.94), or for that matter in a passive construction, must be disjoint from the subject of V_x, while the null subject DP of V_c in restructuring is co-indexed with the subject of V_x (cf. note 45). But by Economy of Representation (7.79), all these constructions (Italian and Spanish restructuring, passives, and *faire...par*) are *alike* in containing a single VP whose complement V_c has a subject outside of V′. By the Phrase Mate Hypothesis (7.57) all (non-reflexive) clitics corresponding to internal arguments and adjuncts of V_c in (7.94) then appear on V_x, the PF head of this VP.

In this section, three structures have been derived from applying the lexicalisation theory of sections 7.4.2 and 7.4.3 to a grammatical verb *laisser* with a single frame +___V (D). These structures, together with the Phrase Mate Hypothesis, succeed in predicting the complex patterns of verbal hosts and clitics in causatives. (7.90b) represents the non-climbing structure, (7.91a) the *faire...à* construction, and (7.92a) the *faire...par* construction.

7.4.6 Restrictions on cliticisation in causative/perception complements

An improved version of this section is the appendix to Chapter 6 in Emonds (2000a). Chapter Six, section 7, of this volume contains a summary.

244 *Minimal structures for functional categories*

7.5 Clitics corresponding to complements of adjectives

The fifth construction in section 7.1.1 in which Romance clitics apparently climb to higher V concerns complements of adjectives. Some typical French examples with intransitive verbs from (7.8) are repeated without glosses.

(7.8)   Jean leur restera fidèle (à toutes les deux).
        Elle m'en paraît capable.
        La situation y semble lieé.

As schematised in section 7.1.1, paradigms such as (7.8) require the following pair of structures to be related, where PP is a complement of A.

(7.105) a. ...   V - (DP) - A ... [$_{PP}$ pronoun /adverb] ...
        b. clitic + V - (DP) - A ... [$_{PP}$ Ø] ...

Two problems connected with relating these structures will be addressed. (i) How can the clitic in (7.105b) realise a complement of A if clitics are all subject to the Phrase Mate Hypothesis (7.57), since (7.57) claims that clitics can only replace or double sisters of V^k? (ii) How do we account for the fact that some speakers prefer (7.105b), although (7.105a) can be well-formed, especially with contrastive stress on the PP?

7.5.1 Two lexical projections for French adjectives

Traditional grammars call intransitive verbs with AP complements "linking verbs," and usually attempt to enumerate such verbs, suggesting they are a closed class. There is roughly the same quantity of intransitives realising (7.105b) as there are restructuring verbs, e.g., French *être* 'be', *devenir* 'become', *sembler* 'seem', *paraître* 'appear', *rester* 'stay', *demeurer* 'remain', etc. Thus, linking verbs which can host clitics corresponding to complements of A can plausibly be analysed as grammatical V, in the sense of section 7.3.3. These verbs are then each fully characterised by a small set of syntactic features F_k, and consequently may be inserted either pre-transformationally or in PF just like restructuring verbs.

First we discuss the derivations resulting from PL (7.71); we then come back to derivations with DL (7.72).

(7.106)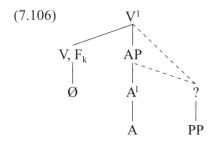

In (7.106), the PP is selected by a subcategorisation feature of a lexical item under A, either +___P or +___D. (In the latter case, P is empty; cf. the definition (7.56) of extended sisterhood.) To test whether cliticisation conforms to the Phrase Mate Hypothesis, we need to determine the mother node of PP. In classical subcategorisation, PP is of course under AP, and according to the revision of section 7.4.3, this still holds:

(7.78) *Extended Classical Subcategorisation. α, X, +___Y is satisfied if and only if Y^0 is the lexical head of a sister to X^0.*

This extension still prevents a complement of an A, say a PP, from being outside AP, and hence from being cliticisable under the Phrase Mate Hypothesis.

However, reasons were presented to dissociate the category of a phrasal head from that of the phrase itself (7.75).

(7.75) *Lexical Head/Projection. Let Y^0 be the highest lexically filled head in Z^j, where $Y^0 = N, V, A, P$. Then Y^0 is the lexical head of Z^j, and Z^j is a lexical projection of Y^0.*

To further exploit this previous step, if complement is defined as "sister to any Z^0", (7.78) can be replaced by a less restrictive (7.107):

(7.107) *Generalised Subcategorisation. α, X, +___Y is satisfied if and only if Y^0 is the lexical head of a complement within a lexical projection of X.*

Inspecting (7.106) in which V is inserted in PF, it appears that both A^1 and V^1 are lexical projections of A; consequently, by (7.107), PP in (7.106) may be a sister to either A or to V, that is, immediately dominated by either A^1 or V^1. Thus, PF lexicalisation of a grammatical linking verb allows both structures in (7.108) to be well-formed. (Late-inserted items are parenthesised.)

246 *Minimal structures for functional categories*

(7.108) a.

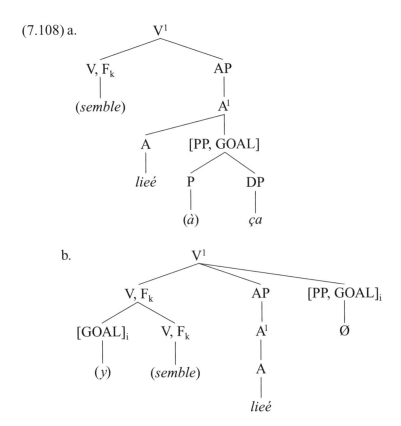

b.

The two trees in (7.108) exactly correspond to the two structures in (7.105), and both result from inserting grammatical linking verbs in PF. The tree in (7.108a) can also result from Deep Lexicalisation of linking verbs, as in section 7.4.4.[50] Since (7.108b) is a representation of (7.106) in which PP is a daughter of V^1 (outside AP), question (i) from the introduction to this section has been answered: cliticisation of a complement to A is consistent with the Phrase Mate Hypothesis.

Question (ii) asks why some speakers prefer the cliticised variant for linking verbs (7.105b, 7.108b) to the construction with an overt embedded PP (7.105a, 7.108a); cf. note 3. The choice here is made by a principle of Economy of Derivation, which has not yet been introduced in this study. This principle nonetheless plays a central role in regulating the appearance of clitic doubling. It is discussed in section 7.6.6, with a brief explanation for question (ii), the preference for (7.105b) over (7.105a). In future work in the AR/in situ framework, Economy of Derivation is certain to be pivotal.

In this section, attention has been focused on complements of adjectives following linking verbs. Additionally, complements of adjectives in secondary predications can sometimes cliticise onto the corresponding governing verb, as noted in Kayne (1975: section 4.6); examples from (7.10) are repeated without glosses.

(7.10)   *Tout le monde en croit Jean digne.*
         On y croit Jean fidèle.
         Cet evènement y a finalement rendu Jean sensible.

Given the range and semantic specificity of verbs whose complements express secondary predication, it is unlikely that they are all grammatical verbs subject to PF lexicalisation. If not, then (7.75) and (7.107) together require that complements of the secondary predicate A be generated within AP in deep structure.[51]

And indeed, Kayne argues in the cited section, with much supporting evidence, that cliticisation of either the secondary predicate adjective itself or its dative complement is excluded in this context by the intervening "specified subject", i.e., the direct object DP, in the same way that such items cannot cliticise in complements to causative verbs. The reformulation of the Specified Subject Condition Emonds (2000a, Ch. 6) and Chapter 6 of this volume has recast Kayne's proposal in the terms of this study. As Kayne notes, only pro-PP clitics as in (7.10) seem to escape this restriction.

But precisely the P-clitics in (7.10) can correspond to empty right-dislocated PPs which have moved in accord with subjacency; that is, they can be analysed as cliticising empty or overt right-dislocated PPs just as other instances of *en* were analysed in section 7.2.

(7.109) *Tout le monde en croit Jean digne (, de ce prix prestigieux).*
        On y croit Jean fidèle (, à ses principes).
        Cet evènement y a finalement rendu Jean sensible (, à son devoir familiale).

The examples in (7.109) suggest sources for the PP clitics in (7.10) which accord with the Phrase Mate Hypothesis (7.57).

248 *Minimal structures for functional categories*

7.5.2 *Two lexical projections for English adjectives*

Outside of Romance, the possible positioning of complements to adjectives in precisely the two positions shown in (7.108) has been extensively argued for in Hendrick (1978).[52] In support of this dual structure, he observes that when an English AP is fronted in questions, a phrasal complement to the adjective can be either preposed or left in situ, exactly as expected if it has the two structural realisations (7.108a) and (7.108b):

(7.110) *AP fronting, with a complement to A inside AP:*
How ready to go is John?
How happy doing that work is he?
How angry at Bill did John seem?
How distrustful of John does Mary feel?
How satisfied with your work did Bill appear yesterday?
Mary asked how mad at John the supervisors got.

(7.111) *AP fronting, with a complement to A outside AP:*
How ready is John to go?
How happy is he doing that work?
How angry did John seem at Bill?
How distrustful does Mary feel of John?
How satisfied did Bill appear with your work yesterday?
Mary asked how mad the supervisors got at John.

The analysis of French APs in section 7.5.1 is thus independently justified by the fact that Wh-fronting reveals the same structural ambiguity in English APs.

The structural contrast between (7.108a) and (7.108b) is reminiscent of paradigms associated with "light verbs", that is, verbs of not fully specified semantic content whose objects are nominalised lexical verbs. The combination of light verb plus nominalised object is a near paraphrase of the lexical verb alone: *take a walk* = *walk; have a look* = *look; make complaints* = *complain*. When a nominalised object of a light verb is questioned, its complement can be preposed with the noun or left in situ, exactly as in (7.110)–(7.111) (Ross 1967).

(7.112) Which complaints about food did they make?
How long a walk into the forest did Mary take?
How serious a look at the exhibit would you have?

(7.113) Which complaints did they make about food?
How long a walk did Mary take into the forest?
How serious a look would you have at the exhibit?

When verbs with the same objects are not themselves "light", question formation cannot separate the objects from their PP complements (again, Ross 1967):

(7.114) Which complaints about food did they ridicule?
How long a walk into the forest did Mary avoid?
How serious a look at the exhibit would you recommend?

(7.115) *Which complaints did they ridicule about food?
*How long a walk did Mary avoid into the forest?
*How serious a look would your recommend at the exhibit?

Much discussion concerning light verbs has been in terms of how they and their object nouns assign theta roles to complement phrases. However, since linking verbs don't assign theta roles like light verbs, the theta role approach does not generalise. On the other hand, by analysing light verbs as grammatical V (lacking purely semantic features) with N complements, parallel to analysing linking V as grammatical V with A complements, the paradigms (7.112)–(7.113) are the fully predicted counterparts of (7.110)–(7.111).

The structure giving rise to (7.113) is (7.116).

(7.116)

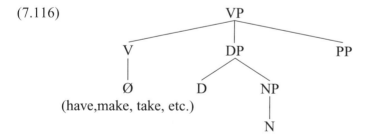

Thus, light verbs are simply special cases of closed class grammatical verbs which undergo either deep or PF insertion. Complements to their deep object N, or equally well to deep predicate attribute N or A, can be optionally realised as sisters of either N or A (Deep Lexicalisation), or of the higher grammatical V (Phonological Lexicalisation), since both N'/A' and V' are extended projections of N/A by (7.75). The lexicalisation theory developed here thus entirely subsume the phenomenon of "light verbs" as the transitive subcase of grammatical verbs.

7.6 Unresolved issues in the in situ framework

The Phrase Mate Hypothesis for Romance verbal clitics (7.57) has now been extended to all the contexts (i)–(v) of section 7.1.1 which previously have been presented as justifying clitic movement. The mechanisms which license clitics are their lexical entries, which conform to Alternative Realisation (7.60); in the presence of these clitics, the Invisible Category Principle (7.61) licenses as empty (sometimes right dislocated) corresponding co-indexed complement and adjunct phrases.

Central to my explanation of clitic placement in restructuring, auxiliary, and causative/perception verb contexts has been a theory of grammatical verbs (sections 7.3.3, 7.4.2 and 7.4.3), which are characterised by their lacking purely semantic features. According to the principles of Deep (7.72) and Phonological (7.71) Lexicalisation, restructuring and causative/perception verbs may be empty prior to s-structure, and auxiliary verbs must be. These empty V give rise to VPs with more than one V, which consequently permit clitics on the first of its verbs to alternatively realise phrases within this VP. Hence, as shown in section 7.4, what appear in previous analyses to be "higher" V in fact share the same VP with their non-finite complement. Consequently, neither clitics nor complements to causative verbs ever actually "climb" or "raise" out of their deep phrases. They are all generated in situ.

While these lexicalisation principles aspire to some measure of completeness, many issues in the generative grammar of Romance clitics remain unresolved; however, several are brought into sharper focus. For example, section 7.4.6 of the original essay parsimoniously recast Kayne's classic Specified Subject Condition treatment of clitics in causatives, eliminating a superfluous and I claim descriptively inadequate mention of any clause-like category which dominates these subjects. To conclude, I now outline how six further questions about Romance clitics relate to this study's lexicalisation theory and in situ analyses, and how some but not all seem close to resolution.

7.6.1 Nominative clitics and finite agreement

As indicated in note 6, this study has not discussed nominative clitics (in French and many Italian dialects), nor the lack of them (in Spanish and Standard Italian), nor clitics of negation. In my terms, such clitics appear to be alternative realisations on the category I (cf. section 7.3.3). In particular, nominative clitics compete with finite agreement morphology to alternatively realise subject DPs. One interesting difference between the two types of bound morphology is that French clitics but not agreement can serve as clause-internal "identifying constituents" for dislocated phrases in the tentative Dislocation Convention (note 15). Another is that nominative (and other) clitics may invert with V, but agreement morphology never can.

In general, one might conjecture that agreement morphemes are X^0–internal heads, while clitics are X^0–internal non-heads. From this fundamental difference their other differences could follow, but this study has not explored this possibility.

7.6.2 Enclisis

Any investigator of Romance is struck by the proclisis on French infinitives vs. the enclisis on Italian and Spanish non-finite forms. Further interesting facts about enclisis are that, unlike inflectional suffixes, Spanish enclitics are stress-neutral and fail to constitute "right hand heads" of the V^0 they occur in.

These characteristics may suggest that enclisis results from moving V leftward over underlying proclitics (i.e., proclitics on a trace of V), as in some studies adopting a minimalist approach. If enclisis thus results from verb fronting, all the standard Romance verbal clitics might be lexically listed as +___V.[53] In any case, the relation between enclisis and proclisis has not formed part in this study.

7.6.3 Clitic ordering

The in situ approach seems well-suited for solving the issue of how clitics are ordered among themselves. Under Alternative Realisation, each clitic is a closed class lexical entry subject to PF lexicalisation (7.71). In principle, internal sequencing of clitics should be easy to express in these entries as a function of their contextual features and/or general ordering conditions on insertion operations.

Assuming that language-learners assign proclitics the feature +___V in the least marked cases, contextual features of individual proclitics might then elaborate on this basic specification. For example, case-marked (φ-feature) French proclitics which replace DPs might be listed as CASE, +___(α)^V, to indicate that other clitics may intervene between them and the V; in contrast, (non-idiomatic) French adverbial (= PP) clitics are strictly V-adjacent. Internal ordering among the CASE clitics might be determined by yet other factors.

Another device that might affect clitic sequencing is that related closed class entries (e.g. CASE clitics) may appear in the lexicon with some kind of internal order (in a formal "paradigm") that influences their ordering in a string. Finally, UG might also dictate some kind of left-to-right or right-to-left insertion order for multiple clitics under a single X^0. To investigate these options with reference to Romance would be related to determining whether proclisis or enclisis is more basic. Usually clitic sequencing is the same in either case, but not entirely. For instance, enclitic order in French affirmative imperatives differs in one perhaps telling way from that of proclitics in the "elsewhere" case (Emonds 1976: Ch. VI).

Exploration of these various possibilities should lead to a design for closed class lexical insertion which nicely captures effects often ascribed to sui generis templates in earlier work (Perlmutter 1971). How to best do this is a non-trivial but highly feasible research task, and one that will shed much light on the mechanisms of both the lexicon and linguistic category theory. The AR/in situ framework, by centrally focusing on characterising individual closed class lexical items, should provide satisfying accounts of these decades-old anomalies.

7.6.4 Choice of host V within restructured VPs

As discussed by Burzio (1986: section 7.4.3, esp. 261–262), the previous literature as well as his own analysis accounts for why clitics can appear on higher verbs, but "provides no explanation for why they *must*." The AR/in situ approach, in contrast, promises to provide an explanation.

Under the analysis of optional PF lexicalisation for restructuring and causative/perception verbs, a single VP dominates two V sisters, V_x and V_c. The Phrase Mate Hypothesis (7.57) has deliberately been formulated so as not to exclude the complement verb V_c from sometimes hosting clitics. Nonetheless, in almost all relevant paradigms, the late-inserted restructuring or causative/perception verb V_x is the clitic host. To reflect this, we might sharpen (7.57) as follows:

(7.117) *Head-driven Phrase Mate Hypothesis. Romance clitics are related and co-indexed only with XP sisters of a projection of a lexical head V_i.*

See (7.75) for the definition of lexical head; such a head cannot be empty. Taking (7.71) and (7.117) together, PF-inserted clitics will invariably appear on V_x, the PF head of VP, as indeed is usually the case.

Rizzi (1978) notes that in a few restructured contexts some clitics may attach to V_c (cf. note 42). Similar patterns are also reported for various Italian dialects. More crucially, a central hypothesis of Kayne (1975: Ch. 6) is that French reflexive *se* appears on V_c in causative constructions with postposed lower subjects; Rouveret and Vergnaud (1980) show that other French clitics, in certain circumstances, do as well. In this study's terms, French reflexives and these others are proclitics on V_c in $[_{VP} V_x \ldots V_c \ldots]$.

If (7.117) is fully general, such facts suggest that *se* and some other clitics on V_c in restructuring and causative/ perception verb contexts are alternatively realised at a point in a derivation when V_c rather than V_x is the lexical head of the single VP, i.e., prior to Spell Out. That is, some clitics, especially reflexives, may well be subject to Deep Lexicalisation (7.72).

In fact, DL for reflexives seems to fit with Kayne's (1975: Ch. 6) extensive argumentation that *se*-cliticisation occurs qualitatively earlier in a derivation (in the cycle) than does other (post-cyclic) clitic placement. If Deep Lexicalisation is simply identified with his cycle, and Phonological Lexicalisation with his post-cycle, Kayne's results transfer into this study's framework. Prior to detailed examination of the paradigms involved, Kayne's distinctions in cyclicity for clitic placement dovetail prima facie with the two levels for closed class lexical insertion of the in situ approach.

7.6.5 The historical persistence of clitic case

There is a pervasive characteristic of Romance clitic systems that, though remarked by Kayne (1975: 87), has not been integrated into a systematic account. In Romance languages, abstract case is nowhere distinctive on DPs: in particular, the "strong pronoun" DPs do not distinguish nominative, accusative, and oblique case unless they are cliticised to V or P.[54] Thus, while Universal Grammar is assumed to assign abstract case to Romance DPs, these case features are never distinctively realised inside DPs.

Nonetheless, the accusative/oblique contrast (and contrasts with nominative in French, in the absence of pro-drop) is distinctively realised in clitic positions (e.g., third person masculine singular French *le/lui/il*, Italian *lo/gli*, Spanish *lo/le*). Moreover, these languages have for centuries steadfastly maintained these case distinctions in and only in these phonologically non-prominent positions. This persistence contradicts conventional wisdom such as "case distinctions are lost in phonologically weak positions" (e.g., on nominal inflections). How can one explain this case persistence in the face of overt case being lost in the rest of the language? A movement approach to clitics would expect identity with base forms, not further distinctions, in a landing site.

In contrast, AR and the ICP not only describe, but explain such persistent case distinctions among special clitics. These principles say nothing about a feature (e.g. a case feature) being morphologically realised on the category with which it is canonically matched by (7.59). But the ICP licenses empty phrases only if all the phrase's syntactic features, including case, are realised elsewhere by a grammatical morpheme. A minimal alternative realisation of say ACCUSATIVE would imply that at least one morpheme in a language is compatible with ACCUSATIVE but no other case. Exemplifying with French, since *il-V* (nominative), *le-V* (accusative), and *lui-V* (oblique) are all distinct for any verb, case features are indeed alternatively realised, as required by the ICP (7.61). Similarly, the gender feature is alternatively realised in French clitics by morphology, since singular accusative *le-V* and *la-V* are distinct (for consonant-initial verbs).

Along these lines, one can verify that all ϕ-features are realised by some overt morpheme in all three Romance clitic systems under discussion. Curiously, the systems meet the AR requirement of the ICP in nearly minimal ways, in that many features are neutralised for several of their values (i.e., the only overt gender and case markings in French clitics are those mentioned just above). In other words, the ICP requires that if the Romance clitic systems are to survive at all, they must continue to exhibit minimal distinctions in case. Remarkably, this state of affairs predicted by AR and the ICP seems to be exactly what has been maintained in these languages for centuries, counter to their otherwise total loss of case morphology.[55]

7.6.6 Economy of Derivation

As discussed in section 7.1.2, a movement approach to Romance clitic placement incorrectly expects complementary distribution between clitics and full DPs, while the in situ licensing approach predicts that clitics may accompany either full phrases (the definition of "doubling") or ICP-sanctioned null phrases. The ICP cannot zero a complement or adjunct XP with content beyond features spelled out by clitics, which then leads to doubling.

Nonetheless, as observed in section 7.3.3, the AR/ICP mechanisms themselves do not fully specify conditions under which overt phrasal – clitic doubled pairs are expected, allowed, or forbidden. These conditions are the task of other grammatical principles and of language-particular lexical entries of the clitics themselves.

One situation where overt doubled pairs seem obligatory was discussed in note 15, repeated here for convenience:

(7.118) *Dislocation Convention. A phrase α adjoined to a clause co-indexed with a constituent α' inside the clause requires that α' be phonological if possible.*

If the adjoined/dislocated phrase is itself overt, then it gives rise to obligatory doubling, provided that the language's closed class lexicon contains an appropriate identifying clitic α'.[56]

From the above, on might conclude that if nothing forces doubling, then AR and the ICP allow optional doubling of any sort of non-dislocated phrase. But in at least two situations this is excluded.

(i) If doubling is not obligatory, then the presence of a Romance clitic typically leads to the possible zeroing of an unstressed pronominal complement or adjunct phrase, since the pronoun's features are all alternatively realised. (It appears that contrastive stress is never alternatively realised; i.e., clitics never bear it.) But while the ICP permits zeroing, it is not formulated so as to require it. As argued in Emonds (1994), zeroing is forced by a more general Economy of Derivation, as follows:

(7.119) *Economy of Derivation. Among alternative derivations from the same deep structure, prefer the derivation with the fewest insertions of free morphemes.*

By this principle, with many implications outside the area of bound morphology (e.g., in the English auxiliary system), a clitic co-indexed with a null phrase is always preferred to a clitic paired with an unstressed pronominal. In this way, the consequences of Chomsky's (1981) "Avoid Pronoun Principle" for clitics are subsumed under a more general principle.

(ii) The unacceptability of doubling with many Romance direct object clitics is well-known, exemplified here in French:

(7.120) *Marie l'a suggéré   le   livre à   Paul.
        Marie it suggested the book to Paul
        *Paul les a proposés les films à des copains.
        Paul them suggested the movies to some friends

To exclude this pattern, Kayne (1981) plausibly suggests that abstract accusative case is unavailable to a direct object DP when a co-indexed clitic is present. It seems likely that this lack is related to the fact that V is the source of accusative case, and is not able in (7.120) to simultaneously case-mark both a clitic and an object DP. In contrast, oblique case for dative DPs is provided by an empty P (cf. section 7.3.2) while AR licenses verbal clitics. Oblique case can perhaps then simply be copied with other φ-features via AR, thus providing case for both members of a doubled indirect object.[57] This explanation for the lack of accusative doubling is schematic; a complete analysis should clarify the more general issue of how bottom-up processing interacts with both canonical assignment and alternative realisation of case features.

Another Romance clitic paradigm which Economy of Derivation can explain is the preference noted by Kayne in section 7.1.1 for (7.105b) over (7.105a); i.e., in the absence of contrastive stress, complements to adjectives should be cliticised if possible.

(7.105) a. ...   V - (DP) - A ... [$_{PP}$ pronoun /adverb] ...
        b. clitic + V - (DP) - A ... [$_{PP}$ Ø] ...

Free morphemes exemplifying (7.105a), e.g., French à elles 'to them', là 'there', à ça 'to that', d'eux 'of them', etc. are less economical in the sense of (7.119) than clitics. Therefore, since the lexicalisation theory of sections 7.4 and 7.5 generate both (7.105a) and (7.105b), it is Economy of Derivation which chooses between the two and favours (7.105b).[58]

Notes

* This paper reports on the research carried out as a member of Group 9 of the European Science Foundation Eurotyp Project. My work in this group was arranged by Henk van Riemsdijk through a Netherlands Science Foundation Fellowship at Tilburg University. There my research seminar was devoted to the clitic systems of Romance, which generative grammar, justly or not, has focused on more than any others. Since then, he and other members of Group 9, as well as research students and colleagues at Durham, have encouraged and constructively critiqued my presentations. For their many commentaries, presentations, and discussions on clitics I am most grateful.

I am indebted to Béatrice Lamiroy, Michèle Mittner, Paula Monachesi, and María del Socorro Franco, who have patiently and insightfully discussed many of the myriad issues and difficulties surrounding the grammar of clitics. I am also grateful to Miori Kubo for reading and commenting on various sections. Finally, I deeply appreciate the facilities provided by President Kazuko Inoue of Kanda University.

1. Due to my limitations, this study deals only with Standard French, Italian, and Spanish. I apologise for using the cover term "Romance" throughout.
2. A principal aim of this study is to bring this characteristic of restructuring and causative verbs out of the shadows and to explain it in terms of linguistic theory. In competing accounts, it has been treated as accidental.
3. P. Monachesi (among other Italian speakers) feels that cliticisation of complements to A is entirely optional. Yet Kayne (1975: 172) reports for French: "In the absence of special stress on the pronoun, the nonapplication of Cl-Pl leads to what are generally considered ungrammatical sentences:"
    *Elle est infidèle à toi.
    'She is unfaithful to you.' (Kayne 1975: 172)
    *Cela est pénible à eux.
    'That is painful for them.' (Kayne 1975: 139)
   This study concentrates on what makes cliticisation possible, rather than when it is obligatory. Nonetheless, section 7.5.1 proposes that complements to adjectives can occupy two structural positions, suggesting that cliticisation is both possible and obligatory from one position and blocked from the other. The relation between preference (Kayne) and optionality (Monachesi) will be related to Economy of Derivation in section 7.6.6.
4. In this study, constituents which have been traditionally referred to in generative studies as NP are notated as DP (Determiner Phrase), in line with Abney (1987). The head of DP is D, which takes an NP sister, analogously to the way in which I, the finiteness constituent which is the head of IP, takes VP as a sister. Thus, "N-bar" in earlier studies of X-bar syntax corresponds to NP here.

5. The term "base-generation" for my approach would cause misunderstanding. As will be seen, feature bundles eventually spelled out by clitics are indeed base-generated on their verbal hosts, but they are licensed only by means of "alternative realisation" (section 7.3). This crucial use of post-movement structure in the present analysis avoids Rizzi's (1978: 151–152) critique "Against a Base Solution", while retaining his arguments against double subcategorisation (148–150).
6. No analysis has proposed that French and Italian nominative clitics can climb, because they clearly always appear no higher than on the I which case-marks them. Therefore, this paper is not concerned with nominative clitics, including the many variations that have come to light in studies of Italian dialects.

    Burzio (1986: 34) and also his note 18 seem mistaken in drawing a distinction between subject and non-subject clitics; the distinction is rather between nominative (I) clitics and verbal (V) clitics.
7. A (adjective) is in this list, since Romance languages can cliticise predicate attributes.
8. Herschensohn (1981) thoroughly catalogues and critiques the devices used by Kayne (1975), Quicoli (1980), and Rouveret and Vergnaud (1980) to predict restrictions on clitic placement using Chomsky's Specified Subject Condition. She reasons that their predictions can be rescued only by *exempting* causative formation from the general conditions on Move α:

    As the SSC/Opacity is a condition on final anaphor-antecedent relations (and thus only indirectly on movement transformations which can be traced at the level of surface structure), causative does not violate the condition, *but rather the trace convention. The aberrant character of this movement can be attributed to the fact that it is a restructuring rule, which I am claiming may have three unusual characteristics: violation of the trace condition, application before unmarked rules ("move α"), and thematic rewriting. These three characteristics substantiate the quasi-lexical character of the amalgamated verb, as well as the almost base-generated nature of the construction as a whole.* (Herschensohn 1981: 262; my italics)

    In other words, the problem with Romance causatives is that they act like a base-generated construction, except that the subject DP of the lower verb acts partly like a subject and partly like an internal argument. While I do not accept Herschensohn's variant of causative formation, her study furnishes valuable perspectives on the analyses she reviews.
9. An additional problem with clitic movement is equally severe whether heads or phrases are involved. In cases (i)–(iii) of putative climbing discussed in section 7.1.1, only certain verbs and not others provide suitable landing sites, even though all verbs in Romance languages can host clitics. Explanatory movement

accounts do not countenance stipulated lexical subclasses of landing sites for short but not long movements.
10. The same holds for negative and nominative clitics.
11. Such lexical statements can plausibly incorporate language-particular ordering restrictions among clitics which, as has long been acknowledged, resist being captured by any general transformational account (Perlmutter 1971).
12. The literature on *en* is often at pains to point out differences in the structural correlates of (i)–(iv), especially focusing on (iv) vs. the others; e.g., the *de* in (iv) is often not explicit. I basically agree with the conclusion of Milner (1978: 164): "Quantitative *en*, as is known, doesn't have the same properties as ordinary *en*; this shouldn't however obscure their formal similarity. In fact, all told, the differences separating them can be traced to a single cause: ordinary *en* pronominalises only N" [DP in present terms], quantitative *en* pronominalises N-bar or N." [my translation]
13. Read without the characteristic comma of dislocation, this sentence may exemplify PP-extraposition: *Paul bought four pounds at the market of potatoes*. But the other examples in (7.31–7.32) are not acceptable right dislocations.
14. If phrasal movements always instantiate universal grammar, the explicandum is not French/Italian dislocation, but rather the absence of NP dislocation in Spanish and English.
15. Additionally, it appears that *en/ne* must double a dislocated phrase whenever they may double one, and more generally, *en/ne* are obligatory whenever they are possible, whether doubling occurs or not (i.e., whether the dislocated phrase is overt or empty). I do not propose to account for the difference between this obligatory doubling and the optional doubling informally described for Spanish non-pronominal objects in Jaeggli (1981: 31)–34. Nonetheless, one determinant seems to be that obligatory doubling occurs with other dislocated and adjoined phrases, such as topics and affected datives. We might envisage an "anti-economy" or "use pronoun" principle such as the following:

Dislocation Convention. A phrase α adjoined to a clause co-indexed with a constituent α' inside the clause requires that α' be phonological if possible.

The corresponding economy or "avoid pronoun" principle would then apply to phrases unrelated to adjoined positions.
16. Couquaux's proposed *underlying post-verbal source* for DP subjects containing gaps corresponding to *en* can be illustrated with a tree for an example from Kayne (1975: 190).

La forme (de ce poème) n'en est pas admirable.
'The form (of that poem) thereof-is not admirable.'
I add the dislocated PP required by hypothesis (7.37):

260 *Minimal structures for functional categories*

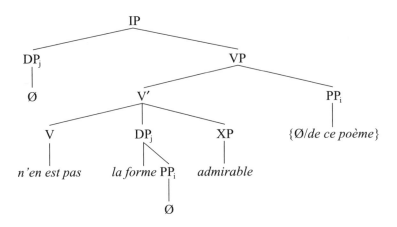

Incidentally nothing in Couquaux's arguments or derivations requires or supports the notion that the VP-internal DP-XP predications as in the above tree form a small-clause constituent that excludes the V.

17. Kayne (1975: 111, note 56) observes that some kind of reanalysis must circumvent subjacency to allow extraction out of a sequence of recursively embedded *de*-phrases:

   On en   peindra le bout du   pied gauche (de la table).
   One thereof will paint   the end of the left foot   (of the table)

   In the present analysis, this reanalysis is a fact about right dislocation, not about clitic placement, for the same embeddings permit right-dislocated phrases:

   On en peindra le bout du pied gauche pour toi, de la table.

18. Kayne's second example in (7.38a) (*Marie se servira du tien alors, de stylo*) might suggest that an adverb intervenes between the DP source and the landing site of dislocation within PP. However, French *alors* 'then' can generally appear within an emphasised DP:

   (i) Kayne (1975: Ch. 2) argues adverbs are excluded between subjects and finite verbs; yet *alors* so appears: *Le mien alors ne vaut pas un sous?*

   (ii) Left dislocation allows a single DP, yet we have: *J'imagine que vous autres alors vous irez à la soirée.*

   (iii) Cleft focus position is also a test for constituency, and still we find: *C'est lui alors que Marie veut engager.*

19. "Bare NP adverbials" of the Italian type *due ore* 'two hours' are PPs with empty Ps, according to the analysis in Emonds (1987). Hence, any dislocation of an NP within this PP will be structurally parallel to (7.46); then, as argued in the text, *ne*-cliticisation of this NP would violate the Genitive Phrase Mate Hypothesis (7.37), giving rise to facts discussed in Belletti and Rizzi (1981):

   Mario ha studiato libri due ore. vs. **Mario ne ha studiate libri due.*
   'Mario has studied books two hours' 'Mario thereof-has studied books two'

20. As indicated in note 15, whenever *en/ne* are possible, they appear to be obligatory. I tentatively ascribed this to a "Dislocation Convention" requiring that, whenever possible, dislocated elements have clause-internal phonologically overt "identifying constituents." We can combine the first formulation in note 15 with the prohibition on two overt co-indexed identifiers as follows:
    Revised Dislocation Convention. A phrase α adjoined to a clause requires, if possible, a *unique* phonological co-indexed element α' inside the clause.
21. Since adverbial clitics attached to V are lower in the tree than the corresponding full phrases, this conclusion provides another argument against a movement approach to clitics, to add to those in section 7.1.2.
22. We return to a detailed treatment of late or PF lexicalisation in section 7.4.2.
23. There are instances in French where *le* seems to cliticise IP (*Il le semble* 'it seems so') and where *y* seems to cliticise VP (*Marie va rejoindre les enfants et Jean y va aussi* 'Marie is going to meet up with the children and Jean is too'). Nothing else in the discussion turns on extending XP to VP and IP, but the symmetry with NP and DP is suggestive.
24. The details of Authier and Reed's analysis do not seem to me to accommodate a minimal English–French contrast. The authors develop a view that affected datives require branching V^1 and are related to V assigning case. In the light of the following this seems unwarranted for English.
    The English lexicon contains a grammatical (PF-inserted) P *on* that heads a PP sister to V^1, which I take to be the structure that defines affected datives. They are compatible with intransitive V^1.
    The windshield cracked on her overnight, so a taxi was called.
    Bill cracked up on his wife, so she got a divorce.
    His supervisor went and retired on one of our best graduate students.
    Standard French has no corresponding lexical P, meaning that the DP sister of the empty P can surface only if alternatively realised as a verbal clitic. This is the well-known fact that French affected datives must be pronominal.
25. Not every language necessarily has four open classes, but many do, and none has more. In generative analyses, the category P is much wider than the traditional term preposition and includes many so-called adverbs. H. van Riemsdijk (personal communication) suggests there are about 300 P in Dutch, and the situation in English is similar. For why the open lexical category P has fewer members than N, V, or A, see the conclusion of Emonds (1986).
26. The actual asymmetry between lexical and non-lexical categories is that only members of the open classes N, V, A, and P may be specified in lexical entries with purely semantic features f that play no role in syntax. In contrast, every feature F on a closed class item can play a syntactic role. Consequently, since each item seems to spell out a specific matrix of syntactic features (e.g., *n't, whether, if, the, else, as, so, how*, etc.), non-lexical categories items almost invariably exhibit unique syntactic behaviour (Emonds 1985: Ch. 4). When open class items

with purely semantic features are used, unique syntactic behaviour (often wrongly termed irregularity) and any justifications for late insertion disappear.

27. I thank Hap Kolb for helpful discussion on how to formulate (7.60) to achieve both empirical coverage and some measure of elegance. In particular, he suggested that an alternatively realised feature might be either a feature on a head or adjoined to a head; hence, here, "under X".

28. (i) and (iii) are discussed in Emonds (1987) and (ii) in Emonds (1994); (iv), as discussed in Chapter 5 of this volume (Emonds, 1993), requires a generalisation of (7.60) not of concern here.

29. Among other things, on the centrality of the three interfaces of Chomsky (1992), a system of bottom-up tree construction and transformational derivation, some variant of Move α which preserves canonical structure, and locating all of language-particular syntax in closed class or functional category lexicons.

30. Napoli (1981) extends Rizzi's tests to Italian auxiliary + participle constructions, thus demonstrating their obligatorily "restructured" nature as well. Abeillé and Godard (1994) argue convincingly, largely independently of their formal framework, that the same holds for French auxiliaries.

31. Rizzi's examples make it clear that an auxiliary with a participle doesn't interfere with NP-preposing; i.e., as established in Napoli (1981), these sequences exemplify "obligatory restructuring."

32. This is not the case with the special Italian enclitic *loro*, whose enclisis even in proclitic environments indicates a separate mechanism is at work.

33. Rizzi observes that his arguments present no reason to choose between (7.67a) and an alternative in which V_x and V_c form a "verbal complex" which is really neither a V nor a verb phrase. He subsequently argues for the latter option, with some misgivings, because of the need to raise a single constituent in a causative formation rule. The analysis of causatives suggested in section 7.4.4 renders such an ad hoc rule and constituent unnecessary. See Zagona (1988) for further arguments against a verbal complex.

34. This proposal for a PF *there*-insertion rule is for the sake of an example; the specifics are unrelated to the argument in the text. The characteristic of the category D is to determine reference, and an expletive such as *there* is marked precisely for lacking this property. The other English expletive *it* is definite. Like other pure pronouns, expletives do not appear with NP sisters. Finally, while the expletive *there* appears only in those DP which either are or bind a subject of an S (= IP), I assume this is related to the combination -REFERENCE, -DEFINITE.

35. This is the late-inserted subpart of the English morpheme *-ing*. The full adequacy of this maximally simple entry is justified in detail in Emonds (1991a), reproduced as Chapter 3 in this volume.

36. Phonological Lexicalisation (7.71) explicitly formalises a possibility long available in a grammatical model with two syntactic levels, but only sporadically uti-

37. lised as a basis for explanation. "This formulation allows later insertion of functional items that are vacuous for LF-interpretation, e.g., the *do* of *do*-support or the *of* of *of*-insertion." (Chomsky 1992: note 22).
37. A third type of lexical entry not covered by (7.71)–(7.72) *will figure crucially* in the argument of this study. A lexical entry in any category may lack purely semantic features f and still be specified for contentful, non-contextual syntactic features F that indeed contribute to interpretation. We return to this possibility in section 7.4.4.
38. These frame could be confused with the "morphological" word-internal frames introduced by Lieber (1980) for bound morphemes. Since left-right order is clearly not an item-specific stipulated relation between heads and phrasal complements, the ordering reflected in classical subcategorisation should be retained for Lieber's frames, while some order-free notation for syntactic frames such as <Y> should replace +___Y. For familarity, I here retain +___Y for phrasal subcategorisation with meaning as in (7.74).
39. At either level of lexical insertion, the sequence of insertion operations is upwards through the tree, as is standard.
40. The tree (7.67b) does not specify that a projection of V_x immediately dominates the lower VP. Although VP is selected via the frame +___V, the non-finite clause actually projected may be a raising or a control infinitival IP sister to V_x.
41. Rizzi (1978: note 6) mentions that various verbs meaning 'try' are marginally acceptable as restructuring verbs. The present framework can account for variability in the triggering classes even in a single speaker's speech as follows. Suppose some verb α with a purely semantic feature f, which consequently requires DL and forbids the "clitic climbing" of (7.67a), is lexically listed as α, V, F (syntactic features), f (semantic feature), +___V. Now, some speakers may modify this entry simply by parenthesising the more specific feature f, yielding α, V, F, (f), +___V. A single speaker in various styles might link the parentheses to other factors. When a derviation containing [$_v$ α] does not include f, then late insertion of α is a possibility. Although the full meaning of α might be pragmatically associated with such a derivation, one could say that restructuring stylistically suggests that a verb has a less specific meaning than it actually does. I believe this corresponds to the "feel" of restructuring, if such can be said to exist.
42. For Rizzi (1978: note 26), some speakers allow some clitics in some restructured sequences as enclitics on the V_c of (7.67a). Such variation does not contravene the Phrase Mate Hypothesis (7.57), although it might bear on the exact formulation of Alternative Realisation (how phrasal sisters of V^k are realised on V). Rizzi refers to then existing discussions of data relevant to determining which V is host as "inconclusive". Cf. section 7.6.6.
43. For the absence of restructuring in Modern French, consult the preceding chapter.

44. When the c/p verbs take object DPs in simplex sentences, they vary as to whether they permit indirect objects, and this property carries over to their use in the complex causative construction. "*Entendre*, etc. ['hear' and other perception verbs, JE] require a direct but prohibit an indirect object in simplex sentences ... The complex sentences [i.e., the causative structures, JE] of all the verbs correspond to their simplex sentences". (Herschensohn 1981: note 47).
45. Even when an infinitive is sole complement to a causative verb, the subject of the infinitive, null or overt, is necessarily disjoint in reference from the subject of the causative. This differentiates causative from restructuring verbs, but is not captured in the present or any previous subcategorisation formalism.
46. Burzio (1986: 333) shows that exactly this structure (7.90b) also occurs with an unaccusative restructuring verb such as *venire* 'come'; when a DP in its base position between the two verbs blocks the possibility of (7.90a), clitics may not climb.
47. The reasoning here is not particular to causatives; Economy of Representation (7.79) always prevents complements of verbs like *persuade* from being realised as **persuade to go away of/to John*.
48. This requirement is Chomsky's (1981) Extended Projection Principle.
49. The present framework as developed to this point does not explain why reflexive clitics in c/p constructions occur on V_c when other clitics may not. Once again, the Phrase Mate Hypothesis does not formally require that V_x rather than V_c be chosen as a verbal host within a single VP, and so is not weakened by less than complete characterisation of this choice of host. Nonetheless, as clitics are licensed in PF (section 7.1.2), we expect that the lexical head of the VP in PF, namely V_x, is a preferred host. If reflexives are licensed earlier in a derivation than other clitics, as Kayne (1975: Ch. 6) argues, it may simply be that Romance clitics invariably attach to whichever V is the lexical head at the point that the clitic is licensed. This idea is pursued briefly in section 7.6.4.
50. When the linking verb, such as *être*, has no interpretable features, only PF insertion is allowed, but this does not affect this section's argument. As explained in section 7.4.4 on restructuring, the complement to a PF-inserted V_x specified as +___V is a bare V not a VP; due to Economy of Representation (7.79), the structure realising +___V with an embedded VP then "loses out" to the flat structure. Here in contrast, the complement to a PF-inserted V_x specified as +___A can not be a bare A rather than AP, since the bar notation requires that any Y^0 not inside some X^0 project to a full YP.
51. There may also be some linking verbs with purely semantic features, which are then consistent only with Deep Lexicalisation. In this case, if a deep-inserted verb has a phrasal complement (here an AP), no cliticisation is possible:
La soupe sent pleine de cela. vs. **La soupe en sent pleine.*
the soup smells full of that. vs. the soup thereof smells full

52. Hendrick seeks to establish that "… adjectives have no posthead complements in the base" (297) and that "… the Adjectival Complement originates as a sister to V" (262). I propose that complements to at least the adjectives following linking verbs may be projected *either* inside or outside AP.
53. If so, the difference between the Italian weak pronoun *loro* 'them' (Cardinaletti and Starke, 1996, 53) and the language's other clitics might be attributed to only *loro* being lexically listed as an enclitic (+V___).
54. For example, the invariant strong forms of Spanish pronouns are *yo* 'me', *tu* 'you', etc. Besides the verbal clitics *me, te*, etc., Spanish also has prepositional clitics *mi, ti*, etc. Invariant strong forms emerge in for example coordinate structures (*para yo y mis hermanos* 'for me and my brothers'), isolated DPs, and predicate attribute DPs, no matter what abstract case is involved.
55. A similar persistence in overt marking under Alternative Realisation can be seen in English number agreement with the subject. Agreement occurs only if the category I is present, yet is not marked on modal verbs canonically generated under I; rather agreement is overt when alternatively realised on V.
56. When no general condition such as (7.118) enforces doubling, the lexical entry of clitics can still bring it about, as briefly discussed in section 7.3.3.
57. The earlier derivational assignment of case by P in the classical model of deep and s-structure has typically been referred to as "inherent" case. In any bottom up model of processing, as argued for in example Emonds (1985: Ch. 2), P automatically assigns case to an indirect or oblique object before V assigns "structural" case to a direct object, so there is no need to differentiate ad hoc the "mode" of case assignment.
58. As noted in section 7.1.1, some Italian speakers consider the clitic/PP alternation entirely optional; hence their grammar does not seem subject to Economy of Derivation in the way presented here. If only speakers rather than languages idiosyncratically differ, this suggests that Economy of Derivation can influence acceptability judgments more or less according to speakers. If instead French and Italian differ on this point, it might be that (7.105a) and (7.105b) do not actually count as the same deep structure for Economy of Derivation.

Chapter 8
English indirect passives*

8.1 Characteristics and scope of structures called "Passive"

According to the classic study of Wasow (1977), English passive clauses are of two types, "verbal" and "adjectival." For example, two options allowed only in verbal passives are agentive *by*-phrases and the use of *get* instead of *be* as an auxiliary.

(8.1)   Her tonsillitis was {being/ getting} treated (by my doctor).
        A back garden is {being/ getting} laid out (by the owner).

The passives in (8.1) are therefore both verbal. Another diagnostic is based on the fact that an inanimate surface subject cannot have a predicate of the form "progressive copula + adjective":

(8.2)   Her tonsillitis was (*being) severe.
        A back garden is (*being) expensive.

Hence progressive passive predicates with an inanimate subject as in (8.1) are again confirmed as verbal.

Many researchers today recognize that *have* is a kind of transitive counterpart to the contentless intransitive copula *be*. It appears from (8.3) that verbal passives with *have* are no exception to this alternation, even though the construction in (8.3) is rarely singled out in grammatical studies as related to the *be*-passive, much less named. Moreover, the relatedness of the two passive structures is reinforced by the fact that *get* equally well replaces either *be* in (8.1) or *have* in (8.3):[1]

(8.3)   She was {having/ getting} her tonsillitis treated (by my doctor).
        We are {having/ getting} a back garden laid out (by the owner).

The verbal passive participle in (8.3) is not just "tacked on" to otherwise independent transitive clauses here, but is rather the essence of the construction. As seen in (8.4), it is precisely the verbal passive in (8.3) that makes the progressive possible.

(8.4) *She was having her tonsillitis.
*We are having a back garden.

The surface subjects in passive sentences like (8.3) receive a "benefactive" theta role with respect to the action named by the participle. For an obligatorily adversative sense, an *on*-phrase, somewhat stigmatized in Standard English, must be added:

(8.5) She was having her tonsillitis treated on her.
We are getting a back garden laid out on us.

These sentences are strange precisely because it is hard to imagine that being treated for tonsillitis or effortlessly acquiring a back garden are negative, but these are indeed the conveyed senses.

The subject matter of this paper is the grammar of the construction in (8.3) and the theoretical implications of a descriptively adequate analysis. An unavoidable conclusion will be that the constructions (8.1)–(8.3) demand unified treatment. That is, they are all passives in the same sense: when certain "auxiliaries" combine with a given participle, certain characteristic syntactic changes follow. [footnote omitted]

Crucially, the phrase expressing the "actor" of the clause loses access to the structurally prominent subject position. This suppression/ demotion of the actor is accorded a central role in Åfarli's (1992, 8) concise statements, which summarize his and much other research on passives [the numbering is mine].[2]

" ... every sentence one might reasonably want to call a passive may be minimally characterized as follows:

(8.6) Relative to its active counterpart, *the passive sentence is marked with special verb morphology.*

(8.7) *The subject of the active sentence never remains subject in the passive counterpart.*"

The second part (8.7) of Åfarli's characterization clearly stresses the relation of passive morphology to the interpretation of the subject phrase.

Inspection shows that the participial morphology of both (8.1) and (8.3) satisfy (8.6) and that both sets of examples satisfy (8.7) as well. Moreover, the constructions in (8.1) and (8.3) exhibit a third familiar hallmark of the passive (8.8) found in many languages, expression of the subject of an active as an object of a grammatical P such as English *by,* French *par* 'by' or *de* 'of', or Japanese *ni* 'to'.

(8.8)   *The subject of an active can be realized in a PP within a verbal passive predicate.*

All the examples in (8.1) and (8.3) permit such PPs.

An adequate analysis of passives should of course show how the properties (8.7) and (8.8) follow from Universal Grammar and some language-particular specification of passive morphology (8.6). The focus of this essay, however, is not passives in general. I aim rather to show that an adequate analysis for traditional passives needs to equally well apply to and explain the construction in (8.3), which I call the "indirect passive." For a general analysis of Germanic and Romance analytic passives, which derives the general syntactic properties (8.7) and (8.8) from the interaction of universal principles with lexical entries for participial morphology (8.6), the reader may refer to Emonds (2000, Ch. 5) or Emonds (2003). [footnote omitted]

8.2   Indirect Passives: a needed concept in English grammar

8.2.1   Genesis of the term "Indirect Passive"

Early studies in Japanese generative syntax reviewed in Kuroda (1979; 208–211) brought into focus an interesting Japanese construction that qualifies as an "indirect passive" (sometimes termed the "adversative passive") precisely because it satisfies (8.6)–(8.8). Here are one of Kuroda's examples and two further examples from Kubo (1992).

(8.9) a. John-ga   ame-ni   hur-are-ta.
         John-NOM rain-DAT fall-PASS-PAST
         'It rained on John.'
     b. Hanako-ga   noraneko-ni   hitobanjuu   nak-are-ta.
         Hanako-NOM stray cat-DAT all night long cry-PASS-PAST
         'Hanako had a stray cat cry all night on her.'
     c. Taro-ga   Hanako-ni   shindou-shuukyoo-o hajime-rare-ta.
         Taro-NOM Hanako-DAT new religion-ACC start-PASS-PAST
         'Taro had Hanako start believing in a new religion (on him).'

In these examples, the verbs all exhibit the same passive suffix *-(r)are* as ordinary "direct" Japanese passives, thus satisfying the morphological characteristic of the passive (8.6). The surface subjects of these indirect passives in (8.9) cannot correspond to the subjects of active clause counterparts, which satisfies characteristic (8.7).[3] They are interpreted rather as additional referents who are "affected" (typically adversely) by the actions indicated in the rest of the proposition or in the corresponding active clause – the presence of this type of surface subject phrase receiving an "affected" theta role is the defining property of the indirect passive. As a result, Japanese indirect passives don't exhibit any movement of deep objects, and often don't even contain such an object. Finally, the agents of the actions in (8.9) can be realized inside the predicate overtly by *ni*-phrases, thus satisfying the third descriptive characteristic of the passive (8.8).

The many analyses of Japanese indirect passives relate them in various ways to the direct passives, i.e. those which more or less translate the traditionally named English passives formed with the auxiliaries *be* or *get*. My purpose here is not to examine these analysis, other than to agree with their general thrust – to provide some kind of unified account of all Japanese passives in terms of some single property of the passive suffix *-(r)are*. The fact that two somewhat different types of Japanese sentences seem to qualify as "passive" by the criteria (8.6)–(8.8) then leads us to inquire, could there be two superficially different types of English sentences which should similarly be analyzed as subcases of a single passive construction?

8.2.2 The English candidates for Indirect Passive status

The English "passive auxiliaries" are *be* and *get*, whose complements are what we may now call direct passives, analogously to the terminology for Japanese. But as seen in section 8.1, these are not the only passive complements in English. The forms in (8.3) and italicized in (8.10) are passives as well, introduced by the six transitive "auxiliary" verbs in bold in the following:

(8.10) The players {**had/ heard/** *let/ *found} the insults *shouted* at them (by fans).
Many customers {**got/ wanted/** *noticed / *felt} their samples *handed* to them (by our employees).
You may {**see/ need/** *watch/ *make} your receipts *put* into the right drawers (by the file clerk).

English indirect passives 271

The transitive grammatical verbs permitted in the English construction in (8.3) and (8.10) aree *have, get, want, need, see* and *hear*. I will call the combination of these transitive V with passive participles the "English indirect passive." They all satisfy the descriptive properties of passives (8.6)–(8.8).

As a preliminary, we want to ensure that the participles in examples like (8.3) and (8.10) are not simply adjuncts *within* the direct object phrases. We can test for this with direct objects that are proper nouns or pronouns, since such DPs cannot then contain participial modifiers. Consequently, the italicized participial phrases in (8.11) are *outside* the bold DP objects.

(8.11) She {had/ got/ wanted/ needed/ saw/ heard/ *noticed/ *felt/ *found} **Jim** *brought in to the judge*.
We {saw/ wanted} **Baghdad** *slowly approached*, but we didn't {see/ want} **it** *handed over*.
The coach didn't want **them** *taken outside*, so he had **Jim** *posted at the door*.

Because the participles in (8.11) are not internal to the noun phrases they modify, these combinations cannot serve as DP subjects of a predicate:[4]

(8.12) *[Jim brought in to the judge] woke me up.
*[Baghdad slowly approached] replaced some talk shows.
*We wondered if [it handed over] would happen.
*[Them taken outside] and [Jim posted at the door] upset the players.

In addition, the sequences in (8.11) do not move as constituents:

(8.13) It was Jim brought in to the judge that she {*had/ ?got/ *wanted/ *needed/ ?saw/ ?heard}.
*Baghdad approached was seen in many countries, but it handed over wasn't.
*Which ones taken outside did he want?
*Who posted at the door did he have?

I conclude that English indirect passives are not simply DPs in object position, though certain passives may for certain speakers be structurally ambiguous, i.e. alternatively interpretable as part of a direct object; these latter structures are irrelevant to the logic of this study. We are interested rather in the following structure as characteristic of English indirect passives.[5]

272 *Minimal structures for functional categories*

(8.14)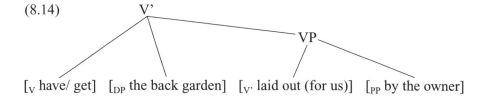

[$_V$ have/ get] [$_{DP}$ the back garden] [$_{V'}$ laid out (for us)] [$_{PP}$ by the owner]

8.2.3 Distinguishing true Indirect Passives from Adjectival Passives

The English indirect passive construction in (8.3) and (8.10) must be sharply distinguished from the adjectival passives in (8.15), which alternate with simple adjective phrases.

(8.15) The tax office {considered/declared} the bonuses {unearned / too generous}.
Many customers {judged/ called} our samples {too gaudily decorated/ well made/ inappropriate}.
You will {find/ imagine} this dish {less salted/ very sweet}.

To demonstrate the separateness of the two constructions, we can apply diagnostics that differentiate so-called "verbal" from "adjectival" passives, which mostly originate with Siegel (1973) and Wasow (1977). These tests typically show that the distribution of adjectival passives is very close to simply being that of APs. Verbal passives, in contrast, have a much more restricted distribution, in particular when they appear as complements (rather than adjuncts). English direct verbal passives are complements to only *be* and *get*.

The tests distinguishing the two types of passives are summarized in current terms in Emonds (2000, Ch. 5), under the following headings.

(8.16) a. An interpretive difference; ongoing activity (verbal) vs. completed activity (adjectival)
b. Different verb classes select them; adjectival passives are selected like AP.
c. Only verbal passives have external arguments.
d. Degree words freely modify only (certain) adjectival passives.
e. Only adjectival passives take the adjectival prefix *un-*.
f. Only verbal passives have the full internal structure of surface VPs.
g. Idiomatic object nouns passivize freely only in verbal passives.

One can already observe that the contrasting examples in (8.10) and (8.15) conform to (8.16a-b), although an intuitive interpretation as "ongoing activities" for the indirect verbal passives in (8.10) must be reinforced by more reliable syntactic testing. The main verbs in (8.15) are typical of those that take a range of secondary predicate APs with their objects, as required by (8.16b).

As predicted by (8.16c), the possibility of overt post-verbal agent phrases in indirect verbal passives (8.10) contrasts with their exclusion in adjectival passives:

(8.17) The tax office declared the bonus unearned (*by the new coach).
You will find this dish less salted (*by the substitute cook).
Many customers called our product well made (*by the supplier).

The adjectival passives in (8.15) are already constructed with adjectival modifiers such as *too, well, less* and *un-*. In accord with (8.16d-e), such modifiers in (indirect) verbal passives as in (8.10) are unacceptable:

(8.18) *The players {had/ heard} insults too shouted at them.
*Many customers {got/ wanted} samples well handed to them.
*You may {see/ need} your receipts less put into the right drawers.
*We {had/ needed} some shelves {well made/ unmade} into desks.

As allowed by (8.16f), verbal passives can contain overt NP second objects, italicized in (8.19), in addition to their passivized objects, represented with traces t_i.

(8.19) The players {had/ wanted/ got} the coach$_i$ sent t_i *that big present.*
You will {see/ want} your children$_i$ prepared t_i *a tasty snack.*

But since adjectival passives are based on an adjectival head, they cannot assign case to such a second NP:

(8.20) *The players {considered/ judged / imagined} the coach$_i$ sent t_i *that big present.* (coach=GOAL)
*You should {find/ judge/ picture} your children$_i$ prepared t_i *a tasty snack.* (children=GOAL)

Finally, (only) verbal passives tolerate direct objects that are parts of an idiom (8.16g). Corresponding adjectival passives are ill-formed.

(8.21) We {had/ saw} too much advantage taken of our hosts.
The new guests {wanted/ got} more attention paid to safety.
*We {judged / declared} too much advantage taken of our hosts.
*The new guests {believed / imagined} more attention paid to safety.

An additional argument that indirect passives are verbal is based on verbs that cannot be used in adjectival passives (Emonds: 2000, Ch.5):

(8.22) *That good dinner felt accompanied by too much drink.
*Many polluted cities remain (un)avoided during the summer.
*The clay looked (too) pressed into a bowl.
*The message appeared slipped to the spy.
*Some basketballs sounded dribbled across the floor.

But such verbs (*accompany, avoid, press, slip, dribble*) appear freely in indirect passives, again indicating that the latter are verbal rather than adjectival:

(8.23) They don't need such a good dinner accompanied by too much drink.
He wants those cities avoided during the summer.
The sculptor {had/ got} the clay pressed into a bowl.
Someone saw the message slipped to the spy.
We all heard the basketballs dribbled across the floor.

On the basis of these many tests (8.16a-g) that distinguish the two types of English passives, we can safely conclude that the indirect passives are *not* adjectival passives. Rather, they are verbal in precisely the same sense as are traditional direct passives formed with *be* and *get*.

8.3 The theoretical components of the Indirect Passive

8.3.1 Characterizing the "Grammatical V" that trigger the Passive

It is often said that science's first step consists of making the familiar strange, and hence in need of explanation. That is, of asking how obvious facts, at the level of observation, actually come to hold. In my view, one such obvious grammatical fact is the restricted distribution of passive participles as complements:

(8.24) Verbal passive participles occur as complements to only a few grammatical verbs.[6]

If the passive participle is just "another non-finite form," why are there not dozens or even hundreds of verbs that select it, like there are dozens or hundreds of verbs that select infinitives, participles and gerunds?

Limiting myself to the "intransitive" English passive auxiliaries *be* and *get* (in line with the generative tradition), I have proposed an answer to this question in Emonds (2000, Ch. 5). The first step in the answer consists in clarifying what is meant by "grammatical verb." After all, the English passive auxiliaries are not simply two random verbs, or even two random verbs that happen to take adjectival complements, such as say *remain* and *appear*.[7] They are rather (and also precisely) the least semantically specified English verbs that take adjectives. Confirming the role of the category A in this characterization is the fact that the passives of many Germanic and Romance languages, which closely resemble the English version, exhibit entirely adjectival agreement morphology.

Accounting for (8.24) thus requires determining the grammatical nature of "least semantically specified" verbs. One revealing property of all such verbs is that each has its own characteristic distribution with respect to other verbs in its language (and each other), i.e., they each have "unique syntactic behavior." Even outside English passive structures, where indeed they are unique, *be* and *get* are items unto themselves. *Be* is the only verb with so many suppletive forms (*are, is, am*, etc.), and the collocation *have got* has special properties as well.

Let's assume that members of some subset Σ of a language's lexicon have no "purely semantic" features, i.e. all features of such items are used somewhere in the language's syntax. Then, any two such items that are truly distinct (i.e., not in free variation) will differ by some feature that appears in some statement of syntactic well-formedness, with respect to which the two items will then behave differently. Holding one item σ constant and letting the other vary over Σ, we see that any σ lacking purely semantic features will have unique syntactic behavior.

Thus, precisely those lexical items that lack "purely semantic features" will have the syntactic property observed for grammatical verbs such as *be* and *get*. And indeed, this lack is consistent with the intuition that they are vague or not semantically specific. Such items share a wide range of other linguistic characteristics that set them apart from the open classes in the Dictionary Đ. In recognition of this clustering of properties, Emonds

(2000) groups together the subset Σ of lexical items that lack purely semantic features:

(8.25) The Syntacticon is the set Σ of lexical items that lack purely semantic features.

This term permits restating the somewhat vague (8.24) as the still puzzling (8.26):

(8.26) Verbal passive participles occur only as *complements to V in the Syntacticon* that are subcategorized for AP complements.

8.3.2 Properties of the Grammatical Lexicon

Much of Emonds (2000) is devoted to justifying and properly formulating a range of properties that distinguish items in the Syntacticon Σ from those in the Dictionary Đ, as summarized in the following table:

(8.27)		Đ=DICT	Σ=SYNT
a.	Items have purely semantic features f	YES	NO
a'.	Items have unique syntactic behavior (converse of a)	NO	YES
b.	Grammatical categories in the inventory	N,V,A,P	ALL
c.	Open classes; coining for adult speakers	YES	NO
d.	Bound morphemes have inherent stress and head compounds	YES	NO
e.	Interface with non-linguistic memory and culture	YES	NO
f.	Full suppletion inside paradigms possible	NO	YES
g.	Phonetically zero morphemes possible	NO	YES
h.	Items must conform phonologically to core vocabulary	NO	YES
i.	Items may have alternatively realized features	NO	YES
j.	Insertion possible during syntactic derivations and at PF	NO	YES

The Syntacticon is thus a mental module that has no access to a relatively open-ended class of purely semantic features, notated *f*. [footnote omitted] While the Dictionary has such access, this module is not without its own limitations. The strongest among these is that the Dictionary has only four primitive categories. That is, I claim that purely semantic features are found only in the four open classes: N, A, V and perhaps P, and that this is what allows these categories to have so many members. Every feature in every other category is used somewhere in syntax; the reason that the other "closed" syntactic categories have so few members is that the syntactic features themselves are severely limited in number.[8]

Returning now to the restriction (8.26), I wish to substantiate the claim that the auxiliaries observed in indirect passives, namely *get, have, want, need, see* and *hear*, all plausibly belong to the Syntacticon. As monosyllables they clearly conform to (8.27h), and they could hardly be said to involve non-linguistic memory or general culture (8.27e). Nor do they participate as heads in any remotely regular type of verb-final compound (8.27d).

In addition, all these auxiliaries have individual grammatical and paradigmatic idiosyncrasies (8.27a') and (8.27f) characteristic of Syntacticon membership. The syntax of *get* is unique in collocations such as *have got* and *get going*, and it is the only passive auxiliary that is both intransitive (the classical passive) and transitive (the indirect passives of this paper). *Have* has special syntax in a number of ways: it forms the English perfect; in certain uses it inverts in questions and contracts to a final consonant (in theory-internal terms, it "raises from V to I"); and it is one of a handful of English verbs whose third singular form is phonologically irregular.

While a skeptic could hardly contest the unique syntactic behavior of *have* and *get*, one might nonetheless hesitate to include *want, need, see* and *hear* among such verbs. However, the hesitation is unjustified. For example, the morpheme *need* doubles as a negative polarity modal in English, a property shared only with *dare* (which is not a passive auxiliary). Since a modal is an I rather than a V, by (8.27b) *need* is in the Syntacticon.

The contraction possibilities of *want* (i.e. *"wanna"*) and the ample literature thereon attest to its syntactic uniqueness. But perhaps a more convincing case for its Syntacticon membership, as well as for that of *see* and *hear*, is based on their Romance counterparts. Italian and Spanish translations of *want, see* and *hear* are among a small set of grammatical verbs that exhibit effects of "restructuring" (alternatively, "clause union" or "clitic climbing"). Many converging justifications for analyzing such verbs in terms of "late insertion" (8.27j) are provided in Emonds (2000, Ch. 6), thus establishing their head verbs as Syntacticon members (Cf. Ch. 6 of this volume). Because there is no reason to doubt the basic similarity of such membership across languages, it is not surprising that these three verbs turn out to be in the English Syntacticon and hence can serve as auxiliaries in indirect passives.[9] It thus seems that all six first verbs in (8.3) and (8.10) have bona fide unique syntactic behavior; that is, they are verbs whose only features are syntactic.

Summarizing, any verb with an indirect passive complement satisfies (8.26): any passive auxiliary in either type of English passive must be (i) a verb in the Syntacticon and (ii) select an AP complement. (The converse isn't implied; see note 19). All the "indirect passive auxiliaries" have a subcategorization frame +___DP^AP as expected. (8.26) thus explains why *do* is not a passive auxiliary; it doesn't take APs: **Bill did his children sad*; **You should do the walls clean(er)*.

Having established that (8.26) adequately describes both transitive (= indirect) as well as classical intransitive (= direct) verbal passives, the question we now need to answer for a full analysis of indirect passives is (8.28):

(8.28) What is the relation of the verbal passive participle to the category adjective such that it satisfies the contextual frames +___AP or +___DP^AP for Syntacticon verbs, but *not for Dictionary verbs*?

8.3.3 The lexical entries for the participial suffixes

Up to this point, we have focused on the "auxiliary" verbs found in the English indirect passive. But the question (8.28) shifts our focus to the grammatical nature, i.e., the Syntacticon entry, of the passive suffix itself. This is natural since an English passive is composed of two items, an auxiliary and a participle, so the construction requires that we understand both parts.

We can begin by treating the passive suffix *-en* as a typical "right hand head" of the word X^0 it appears in. [footnote omitted] In addition, the particularity of this suffix is that it "alternatively realizes" (8.27i) or "absorbs" some minimal or basic feature(s) Φ of a DP sister of X^0. This feature might be the D category itself or, based on a comparison with what is overt in similar constructions in Romance, the phi-features of D (i.e., gender and number). It thus appears in the configuration (8.29) by virtue of a lexical entry roughly as in (8.30):[10]

(8.29)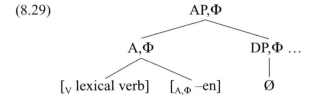

(8.30) English passive participle (tentative): -en, A, +V___, Φ

The sub-tree in (8.29) reflects the fact that the alternative realization of an object's features by the passive suffix is always accompanied (in English) by the zeroing of that object. That is, every English passive participle must be a sister of an empty DP "trace" bearing the feature(s) Φ, in indirect as well as direct passives.[11] In a more general analysis of passives (my own cited in section 8.1 and several others), this object trace is forced to be co-indexed with the participle's subject position, thereby making that position incompatible with the theta-role of a verb's deep subject – i.e. this trace is the source of the other passive properties (8.7) and (8.8). In an English indirect passive, the subject of the participle is the object of the auxiliary, whereas in a direct passive, it is the subject of the auxiliary as well.

There is a problem with the entry (8.30), however. Left as it stands, it implies that every passive participle in English is interpreted as adjectival, i.e., as ascribing a property to its subject, since this is plausibly what the category A conveys in LF. But we know that verbal passives lack exactly this property (8.16a). Emonds (2002) proposes a lexical notation for both the Dictionary and the Syntacticon whereby *parenthesizing* grammatical categories such as A ("property"), D ("reference"), V ("activity") in lexical entries *optionally voids* these categories in LF interpretations.

Thus, while a member of the syntactic category V typically conveys activity (e.g., *pester*), an optionally stative verb (*bother*) is lexically marked as follows: *bother*, (V), +___[ANIMATE], ... Similarly, a preposition such as *in* that can lack spatial or temporal import is listed as (P), in contrast to a purely locative P such as *on*: {in/ *on} *careful fashion;* {in/ *on} *sorrow,* etc. [footnote omitted]

This notation thus leads to a revision of (8.30) that permits -*en* to optionally lack a property interpretation in LF, i.e., to be interpreted as a verbal passive:

(8.31) English passive participle (final): -en, (A), +V___, Φ

We will see below that this entry, in conjunction with the theory of multi-level insertion for Syntacticon items (8.27j), will satisfactorily answer the question (8.28) and hence provide a complete analysis of both English direct and indirect passives.

This analysis and its component parts (the theory of multi-level insertion, with two principles of lexical selection and the lexical notations themselves) permit an interesting account of the grammar of the English "active participle" morpheme *-ing*. The lexical entry of this morpheme differs from (8.31) in only one particular, but its resulting grammatical behavior is quite different from *-en*.

(8.32) English active participle: -ing, (A), +V___

What differentiates the active from the passive participle is that *-ing* is not specified to carry any D feature Φ. Strong support for postulating this difference comes from the almost exact Spanish counterparts of *-en* and *-ing*: *-do* is the Spanish passive participle suffix and *-ndo* is its active participle. Exactly as reflected by the presence/ absence of Φ in (8.31)–(8.32), the passive suffix *-do* inflects for gender and number while the active suffix (8.32) *-ndo* is an invariant form. [footnote omitted]

The two adjective-forming verbal suffixes are both Syntacticon members, since neither entry has any purely semantic feature *f*; moreover, both generally conform to the principles of grammatical lexicalization specified in more detail in the next section. But in addition, it appears that active participles cannot be selected as APs simply by virtue of the category A of *-ing*; to be selected as adjectives, they must appear in lexicalized combinations such as *exciting, intriguing, moving, retiring*. This suggests that a head X^0 of a phrase is not visible for selection if it entirely lacks features:

(8.33) *Visible Right Hand Heads. An X^0 is visible for selection as head of a phrase only if it is the rightmost X^0 in the phrase having additional feature content.*

The principle (8.33) has two dramatically different correct consequences for (8.31) and (8.32). Since the passive suffix *-en* always carries the additional feature(s) Φ, *a passive participle is always selected as an AP* (or not at all), which accounts for one part of the earlier statement (8.26). In striking contrast, because *-ing* carries no inherent feature, it can be selected as an AP only if lexically associated with the content of its V stem. Otherwise, an active participle is selected rather by virtue of the V^0 stem of *-ing*; that is, a present participle is selected as *a V-headed construction*, and not as one that is A-headed.[12] Consequently, there is no restriction on the distribution of active participles comparable to (8.26) or (8.28).

8.3.4 The relation of the Syntacticon to levels of Lexical Insertion

My own and other previous works on the Syntacticon (e.g., Caink, 1998; Veselovská, 2001 and 2003; Whong-Barr, 2002) argue that its members have privileges regarding insertion during derivations that are not shared with the open class items of the Dictionary; this is indicated by property (8.27j). In particular, Dictionary items can be inserted *only* at the start of a derivation on some domain (at the beginning of a minimalist derivational "phase"), while Syntacticon items can be inserted (i.e. satisfy their contextual restrictions) throughout a derivation.

(8.34) *Lexical Accessibility. The Dictionary can be accessed on a domain only before syntactic processing. The Syntacticon, and in particular its contextual frames, can be accessed at all derivational levels.* [footnote omitted]

This difference in accessibility implies that Syntacticon items have a range of insertion options:

(8.35) a. A grammatical item α can be (part of) a Dictionary item with a semantic feature *f* and hence like them can be inserted *before* processing of the syntactic domain Δ in which it occurs.[13]
b. A grammatical item α can be inserted *during* syntactic processing of a domain Δ.
c. A grammatical item α can be inserted in Δ at PF *after* syntactic processing of a domain Δ (i.e., after Δ has been sent to the PF and LF interfaces).

Recall now the remaining question about the limited distribution of passive participles that the "tripartite insertion" theory above can hopefully answer.

282   *Minimal structures for functional categories*

(8.28)   What is the relation of the verbal passive participle to the category adjective such that it satisfies the contextual frames +___AP or +___DP^AP for Syntacticon verbs, but *not for Dictionary verbs*?

Visible Right Hand Heads (8.33) accounts for why all passive participles, verbal and adjectival, satisfy only frames calling for an AP. We have also seen that in adjectival passives the head [$_A$ -*en*] receives a standard "property" interpretation of in LF, while the specificity of verbal passives is that [$_A$ -*en*] is not interpreted. What is needed is a relation between the optional interpretation of an item's category and when it enters a derivation. The following condition provides this.

(8.36)   *Condition on Selection and Interpretation. A category X^0 can be selected* and *interpreted at an interface level only if it is associated with lexical material.*[14]

Clearly, the passive suffix (8.31) is a Syntacticon item lacking any *f*. Suppose first that -*en* is chosen as the head of a domain Δ (= AP) according to either (8.35a) – as part of a lexicalized adjectival passive such as (*mentally*) *disturbed* or *animated (film)* – or to (8.35b), during syntactic processing.[15] Its A head then arrives at the LF and PF interfaces associated with lexical material, so no matter whether the V that selects it on the next larger domain Δ' is from the Dictionary or the Syntacticon, this AP will be interpreted as an A, i.e. as a "property" or adjectival passive, and occur in essentially any position that allows an A.

But now, precisely because -*en* lacks any other interpretable features (see note 10 on the nature of Φ), it can also be inserted according to (8.35c) *after* the AP of which it is the head is sent to the LF interface. This means that as the derivation of the next larger domain Δ' starts, the head of AP is bereft of lexical material. Now by (8.36) an AP in this form cannot be selected at all – by any predicate in Δ'.

But there is one way that this empty-headed AP can be "saved," i.e., selected. *After* syntactic processing of Δ' begins (when it is "too late" for a Dictionary verb to enter Δ'), -*en* can still be inserted in the PF of the lower AP domain Δ by virtue of its Syntacticon membership (8.35c). This insertion has no effect on the LF copy of this AP, whose head A dominates no lexical material and hence is *not interpreted*.[16] In this situation then, -*en* will head an AP with the PF form of an adjectival passive but the LF interpretation of a V-headed phrase, i.e., a verbal passive. A V that is also insertable in PF, namely a Syntacticon member, can then select such an AP. This provides the answer to (8.28).

Let me rephrase this rather dense treatment, as it is the crux of my analysis. A passive participle AP has two representations prior to its being selected as a higher predicate. In cases where -*en* either associates with a V to form lexicalized adjectives with a feature *f* (8.35a), or when -*en* is inserted just prior to Spell Out (8.35b), its category A satisfies Condition (8.36) and so is interpreted as a "property" in LF, a characteristic of all adjectival passives. It is moreover selected as an AP in the next containing domain.

(8.37) a. Adjectival passives at both LF and PF (and also verbal passives at PF):

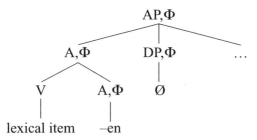

But when -*en* is inserted later in PF, its category A remains empty at LF, so a participle has no interpretation as a property and forms rather a verbal passive.

(8.37) b. Verbal passives at LF:

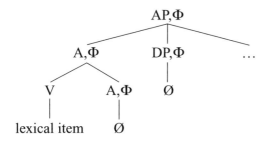

Here Syntacticon verbs play a crucial role in the selection of verbal passives. The Condition on Selection (8.36) requires that in order to satisfy +___AP or +___DP^AP, an A head must dominate lexical material. Because the -*en* of a verbal passive is not present under A before PF, only verbs with access to these contextual frames *throughout derivations* can accept such an AP. That is, only a V in the Syntacticon can select a verbal passive, because only such Vs can select their AP in PF. In contrast, Dictionary items can only access LF representations, not PF representations, and so they *cannot* select a verbal passive complement.

This analysis of passive morphology and its characteristic "DP gap" in terms of the properties of the Syntacticon and two plausible quite general principles, (8.33) and (8.36), thus succeeds in accounting for the mysterious restricted distribution of both indirect and direct verbal passives (8.26). It similarly answers the sharpened question (8.28) based on this property.

8.4 Countering possible objections

8.4.1 Objection: grouping Japanese and English Indirect Passives is misleading.

There nonetheless remains a difference between the indirect passives of English and Japanese. The analysis of the English passive in section 8.3 claims that its passive suffix [$_A$ -*en*] forces some post-verbal DP object position to be empty.[17] *This DP must then be a trace*, either of the auxiliary verb's surface subject as in the classical direct passive or of its object as in the indirect passive.

In Japanese indirect passives (section 8.2.1) on the other hand, the suffix -*(r)are* is itself a V with no role in any Alternative Realization or absorption that forces movement.[18] As mentioned earlier, the crucial characteristic of a Japanese passive is rather the presence of an "extra DP position," the surface subject of this -*(r)are*, which can be filled either by movement from several different positions or by an additional lexical DP, which is assigned an extra adversative or "malefactive" theta-role. Consequently, Japanese passives can perfectly well contain overt objects with accusative case and sometimes have no DP gap at all (Kubo, 1992).

One might therefore feel that using the same term for indirect passives in Japanese (no movement) and English (movement) is somehow conflating apples and oranges. However, this reaction is unjustified. What is different between the two languages is the syntactic character of the passive suffix itself, an alternatively realizing (or case-absorbing) adjective in English and an "extra argument" inducing verb in Japanese, more akin in structure and effect to a causative suffix. But what is the same in the two variants of indirect passives is *the extra theta-role position*. The English indirect passive auxiliaries, *have, get, want, need, see* and *hear*, have exactly the same property as *-(r)are*: their surface subject provides an extra theta-role (of agent or experiencer) missing in the active counterparts.

Therefore, all constructions called passive in this paper uniformly exhibit the three properties of passives (8.6)–(8.8) mentioned at the outset. The long-standing and vague pre-generative idea (still widespread) that Japanese and English share direct passives but differ with respect to indirect passives is topsy-turvy. Rather, their direct passives employ different morphosyntactic mechanisms, while the "extra arguments" in the surface subjects of their indirect passives are entirely analogous.

8.4.2 Objection: the structures examined aren't really Passives.

There seem to be two different movement processes in English that extract post-verbal noun phrases, often termed "NP Movement" (or "A Movement") and "WH Movement" (or "A-bar Movement"). These names date from Chomsky's (1977) analysis of their differences, whereby the landing sites in the first type (8.38a) involve only "argument (=A) positions," while the second type (8.38b) includes at least an intermediate landing site in a "non-argument (=A-bar) position," often claimed to be SPEC(CP).

(8.38) a. [A manager]$_i$ should be spoken to t$_i$ about the service.
 b. We found [a manager]$_i$ [$_{CP}$ t$_i$ [$_{IP}$ to speak to t$_i$ about the service]].

The customary names are a bit odd, since both types of movement chains can be c-commanded by co-indexed *arguments* as in (8.38a-b); both types can equally well affect NPs and WH-phrases – there is no WH in (8.38b) – and both types can also move a PP: *In the other room seems to be a better place; In how many rooms are there TVs?* A more transparent nomenclature would be passive-like movement for (8.38a) and WH-like movement for (8.38b) [footnote omitted].

Whatever their names, the two types of movement indeed differ, and their differences confirm the claim that indirect passives are truly passives.

(i) First, English stranded Ps, italic in (8.39), must be adjacent to a V only in passive-like movement (8.39a-b) but not in WH-like movement (8.39c):

(8.39) a. The students were spoken *to* about that topic.
New problems should be thought *about* with colleagues.
b. *That topic was spoken to the students *about*.
*Colleagues should be thought about new problems *with*.
*Some violins are often played difficult sonatas *on*.
c. We found a topic to speak to the students *about*.
Top researchers have colleagues to think about problems *with*.
We need some violins to play difficult sonatas *on*.

This diagnostic confirms that indirect passives are indeed passive-like:

(8.40) a. We {saw/ wanted} the students spoken to about that topic.
Top researchers have problems thought about with colleagues.
b. *We {saw/ wanted} that topic spoken to the students about.
*Top researchers have colleagues thought about problems with.
*We {heard/ needed} some violins played difficult sonatas on.

(ii) Secondly, there is a weak cross-linguistic ungrammaticality associated with WH-like movement of indirect objects "promoted" to direct object position, well documented for both English (8.41a) and many languages with "applicative" constructions (reviewed in Emonds and Ostler, 2003). No such problem exists for passive-like movement (8.41b).

(8.41) a. ??Who$_i$ did they send t_i a radio last week?
??We're looking for new customers$_i$ to hand t_i leaflets next week.
??They$_i$ won't be easy to send t_i radios.
b. John$_i$ {was/ got} sent t_i a radio last week.
New customers$_i$ won't be handed t_i leaflets.

Again, the indirect passives of this study are indeed passive-like:

(8.42) a. We {had/ got} John sent a radio last week.
b. The manager {saw/ wanted} new customers handed leaflets.

(iii) Finally, certain "bare-NP adverbials" can perfectly well undergo WH-like movement (8.43a), but are totally impervious to passive-like movement (8.43b).

English indirect passives 287

(8.43) a. We have found [some Saturday]$_i$ to meet (with you) t$_i$ for coffee.
[Which place]$_i$ did Mary live the longest t$_i$?
b. *Some Saturday should be met (with us) for coffee.
*That place got lived the longest (by Mary).

As by now expected, English indirect passives pattern like other passives:

(8.44) a. *They {want/ need} some Saturday met (with you) for coffee.
b. *We {got/ saw} that place lived the longest (by Mary).

In the light of the consistent results from these three tests, there can remain no doubt that what are here called indirect passives fully qualify as "passive-like," i.e., as instances of "A movement" or "NP movement." They do *not* have the WH-like properties widely ascribed to null operator constructions.

8.4.3 Objection: The structures examined are Passives in Small Clauses.

A central conclusion of this study is that the English indirect passives are *not* simply more complex constructions that contain direct passives of a familiar sort. One seeking to avoid this conclusion might claim that indirect passives as in (8.3) are built around direct passive small clause ("SC") complements, with the following internal bracketing:

(8.3) She was {having/ getting} [$_{SC}$ her illness treated (by my doctor)].
We are {having/ getting} [$_{SC}$ a back garden laid out (by the owner)].

Beyond an observation that such Small Clauses fit into no independently justified scheme of grammatical categories, several additional empirical considerations militate against this approach, some already mentioned.

(i) Under more sober approaches to tree construction, a test for constituency is possible movement (Ross, 1967). The postulated small clauses fail this classical diagnostic for constituency; they never move:

(8.45) *What she had was [$_{SC}$ her illness treated (by my doctor)].
*What the press wanted was [$_{SC}$ Baghdad slowly approached].
*What no one could see was [$_{SC}$ it handed over by some commander].

Under the approach in this paper, since the sequences labeled SC above are not constituents, they are correctly predicted *not* to undergo movement.

(ii) Second, in the analysis of this study, independently determined subcategorizations of the Syntacticon verbs such as *get, have, want, need, be, go, do* automatically predict whether or not indirect or direct passives occur as their complements. A grammatical verb with the frame +___AP (*be, get*) will form a direct passive, while ones subcategorized as +___DP^AP will give rise to an indirect passive.[19] That is, we can predict which verbs are passive auxiliaries. But with small clauses in the way we cannot. An extra construct like an SC and a range of unconstrained lexical features to select it are ad hoc and entirely superfluous.

(iii) Third, examples like (8.5) are inconsistent with merging the higher verb *after* putative small clauses (here in italics) are independently constructed, because stative *have* does not accept a progressive form.

(8.5)   She was having *her tonsillitis treated on her.*
        We are having *a back garden laid out on us.*

The proper descriptive generalization is that activity verbs, whether active or passive, accept the progressive *in the very clause being syntactically processed;* consequently the passive combinations *have ... treated* and *have ... laid* in (8.5) must be together in a single clause or "derivational phase."

(iv) Finally, under the analysis of this study the English suffix *-en* expresses some feature(s) of an object DP (8.30); in several analogous Romance and Slavic constructions this is reflected in overt agreement. When *-en* is used in a (personal) passive, these features of the participle are also those of the surface subject DP. Now a curious, very pervasive, and previously unremarked pattern in indirect passives shows that this latter co-indexing (of *-en* with a surface subject) *cannot be mediated by any intermediate -en, trace or PRO.* As the ungrammatical sequences in (8.46) show, the co-indexed pairs must apparently be *directly* related.[20]

(8.46) The receipts$_i$ should be {seen$_i$ / put$_i$ / *seen put} in the right drawers.
        More samples$_i$ will be {needed$_i$ / handed$_i$ to them/ *needed handed to them}.
        They had a good time provided for them by the main office.
        A good time$_i$ was {had$_i$ / provided$_i$ / *had provided} by the office.

Before noon, they got the leaflets distributed even in the suburbs.
Before noon, the leaflets$_i$ were {gotten$_i$ / distributed$_i$ / *gotten distributed} even in the suburbs.
We heard them$_i$ (get) interrogated$_i$. They$_i$ got interrogated$_i$.
*We heard them$_i$ gotten interrogated$_i$.

Under the "small clause + direct passive" conception of indirect passives, this generalization is practically inexpressible and in any case entirely obscured. For suppose that the only passives are direct passives inside small clauses. Evidently, *need* can take such a passive small clause:

(8.47)   We will need [$_{SC}$ more samples$_i$ handed t$_i$ to them].

Nothing now prevents straightforward successive cyclic passivization of *need* in (8.47), which incorrectly yields exactly the kind of excluded structure in (8.46):

(8.48)   *More samples$_i$ will be needed [$_{SC}$ t$_i$ handed t$_i$ to them].

The only way the small clause hypothesis can avoid systematically generating this excluded paradigm (8.46) is to elaborate an already ad hoc analysis: "A verb with a passive in its SC complement cannot be passivized." As always, the appeal of a convoluted and exception-ridden small clause approach, and its status as almost a default analysis of choice among those who otherwise claim that language systems are simple, eludes me.

8.5 Conclusion: English Indirect Passives confirm Late Insertion.

Standing back somewhat from the specific properties and analysis of the indirect passives, an obvious question poses itself: How has a close syntactic relative of the intensively studied English (direct) passive escaped labeling and scrutiny for essentially a half century, during a period when English grammar has been studied and dissected from every possible angle? Somewhat unreflectively, grammarians including the present author have no doubt felt that the indirect passive somehow combines direct passives (formed with *be* and *get*) with some unexplained absence (or "deletion") of *be* in a range of unstudied and unformalized contexts, and at bottom involves no revealing or puzzling special properties.

Whenever constructions come to the attention of grammarians, it is because they initially at least seem to have such properties. In the present case, a focus on the differences between grammatical and open class morphemes has revealed such a property of indirect passives, namely (8.26).

(8.26)   Verbal passive participles occur only as *complements to V in the Syntacticon* that are subcategorized for AP complements.

The number of such transitive verbs (six) has previously been too many to attract attention, especially since the grammatical properties of indirect passives are not so salient as are those of say, Romance causatives. See again note 9.

However, once it is appreciated that grammatical verbs share many properties (8.27) that set them off from open class items, it behooves us to assign them to a special mental component of language, here called the Syntacticon. One central grammatical property of Syntacticon members is then the possibility of being inserted (= satisfying contextual frame conditions) *late in a syntactic derivation*. In the light of this hypothesis, comments by L. Veselovská on using different insertion levels to account for a Czech construction partly similar to English indirect passives refocused my attention on this study's topic.

Section 8.3.4 here, which contains the heart of this study's analysis, explains what is meant by "late insertion" and "PF insertion" during a derivational phase, and how these operations automatically account for the at first mysterious limitation (8.26) on both direct and indirect verbal passives, which distinguishes them from both adjectival passives and active participles.

Notes

* This essay reproduces my contribution to the volume *Facts and Explanations in Linguistic Theory: A Festschrift for Masaru Kajita*. Chiba et al., 2003. The only changes here are a revision of the introductory paragraphs and omission of several footnotes. (As a result, the remaining notes don't carry the same numbers as they did in the original.)

    No linguist I know of better exemplifies a simultaneous insistence on careful empirical investigation and interesting theoretical consequences than Masaru Kajita. His rigorous appreciation and critical evaluations of generative syntax have been an inspiration for almost thirty years.

1. Kimball (1973) argues that *get* is systematically the inchoative of both *have* and *be*. While this semantic claim is defensible in most alternations, it seems that passive pairs such as (8.1) and (8.3) are even more closely related, since they exhibit no truth value differences whatsoever between *be/have* and *get*.
2. For example, Keenan's (1985) broad overview of passive formation and its properties in different languages claims that passives are operations on verb phrases rather than on sentences (247) for which a characteristic morphological marking is central (251). Current theoretical approaches to passives in terms of "de-thematized" subjects stem from Roberts (1987).
3. Kubo (1992) observes that one honorific use of the suffix *-(r)are* actually does permit an active clause subject to remain in the same position in a passive.
4. Perhaps some speakers accept similar phrases as "small clause subjects" of a predicate, but my judgment excludes the examples in (8.12).
5. Section 8.4.3 enumerates the difficulties of analyzing DP-VP sequences as in (8.11) as "small clauses" which contain their DP subject.
6. Another interesting but as far as I know unremarked property of passives is that they do not occur as "bare" complements of N or A:
   (i) *[$_{DP}$ John's deep need praised by his friends] is annoying.
   *She finally expressed [$_{DP}$ a want taken to an expensive restaurant].
   (ii) *Mary seems [$_{AP}$ happy vaccinated for free].
   *John felt [$_{AP}$ guilty arrested for fraud].
   The examples (ii) should not be confused with sentences in which *vaccinated for free* and *arrested for fraud* are adjuncts outside AP. In (ii), WH-fronting of putative APs fails: **How happy vaccinated for free did Mary seem?*
   The restriction in (i)–(ii) follows if passives are analyzed as APs, as in this study. For in general, N and A do not take AP complements:
   (iii) *[$_{DP}$ John's deep need talkative in company] is annoying.
   *She finally expressed [$_{DP}$ a want richer than her best friends].
   (iv) *Mary seems [$_{AP}$ happy able to buy tickets].
   *John felt [$_{AP}$ guilty too poor to help].
   These paradigms undermine attempts to analyze passive participles without a central role for the category A, i.e. as simply a sub-type of non-finite verb.
7. No previous *transformation-based* treatment of passives, to my knowledge, accounts for or even asks why passive auxiliaries happen to be V that also take adjectival complements. Thus, in previous transformational analyses, the English passive auxiliaries could as well be *innovate* and *devastate* as *be* and *get*.
8. With regard to "purely semantic features" (8.27a), we don't know prior to investigation how many features are used in syntax and how many are not (i.e., exactly which ones are *purely* semantic). This uncertainty is natural in science; for example generative phonology didn't "wait" until it knew exactly the list of distinctive features before undertaking research (counter to exhortations from leading structuralists and phoneticians). Nor did modern chemistry "wait" until

it encountered all the elements before it further developed valence theory based on a preliminary periodic table.

Nonetheless, we expect that limits on syntactic features will keep the membership of a Syntacticon category such as V not much greater than that of non-lexical categories such as MODAL or D. Moreover, a Syntacticon item cannot be more semantically specific than a Dictionary item. Indeed, the semantics of at least *be, have, get* and *want* are about as general as one can imagine, and *need* and *see* are certainly less specific than verbs such as *miss, long for* and *observe, inspect*.

9. The most common and least semantically specific perception verbs of Romance, e.g., French *voir* 'see' and *entendre* 'hear' but not its other perception verbs, share a range of properties with the "causative" verbs *faire* 'make' and *laisser* 'let', which more semantically specific verbs with causal meanings do *not* share. This grouping indicates that the meanings of "causative" or "perception" verbs are irrelevant for describing grammar; what counts is their lack of semantically specific features.

    The verb *voir* has another syntactic idiosyncrasy indicative of Syntacticon membership. Its special imperative forms combining locative enclitics with pronoun proclitics (*le voiçi, te voilà*) are not found elsewhere in French grammar.

10. Syntactic features, such as the gender and number of a DP, are interpretable in their base positions where they are "canonically realized." "Alternative realization" (8.27i) consists in spelling out such features on some adjacent (higher or lower) head where they *cannot* be interpreted (Emonds, 2000: Ch. 4). Since neither D (= "reference") nor the gender and number of D can be interpreted on an A, the presence of Φ with A in (8.30) necessarily implies that this Φ alternatively realizes features of a D-projection adjacent to A, i.e., a DP sister (object) of the passive participle.

11. The passive participle morpheme in other Germanic languages sometimes appears with overt DP objects (e.g., Norwegian) and sometimes with intransitive verbs (e.g, Norwegian, German), in constructions termed impersonal (verbal) passives. In neither case is there any "DP gap." For treatment of these variants, see Åfarli (1989) and Emonds (2000, Ch. 5).

12. Thus, intransitive temporal aspect verbs (*begin, continue, finish*, the progressive *be*, etc.) and transitive perception verbs (*watch, notice, taste*, etc.) are lexically specified for V-headed complements (active participles). Emonds (1991a), which is Chapter 3 in this volume, presents an integrated analysis of English constructions based on *-ing*.

13. Examples range from verbs like *come* 'experience orgasm', *come at* 'attack', *come to* 'recover consciousness', *do in* 'ruin', *do away with* 'eliminate', *get over* 'recover' and *get up* 'stand up or sit up' to all kinds of lexicalized formations in derivational morphology such as *nothingness, seemly, overdo, outing, iffy, outcome, income, haves and have nots, so-so, ins and outs, (an) upper/downer*, etc.

The morphemes in these examples are all from the Syntacticon.

It is not surprising that the Dictionary cannibalizes Syntacticon items (from a different mental module) as raw material to construct ever more entries with purely semantic and encyclopedic features. The word-forming capacity voraciously uses the meaningless phonemes of phonology, acronyms, borrowings from other languages, and basically anything it can lay its synapses on.

14. The standard way to be "associated with lexical material" is to dominate a lexical item. Two special situations can arise, but neither is relevant to the logic of this essay. First, lexical material can be a *stipulated null morpheme* – it need not be phonological. Second, an empty X^0 can be associated with lexical material, not by virtue of dominating it, but by being anaphorically related to such material elsewhere in a tree, e.g., gapping, null pronominals, etc.

15. The latter choice gives rise to adjectival passives that are not lexical, but rather syntactically generated. Such formations typically do not accept "degree word" modification: *The window seemed {(*very/*too) painted/ (*so/*less) sold}*.

16. The lack of interpretation is permitted by the parentheses around A in the lexical entry of *-en*. The categorial notation (X^0) in lexical entries that lack other interpretable features, such as (8.31), is thus tantamount to stipulating optional PF insertion of the entry. This use of the parentheses succinctly expresses the "Polyfunctional Morphology" found cross-linguistically as part of many passive systems, for example in Schoorlemmer's (1995) study of Russian and Veselovská and Karlik's (2003) study of Czech.

17. In this study, *-en* is a PF spell out of the φ-features of a caseless DP A morpheme that thus "alternatively realizes" features by spelling them out in a non-base position typically *forces* their base position to be empty (i.e. unless the morpheme is marked otherwise in the Syntacticon). That is, at the level that *-en* is inserted, a V with a suffix *-en* requires a caseless sister [$_{DP}$ Ø] But caseless empty DPs in object position can only be traces of moved DPs.

18. Analyses of the English passive in later government and binding (e.g., Jaeggli, 1986; Roberts, 1987) claimed that the passive *-en* necessarily "absorbs accusative case" from some DP. Absorption was similar to Alternative Realization, but was not integrated into a formal theory; it remained a rather hazy concept.

19. The lone apparent exception to this generalization underscores the closeness of the fit. The verb *make* is in all probability also a Syntacticon item, and it indeed accepts the frame ___DP^AP: *Bill made his children sad; You should make the walls clean(er)*. Yet it does not allow indirect passives:
    (i) *Bill made his children sent to school.
    　　*You should make the walls cleaned with the new product.
    Only *make* hinders stating (8.26) as a two-way implication.

20. The pattern in (8.46) is plausibly related to the inability of adjectives to directly take adjectival complements; cf. note 6 for detailed discussion.

Part III
Landing sites of phrasal movements

Chapter 9: "A theory of phrase structure based on Extended Projections." Reprinted from Section 1.3 of *Lexicon and Grammar*, Mouton de Gruyter, 2000a, 12–21

This short introductory chapter sets the stage as the structural framework for the several hypotheses and conclusions of the following two chapters.

Chapter 10: "The lower operator position with parasitic gaps." Reprinted from *Features and Interfaces in Romance*. J. Herschensohn, E. Mallén and K. Zagona (eds.), 85–106. John Benjamins, 2001. (permission obtained)

This chapter first shows that fully grammatical parasitic gaps occur only in *non-finite* clauses. It then shows that the SPEC positions of DP in gerunds and of IP in infinitives (see previous chapter) are the actual locations for the "lower" operator whose existence was established in the mid-eighties, and that this lower operation is actually deleted in LF. This latter step re-establishes the generalizations of Chomsky's earlier elegant treatment of variables in *Concepts and Consequences*. The chapter also crucially uses the results of Chapter 3 on selection of non-finite clauses, comparing English with Spanish participles.

Chapter 11: "Unspecified categories as the key to root constructions,*"* Reprinted from *Peripheries: Syntactic Edges and their Effects*. D. Adger, C. de Cat and G. Tsoulas (eds.), 75–120. Kluwer Academic Publishers, 2004. (permission obtained)

This chapter shows how "label-less projections" above root clauses accommodate the many properties of root constructions better than, e.g., the labeled discourse projections in Rizzi (1997). Next a property of Chomsky's original formulation of the Tensed S Constraint is shown to account for a wide range of restrictions on movement. The strongly contrasting properties of German and English root clauses are analyzed and attributed to subtle differences in their Syntacticon entries for the unmarked complementizers.

Chapter 9
A theory of phrase structure based on Extended Projections*

9.1 Lexical Projections

Around 1986, generative grammar reached a seeming consensus that a restrictive and universal set of syntactic categories, called the "bar notation," was empirically adequate and cross-linguistically appropriate. Under this conception, any language contains at most the four lexical heads X, a very few functional heads such as D (associated with NP) and I (associated with VP), non-maximal or maximal projections of these six or so heads (respectively X' and XP), and specifier (SPEC) daughter nodes of XP. As argued in Speas (1990, section 2.2), non-maximal X' differ from maximal projections XP only in that the latter do not head some larger XP; i.e., adjoining α to a phrase renders this phrase non-maximal. My own research has argued that an additional functional head C for introducing clauses ("complementizer") reduces to a class of grammatical P with sentence complements (Emonds, 1985, Ch. 7); this revision of the bar notation is adopted throughout this work.

Such a conception of syntax suggests strong restrictions on the category inventories available in Universal Grammar. Consequently, in that work's Introduction, I formulated two principles which are still tenable if, as just outlined, we are justified in postulating only a very small set of syntactic categories.

(9.1) *Categorial Uniformity. The categories defined in terms of the bar notation, X^j and SPECIFIER(X), do not differ from language to language, but their subcategories which are realized in each language's syntax may vary.*

(9.2) *Hierarchical Universality. The range of hierarchical combinations of syntactic categories does not vary from language to language at the level of deep structure.*

Although many analysts in intervening years have reanalyzed the syntactic features of the six or so lexical and functional heads as a greatly expanded set of functional heads and projections, I remain unconvinced of the fruitfulness of this line of research.[1] Rather, the earlier, more parsimonious theory retains its appeal and promise. I thus utilize a conservative category system, elaborated along the following lines:

(9.4) Lexical category heads X together with their complements and adjunct phrases constitute units of syntax, called *maximal projections* XP of these X.

(9.5) Finite verbs V and *all* their arguments are syntactic units, called clauses IPs.

(9.6) Analogously, nouns N including derived nominals and all their linguistic (as opposed to pragmatic) arguments are syntactic units, called DPs.

Formally specifying how these heads combine with complements has been the subject matter of Part I, where each chapter refined the mechanics of subcategorization. For a discussion of adjuncts, i.e. phrases which are both a sister and a daughter of the same type of phrase, see Emonds (2000, Ch. 7). Provided that CPs are special cases of PPs, one may impose a general syntactic restriction: *Adjuncts are always PPs or APs.*[2] APs are sometimes "adjectival" (they agree with a modified NP) and sometimes "adverbial" (they lack such agreement).

This chapter focuses not on the internal structure of XP, but rather on how XP containing all of X's complements and adjuncts combine into larger phrases with functional heads, namely IP and DP. The divisions in (9.4)–(9.6) suggest that certain "external arguments" of V and N in these "functional projections" are generated outside VP and NP.

9.2 The Subject as a special phrase: I and IP

Within finite clauses, one argument NP/DP of the verb, a "subject phrase," is external to the VP. Indirect evidence for its special status is of many sorts: (i) the role of the subject – predicate pairing in Aristotle's logic and its wide and long-standing acceptance; (ii) its central role in Cartesian *grammaire générale* and the resulting "traditional grammar"; and (iii) the still valid descriptive value of Chomsky's (1957) original phrase structure rule, S → NP – VP. Many of the thirty odd properties examined in Keenan (1976) that "cluster" around subjecthood are prototypically exhibited by subjects of finite clauses.

Several direct, empirical syntactic arguments for the VP-external nature of the subject are provided by processes such as e.g. VP-fronting and VP-ellipsis in English and Japanese, English tag questions, widespread subject-verb agreement in languages lacking other agreement patterns, etc. Notably, these arguments all concern or work best with the subject phrase of *finite* clauses.

By the same arguments and others, the finite elements I are just as external to VP as the subject phrase is. This can be seen easily with English modals, which are prototypical instances of the finiteness category. Like subject phrases, modals don't front or ellipt with VPs and they appear in tag questions. They furthermore contract with the subject and with the negative (in the form *n't*) in ways that Vs do not.

(9.7) *Deep finite clauses are of the form IP = DP – I – VP, where I is a grammatical "finiteness" head paired with V.*

For uniformity with the rest of the bar notation, we can assume that this DP is in SPEC(IP) and that the combination I + VP constitutes an I' (Chomsky, 1986).[3]

The structure in (9.7) differentiates a special argument called the subject from other "internal arguments" or complements, which is then defined by (9.8).

(9.8) *Definition of Subject (tentative): The subject (or external argument) of a head V is a DP/NP which c-commands VP within the minimal IP containing V.*

In most cases, Keenan's (1976) special properties of a subject can be related to its VP-external status. In any case, some variant of definition (9.8) is needed in any theory of grammatical relations which can at least differentiate subjects and objects.

9.3 The DP Hypothesis and generalizing the definition of Subject

Chomsky (1970), Jackendoff (1977), George and Kornfilt (1981) and Abney (1987) all argue that the internal structure of noun phrases parallels that of sentences (IP), in that many classes of head nouns have a "subject", analogous to the subject of verbs, realized as a possessive noun phrase within a traditionally conceived larger noun phrase. Abney further proposes, following Brame (1984), that the noun phrases of the earlier generative literature contain two heads, where one is a grammatical "reference or quantification" head, say D (= Determiner), paired with N much as I is paired with V. This is Abney's DP-hypothesis. Under this conception, the earlier noun phrases have the form (9.9) analogous to finite clauses as in (9.7). This structure then defines an external argument for N, which we call SPEC(DP).[4]

(9.9) *Deep nominal phrases are of the form DP = (DP) – D – NP, where D is a grammatical "reference or quantification" head paired with N.*

The parentheses around the possessive DP in (9.9), in contrast to an IP subject's obligatory status in (9.7), reflect the fact that nouns, including derived nominalizations of verbs, often lack a linguistic subject within the larger DP (Wasow and Roeper, 1972). That is, their understood subject can only be pragmatically determined.

One argument for this is that a syntactically represented understood subject, a so-called "arbitrary PRO," must have animate reference at least in the positions SPEC(IP) and SPEC(DP), as shown in (9.10–9.11). In contrast, the understood subjects of derived nominals are often inanimate (9.12).

(9.10) Inferred PRO must be animate; the following clausal subjects cannot refer to inanimate events such as volcanic eruptions:
[PRO To explode like that] does a lot of harm.
[PRO Exploding like that] does a lot of harm.

(9.11) A V which cannot have an animate subject is incompatible with a PRO subject:
*Few people like to unexpectedly occur.
*Few people like unexpectedly occurring.

(9.12) Noun-headed nominalizations, which have no PRO, may have a pragmatic subject that is either ±ANIMATE or no subject at all:
An explosion like that does a lot of harm.
Few people like unexpected occurrences.

Serious questions remain as to exactly which morpheme classes realize the functional head D paired with N (= Determiner). Often without argument, the best candidates are assumed to be the definite demonstratives and articles. Nonetheless, Jackendoff's (1977, Ch. 5) detailed empirical work on English noun phrase specifiers isolates two distinct closed class or functional category positions which can occur in sequence, a definiteness/ quantifier position and a numeral/ quantifier position. Both are exemplified in the sequences *those many books, any three vertices, the little nitrogen remaining*.

On the face of it, both classes of morphemes might qualify for D, or there may be two rather than one functional projections matched with N. For example, Szabolcsi (1987) argues on the basis of extractions in Hungarian that a definiteness category D shares properties of C, while an additional functional head between D and N, analogous to I, assigns case to subjects. In other work in principle compatible with this analysis, Cardinaletti and Giusti (1991) and Giusti (1991) argue that both the definiteness and numeral positions should be functional heads.

On the other hand, these approaches seem to exclude a priori a possibility I retain, that closed classes of morphemes might be listed as SPEC(DP) or SPEC(NP). Lobeck (1995) explores parallelisms between English VP and NP ellipsis, both presumably licensed only if a functional head is present outside the ellipted phrase. Clearly, Jackendoff's second numeral/ quantifier position may play this role and thus qualify as D, while his first position (for definite elements and certain quantifier morphemes) might conceivably be SPEC(DP).[5] In this work I will not try to definitively establish criteria for membership in D, nor determine whether two independent functional heads can appear above nouns in a DP.

Leaving aside the exact nature of D, let us proceed to formalize further parallels between NP and VP, besides the fact that each is the complement of a functional head. For these we need definitions.

(9.13) *a. N and the projections of N and D are "N-projections"; V and the projections of V and I are "V-projections."*
b. DPs and IPs are "extended projections" of N and V respectively.

(9.14) *Cyclic domains. IP and DP are "cyclic domains" of V and N respectively.*

It is a natural step to extend the notion of "subject of V" in (9.8) so as to encompass "subject of N", including of nominalizations:

(9.15) *Generalized Subjects: The subject or external argument of a head X is the lowest N-projection which c-commands a phrasal projection of X within its minimal cyclic domain.*[6]

The definition (9.15) correctly requires that a *linguistic* subject of N (including nominalizations) must be inside DP. It further predicts that if a head noun has no such DP-internal subject, it can only have an unprojected, pragmatic subject (Wasow and Roeper, 1972). This generalized definition of subject plays an important and recurring role throughout this study.

The construction known as "subject small clauses" confirms the appropriateness of (9.15). Kubo (1993, 103–107) provides evidence that such predications have both the internal structure and external distribution not of clauses but of DPs. In her structures (9.16), the brackets indicate the smallest cyclic DP domains containing italicized heads X of predicate phrases; the bold N or N' are the nominal projections which are the subjects of these X.

(9.16) [**Young workers** *angry* over their pay] looks revolutionary.
[**Children** *in* dangerous parks] is a scene used to convince women to quit jobs.
[The **flags of many lands** *flying* over the plaza] is a good scene for a postcard.
[**Paris** *and* its perfumes] fascinates American women.
[**Sake** *and* tofu (together)] makes me sick.

By interpreting the predicate category as covering A, P, non-finite V and even co-ordinate conjunctions, Kubo shows that a definition similar to (9.15) correctly characterizes the (bold) nominal projections in (9.16) as the subjects of the italicized predicates. Her analysis makes no appeal to any clause-like structure not independently motivated as DP-internal.

9.4 The EPP: explaining the "strong D feature on Tense"

Let us now return to the discrepancy between (9.7) and (9.9): subjects of IPs are obligatory while those of DPs are optional. To maintain that, uniformly, only heads of projections and extended projections are obligatory and that argument positions are optional, we can revise (9.7) to IP = (DP) – I – VP, parallel to the formula for DP (9.9). The obligatory linguistic presence of the subject of a V under IP is then factored out as Chomsky's (1981) Extended Projection Principle, which can be expressed as (9.17).

(9.17) *Extended Projection Principle. Every head verb present in Logical Form must have a structural subject phrase to which a semantic role may be assigned.*[7]

In many other constructions, the EPP plays an explanatory role beyond allowing the IP projection (i) to parallel that of DP and (ii) to conform to the generalization that only heads are structurally obligatory.

The EPP and the formulation of Generalized Subjects (9.15) guarantee that the SPEC(IP) will always contain a structural DP subject for the highest V in IP. While this seems correct for English and many languages whose finite I obligatorily agrees with its subject, there is evidence that SPEC(IP) in a non-agreeing language such as Japanese can be absent, i.e. Japanese seems to directly reflect the optionality in the formula IP = (DP) – I – VP.

Sells (1996) contrasts two types of raising and obligatory control complements of Japanese verbs, both of which are uniformly IPs with past – non-past tense alternations. He shows how one type permits an overt (reflexive) subject DP presumably in SPEC(IP), while the other entirely lacks such a DP position. This latter type of IP, for which he constructs it seems incontrovertible arguments, Sells calls "sub-clausal" and observes that their understood subject appears in either subject or object position in the main clause. His arguments thus establish that Japanese robustly instantiates a subjectless (head-final) structure [VP – I]. In a somewhat more general and theory-based treatment, Kuroda (1992, 321) reaches the same conclusion: SPEC(IP) "can be left vacant" in Japanese but not English.

These arguments, taken at face value, suggest that a Generalized Subject α of a V need not always be present within the smallest finite IP; i.e., α can be the lowest DP which c-commands VP within some domain *larger* (in Japanese) than its minimal IP.[8] We get this consequence if we add a condition to (9.14) that a cyclic domain of V must additionally contain *a potential subject for XP,* i.e. a DP c-commanding V^k. Under this condition, SPEC(IP) can, like SPEC(DP), be entirely absent in certain instances. Nonetheless, cyclic domains for a VP do not under this conception extend upward in the tree without limit; the lowest IP containing a potential DP controller of VP will then be the latter's cyclic domain, and the EPP guarantees that there must be such a DP.

This now raises the question: if the EPP doesn't force every SPEC(IP) to contain DP, why must it do so in English and other agreeing languages? To account for this, I extract a part of a general hypothesis of Kuroda (1992, 325) that "English is a forced Agreement language." While he derives several contrasting properties of English and Japanese from the respective presence and absence of his generalized notion of agreement, I focus here on perhaps the morphologically most salient difference between the two languages:

(9.18) *Number Filter. Overt functional heads (I and D) must be specified for number (±PLURAL) at PF in certain languages (e.g., English but not Japanese).*

Now, the cognitive syntactic feature PLURAL is canonically associated with D – at least for this discussion D should be the canonical locus for realizing PLURAL as in (1.5) of Chapter 1. (9.18) then specifies the fairly uncontroversial property that the English but not the Japanese DP must express the ±PLUR distinction; for related discussion of (optional) Japanese noun classifiers, see Kubo (1996).

But equally, PLURAL is *not* a canonical feature of I. Number can only surface on I and hence satisfy (9.18) when the latter *agrees* with some phrasal projection in its SPEC which *is* specified for ±PLUR, i.e. SPEC(IP) must be a DP in a "Number Filter" language. We thus derive not only the obligatory presence of a phrase in SPEC(IP) from a more general property of English but also the fact that its SPEC(IP) must be DP rather than just any XP.[9] In light of (9.18), the specifiers of both IP and DP can remain optional at the level of UG, as can all non-heads in the bar notation.

In conclusion, the combinations of the basic syntactic categories discussed in Chapter 1 are the classic bar notation XP projections of the four lexical heads N, V, A and P, and the extended projections given by the formula (9.19). Strictly speaking, these latter expansions are not rules, but simply definitions of the extended projections of N and V.

(9.19) *Functional Projections. FP = (DP) – F – XP; when F is I, then X is V and when F is D, then X is N.*[10]

The subject positions of FP can be referred to as SPEC(IP) and SPEC(DP). The left to right order of the elements in these projections is related to general word order principles. Beyond projections of these six heads, I do not envision greatly expanding the inventory of possible phrases.

9.5 Transformational derivations

The descriptive and explanatory successes of transformational generative grammar have been based on a model which assembles choices from a lexicon, puts them together in trees (or phrase markers) in terms of a theory of phrase structure, and then subjects these underlying trees to a sequence of Chomskyan transformational operations which maps them into some sort of "well-formed surface structures" in which, possibly among other elements, overt morphemes appear in the order pronounced. Abstracting away from actual phonological processes (e.g. assimilations, epentheses, deletions, aspirations, etc.), we can, along with many syntacticians, still refer to the results of these transformational derivations as "Phonological Form" or "PF".

Chomsky (1976) and Chomsky and Lasnik (1977), building on a decade of "interpretivist semantics" on the relation of syntax to a range of generalizations about meaning, codified the notion that the basic locus of the interface of syntactic structure with the use and understanding of language was "late" in a transformational derivation, i.e. subsequent to most or all of the transformations that had been scrutinized up to that time. The transformationally derived syntactic structures which speakers use to interpret and understand language are widely called Logical Form or "LF", following Chomsky (1976).

A number of often rather abstract debates have surrounded the relation between LF and PF. The most usual positions are that a transformational derivation of PF "branches" to LF (or vice-versa, depending on one's point of view), and that subsequent to this branching, a number of invisible or "covert" transformational operations further rearrange syntactic structure before it reaches the LF interface with understanding and use. Many minimalist models postulate even more covert syntax than is observed in the overt part of derivations. At the other extreme, the "linear model" of van Riemsdijk and Williams (1981) and van Riemsdijk (1982) simply defines LF as a certain intermediate point in the derivation of PF; this model does not countenance covert movements.

However these debates are eventually settled, cyclic domains (9.14) at the branch point (also called Spell Out) can be called s-structures, without claiming or denying that they exhibit interesting sets of properties. In current competing derivational models (i.e. those which transformationally map combinations of lexical choices to PF), the derivational structures at the branch point, whether close or far from either LF or PF in terms of operations, are agreed to contain various types of phonologically empty categories (traces, empty pronouns, empty discourse anaphors, certain null morphs or allomorphs), as well as indices (or their equivalents) which link these empty categories (and other co-referring categories) to antecedents of various sorts. That is, current derivational conceptions of s-structures are much more than structuralist-style trees, whose only function is to impose structure and classification on sequences of overt morphemes.

Throughout this work, I adhere to such a derivational model, in which transformations map sets of lexical choices combined in phrase structures into s-structures with empty categories and co-indexing and subsequently into LF and PF; hence I frequently employ the acronyms PF and LF. A transformational operation which precedes s-structure is said to occur "in syntax," while one which applies subsequent to s-structure in deriving PF is said to take place "on the way to PF" or "late" or even, somewhat misleadingly, "at PF."[11]

Notes

* This brief introduction to Part III reprints section 1.3 of Emonds (2000a). The analyses of subsequent chapters here crucially use the landing sites provided by this chapter's theory of functional category projections.
1. Chomsky (1995, section 4.10) seems less enthusiastic about such analyses, e.g. about separate projections for agreement features. My skepticism about a greatly expanded set of functional categories does not preclude the possibility that the set widely recognized in the mid-eighties is too small.
2. Finite adverbial clauses are invariably introduced by complementizers, and in turn, as mentioned above, CPs can be shown to be PPs. "Bare NP adverbials" as well as adjunct purpose clause infinitivals are argued to be PPs with empty heads in Emonds (1987). Present participles, which might be thought of as adjunct VPs or reduced IPs, are argued to have the structural form of APs is Emonds (1991a); Emonds (2000a, Ch. 5) extends this idea to passive participles.

3. CPs and PPs can appear to be in subject position in English finite clauses. However, investigation of embedded contexts reveals these apparent non-DP subjects to be a root phenomenon akin to topicalization (See Emonds, 1976, Ch. 4 for CPs and Emonds, 1985, Ch. 7 for PPs). Moreover, Higgins (1973) shows that these topicalized CPs have their source *only* in DP positions: *That Mary would be late {*it didn't seem/ few believed (*it) / we thought (*it) obvious}*.
4. The advent of the DP hypothesis has given rise to especially interesting work on Semitic languages focusing on the "construct state" of DPs which modify Ns: Borer (1984, 1989), Ritter (1988), Fassi-Fehri (1993), and Siloni (1997), among others.
5. Under this view (to which I am not committed), the ellipsis in *Your wine but not Sam's was tasty* would require a null functional head D. Such null heads might then be licensed by the possessive morpheme -*'s* as an "alternative realization" of D on the SPEC(DP) sister of D', as in Emonds (2000a, section 4.3.2).
6. Generalized Subjects permits subjects of X to be within maximal projections of X but does not require them to be. It is thus neutral with respect to the issue of the "VP-internal subject hypothesis" (Zagona, 1982) and in fact allows for the possibility that in some constructions a subject is outside VP and in others within it.
7. Impersonal verbs with so-called "theta-bar" subjects (like *seem* and French *falloir* 'be necessary') do not actually assign such roles in LF, but they still require a DP subject position.

    The EPP has come to be known in the Minimalist Program as the "strong D feature on Tense," i.e. the Tense projection (here IP) in many languages must have a DP in its Specifier position at Spell Out. As far as I can tell, this is simply stipulated and is moreover significantly less general than (9.17). For example, (9.17) will crucially explain why the lower lexical verbs in both verbal passives and Romance causatives (Emonds, 2000a, Chs. 5–6) must have (possibly understood) structural subjects, which are located outside SPEC(IP).
8. Neither Kuroda's nor Sells' framework can accept this conclusion because of commitments to other hypotheses (VP-internal subjects and argument structures respectively).
9. If the XP in SPEC(IP) need not be DP in certain "V second" languages such as Icelandic and Yiddish, then number ageement on their I must be ensured differently than in English. This obviously holds independently of (9.18).

    It is tempting to say that a null and caseless DP in SPEC(IP), though sufficiently specified for number for ensuring compliance with the Number Filter (9.18), is not a visible source at PF for any concrete morphemes which realize agreement on I. From this would follow the correct result that a null caseless subject in English implies a null I. (The converse of course doesn't hold.)
10. In my view, A and P do not have extended projections, at least in the sense that these extended projections *contain DP subjects of A and P.* In English, no

movement of an AP or a PP which may happen to be adjacent to its subject, as in *We consider Bill stupid* or *We found John in the library* ever includes that subject:
   (i) *What we considered was Bill stupid.
        *Bill stupid though she considered, she married him anyway.
   (ii) *It was John in the library that we found.
        *Whose father in the library did they find?
        Cf. How many feet behind the house was it placed?
I don't exclude the possibility that full APs and PPs include functional projections, but such projections, unlike those of N and V, don't contain subjects of A and P. My use of the term "extended projection" covers only functional projections which include subjects.

11. Since I am unconvinced that morphemes are actually reordered between Spell Out and LF, my operations "on the way to LF" or "in LF" refer, unless explicit mention is made of movement, to either deletions or to copyings.

Chapter 10
The lower operator position with parasitic gaps*

This study presupposes some familiarity with parasitic gaps ('PG'), as presented for example in Chomsky (1982, section 4) or Engdahl (1983). More recent comprehensive overviews are Culicover (2001) and Postal (1994). I limit discussion in this study to English PG. We can begin with the descriptive generalization (10.1), i.e., Chomsky's (56), for which that author credits Taraldsen (1981).

(10.1) *No C-command Condition. A trace of the operator binding a PG cannot C-command the PG.*

The brackets in the following examples demonstrate how structures conform to (10.1). The operators are in bold, the traces are represented as *t* and the PG as *e*.

(10.2) a. **Who** did he give [a picture of *t*] [to *e*]?
      b. I prefer hosts **who** [letters to *e*] don't [make *t* sarcastic].
      c. **Who** did the professor strike [friends of *t*] as [unfair to *e*]?
      d. **Which candidate** did Bill [dismiss *t*] [without interviewing *e*]?
      e. **Which one** did she [criticize *t*] [right after introducing *e*]?
      f. ?Here is the author **who** John [sent a manuscript to *t*] [in order to impress *e*].
      g. ?**Which guest** did Bill [invite *t*] [before recalling that Sue hated *e*]?

I will be mainly concerned here with PGs which are not themselves permissible traces, such as those in adverbial adjuncts as in (10.2d-g).

(10.3) *Which candidate did Bill [dismiss the issues] [without interviewing *t*]?
      *Which student did she [criticize the supervisor] [right after introducing *t*]?
      *Here is the author John [got a haircut] [in order to impress *t*].
      *Which guest did Bill [go out] after recalling that Sue [hated *t*]?

Throughout, I treat what Postal (1994) calls "true P-gaps", i.e. those licensed by some type of leftward movement, and not what he shows are "pseudo-P-gaps", those licensed by rightward movement.

Chomsky (1982, 45) proposes that the necessary No C-command Condition between an A-bar bound trace t and a co-referential parasitic gap e is due to the very definition of an LF variable.[1] That is, all well-formed LF variables are subject to (10.4):

(10.4) *A locally A-bar bound empty XP in a theta position is a well-formed LF variable.*

I interpret (10.4) as follows: an empty XP in a theta (argument) position is a well-formed LF variable only if it has a closest binder, which determines its range, in an A-bar (non-argument) position.[2] It then becomes unnecessary to use Principle C (Chomsky, 1981) to account for Strong Crossover (10.5) by somewhat dubiously baptizing LF variables as "referring expressions." (10.5) follows rather from (10.4).

(10.5) Strong Crossover. An empty XP variable in a theta position cannot have a local binder in an argument position.[3]

According to (10.4), both the traces and the PGs in (10.2) are claimed to be LF variables bound by the WH antecedents of the traces. If an intervening trace additionally c-commands a putative variable as in (10.6), the antecedent of the trace fails to *locally* bind the PG and this violates (10.4).

(10.6) *Who did he describe t to (a friend of) e?
 *I like discussion hosts who t insist that you respond to e.
 *Which candidate did Bill persuade t to ask Hillary to help e?
 *Who did Bill criticize t for recalling that Sue had betrayed e?
 *Which city did John prefer t to the residents of e?
 *Who did the professor strike t as unfair to e?

(10.4) requires that the bold LF operator in the grammatical examples of (10.2) be the *local* binder of XP=e.[4] If the closest binder of e is rather the trace, then (10.4) fails. (10.4) thus entails the No C-command Condition (10.1).

10.1 Subjacency effects on parasitic gaps

As observed in Kayne (1983), Contreras (1984), Stowell (1985) and Chomsky (1986), parasitic gaps exhibit subjacency effects induced by islands, as in (10.7):

(10.7) a. *Which guest did Bill criticize *t* while recalling [$_{DP}$ the fact that Sue supported *e*]?
b. *Which one did Bill encourage *t* without saying [$_{CP}$ where he would publicly support *e*]?
c. *What student did she criticize *t* right after [$_{DP}$ introducing *e* to a professor] was suggested?

Thus, *at least some* parasitic gaps must be additionally bound in syntax at s-structure to a lower operator O_i in the clause containing the parasitic gap.[5] In these cases, *e* is an s-structure trace of O_i.

(10.8) a. Which one did Bill dismiss *t* without [O_i interviewing *e*]?
b. ?Which guest did Bill criticize *t* while recalling [O_i that Sue had supported *e*]?
c. Which one did she criticize *t* right after [O_i introducing *e*]?

This lower operator also explains why PGs apparently violate the Condition on Extraction Domains (cf. section 10.3), since in fact a lower operator *inside* the adverbial clause binds the PGs. No movement can occur out of this type of domain.

Two questions must now be posed about this lower operator with PGs:

(10.9) What can be the location of the lower operators O_i?

Moreover, if we want the general definition of a variable (10.4) to continue to describe the relation interpreted in LF between the higher bold operators in (10.2) and the parasitic gaps *e,* then the s-structure lower operators O_i must be deleted in LF.

(10.10) How do the lower operators O_i come to be deleted in LF?

For if these O_i are *not* deleted in LF, then parasitic gaps as in (10.8) are in reality not parasitic and the definition (10.4) lacks generality and hence interest. We can refer to this lower operator as a "parasitic operator."

312 *Landing Sites of Phrasal Movements*

10.2 The location of the parasitic operator O_i

It is often too quickly concluded that parasitic gaps can occur freely in various types of adverbial adjunct clauses. This is far from being the case, and the limitations on where they can occur provide important clues as to the location of the parasitic operator. Since we are focusing here on PGs which are not permissible traces, I in fact take the presence of PGs to be *crucially licensed* by the possibility of the lower null operator O_i. Then, I attribute the lack of PGs in various constructions to the lack of this O_i. Emonds (1985, Ch. 2) notes the following four properties of PGs:

10.2.1 No operator O_i in finite clauses

Contrary to commentary about all PG clauses being marginal, the real contrast in English is this: simple participial PG clauses (10.11) are fine while simple finite ones (10.12) are not.[6]

(10.11) a. I liked the painting that the expert scrutinized *t* before *describing e to the owner.*
b. Which books did he make a list of *t* while *putting e away?*
c. Which students did she criticize *t* after *introducing e to the professor?*

(10.12) a. *I liked the painting that the expert scrutinized *t* before *Mary described e to the owner.*
b. *Which books should I make a list of *t* while *we are putting e away?*
c. *Which students did she criticize *t* after *the boss had introduced e to the professor?*

Not only are finite temporal clauses incompatible with PGs, so also are other finite adjunct clauses:

(10.13) a. *Which books did so many people take out *t* that *Sue had to rebind e?*
b. *I didn't meet the people John invited *t* in order that *I might speak to e about a job.*
c. *How many tools did you bring *t* in case *the remodelers need e?*

10.2.2 No operator O_i in infinitives with overt subjects

The contrast in (10.11)–(10.12) can't simply be attributed to non-finiteness, since PGs are also unacceptable in infinitival clauses with overt subjects:

(10.14) Who do we have to take *t* to a jazz club in order (*for you) to impress *e*?
  The computer they bought *t* in order (*for their kids) to take *e* on their trip was faulty.

Bordelois (1985) notes a similar restriction for Spanish. Her paradigm and (10.14) show, contra Culicover (2001: 55), that PGs in both languages require an empty subject.

10.2.3 No operataor O_i in bare adverbial participles

Nor can we attribute the well-formedness in (10.2) and (10.11) to *-ing* forms. It has gone unnoticed that PGs are not good in adverbial participles lacking conjunctions, italicized in (10.15).

(10.15) *I disliked the one that she scrutinized *t describing e to the owner.*
  *What dishes should I dry *t putting e away*?
  *Which students can we describe *t introducing e to you*?

10.2.4 No operator O_i in absolute constructions

Nor has the literature mentioned that PGs are excluded in the italicized absolute constructions (10.16) introduced by *with*:

(10.16) a. *The papers I can't locate *t* with *the staff putting e away so soon* are important.
  b. *Which supplies don't you trust *t* with *Bill getting e so cheap*?

These four puzzles suggest that exactly the sequence: *overt P + non-finite V* plays a curious role in allowing PGs with parasitic operators O_i. This general factor has not been previously recognized, and will be the basis of the analysis to be given here.

10.3 Puzzle: the lower operator O_i is not in SPEC(CP)

PGs are structurally relatively far from the (possibly overt) operator which binds them in LF, farther than what is ordinarily allowed between a moved element and its trace. Ordinarily, we think of such long distance relationships in syntax as being mediated by elements in SPEC(CP), long taken to be the "escape hatch" for syntactic movement. However, the adverbial constructions introduced by overt P + non-finite V, in particular by the sequence P + V + *ing* which so favors parasitic gaps, otherwise exhibit no COMP phenomena whatsoever. That is, strong islands are the very constructions that best tolerate parasitic gaps:

(i) The constructions P + non-finite V show no evidence of long distance movement, as seen in (10.3). These restrictions on movement motivate Huang's (1982) Condition on Extraction Domains or 'CED'. This alone suggests there is no SPEC(CP) escape hatch for A-bar movement in the construction.

(ii) Nor do these adjunct constructions show any evidence of housing null operators (other than the PG lower operator itself) which might themselves play a role in LF.

(10.17) *Bill had to find a wall$_i$ O_i before leaning the boards against t_i.
*We must justify more receipts$_i$ O_i in order to list t_i for the tax investigation.

In contrast, so-called "lower purpose clauses," as seen in (10.18), are well motivated as *complements*: only certain verb classes select them, they are incompatible with *do so*, and cannot be preposed with comma intonation (for paradigms, see Emonds 2000a, Ch. 9). Unlike the adjunct constructions which favor parasitic gaps, these lower purpose clauses *do* exhibit null operator dependencies characteristic of SPEC(CP):

(10.18) Bill had to find a wall$_i$ O_i to lean the boards against t_i.
We must send more receipts$_i$ O_i to list t_i for the tax investigation.

(iii) The PG-licensing construction "P + non-finite V" can contain no overt WH phrases, which is expected if it contains no SPEC(CP).

(10.19) *Bill hired the candidate in order who to please in his home state.
*She might criticize us after whatever tasks doing for low pay.

These three restrictions all follow if there is no SPEC(CP) in PG constructions to house a lower operator. The absence of SPEC(CP) and C in these constructions can in fact be explained by assimilating C more generally to a special case of P, as argued on other grounds in Emonds (1985, Ch. 7). According to that analysis, lexical or "semantically specified" P with IP complements, i.e. the type that favor the PG construction, compete with so-called complementizers for a single P slot in $[_{PP} P - IP]$. The traditional complementizers C are those P which are inserted "late" (in PF) and are, crucially, the only P which license SPECs with a potential for A-bar binding. Hence there can be no SPEC(CP) to house an A-bar binding operator O_i in a clause introduced by a lexical P.

10.4 The lower operator is in SPEC(IP) or SPEC(DP)

We thus need to find some other landing site, presumably a SPEC position, to house the lower operator in the parasitic gap construction. The contrast in (10.14) above is suggestive:

(10.14) Who do we have to take *t* to a jazz club in order (*for you) to impress *e*?
The computer they bought *t* in order (*for their kids) to take *e* on their trip was faulty.

Superficially, it looks like the lower operator alternates with and hence is possibly housed in SPEC(IP) in these "higher (adjunct) purpose clauses." In fact, the same paradigm can be reproduced with participles. Certain subordinating conjunctions P do not impose obligatory control on their DP-gerund (V + *ing*) complements (10.20), yet *with parasitic gaps, these same gerunds tolerate no overt subject* (10.21):[7]

(10.20) She scrutinized the paintings without the owner('s) knowing it.
Instead of John putting away the dishes, let's leave now.

(10.21) Which paintings could she scrutinize without (*the owner) bringing to the gallery?
These are the dishes you should take instead of (*John) putting away.

Hence, a first, descriptive version of my hypothesis for the lower operator in parasitic gaps:

(10.22) *Tentative Lower Operator Hypothesis: A non-case-marked SPEC(IP) can house a lower or parasitic operator for PGs.*

(10.22) immediately explains why parasitic gaps are not well-formed in finite clauses (10.12)–(10.13) or infinitival clauses with overt subjects (10.14). Similarly, parasitic gaps don't occur in absolute constructions (10.16) because a subject in an absolute construction is always overt.

Let us now turn to the temporal adverbial clauses P + V + *ing*; their P heads impose obligatory control, so that it is not possible to construct patterns like (10–20)–(10.21), in which PGs alternate with overt subjects. English clauses introduced and headed by V + *ing* are generally of two types:

(A) DP gerunds occur freely in structural DP positions, including embedded ones. They move, coordinate, are modified by adjectives, receive case, etc. like DPs.[8] And independently of these properties, DP gerunds headed by V + *ing* have structurally present subject SPEC positions, overt or null (Wasow & Roeper, 1972).

However in five other positions, English V + *ing* clauses have participial, non-DP status according to Emonds (1985, Ch. 2), which contrasts their distribution with that of DP gerunds. Thus:

(B) Non-DP participles occur freely in structural AP positions. Moreover, as argued in the cited study, such participial XPs headed by V + *ing* completely lack internal subject (SPEC) positions.

The five positions for non-DP, participial V + *ing* clauses in English are as follows:[9]

(10.23)   a. in subject-modifying adjuncts outside V-bar with no introductory P,
  b. in absolute constructions,
  c. as complements of certain aspectual verbs,
  d. as secondary predications after certain perception verbs,
  e. as reduced relative clauses or in scene titles such as *Man washing his son in a river.*

We can't easily tell which of these two types the adverbial sequence of interest here, namely "overt P + V + *ing*," belongs to, because the CED independently stops us from testing for DP status by movement:

(10.24) *It's {the dinner party/ introducing me} that you should reveal our secret after.
*It was {a fair interview/ reviewing her book} that Bill dismissed her without.

But comparison of the forms taken on by a wide range of non-finite clauses of English and Spanish indicates rather clearly that the sequence P + V must involve a gerund (DP) rather than a participle (a non-DP):

(10.25) In translating all five uses of English participles in (10.23), Spanish uses the traditionally named *gerundio* (V + *ndo* + ...), which has no DP properties (Emonds 1985, Ch. 2).

(10.26) On the other hand, a wide variety of English DP gerunds are translated as Spanish infinitives, e.g., as subjects, objects of V, objects of P, etc; see especially Plann (1981).

In crucial contrast to (10.25), English subordinating P + V + *ing* translate as Spanish infinitives, not as *gerundios*:

(10.27) *Cuantos poemas debería publicar antes de {escribir/ *escribiendo} un libro?*
'How many poems should he publish before writing a book?'
Esta mujer no dice nada después de {describirte/ *describiéndote} el cuadro.
'That woman is saying nothing after{to describe/describing} the painting to you.'

Putting together (10.25)–(10.26) suggests that English non-finite V + *ing* complements of overt Ps are actually gerunds. That is, English V + *ing* clauses containing well-formed parasitic gaps are DPs. If they were not, we would expect that they translate into Spanish as *gerundios*.

Why have parasitic gap clauses in V + *ing* not been recognized as gerunds, i.e. as DPs? Partly because of the lack of discriminating CED paradigms

(10.24) and partly because temporal subordinating P force obligatory control on the possessive DP position.

(10.28) She scrutinized the painting before (*the owner's) selling it.
The teacher criticized the students while (*my) lecturing them.

Because of this obligatory control, non-finite temporal adverbial clauses appear to lack internal subject positions, which would be characteristic of non-DP participles as in (B) above. But some gerund complements of V, e.g., in (10.29), which are uncontroversially DPs because they passivize and freely appear as the focus of cleft sentences, can also exhibit obligatory control. Therefore the pattern in (10.28) actually says nothing about whether the sequence P + V + *ing* is a DP (A) or not (B).

(10.29) She avoided (*the owner's) selling the painting.
Sue tried (*my) lecturing the new students.

I thus conclude that adverbial temporal V + *ing* clauses are gerund DPs which, as in (A), have (always empty) structural subject positions SPEC(DP).When these clauses contain PGs, this SPEC position is apparently also available for housing the lower operator. Thus the Lower Operator Hypothesis (10.22) can be extended from infinitive clauses to all non-finite clauses:

(10.30) *Lower Operator Hypothesis: A non-case-marked SPEC(IP) in infinitives or SPEC(DP) with V + ing can house a lower or parasitic (A-bar) operator for PGs.*

This generalization of (10.22) accords well with studies which claim a parallel structure for IP and DP, as reviewed for example in Emonds (2000a, Ch. 1). The more general (10.30) also explains paradigm (10.15) in section 2 above, which (10.22) alone doesn't cover: Since these bare adverbial participles are not DPs, but rather one of the five cases of V + *ing* clauses generated in AP positions (10.23), it follows from (B) that these participles lack the SPEC position which (10.30) requires.

10.5 Why parasitic gaps must be DPs

It is well-known that a SPEC(DP) or a SPEC(IP) position must be a DP. If this DP is an operator O_i binding a parasitic gap, (10.30) immediately explains an earlier observation of Emonds (1985) and Lasnik & Stowell (1991): PGs are limited to DPs and cannot be PPs or APs.

(10.31) a. *This is a neighborhood in which you should look around *t* before residing [$_{PP}$ *e*].
This is a neighborhood which you should look over *t* before residing in [$_{DP}$ *e*].
b. *For whom did he ever work *t* without praying [$_{PP}$ *e*]?
Who would he ever work with *t* without praying for [$_{DP}$ *e*]?
c. *How sick did John say he felt *t* before getting [$_{AP}$ *e*]?
d. *How clever does she look *t* while acting [$_{AP}$ *e*]?

Lasnik & Stowell's proposal is that PGs are limited to DPs because empty operators O_i only bind names and names are DPs; but this stipulation is incorrect for many O_i beyond PGs:

(10.32) In the hall would be a good place O_i to put it [$_{PP}$ e_i].
Less abrasive would be an appropriate way O_i to act [$_{AP}$ e_i].

The account based on (10.30) has now successfully explained the DP status of PGs, the paradigms (10.11)–(10.16) of section 10.2, the paradigms (i)–(iii) of section 10.3, the subjacency effects on PGs and the No C-command Condition (10.1). No competing account of PGs makes so many predictions, which here follow without any auxiliary stipulations beyond the Lower Operator Hypothesis (10.30) itself and the remaining question (10.10).

(10.10) How do the lower operators O_i come to be deleted in LF?

Even if (10.30) remains puzzling, it seems so strongly supported that theory should be made to accommodate it and not vice-versa.
But still, the SPEC(IP) position in infinitives and the possessive position in DPs are typically argument (subject) rather than A-bar positions. Thus, (10.30) and (10.10) reduce to the two intriguing research problems in (10.33), best conceived as statements still to be derived:

(10.33) a. In the structure [$_{\text{IP/DP}}$ (DP′) – I/D – XP], the SPEC position DP′ may have binding properties of an A-bar (non-argument) position, provided it is deleted in LF.[10]
b. In this same structure, if DP′ is an A-bar position, the subject cannot be in this SPEC position but must be elsewhere.

10.6 The sequence of T-model operations on a cyclic domain

This section deals with (10.33a). This statement becomes less puzzling if we conceptualize Chomsky & Lasnik's (1977) T-model of derivations as applying not to deep structures but rather to a series of derivational "phases," such as the cyclic domains IP, DP and perhaps CP. In terms of such "bottom up" processing, as first proposed I believe in E. Klima's 1967 lectures, the following T-model operations apply in sequence on a given cyclic domain YP.[11]

(10.34) *First,* heads of YP are selected in terms of subcategorized complements of Y (Merge).

(10.35) *Second,* phrases can Move to SPEC(YP) positions, including to SPEC(IP) and SPEC(DP).

This second step becomes A-movement (to an argument position) if and only if case is directly assigned to the SPEC position. I assume case assignment is always optional, resulting in Case Filter violations in argument chains if not applied. If case is not assigned, movement to SPEC is A-bar movement, as required in (10.33a).

Thus, in a DP domain, when a DP moves to a subject position SPEC(DP) by the strict structure-preservation of Emonds (1976), SPEC can be an A-bar position just in case that D or some external case assigner fails to assign case. Similarly on an IP domain: if I or some external case assigner fails to assign case, SPEC(IP) can also be an A-bar position. That is, in the absence of case assignment, these SPEC positions can house null (caseless) operators which are A-bar binders.

However, these A-bar SPEC positions are not automatically *interpretable* operators in LF, due to (10.36).

(10.36) Specific interpretive rules for LF must license any configurations which are not licensed by Merge. For example, *English operators are licensed in LF only in SPEC(CP)*.

Consequently A-bar DPs in SPEC(DP) or SPEC(IP), i.e., the lower operators with parasitic gaps, must eventually delete prior to LF.

Returning now to the bottom up sequencing of operations on cyclic domains:

(10.37) *Third,* Spell Out derives Phonological Form on the YP domain.

(10.38) *Fourth*, Logical Form on the YP domain is derived after Spell Out, in part by (10.36) and then by deleting uninterpretable empty elements under appropriate identity of indexing.

When the fourth step (10.38) processes a domain YP whose SPEC contains an empty (parasitic) operator, nothing happens as far as preparing this operator for LF. However, on the *next largest* domain XP, which always exists in the case of parasitic operators, this now "lower" operator O_i can be deleted if it is co-indexed with (i.e., locally bound by) some ZP_i in XP.[12] There are limitations on permissible positions for ZP, but generally any ZP not in a position where it receives its theta role, in particular one which is a WH-phrase in SPEC(CP), seems to be a candidate for properly binding O_i in SPEC(YP).

In fact, this deletion in the higher XP domain essentially conforms to the system of deleting "intermediate traces" in COMP proposed by Lasnik & Saito (1984). Although their proposal that the derivation of LF deletes uninterpretable elements is generally thought of as applying to a chain of traces (excluding the lowest), there is no reason not to consider it rather as applying to a chain of operators (save the highest).[13]

In particular, a lower operator binding parasitic gaps fulfills the same range of conditions as does an "intermediate operator" in successive cyclic chains of WH-movement:

(10.39) a. Both are empty categories in the highest SPEC position of a cyclic domain α.
b. Both are locally bound by an operator not in a theta position in the smallest cyclic domain above α.
c. Neither is in a case-marked position.

d. Both are in a position where they typically alternate (and cannot co-occur) with a phonologically realized phrase.
e. Both are freely generated only when they bind arguments, not when they bind adjuncts.

This last condition (10.39e) is in fact an important empirical property in the Lasnik & Saito system. The cyclic deletion of intermediate operators is de facto optional; empty operators may be retained if needed in LF, as these authors indeed claim they are for interpreting lower adjuncts in successive cyclic A-bar chains. However, we will see below a separate reason based on proper LF representations which *forces* parasitic operators to delete. Consequently, adjuncts bound by these operators in PG constructions are simply ill-formed in the absence of the needed lower operator. This empirical prediction is correct:[14]

(10.40) *Which room did the artist move out of *t* before painting her portraits in *e*?
?This is the car that Joan wants to sell *t* instead of driving to work in *e*.
?Who are they preparing to see now *t* in order to visit museums with *e* next week?

A crucial final step in deriving LF (10.38) consists in taking into account the effects of LF deletion of intermediate operators in SPEC positions. The most plausible notion of "pruning," i.e. the loss of phrasal nodes resulting from steps in a derivation, is a proposal by S.-Y. Kuroda in early unpublished work to the effect that, in current terms, a YP disappears when its head has no marked features (phonological or syntactic) and its SPEC is deleted.

(10.41) *Fifth*, Pruning (= deletion) of Y^k occurs at any point in a derivation at which a YP whose head is completely unspecified comes to lose its SPEC.

Strictly speaking, this final step is not part of a derivation but simply part of the definition of projection.

As we have just seen, an intermediate, non-case-marked operator in the SPEC(YP) of a functional category such as I or D can delete at LF, if bound by a similar operator in the SPEC of the next highest cyclic domain. By (10.41), when such an I or D is neither specified for features nor assigns

Case, it then constitutes an uninterpretable empty element, and hence all projections of Y delete in deriving the final form of LF.

Thus in constructing LF, a clause with a typical PG looks like (10.42). In particular, the bold nodes delete/ prune in LF and are absent in the final interface representation (ø represents empty categories). For exposition, some intermediate projections are omitted, and the representation of gerunds as VPs in an NP position is simplified.[15]

Due to this LF deletion, a final LF representation for PG constructions lacks a lower operator, the one whose presence in syntax is justified by the subjacency effects seen in (10.3) and (10.8), but one which must be absent in LF in order for the definition of variable (10.4) to remain a valid description of the relation between a parasitic gap and the higher operator which binds it.

Therefore, the No C-command Condition (10.1) again holds in full generality: the two empty non-bold DP_k in (10.42) are not in a c-command relation, and both are locally bound by the same LF operator *which candidate,* exactly as in *Concepts and Consequences* (Chomsky 1982).

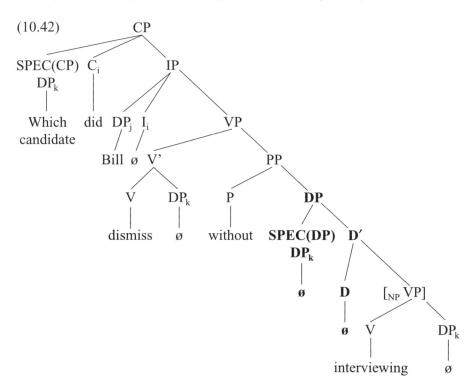

10.7 A generalized definition of subject

We must return now to the final issue to be resolved in solving the puzzle of the lower operator in parasitic gaps. While we have adequate and non ad hoc mechanisms for first generating and then disposing of the operator DP in (10.33a), we still lack a full account of the second issue outstanding from section 10.5:

(10.33) b. In a structure [$_{\text{IP/DP}}$ (DP') – I/D – XP], if DP' is an A-bar position, the subject cannot be in this SPEC but must be elsewhere.

First, I maintain the view that *every interpreted V which heads a phrasal projection must have a subject*. That is, the Extended Projection Principle (EPP) of Chomsky (1981) is more general and explanatory than its successor in the minimalist program (see Emonds 2000, Chs. 1, 6, 10). It is furthermore clear that clauses with PGs as in (10.2d-g), (10.21), etc. always have an unambiguously determined subject, namely the subject of the main clause they appear in.

In discussions just cited and in Ch. 6 of this volume, I argue that generative studies have been laboring for decades under a misconception, namely that structural subjects, e.g. those which satisfy the EPP, must somehow be specified as such early in or even at the beginning of derivations. Using a variety of constructions (passives and Romance causatives with postposed agent phrases, Romance restructuring constructions, auxiliaries), I try to show that superior accounts emerge if we identify subjects of Vs *only in the final LF interface representations* such as (10.42), i.e., in which *the bolded nodes are absent*. Consequently, in a really broad range of constructions, DP subjects are not sisters of predicates but are rather the lowest DPs which c-command them, as determined by the following definition:[16]

(10.43) *Generalized definition of Subject. DP_j is the subject of X^0 in LF if and only if it is the lowest DP c-commanding X^1 such that DP_j and X^1 are in all the same DP and IP.*[17]

Given the absence of the bold nodes in the LF of (10.42), this general definition of subject successfully relates the verb in an adverbial clause with the higher subject DP_j.

Since every head V interpreted in LF must have its own subject position in LF (by the Extended Projection Principle), without deletion of DP' in

(10.33a), the structure cannot survive. For in this case DP′ would be the subject of the lower verb, by (10.43). Then either this DP′ would not have the index k, in which case movement of the object to the subject position would not take place and a lower DP_k would be unlicensed,[18] or DP′ would have the index k and the empty object of the lower V would be co-indexed with its own subject. This latter situation can in fact happen (only) with "unaccusative verbs" (which thereby satisfy the EPP), but such DP′ still satisfy the conditions (10.39) for deletion at LF.[19]

The generalized definition of Subject (10.43) thus forces deletion of a parasitic operator and the consequent Pruning (10.41) of the DP (or IP) over a non-finite adverbial clause containing a PG. This is the factor that explains the marginality of PGs which are themselves in adjuncts, as exemplified in (10.40). The specification of subjecthood (10.43), in particular its "late" ordering in a derivation after steps (10.34)–(10.38) and (10.41), successfully locates the "missing subject" in non-finite PG clauses as required by (10.33b), and thus completes the present analysis.

10.8 Extending the analysis to long distance movement

The above analysis of parasitic gaps is promising for extension to other troublesome grammatical puzzles. Most likely, we must consider A-bar positions as elsewhere positions in the following sense: any SPEC position unneeded for the Projection Principle or the Extended Projection Principle (i.e., for assigning arguments) can revert to A-bar status.

Limiting the discussion to DPs but lifting the limitation to PGs, we can observe the same processes in arguments as are at work in adjuncts.

(10.44) *Lower Operator Hypothesis (extended): A non-case-marked SPEC(IP) or SPEC(DP) can house a lower or parasitic (A-bar) operator.*

Thus, the phenomena treated in the main part of this work extend beyond PGs. Hypothesis (10.44) suggests that English DP gerunds which are arguments should behave like non-finite clauses with PGs. From this emerges a new descriptive generalization:

(10.45) The possessive position in English DP gerunds can act like a deletable intermediate operator.

When SPEC(DP) is a subject (with its own theta role), i.e., disjoint in reference from a higher subject, it must survive at LF. This makes long distance movement through SPEC(DP) impossible.

(10.46) *Which prisoners$_i$ did they criticize PRO$_j$ executing t_i for petty crimes?
*What$_i$ did John enjoy Mary's showing off t_i at the party?
*The jobs$_i$ we talked about Bill's having lost t_i never paid well.

However, if the generalized definition of Subject (10.43) can associate a V head of a gerund object in LF with a subject outside the gerund, the SPEC position of this gerund can indeed serve as a deletable intermediate trace, exactly as in PG constructions:

(10.47) Which prisoners$_i$ did they avoid executing t_i for petty crimes?
What$_i$ did John enjoy showing off t_i at the party?
He asked which letters$_i$ I was worried about having lost t_i.

That is, the long distance movement that is blocked by unlike subjects in (10.46) is suddenly perfect when the subjects are the same in (10.47).[20] The mechanisms at work in the contrast (10.46)–(10.47) appear to be exactly those of sections 10.6 and 10.7.

Notes

* This essay is a contribution to the Festschrift for Heles Contreras, *Features and Interfaces in Romance*, edited by J. Herschensohn, E. Mallén and K. Zagona and published with John Benjamins (2001). I have made only editorial changes.
    I would like to thank Heles Contreras, Noam Chomsky and Miori Kubo for discussing various aspects of earlier versions of this material with me – as linguistics goes, in the rather remote past. I also appreciate the comments of an anonymous reviewer.
1. Lack of c-command by a trace is not always sufficient to permit a potential parasitic gap. The following two structurally similar examples contrast with respect to permitting a PG.
    (i) *Who did the professor speak with t about (friends of) e?
    (ii) Which neighborhood did the councilman talk about t with the residents of e?
2. It might be thought that the bolded A-bar binders for the variables e in the following examples are not local, because of the intervening *who*.

(i) This is the type of book **which** [laymen [who try to read *e*]] usually can't understand *t*. (Stowell 1985:315)
(ii) John is a man that **O**$_i$ [anyone [who talks to *e*]] usually ends up liking t. (Chomsky 1986:58)
However, the relative *who* may simply not be raised here out of IP into the CP. When CP clearly contains a closer potential A-bar binder, a PG is impossible:
(iii) *This is the type of book **which** [laymen [who we consult about *e*]] usually can't understand *t*.
(iv) *John is a man that **O**$_i$ [anyone who Bill sends to *e*]] ends up liking t.
3. Thus in (i), the local binder of t_i is *he*:
   (i) *Which candidate$_i$ did Hillary think that he$_i$ had tricked Bill into hiring t$_i$?
4. Contreras (1984) and Chomsky (1986) use the Binding Theory Principles (Chomsky, 1981, Ch. 3) to question the No C-command Condition (10.1) between a trace *t* and a PG *e,* but these principles of disjoint reference are better characterized, at least in certain cases, in terms of C^{max}-command. Thus, Principle C must have the consequence that a referring expression can't be C^{max}-*commanded* by an antecedent:
   (i) *Mary [$_{VP}$ [$_{V'}$ criticized him$_i$] after introducing John$_i$ to us].
   *John [$_{VP}$ [$_{V'}$ read them$_i$] without buying those books$_i$].
   Nor, according to Principle B, can a pronoun be C^{max}-commanded by an antecedent in its Governing Category (roughly, the same IP) in similar configurations:
   (ii) *Bill recalled that [$_{IP}$ Mary [$_{VP}$ [$_{V'}$ criticized John$_i$] right in front of him$_i$]].
   *Bill was happy that [$_{IP}$ Mary [$_{VP}$ [$_{V'}$ had found John$_i$ a room] for him$_i$]].
   Both these Binding Conditions should be redefined using C^{max}-command, where VPs are the lowest C^{max} containing antecedents of the referring expressions in (i) and the pronouns in (ii). Thus, although their antecedents fail to c-command *John, books* and *him*, they nonetheless (improperly) C^{max}-command these expressions, accounting for (i) and (ii).
5. This is not the position of Kayne (1983), but Stowell (1985, section 2) argues that Kayne does not succeed in rendering an empty operator unnecessary.
6. The often cited example, *This is the kind of food you must cook before you eat*, sounds better than the more typical structures in (i) below, because two overt subjects are identical unstressed pronouns and because intransitive *eat* can pragmatically be construed as referring to the food being cooked (*John cooked the fish and then we ate*).
   (i) *These are the tools that I broke before Mary sold cheap.
   *Which articles did she file if the boss put to the side?
   *Here's the editor we sent your manuscript to after Mary contacted.
   *This is the kind of food he overcooks when we really want.
   Some analysts report certain parasitic gaps in tensed adjuncts as well-formed:

(ii) Which man did you look at *t* after Mary had spoken to *e*? (Lasnik & Stowell, 1991)

a person that they spoke to *t* because they admired *e* (Kayne, 1983)

I find these examples marginal, and corresponding full sentences with subjects containing lexical nouns or contrasting pronouns seem ungrammatical, like the examples in (i):

(iii) ?Which man did the girls look at *t* after Mary had spoken to *e*?

*Jane saw the person who I spoke to *t* because you admired *e*.

7. Again, unstressed pronominal subjects ameliorate the judgment, as in example (i) from Lasnik & Stowell (1991). Nonetheless, I find (i) marginal, in comparison to (ii):

(i) ?Who did Mary gossip about *t* despite your having vouched for *e*?

(ii) Who did Mary gossip about *t* despite having vouched for *e*?

8. Chomsky (1970) contrasts the internal V-headed properties of gerunds with the N-headed properties of derived nominals; Emonds (1976, Ch. 4) contrasts the external NP distribution of gerunds with the clause-like distribution of infinitives.

9. The non-DP status of these five constructions is non-controversial. Rosenbaum (1967) argues that the complements in (10.23c) and (10.23d) are not DPs (NPs in his terms) because they can not passivize or become the focus constituent in clefts or pseudo-clefts.

10. The proviso is not universal, if languages such as Icelandic and Yiddish treat any SPEC(IP) as an A-bar position, as is widely claimed in the literature. The focus in this article is English.

11. The sequence of operations (10.34)–(10.38) abstracts away from head-to-head movement.

12. In contrast, the lowest trace of O_i must *remain* in order that the chain receive a theta role.

13. Horvath (1992) is an earlier use of Lasnik and Saito's deletion mechanism. In fact, there may be reasons to restrict LF deletion to non-argument positions, i.e., to operators. The intermediate argument trace t_i' in (i) must remain in LF to properly bind an anaphor:

(i) John$_i$ is likely t_i' to seem to himself t_i to be incompetent.

14. The examples (10.40) whose PGs are adjuncts can be contrasted with the following PGs in complements:

?Which room did the artist move out of before putting her portraits in?

This is the road that Joan avoids instead of driving along.

Who are they telephoning now in order to visit next week?

15. Chapter 3 of this volume provides a more precise analysis of how a derivational suffix *ing* can "license" a V-headed construction in an otherwise N-headed context.

16. Emonds (2000, Ch. 1) argues that subjects of various DP-internal predicates are not always full DPs but are sometimes simply non-maximal N-projections within the DP.
17. In both Emonds (1985, Ch. 2) and Emonds (2000, Ch. 7), there remains a restriction against a single DP receiving a theta role from two separate predicates: the two predicates cannot themselves be in a theta role assigning relation. I call this restriction the Revised Theta Criterion. Since verbs do not assign theta roles to the heads of clausal adjuncts, all the constructions in this paper satisfy it.
18. I assume the empty categories cannot be accidentally co-indexed with operators unless they are subject to some sort of co-indexing condition. That is, "accidental" violations of subjacency such as *John is hard to describe how much Mary hates* are excluded.
19. That is, assuming that *arrive* is 'unaccusative,' *John should call before arriving* may have two representations, one in which *arriving* has a null controlled subject DP and one in which (10.39) deletes this DP, leaving (10.43) to determine that the subject of *arriving* in LF is the overt DP *John*.
20. In order to fully integrate this solution into the framework being developed here, the Revised Theta Criterion in note 17 be sharpened in some way.

Chapter 11
Unspecified categories as the key to root constructions*

11.1 Root vs. embedded clause asymmetry

Syntactic theory has never fully come to grips with the robust asymmetry between "root" (essentially non-embedded) and embedded clauses: the fact that in many well studied languages, main clauses exhibit a wider variety of non-canonical structures than do most dependent clause types. This asymmetry was expressed in earlier transformational grammar as the *Structure Preserving Constraint* (Emonds, 1976): only restricted types of operations can apply freely in all clauses, whereas transformations in root clauses seemingly exhibit a wider range of adjunctions and copyings.

Grammatical analyses have never managed to go much beyond stipulating this root clause property. One language-particular proposal, reviewed and elaborated in Roberts (1993: 52–57), relates several fronting processes to verb raising: main clause C "is associated with Agr(eement) in Germanic." Other approaches claim counterfactually that the asymmetry doesn't really exist; i.e., it is a mere tendency or "squish." Yet other analyses associate root properties with special types of categories, such as iterated CPs in certain contexts only (Authier, 1992), or the TOP (topic) and FOC (focus) projections of Rizzi (1997). However, in the absence of general principles that predict their distribution, labels alone do not actually explain grammatical behaviour, but simply provide names for it.

This study proposes that essentially all of the apparently varied properties of root transformations, in at least English, French and German, can actually be understood and explained if (i) main and certain embedded clauses are associated with *a-categorial shells* that otherwise conform in every way to standard tree architecture, and (ii) all movements used in deriving them are assimilated to a slightly revised notion of generalized structure-preservation.

11.1.1 Variation in root domains across languages

The asymmetric *root transformational* properties of main clauses are documented for English in Emonds (1970: Ch. 1 or 1976: Ch. II). Koster (1978) shows that the main-embedded contrast is if anything stronger in Dutch, where few if any dependent clauses qualify as *root-like*. Banfield (1982: Ch. 1) links more such properties to an unembeddable *E node* ("Expression"). Along a different dimension, Ronat (1973) shows that French root structures seem more limited in kind, comprised of only certain deletions, clitic inversions and rightward movements.[1]

Japanese seems to exhibit a somewhat different asymmetry. Kubo (1994: Ch. 7) proposes that it has two different clausal types, a larger type ("CP") permitting several constructions excluded in the other ("IP").[2] These "CP constructions" she naturally enough associates with either the SPEC or the head position of CPs, which are excluded in certain embedded contexts such as relative clauses and complements to the grammatical N *koto* and *no*. In what follows, I re-interpret these embedded CPs as root-like clauses, i.e., Kubo's CPs are the main and root-like clauses of Japanese. I will suggest that this richer range of structures reflects the same universal tendencies as do the more familiar root transformations of English and German.

11.1.2 Variation across clausal types

Individual speakers as well as languages exhibit variation in how root transformations apply. English speakers, some more than others, judge many root structures as acceptable in *certain types of* structurally simple embedded clauses. Early analyses (Emonds: 1970, 1976) observed that for many speakers dependent clause contexts like *warn someone that ___* and *make a promise that ___* mimic the freedom of root structures in what traditional grammar calls *indirect discourse*. Subsequent studies of such "embedded root phenomena" beginning with Hooper and Thompson (1973) elaborate in various ways on this first rough characterisation.

Nonetheless, such root-like indirect discourse embedding ("RIDE") is incompatible with most dependent clause positions. At least in the languages under discussion, RIDEs as in (11.1) are always (a) finite, (b) complements rather than adjuncts, and (c) tend to be governed by V or A rather than by lexical N or P.[3] Moreover, (d) some argument of these governing V and A must be animate.

(11.1) Topicalisation:
Bill warned us that [$_{RIDE}$ *flights to Chicago* we should try to avoid].
Negative preposing:
I made a promise that [$_{RIDE}$ *only until five would* we work].

When embedded clauses don't satisfy *all four* of these conditions on RIDE positions, root transformations produce clear unacceptability.[4]

(11.2) a. Non-finite IP:
*Bill warned us [flights to Chicago to try to avoid].
*We will propose [only until five working] to the management.

b. Adjunct IP:
*Mary used another company since [flights to Chicago they could avoid].
*I ignored the boss who was so angry that [only until five did we work].

c. Complements to N:
*A warning that [flights to Chicago they should avoid] will soon be posted.
*Their promise that [only until five will they work] will be hard to keep.

d. No animate argument of governing V:
*No experiment showed that [such material this metal would react with].
*The weather meant that [flights to Chicago travellers carefully avoided].

Given the variations in root phenomena, both across languages and between different types of root and embedded clauses, two questions arise:

(11.3) *Question 1: Lexical differences.* Can lexical specifications of grammatical items account for different cross-linguistic behaviours in root and embedded clauses?

(11.4) *Question 2: Parametric differences.* Should (other) parameterised principles differentiate root and embedded clause syntax for different languages and/or speakers?

Since root transformations often affect material set off by commas from the main clause (so-called dislocated, appositive and parenthetical constituents), another question related to root behaviour is (11.5).

(11.5) *Question 3: Pauses.* What gives rise to and determines the distribution of comma intonation?

This study elaborates a general framework for analysing root phenomena, and then tries to give answers to these three questions for at least Standard English, French and German. For reasons that will become clear later, I first compare English and German. Section 11.3.3 makes a suggestion as to why French root phenomena seem more restricted.

11.1.3 An inventory of root transformational operations

For discussion, we can divide the root transformational operations and constructions found for example in English and German into the following seven subcases. For many more examples of these constructions, consult Emonds (1976: Ch. II).[5]

(11.6) a. *Leftward movement to pre-subject position with no verb inversion (English but not German):* Topicalisation, VP-preposing, exclamative WH-fronting, directional PP preposing.

b. *Leftward movement to pre-subject position with obligatory finite verb fronting:* English direct question formation and preposed negative constituents; German topicalisation.

c. *Finite verb inversions:* German "Verb Second"; English auxiliary inversion ("I to C movement") and V inversion for quotes and directional PPs as in *Bill is silly, exclaimed Sue* and *Away ran John*.

d. *Leftward movement (or expletives) with clause-final subjects:* Preposing of AP over *be* and of locative PPs; *there*-insertion with clause-final subjects.

(11.7) *Left dislocated phrases with commas:* Left dislocation; sentential complement preposing, yielding clause-final parentheticals as in *Bill was late, it seems to me.*

(11.8) *Phrases in final position with comma intonation:* Right dislocation (Ross, 1967); parenthetical PPs (*just between us, to my knowledge,* etc.); English tag questions.[6]

(11.9) *Phrases moved to clause-final position with comma intonation:* Rightward movements over internal parenthetical and appositive relative clauses.

In Emonds (2004), I collect into an appendix all analysis of constructions such as in (11.8) and (11.9) that may require rightward transformational movement. Therefore this chapter does not further mention rightward movement as in (11.9).[7]

A final question of main clause syntax concerns why certain null allomorphs occur only in root clauses. Null realisations are possible for several grammatical items in root contexts, such as second person subjects and understood modals in imperatives, initial English auxiliaries in yes-no questions, and first and second person subjects with these empty I (*Lost your temper lately? Working myself too hard lately*). Emonds (2002: section 3.1) provides a lexical entry based analysis of these "root deletions" consistent with this study, so they will not be further treated here.

In this study, we first focus on the frontings and inversions in (11.6)–(11.7). The main line of argument is presented in sections 11.2 and 11.3, which provide a structure-preserving analysis of the root frontings lacking comma intonation (11.6) and contrast the root operations of Standard English, German and French. Sections 11.4.1 and 11.4.2 then turn to the question of what determines the highest functional head in root constructions (11.6c): when is it null and when is it a fronted finite form? Section 11.4.3 completes the analysis of root categories, discussing "residual WH-movement.". Section 11.5.1 analyses left dislocated phrases set off by commas (11.7), and section 11.5.2 treats right-dislocated phrases (11.8).

11.2 Leftward movements without commas

This study aims to analyse the highly varied root configurations in (11.6)–(11.7) as special cases of the same general structural types as found in embedded positions. The crux of my proposal is that the standard basis of root constructions, a finite clause, can be "housed" in progressively larger projections of standard bar notation architecture, which I call "Discourse Shells." This study will show how these shells, appropriately theorised, provide a restricted set of landing sites for the various root transformations and yet are unavailable for free embedding.

11.2.1 The domains of root movements: "Discourse Projections"

Prior to introducing Discourse Shells, I first define standard root clauses as Discourse Projections. The choice of this term reflects a conviction that ultimately, the constituents of a root clause stand in privileged relations with surrounding categories of discourse: focus constituents, topics, other Discourse Shells, sentence fragments, speaker-oriented interjections and PPs, etc.

(11.10) *Root clauses.* Unembedded finite clauses IP are *Discourse Projections* in all languages.[8]

A little reflection shows that "finite" is a rather misleading term for the important property of the grammatical items it refers to. In a main clause, the choice of the ±MODAL feature value of finiteness (i.e., of the I head of IP) indicates whether or not the speaker claims the sentence's content is a "real event." Only secondarily does finiteness refer to time. That is, the lexical item in a root I expresses a (Fregean) judgment of "eventhood" concerning the proposition represented in the rest of IP.[9] According to (11.10), it is exactly this assertion about eventhood, either realis or non-realis (using O. Jespersen's terms), that triggers the possibility of root transformations, which are associated here with the status of IP as a Discourse Projection.

In contrast to finite I, a non-finite form such as English *to* is an unspecified (empty) I in Logical Form ("LF"), as argued in syntactic grounds in Lobeck (1986) and Emonds (2000, Ch. 1). As such, it gives no information about eventhood, so its projection IP cannot serve as a Discourse Projection. Hence, the definition (11.10) amounts to defining Discourse Projections as phrases whose lexical heads specify the nature of LF events. Understood in these terms rather than in terms of Tense or time, the rationale for the presence of "finite" in (11.10) becomes less arbitrary.

In the languages under consideration, the root-like dependent clauses (RIDEs) of section 11.1 also have the status of Discourse Projections, i.e. they exhibit the behaviour of "embedded roots."

(11.11) *Discourse Projection Parameter.* Particular languages may specify larger classes of finite clauses as Discourse Projections.

(11.12) *Indirect Discourse.*
   a. Standard German and typical idiolects of English permit IPs of indirect discourse (RIDEs) to be Discourse Projections.[10]
   b. Japanese may have a larger class of RIDEs that include the complement *to*-clauses and adjunct *kara*-clauses analysed as CPs in Kubo (1994: Ch. 7).

Even prior to its formal analysis, the German "Verb Second" phenomenon can serve as a diagnostic for whether an embedded clause is a Discourse Projection. Traditional German grammar discusses embedded root transformational behaviour under the rubric of contrasting two types of indirect discourse; thus Grebe et al. (1973: section K) distinguish between the grammar of *einegebettete Sätze ohne Einleitewort* 'embedded sentences without complementiser' (11.13a) and *einegebettete Sätze mit einem Einleitewort* 'embedded sentences with a complementiser' (11.13b). Roberts (1993: 57–58) reviews the main points of this contrast and generative analyses of it.

German pairs exemplifying these types in (11.13) are synonymous.[11]

(11.13) a. German indirect discourse with an embedded Discourse Projection; the Verb is obligatorily second and *dass* 'that' is excluded:
   Hans sagte, (*dass) [$_{RIDE}$ [$_{DP}$ seiner Mutter] [$_V$ würden] die Kinder sehr oft helfen].
   Hans said (*that)   his mother   would the children quite often help
   'Hans said that the children would quite often help his mother.'

   b. German indirect discourse without an embedded Discourse Projection; the Verb is obligatorily last and *dass* 'that' is required:

Hans sagte *(dass) [IP die Kinder sehr oft seiner Mutter helfen würden].
Hans said   that   the children quite often his mother help would

Although English indirect discourse lacks the salient word order contrasts and subjunctive morphology of German, it exhibits similar possibilities:¹²

(11.14) a. English indirect discourse with a Discourse Projection and root frontings:
John said that [RIDE his mother the children often helped].
John said that [RIDE never did the children help his mother].

b. English indirect discourse without a Discourse Projection:
John said that [IP the children {often/ never} helped his mother].

Both languages permit fronting as in (11.13a)–(11.14a) only in those embedded clauses that can be construed as reporting the speech or thought of another party. We saw this for English in (11.2), and similar data holds for German. If we violate the four conditions on RIDEs given there and at the same time prepose an XP into first position, German word orders that are acceptable in RIDEs become unacceptable:

(11.15) a. Non-finite IP:
*Er empfahl [IP [DP das Buch] ihr bald zu geben].
He recommended   [the book   her soon to give]

b. Adjunct IP:
*Wir werden eine andere Fluggesellschaft brauchen bis [IP [DP Flüge nach Chicago] wir vermeiden können].
We will another company use until
[flights to Chicago we avoid can]

c. Complements to N; cf. the acceptable (11.13a):
*Die Wahrscheinlichkeit dass [IP [DP seiner Mutter] die Kinder sehr oft   helfen würden] ist zu vernachlässigen.
The possibility that [his mother the children very often help   would   is to disregard]

d. No animate argument of governing V:
*Kein Experiment hat gezeigt, [$_{IP}$ [$_{PP}$ mit solch einem Stoff] würde dieses Metall reagieren].
No experiment has shown, [with such material would this metal react]

Thus, the variety of fronted constituents permitted in both English and German Discourse Projections, i.e. main clauses and RIDEs, are *not otherwise permitted* in embedded contexts.

It is not unusual to find authors giving instances of RIDE in rather simple structures that are less amenable to being characterized as indirect discourse. For example, Rizzi (1997, 298) provides the Italian *Ecco un uomo [$_{CP}$ a cui il Premio Nobel dovrebbero dare.]* 'Here is a man to whom the Nobel Prize they should give.' As predicted by (11.12a), the English translation seems unacceptable, although easy enough to understand with enough stress on *Nobel Prize* (as is also the ungrammatical *Few people would THE NOBEL PRIZE turn down*). Rizzi indicates that contrastive stress is needed in his Italian example as well. If such sentences are systematically better in Italian than in English – and if the focused DP is not in SPEC(IP) in Italian – then that language simply has a larger set of Discourse Projections than English, as permitted by (11.11).

11.2.2 The landing sites of root movements: "Discourse Shells"

In order to develop a structural analysis of the root phenomena such as the frontings just reviewed, I propose the following "categorially unspecified" extension of the bar notation in root clauses and RIDES.

(11.16) *Discourse Shells.* Categorially unspecified projections termed "Discourse Shells" may immediately dominate (only) IPs specified as Discourse Projections.[13]

Under this hypothesis, the many classical leftward root transformations without commas in (11.6), those permitted in Discourse Projections, have landing sites in a bar notation projection [$_{XP}$ SPEC(XP) – X – root IP]. Prior to these movements, such a projection completely lacks any category specification. In English, the root X^0 in these projections must more often than not be null in Phonological Form ("PF"). What licenses this null X^0 will be treated in section 11.4.

(11.17)

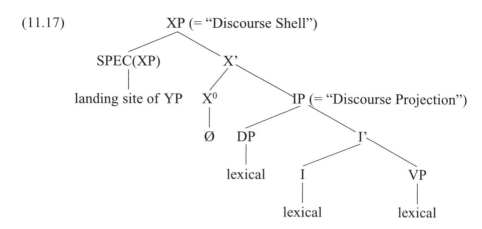

All values of YP for the structure in (11.17) are instantiated by the English root structures in (11.18), with the exception of YP = IP. None of these constructions occur freely in dependent clauses. Section 11.5.2 will exemplify the possibility of fronted IPs as well; that is, all types of YPs can end up in SPEC(XP) in (11.17).

(11.18) a. Exclamative WH-fronting, with DP or AP in SPEC(XP):
[$_{DP}$ What beautiful skirts]$_i$ [$_X$ Ø] that girl wears t$_i$!
[$_{AP}$ How long]$_i$ [$_X$ Ø] the professor droned on t$_i$!

b. Topicalised DPs or NPs in SPEC(XP):
[$_{DP}$ The first part of the movie]$_i$ [$_X$ Ø] John missed out on t$_i$.
[$_{DP}$ Those beautiful skirts]$_i$ [$_X$ Ø] she wouldn't dare wear t$_i$!
[$_{DP}$ A city like that]$_i$ [$_X$ Ø] the professor denied t$_i$ could be dangerous.
[$_{NP}$ Good books]$_i$ [$_X$ Ø] we don't have {many/ any} of t$_i$.

c. VP preposing (allowed in English in very limited contexts):
..., and [$_{VP}$ buy such books]$_i$ [$_X$ Ø] John already has t$_i$.
..., but [$_{VP}$ eaten that candy]$_i$ [$_X$ Ø] she couldn't have t$_i$.

d. Directional PP preposing without subject inversion:
[$_{PP}$ Into the pool]$_i$ [$_X$ Ø] Mary jumped t$_i$.
[$_{PP}$ Down the street]$_i$ [$_X$ Ø] the baby carriage rolled t$_i$.

Unspecified categories as the key to root constructions 341

The same Discourse Shell structures (11.17) are also the basis for English auxiliary inversion in direct questions and negative constituent preposing (11.6b), as well as for the optional simple verb inversion with directional PP preposing (11.6c). In these cases, however, I^0 or V^0 moves to replace the empty X^0.

(11.19) a. [$_{PP}$ To which child]$_i$ [$_I$ should] John give a book t_i?
 [$_{DP}$ Not one book]$_i$ [$_I$ did] John give t_i to this child.

 b. [$_{PP}$ Into the pool]$_i$ [$_V$ jumped]$_j$ Mary t_j t_i.
 [$_{PP}$ Down the street]$_i$ [$_V$ rolled]$_j$ the baby carriage t_j t_i.

Section 11.4 returns to the contrast between phrasal frontings without inversion (11.18) and those with inversion (11.19).

All the types of phrasal constituents that can be fronted in root and rootlike English clauses can also so appear in German Discourse Projections, as in (11.20). However, a German *Verb Second rule* always guarantees that the highest finite V moves to become the surface head of any XP Discourse Shell that immediately dominates a Discourse Projection. This German pattern makes no distinction between topicalised constituents as in (11.20a-c) and the two constructions (11.20d) that require fronted auxiliaries in English, namely WH-fronting and Negative Constituent Preposing.[14]

(11.20) a. Topicalised DPs or NPs in SPEC(XP):
 [$_{DP}$ Den ersten Teil]$_i$ [$_V$ hat] Hans t_i verpasst
  The first part   has   Hans   missed
 'The first part Hans has missed.'
 [$_{NP}$ Gute Bücher]$_i$ [$_V$ haben] wir {nicht viele/ keine} t_i.
  Good books   have   we   not many/ none
 'Good books we don't have {many/ any} of.'

 b. VP preposing:
 …, und [$_{VP}$ solche Bücher gekauft]$_i$ [$_V$ hat] Hans schon t_i.
       and   such   books   bought   has   Hans already
 ' … and such books Hans has already bought.'

 c. Directional PP preposing:
 [$_{PP}$ Ins Schwimmbad]$_i$ [$_V$ sprang] Marie t_i.
  into the swim-bath   jumped   Mary
 'Into the pool jumped Mary.'

d. [$_{DP}$ Welchem Kind]$_i$ [$_V$ soll] Hans ein Buch t$_i$ geben?
    Which   child   should Hans   a   book give
'To which child should Hans give a book?'
[$_{DP}$ Kein einziges Buch]$_i$ [$_V$ gab] Hans diesem Kind t$_i$.
    Not   single   book   gave Hans this   child
'Not a single book did Hans give to this child.'

The fronted Vs in all these examples have been typically analysed as undergoing *V to I to C movement*, for example in Roberts (1993) and in Vikner's (1995) comparative analyses of Verb Second systems.

Formulating root transformations in terms of the Discourse Shell XPs in (11.17) automatically expresses properties that are otherwise accidental. For example, it is well-known that in *non-root contexts*, heads categorially constrain the type of phrases permitted in Specifiers: SPEC(IP) must contain a DP, plausibly so as to potentially enter into agreement with I or to receive nominative case, and phrases in embedded SPEC(CP) must have the feature WH in indirect questions. Less often discussed is the restriction that SPEC(AP) and SPEC(PP) tolerate only measure phrases.[15]

In contrast to these category-specific restrictions on embedded SPEC(XP), the root constructions in (11.18)–(11.20) instantiate *all* major types of YP in SPEC. The hypothesis that a Discourse Shell is an XP *without category* serves to explain why essentially any type of maximal projection can move to its Specifier. Such "category-free" movement is then predicted to occur in root contexts only. If the categorial limitations on phrasal types in various SPEC(BP) are functions of particular categories B, it follows that these limitations will disappear in categorially unspecified XP – precisely what happens in root constructions. Discourse Shells thus *explain* the variety of frontable phrasal types in root contexts. Exactly the same reasoning permits the variety of phrasal types found in the German and Dutch "first positions" or *Vorfeld*.[16]

I haven't yet specified exactly the formal mechanism that allows all these phrases to substitute for category-free landing sites. Nor have I accounted for the null or head movement options for X^0 in the Discourse Projection structures (11.17). We turn to a restrictive answer to these questions after a brief comment on variation in root behaviour across languages.

11.2.3 Cross-linguistic variation in Discourse Projections?

The structures assigned to embedded RIDE XPs (11.13a)–(11.14a) in this study are of the form C-[$_{XP}$ IP]. Because of the a-categorial nature of XP, the widely noted selectional relation between C and the form of IP (Rizzi, 1997: 283–284) can then be easily defined: intermediate a-categorial shells don't interfere with selection. In contrast, this important relation between C and IP is obscured in analyses that express RIDE with full categorial projections such as TopP, FocP or iterated CPs. In fact, the more a language utilizes embedded RIDEs, e.g., Italian as reported by Rizzi, the more crucial it is to *avoid analyses in which labeled categorial projections intervene between C and IP*, and to use Discourse Shells (11.16) instead.

Let us turn now to proposals for particular systems that interact with Discourse Projections in special ways. According to syntactic literature on Icelandic and Yiddish reviewed in Roberts (1993: 58–60), a wider range of clauses in these languages permit V-second than in English or German. Some analyses have consequently claimed that these languages use SPEC(IP) as a landing site for topicalisation, rather than SPEC(CP) as in German and Dutch. I would suggest rather that Icelandic and Yiddish have larger sets of embedded RIDEs than does English, as permitted by the Discourse Projection Parameter (11.11). If so, embedded clauses, beyond those that serve for conveying indirect discourse, may additionally qualify as Discourse Projections in Icelandic and Yiddish. As a result, a finite V in these languages moves to second position in more types of clauses.

In a head-final language like Japanese, the counterpart of V inversion or fronting is raising of V out of IP to a higher *final* head position. Kubo's (1994) analysis of Japanese clausal typology in terms of differing "constructional meanings" is crucially based on V raising through I and sometimes to C. For example, the Japanese copula is expressed by the suppletive form *da* in her system only when it is in C. In the present framework, her CPs can be reanalysed as category-less XP Discourse Shells (11.12b). This different categorial status may be why the properties of Japanese CPs that she inventories do not correlate so well with the properties of CPs found in Indo-European languages. The latter, after all, have been largely associated with embedded clause constructions, especially indirect questions, while some of Kubo's CP properties seem more related to attitudes of a speaker such as strength of assertion, which constituents are possible topics, etc; cf. note 2.

In sum, some languages may allow significantly wider classes of finite clauses – perhaps even all finite clauses – to be Discourse Projections.[17] I have formulated condition (11.12b) for Japanese as a tentative example of this option. Of course, if deeper investigation shows that all languages have exactly the same range of Discourse Projections, so much the better. The answer to Question 2 in (11.4) then changes to simply "no," and the English/ German "parameter setting" (11.12a) is elevated to Universal Grammar.

11.3 Extending Structure Preservation

I now turn to developing a unified and yet constrained transformational system that encompasses both freely embeddable operations (passive movement, WH movement, etc.) and the root operations just reviewed, which are restricted to Discourse Projections. The original structure-preserving constraint (Emonds, 1976: 5) keeps them separate, in claiming that transformational operations are limited to three essentially disparate types:

(11.21) *The structure-preserving constraint (SPC).* Major grammatical transformational operations are either root or structure-preserving operations.

This formulation does not reveal the considerable formal differences among the three permitted types of operations: "root," "structure-preserving" and "non-major."[18] *Root transformations* are only required to attach, copy or delete nodes under a root, with no restriction *on the type of formal operation.* In contrast, the familiar freely occurring transformational operations (passive, etc.) must preserve structure, i.e. they can only *substitute* a constituent B for a constituent of *exactly the same category.* Clearly, the structure-preserving operations are the more restricted of the two, so we want to assimilate root operations to them as much as possible.[19]

We must however first clarify the term *structure-preserving* in current syntax. It now often refers to Chomsky's (1986) influential usage, which is that any moved category can *substitute for or adjoin to any other*, excluding *only* phrasal movements to a head position and head movements to a phrasal position. If this is adopted, most of the predictive content of the SPC then disappears. Apparently this revision of the SPC was thought to be necessitated by that monograph's movement to COMP via VP adjunction. But intermediate traces do not interact with structure-preservation, so this weakening of the original SPC is in fact entirely unmotivated.[20]

In any case, according to Lightfoot and Weinberg's (1988) otherwise favourable review of Chomsky (1986), while "Adjunction to VP is required by Ch[omsky]'s approach; ... So far there is no real independent motivation for this notion, and it raises many questions."(370)[21] They conclude that "*Barriers* uses adjunction as something of a wild card." (382) To my knowledge, no one has ever proposed some other theory-based justification for weakening the original SPC.

Empirically, the structure-preservation of *Barriers* is not only broadly speaking too weak; in root contexts it is too strong. In languages such as Breton, a focused non-finite V^0 can move into the supposedly phrasal SPEC of a clausal projection, with an auxiliary in the following head position (cf. Anderson and Chung, 1977). Van Riemsdijk (1989) discusses several paradigms and analyses of non-maximal projections N^1 and V^1 moving to clausal SPEC positions.

The *Barriers* revision of the notion "structure-preservation" opened the gates for a much looser range of transformational operations, and so was then followed by ad hoc tightenings such as "TENSE has a strong D feature." Minimalism's strong features, when motivated by more than one construction, are in fact equivalent to stipulating structure-preservation locally at each landing site.[22] Under this weak structure-preservation bolstered by feature checking, nothing but lack of imagination prevents rather fantastic structures in which TENSE could have a strong A feature, D a strong P feature, NUM a strong vP feature, etc.

There thus remain strong and unchanging motivations for maintaining my original restrictive version of structure-preservation. Movement and copying operations to non-adjacent positions can involve only *substitutions of a category α for another of exactly the same type*, except when the landing site of α is immediately dominated by a root node. My attempt here to eliminate a special category of root operations thus starts from the SPC (11.21) as originally formulated.

11.3.1 Deriving local and root operations from structure preservation

In order to strengthen and simplify the structure-preserving framework along the above lines, I must first discuss local transformations, one of the three types allowed by the original SPC (11.21). These rules required *adjacency* between affected elements, one of which had to be non-phrasal. Local rules that are today still considered transformational have been subsumed under head movement, usually along the lines of Baker (1988).

346 *Landing sites of phrasal movements*

With respect to such head movement, the careful cross-linguistic study of van Riemsdijk (1998a) comes very close to justifying the SPC in its original form. He concludes that head movement either involves adjacent nodes (11.22a) – a *local* operation – or it is a substitution (11.22b).

(11.22) *The Head Adjacency Principle* ("HAP"; van Riemsdijk, 1998a: 645).
    a. *Head Adjunction*: Two phonetically identified heads are joined, yielding an adjunction structure, in which case the two heads must be strictly linear adjacent at the moment of application of the rule.
    b. *Head Substitution:* A head is moved into a head position, which is phonetically empty but which may contain φ-features, thereby unifying the two morpho-syntactic feature matrices.

As justification, his study encompasses the Head Substitutions listed in (11.23):

(11.23) a. The main clause operations of English subject-auxiliary inversion and Germanic Verb Second
        b. The freer raisings of V-to-I:
           French finite verb raising (i.e., V-to-Tense)
           V-to-Tense in Vata (Koopman, 1984)
           V-to-Tense in Bantu languages (Ndayiragije, 1999)
        c. N-to-D movement (Longobardi, 1994), a process also often proposed for the N-initial DPs of Semitic languages

If the substitutions of V and N in (11.23b-c) can be argued to preserve structure, then the HAP (11.22) is fully compatible with the original SPC (11.21) since (11.22a) are local rules and (11.23a) are root operations.[23]

To this end, I propose to slightly weaken the absolute categorial identity in the original SPC (11.21) between a moved category and its landing site. Since some minimal difference must distinguish V from I and N from D, it is plausible that lexically empty I and D are respectively simply *less specified* categorial variants of V and N. In fact, van Riemsdijk (1998a, note 5) views such movement exactly this way: " ... the resulting node after substitution will contain a feature matrix which is an amalgam of the feature matrices of I and V, or, to put it differently, *an I with some of the features of V added to it.*" [my emphasis] Under this view then, V-to-I (11.23b) and N-to-D (11.23c) are movements whose (empty) landing sites have *fewer* categorial features than the elements moving into them.

In particular, I lacks V's unmarked LF interpretation as ACTIVITY, and D lacks N's unmarked interpretation of permanent reference.[24] Thus, while the English grammatical verb *do* under V is proto-typically +ACTIVITY, the auxiliary *do* under I has no such interpretation. Similarly, in correlating Japanese case-marking patterns and verbal interpretation, Kubo (1994: 103) concludes: " ... when a verb is under V at s-structure, it has an activity interpretation, while a verb which is raised to I has a stative interpretation."

I therefore propose that structure-preservation be henceforth understood as substituting a category α for another β with the exactly the same *or fewer* categorial features. Movement *preserves* the categories of all its landing sites, but can also have the effect of *specifying them further*:

(11.24) *Definition of Structure-Preservation.* A structure-preserving transformational operation is one in which α substitutes for β, where β cannot be specified for a feature differently than α.

According to (11.24), V to I and N to D preserve structure because, as proposed above, D and I have fewer categorial features than their lexical counterparts N and V. Elsewhere in non-root domains, this modified definition has no effect since in all ordinary cases categories such as N^j, A^j, V^j and P^j simply differ in features, and according to classical structure-preservation, projections of one cannot substitute for another.[25] With this modification, *all of van Riemsdijk's Head Substitutions over variables (11.23) are either root (I or V to C) or structure-preserving operations*. Consequently they fully accord with the original SPC (11.21).

With this modification of structure-preservation, let us now review the inventory of transformational movement or copying operations. The only remaining local rules that are not root or structure-preserving operations are van Riemsdijk's Head Adjunctions (11.22a).The following subclasses thus seem instantiated:

(11.25) a. Structure-preserving operations satisfying (11.24)
        b. Root operations
        c. Strictly local Head Adjunctions

In fact, a review of the literature now cries out for *eliminating* any special class of local adjunctions from the range of movement operations. According to van Riemsdijk (1998a), those that move feature bundles *leftward* include German P-DET Contraction, Dutch pre-head Adjectival Agreement, and possibly Romance clitic climbing. These are all better treated I feel as instances of Alternative Realisation, basically a type of lexical insertion developed in Emonds (2000a: Ch. 4); in this perspective they are not movements at all. For a rather complete treatment of Romance clitics in these terms, consult Chapter 7 of this volume.

The *rightward* adjunctions cited by van Riemsdijk are Dutch Verb Raising and Inuit Noun Incorporation. Interestingly, other research has called into question on independent grounds whether these rules have transformational status. Van Riemsdijk in fact cites extensive work by himself and others arguing that they result from "reanalysis" rather than movement. A second possibility is that both processes instantiate productive compounding patterns.[26] Finally, I myself favour analysing Verb Raising with a base-generated "flat structure" along the lines of Italian and Spanish restructuring, as in Emonds (2000a: Ch. 6 and Chapter 6 of this volume). Given these highly plausible alternatives, the remainder of this study assumes that no category of local movements needs to be exempted from the SPC, i.e. the word "major" in the original SPC (11.21) is unnecessary.

The only truly transformational local movements are thus substitutions for I, D and C, and these are subsumed under (11.25a-b). This ends the need for any local transformations. It is now clear that any remaining open-endedness in the structure-preserving framework rests squarely with the unconstrained root transformational operations.

By using the category-less properties of Discourse Shells (11.16), we can now finally remove this longstanding weakness in transformational theory. In the prototypical Discourse Shell at a root (11.17), a YP of any type can substitute for SPEC(XP), while an I (or a V previously moved to I, as in German) can similarly substitute for X^0. Subject auxiliary inversion in English and Verb Second in German both instantiate such head movement. Therefore, the new definition of Structure Preservation (11.24) *already encompasses* not only (i) classic structure preservation and (ii) van Riemsdijk's Head Substitutions (11.22b), but also (iii) the root and root-like movements into the a-categorial heads and specifiers of Discourse Shells. We can therefore fully simplify the original Structure Preserving Constraint as follows:

(11.26)   *The Augmented Structure Preserving Constraint ("ASP")*. Movements must always be structure-preserving substitutions, as defined in (11.24).

Unspecified categories as the key to root constructions   349

What accounts for root movements is thus the availability of the category-less landing sites X^0 and SPEC(XP) in Discourse Shells (11.16), both in main clauses by (11.10) and in RIDEs (11.12). All leftward root movements listed earlier in (11.6a-d) automatically fall under the ASP (11.26). Section 11.5 will use the hypothesis of Discourse Shells to also subsume under ASP the left dislocated phrases derived by movement (11.7).

There remains the possibility of rightward phrasal movements, including (i) Ross's (1967) Heavy NP Shift, (ii) rightward movement for certain clause-final subjects, (iii) right dislocations of various sorts (11.8), and (iv) parenthetical formation (11.9). Since these cannot be straightforwardly motivated as substitutions, they are not easily assimilated to the ASP and seem at first sight to indicate a second option for rightward movement. The appendix to this essay (in Emonds, 2004) investigates whether transformational theory actually requires this second non-structure preserving type of movement. It then uses the theory of Saito and Fukui (1998) to assimilate rightward movement to minimalist Merge rather than Move. This step allows us to *maintain an Augmented Structure Preserving Constraint in its strongest form* (11.26).

11.3.2 Unique landing sites for frontings without comma intonation

There remains an important pattern of fronting rules that the ASP framework needs to capture. The earliest work on structure-preservation emphasized the mutual incompatibility of many root transformations. In particular, all the phrasal frontings without comma intonation in (11.6a-b) and (11.6d) are pairwise incompatible. This very general paradigm argues that these processes are all competing for the same landing site, namely the SPEC(XP) of a single discourse shell in tree (11.17).

Since I have listed eight distinct subcases of root frontings, fully demonstrating the incompatibility of each with all the others would require around 30 different sets of examples, obviously beyond normal space limitations. A few examples will have to suffice; several more can be found in Emonds (1976: Ch. II).

(11.27) a. Exclamative fronting + topicalisation:
           *[What a stupid campaign]$_i$ [that whole weekend]$_j$ Mary spent t$_j$ on t$_i$.
           *[That whole weekend]$_j$ [what a stupid campaign]$_i$ Mary spent t$_j$ on t$_i$.

b. Topicalisation + question fronting:
*[That house]$_i$ [which cousin]$_j$ did Mary buy t$_i$ for t$_j$?
*[Which cousin]$_j$ [that house]$_i$ did Mary buy t$_i$ for t$_j$?

c. Double topicalisation:
*[Bill]$_i$ [that house]$_j$ she took t$_i$ to t$_j$ for the weekend.
*[That house]$_j$ [Bill]$_i$ she took t$_i$ to t$_j$ for the weekend.

d. Topicalisation + directional PP preposing:
*That big toy into the pool {Mary jumped with/ jumped Mary with}!
*Into the pool that big toy {Mary jumped with/ jumped Mary with}!

e. VP preposing + topicalisation:
… and the old house he was sure would increase in value.
… and increase in value he was sure the old house would.
… *and [$_{VP}$ increase in value]$_i$ [$_{DP}$ the old house]$_j$ he was sure t$_j$ would t$_i$.

f. Negative preposing + question fronting:
Only from the suburbs did they confiscate the political banners.
Which banners did they confiscate only from the suburbs?
*Only from the suburbs which banners did they confiscate?
*Which banners only from the suburbs did they confiscate?

The uniqueness of the landing site for these English preposings recalls the better known unique "first position" (*Vorfeld*) of German and Dutch traditional as well as generative grammar. The fact that the same overriding pattern occurs in both declarative and question clauses in German and Dutch and with or without inversion in English suggests that universal grammar itself *restricts root phrasal movements to a single landing site.*[27]

Moreover, this pattern is exactly reproduced in English, German and Dutch indirect questions and relative clause CPs; overt movement permits only one fronted WH-phrase. The unique landing site in all these paradigms is thus the SPEC(XP) or SPEC(CP) in the tree below:

(11.28)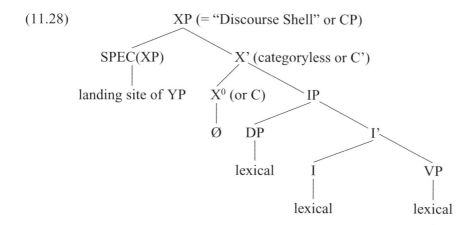

In an interesting juxtaposition, this hypothesis combined with Chomsky's (1973) venerable Tensed S Constraint accounts automatically for all the restrictions seen in (11.27). Although research using this constraint has often focused on the category "Tense," it originally included another crucial property, the idea of a single escape hatch per finite clause for long distance movement. My rephrasing:

(11.29) *Tensed S Constraint,* or *"Unique Traces Constraint."* A trace inside a finite complement of X^0 must be bound within XP.

This formulation correctly implies that SPEC(XP) is a *unique escape hatch* for movement from within IP to outside XP. This restriction has been lost in subsequent reconceptualisations. In order to capture robust paradigms such as (11.27) and others, we must use Chomsky's original idea.

Since all Discourse Projections including RIDEs and their Discourse Shells are necessarily finite, the generalised landing site SPEC(XP) in a Discourse Shell (11.28) can serve as the counterpart to Chomsky's single escape hatch in a CP.[28] If each SPEC in two successive Discourse Shells – with another ZP atop XP in (11.28) – would bind different traces in a single IP, the trace of the phrase in SPEC(ZP) would not be bound within XP, counter to (11.29). In fact, even if the lower SPEC(XP) bound no trace (for example, it might house a simple fronted adverbial PP), the trace of the higher SPEC(ZP) would still be free in XP and violate (11.29). Therefore, if SPEC(XP) in a Discourse Shell contains an overt phrase, it cannot additionally house an intermediate trace in a successive cyclic chain.[29] This simple statement nicely accounts for all the data patterns in (11.27).

From this reasoning we also deduce that left dislocations, which are widely considered to not bind traces, must precede the various fronted constituents in (11.6), and in fact they do. Moreover, since fronted WH phrases clearly compete with root operations for the same position, as seen in examples (11.27b) and (11.27f), they also should appear to the right of any left dislocation. In confirmation, De Cat (2002: 96) presents data that left dislocated topics must precede fronted WH elements in French and cites a number of authors who make similar claims for other languages. For Rizzi's (1997) claim to the contrary, see note 39.

Finally, the Tensed S Constraint (11.29) explains paradigm (iii) in note 4, repeated here.

(11.30) *[Which company]$_i$ did Bill warn you (that) [$_{XP}$ flights to Chicago [$_{IP}$ t$_i$ had cancelled]]?
*[Who]$_i$ is it shocking to Sue that [$_{XP}$ not once has [$_{IP}$ Mary heard from t$_i$]]?

In (11.30), the traces t$_i$ of the WH-phrases are not locally bound in XP and hence violate (11.29).

11.3.3 Exclusion or rarity of French frontings without verb inversion

Modern French seems to be different from Germanic systems with respect to root phenomena. Ronat's (1973) early study of clausal types and root transformations concludes that Standard French lacks the frontings in (11.6), those with neither inverted verbs nor resumptive pronouns. French does of course exhibit WH-fronting, but this operation can be conflated with the same non-root operation in indirect questions. As explained in note 33 below, WH-fronting as a movement operation preserves structure both in the sense of Emonds (1976) and of Chomsky (1986).

The issue is thus whether French excludes counterparts to the English examples (11.18a-d):

(11.31) a. ??Quelles belles jupes cette fille porte!
  'What beautiful skirts that girl wears!'

  b. ??Ma mère les enfants aident souvent.
  'My mother the children help often.'

??Des vols vers Chicago nous devrions éviter.
'Flights to Chicago we should avoid.'
??Une ville comme ça le professeur a voulu visiter.
'A city like that the professor wanted to visit.'

c. ??... et acheter de tels livres Jean n'a pas pu.
'... and buy such books John couldn't.'

d. ??Dehors Jean s'est précipité.
'Outside John rushed.'
??Vers le boulevard le pousse-pousse roulait.
'Toward the boulevard the pram rolled.'

Whether or not speakers consistently reject these patterns, many speakers do reject them, as well as their counterparts with inverted verbs. I suggest there is a clash between the universal factors in (11.32) and a principle of French intonation (11.33).

(11.32) a. Constituents in Discourse Shell Specifiers that bind traces are universally focused, as proposed in Rizzi (1997, 291).
b. Within their intonational phrase, focused constituents universally receive prominent stress.

(11.33) French stress in declarative intonational phrases is invariably on the right.

These three statements taken together imply that French declarative sentences do not toleration fronted phrasal antecedents of traces; this excludes the examples of (11.31).

In any case, it seems fair to conclude that the questionable status of the French patterns in (11.31) is orthogonal to the main hypotheses of this study.[30]

11.4 Licensing the root X^0 position: English Ø vs. German V

Sections 11.2 and 11.3 have restrictively extended the original notion of structure-preservation so that at least leftward phrasal root transformations fall under its scope. But they mention only descriptively an important difference that separates English, where verb inversions are restricted, from German, where Verb Second is pervasive. Nor has anything been said about the empty head X⁰ in English Discourse Shells, as seen throughout (11.18) for example.

In order to characterize these differing root behaviours, I will exploit a difference in the lexical specifications between the unmarked English complementiser *that* and its German counterpart *dass*.

11.4.1 Lexical entries for Complementisers

A somewhat detailed study of lexical notation in Emonds (2002) pays particular attention to formally representing two independent interface notions: "null at LF" and "null at PF." These both play an important role in the analysis of *that/ dass*.

Let us first consider *null at LF*. It seems that the main semantic features typically associated with basic grammatical categories (such as PLACE or PATH with P, ACTIVITY with V, REFERENCE with D, EVENT with I, and PROPERTY with A) are simply intuitive labels for their usual interpretations. That is, if nothing else is said, each such category is interpreted roughly as the corresponding word in capitals in the above list. In this sense, these "features" are nothing beyond the grammatical categories themselves instantiated and interpreted in LF.

These typical interpretations are nonetheless suspended for certain special lexical items: a few P such as *of* indicate neither PLACE nor PATH; a marked minority of verbs are stative; the expletive DET forms *it* and *there* lack reference; the infinitive marker *to* of category I is unrelated to eventhood, etc. Emonds (2002) formally relates all these possibilities by introducing a symbol Ø as a marked syntactic feature in lexical entries to indicate that an item's syntactic category B is *not* part of its interpretation, i.e. the category [B, Ø] then means B is not interpreted or is "cancelled at LF" or is "null at LF."[31]

Among complementisers, *that/ dass* seems to be simply a subordinating conjunction C with a context feature +___IP and otherwise lacking in semantic content.[32] What then distinguishes the declarative C *that/ dass* from an interrogative C *if/ ob* in their shared context of a finite IP sister? It begs the question to respond with "±WH," since this feature used for distinguishing complementisers is at bottom nothing but a diacritic. A better motivated dichotomy is that between an interpreted and non-interpreted category, as just introduced. That is, a so-called "WH feature on C" reduces to an unmarked LF interpretation of C in the context ___IP. In contrast, C, -WH reduces to an uninterpreted C.

In this perspective, corresponding English and German complementisers both have extremely simple lexical entries, which eliminates specifying any feature WH on C.[33]

(11.34) a. *LF-Interpreted Complementisers*, previously [C, +WH]
English: if, C, +___IP   German: ob, C, +___IP
b. *Uninterpreted Complementisers,* preliminary version
English: that, C, Ø, +___IP   German: dass, C, Ø, +___IP

I take the notation +___IP to mean selection of a complement whose head is specified for I features, i.e., a finite clause. A head can take a non-finite clausal complement only if its lexical entry explicitly calls for an I that is "null at LF," e.g., an English infinitive headed by "*to*, I, Ø" can be explicitly selected only by a context feature +___[I, Ø].

To find a motivated *difference* between the English and German Cs in (11.34), we can turn to the second notion, *null at PF*. It is a commonplace that, while the English C *that* can optionally "delete" in a complement (11.35a), its counterparts in German (11.35b) and French (11.35c) translations cannot.

(11.35) a. John persuaded Mary (that) she would easily get the job.
We explained (to her) (that) they should stay outside.

b. Hans hat Marie überzeugt *(daß) sie die Stelle leicht bekommen würde.
Wir haben (ihr) erklärt *(daß) sie draussen bleiben müssen.

c. Jean a persuadé Marie *(qu') elle aurait le poste facilement.
Nous (lui) avons expliqué *(qu') ils devraient rester dehors.

The lexical statement of this (learned) language-particular property of *that* but not *dass* should be simply an option of being null at PF. I propose that this *null at PF* property, which is shared by many grammatical formatives reviewed in Emonds (2002), is notated by *parentheses around the phonological representation* in a lexical entry. The French and German counterparts of *that*, whose contentless complementisers must be overt, have no such parentheses.[34]

(11.36) *Uninterpreted Complementisers,* final version
    a. English: (that), C, Ø, +___IP
    b. German: dass, C, Ø, +___IP

Let us return now to the X^0 heads of Discourse Shells in these two languages, where previous analyses often hypothesise a root clause C. The formal notations in these lexical entries turn out to have an important role in predicting a central difference between English and German root sentences.

Throughout this volume, I have shown how grammatical items as in (11.36) are listed in the Lexicon differently from open class items. The latter can be argued to be accessed by their initial phonological clusters, similarly to standard dictionary practice. But closed class items in the Syntacticon have different properties and are accessed rather by their syntactic addresses. That is, (11.36a-b) should be read as instructions for *spelling out C heads* (i) whose complement sisters are IP, and (ii) which are not interpreted at LF.

Schematically, (11.36a) then means that the LF combination $[X^0, \emptyset]$ in the context ___IP can be spelled out at PF as either $[_C \textit{that}]$ or Ø. That is, this instruction applies to *any sister of IP with no category features at LF:*

(11.37) *Corollary of (11.36a).* In English, an X^0 sister of IP that lacks category features at LF can be either Ø or $[_C \textit{that}]$ in PF.

In a generic Discourse Shell as in (11.17), the X^0 head is not a C but is rather *unspecified* for category; but even so, it satisfies the reading (11.37) of the lexical specifications for C in (11.36a). Thus, not only can an unmarked C be optionally unpronounced, as in (11.35a), but so also can any X^0 with no category features at LF, i.e. the head of a Discourse Shell. This prediction thus accounts for the lack of any overt realization of the root X^0 in a wide variety of root fronting constructions in English (11.18).

At the same time we must still explain why such root clauses firmly exclude *that* even as an option. Along the same lines, interpreting (11.36b), which lacks parentheses, parallel to (11.36a) would imply that a head of a German Discourse Shell would necessarily be *dass*, contrary to fact. The lexical entry (11.36) can be claimed to provide an account of the difference between English and German root clauses (i.e., X^0 can be null in only the former) if and only if some *separate factor* disallows an overt *that/dass* at the root in *both languages*.

In fact, a quite simple conception of Economy accounts for this in English. This version is motivated in Emonds (2000a: Chs. 4, 7) with many constructions ranging from *do*-support to porte-manteau morphemes.

(11.38) *Economy of Derivation.* Among alternative derivations from the same deep structure, prefer the derivation with the fewest insertions of overt free morphemes.

From the two options in English provided by the Corollary (11.37), Economy selects a phonologically empty head X^0 of a Discourse Shell. We turn in the next subsection to why German root clauses exclude *dass*.[35]

11.4.2 A grammatical moral based on Germanic Verb Second

Since the German lexical entry (11.36b) doesn't license a null X^0, a second strategy for filling a root X^0 in a Discourse Shell is necessary; it consists of movement to X^0 from the nearest lower head, i.e., from I. *This constitutes the theoretical motivation for the Verb Second rule of German.* As a leftward movement, it is licensed by the Augmented Structure Preserving Constraint (11.26)); an I can substitute for an X^0 because the latter has fewer categorial specifications. Economy of Derivation (11.38) correctly prefers this movement of $[_I V]$ to X^0 in a Discourse Shell to insertion of an extra morpheme, whether or not its lexical entry would allow *dass* to be a-categorial at LF. It follows that the option of licensing a root X^0 in any German Discourse Shell by means of a moved I, namely Verb Second, is obligatory.

Of course, it is even more economical to do nothing (when a lexicon permits a null X^0 at PF) than to move. Hence English lacks Verb Second precisely because its lexicon entry for *that* in (11.36a) contains parentheses.

It is now of some interest to stand back and look at the implications of this analysis. In the two decades since Borer (1984), syntactic theorists have tried to maintain the interesting hypothesis that language-particular syntax largely or completely reduces to lexical specifications of closed class items. Yet most studies adhering to this hypothesis direct almost no theoretical effort toward how individual grammatical items are specified or how these specifications interact with general syntactic principles. Consequently, it is not surprising that current syntactic theory, whatever the validity of its claims to reveal deep mental properties, generally fails to account for even the most familiar grammatical differences among languages.

This study is part of an ongoing effort to remedy this defect. I have concluded above that the behaviour of embedded *that* vs. *dass* is actually the cause of the quite different grammars of root contexts in English and German. Recall that one of the main questions this study tries to answer is (11.3):

(11.3) *Question 1: Lexical differences.* Can lexical specifications of grammatical items fully account for different cross-linguistic behaviours in root and embedded clauses?

Examining only root contexts, it is very difficult to see which lexical items might differentiate between German's general Verb Second rule and the English lack of it. But careful attention to the formalisms used in the closed class lexicon (of course in conjunction with plausible universal principles) has in fact seemed to lead to descriptive and even explanatory particular grammars for the two systems.

In the present case, the specifications of the lexical entries for basic Cs (11.36a-b), which allow the unmarked English subordinator but not its German counterpart to alternate with Ø in PF, are far removed from the complex arena of root clauses and constructions. Yet the entry (11.36a) has turned out to be the crucial factor that eliminates Germanic Verb Second from Modern English. Without attention to *lexical formalisms* such as the syntactic "cancellation" feature Ø and the possibility of parenthesising PF material, this minimal and elegant account would not even suggest itself.

11.4.3 "Residual" English verb inversions in root and root-like clauses

Earlier in its history, English had a Verb Second system. The fifteenth century passage from Middle English to Modern English syntax is practically identified with the simultaneous disappearance of much verbal morphology and of the Verb Second system (van Kemenade, 1987).

But what has been said so far now actually leads us to expect that Modern English should retain no vestiges of Germanic Verb Second whatsoever. Although the Augmented Structure Preserving Constraint (11.26) *permits* I movements to X^0, we have as yet no motivation for the familiar English inversion of I with the subject in Direct Questions and after Preposed Negative Constituents (11.6c), in either main clauses or RIDEs. As with German Verb

Second, such root frontings are indeed more economical than inserting an extra morpheme like *that* or *if* into the head X^0 of a Discourse Shell. But a null X^0 might seem a still better way to license English Direct Questions and Preposed Negated Constituents. Given the availability of null heads of Discourse Shells in Modern English, the question then is: why do two clausal types show remnants of finiteness in pre-subject position?

The answer may lie in a cross-linguistic pattern of affinity in Discourse Projections between finiteness and both Questioned Phrases and Preposed Negative Constituents. This pattern recurs throughout European languages, even in non-Indo-European Basque (Artiagoitia, 1992). Whether indirect (dependent) questions are Discourse Projections or not, WH-phrases in their SPEC(CP) are presumably licensed in part by the fact that the lexical entries for *if/ ob* (11.34a) *do not undergo any C-deletion at LF.* That is, their WH complementisers retain LF content.

Something like this LF content is apparently needed in direct questions as well. To make this precise, I define a notion of "link" in terms of the Tensed S Constraint (11.29), a centrepiece of this study.

(11.39) *Definition of Link.* An X^0 whose SPEC(XP) *binds a trace* t_i inside a finite complement of X^0 is called a *link* between SPEC and t_i.

It seems that Questioned Phrases and Negative Constituents in a root or a RIDE, at least in German and English, require their links to have features, or in other words, some kind of content:

(11.40) *Visible Links.* WH and NEG phrases in Discourse Shell Specifiers require links specified for syntactic features at some interface.

The WH complementisers *if/ ob* in English/ German indirect questions serve to satisfy (11.40) in LF, as do fronted Vs at PF in a Verb Second system. But even though the null allomorph of English *that* might be available as X^0 in a main clause by (11.37), the problem for Visible Links (11.40) is that this allomorph retains *no* feature at either PF or LF, since it realises the complex [C, Ø] (11.36a). Consequently, the only way to satisfy Visible Links in English direct question Discourse Shells is to move I^0 to X^0 in accord with the ASP (11.26). Thus, English subject-auxiliary inversion actually follows from (11.40).[36]

This way of reconceptualising the oft-noted complementarity between lexical complementisers and inverted finite verbs now explains a puzzling asymmetry in English indirect discourse, i.e., embedded Discourse Projections. Embedded Preposed Negated Constituents *require* inversion (11.41a) while Standard English embedded WH-fronting *forbids* it (11.41b).

(11.41) a. The guard repeated that not once could her husband visit her.
*The guard repeated that not once her husband could visit her.

b. *Mary forgets when may her husband visit her.
Mary forgets when her husband may visit her.

The reason for this asymmetry is as follows: According to the entry (11.34a) for *if*, the C head of any indirect question is visible in LF (= not cancelled by the feature Ø) and so can satisfy Visible Links (11.40). But the syntactic feature Ø renders the head of a *that*-clause invisible at LF, whether in a Discourse Shell or not. Therefore a Preposed Negated Constituent in *any* Discourse Shell, embedded or not, requires I to raise to X^0 so as to satisfy (11.40). In sum, direct questions and clauses with preposed negative constituents exclude null C because their interpretations *crucially require their head X^0 or C^0 to be grammatically visible at some interface*. Indirect questions have a C that is visible at LF, while English subject – auxiliary inversion provides an X^0 visible at PF when no C is visible in LF.

Visible Links (11.40) thus provides an answer to why English retains residual I to C movement in clauses with preposed negated constituents and in direct questions.

A question arises, is Visible Links a parameter or a part of UG? The more interesting perspective, that it is universal, suggests that it may be vacuous in languages whose Discourse Projections lack overtly fronted WH or NEG constituents. But there are reportedly languages where root clause WH-fronting doesn't entail inverted verbs, such as Indonesian and Thai. If Visible Links is indeed language-particular, it most likely relates to conditions on inserting WH and NEG operators in fronted positions, i.e. it could be part of the lexical entries for abstract WH and NEG morphemes. I do not try to resolve this question.

If Visible Links (11.40) remains a parameter, then it together with (11.11), repeated for convenience, are plausibly the *only* Universal Grammar principles that group together root clauses and subsets of root-like dependent clauses (RIDEs). They hence combine to constitute an answer the second guiding question posed at the outset.

(11.11) *Discourse Projection Parameter.* Particular languages may specify larger classes of finite clauses as Discourse Projections.

(11.4) *Question 2: Parametric differences.* Should (other) parameterised principles differentiate root and embedded clause syntax for different languages and/or speakers?

I hypothesize that Universal Grammar and its parameters do not differentiate root and embedded clause syntax beyond the possibilities in the Discourse Projection Parameter (11.11) and Visible Links (11.40). In the discussions of each, we have moreover seen that both may ultimately turn out to be reflections of Universal Grammar and not parameters at all.[37]

11.5 Left dislocations with commas

11.5.1 Iterative a-categorial root clauses

Sections 11.2 and 11.3 have analysed leftward root phrasal movements without commas in terms of Discourse Shells and Augmented Structure-Preservation. Section 11.4 has accounted for inversions of the finiteness constituent I in terms of the same principles, with an added role for Economy of Derivation (11.38) and a new principle (or parameter) called Visible Links (11.40).

To complete the analysis of initial constituents in root contexts, we need to account for left dislocations set off by commas. Such root structures occur in all three languages under discussion and are bold in (11.42). Left dislocations often occur with co-referential resumptive pronouns, which are italicised in these examples.[38]

(11.42) a. [$_{XP}$ **[Mary]**$_i$, [$_{XP}$ why [$_X$ must] [$_{IP}$ [*she*]$_i$ always be late]]]?
[$_{XP}$**[Because he phoned]**, [$_{XP}$[the first part of the movie] [$_X$ Ø] [$_{IP}$ Jim missed out on]]].
John thinks [$_{CP}$ that [$_{XP}$ **[such a car,]**$_i$ [$_{IP}$ you shouldn't buy *it*$_i$]]].

  b. French:
On croit [$_{CP}$ que [$_{XP}$ **[ce type-là,]**$_i$ [$_{IP}$ le patron va *le*$_i$ mettre à la porte]]].
One thinks that   that guy-there the boss goes him+put to the door
'One thinks that that fellow, the boss is going to fire him.'

c. German (adapted from Vikner, 1995, 239):
[$_{XP}$ [$_{CP}$ **Dass du gekommen bist**]$_i$, [$_{XP}$ *das$_i$* [$_V$ ärgert] [$_{IP}$ hier alles]]].
   That you come   are   that   bothers
   here everyone
'That you have come, that is bothering everyone here.'

An obvious question is whether left dislocation also exemplifies Discourse Shells as in (11.17), or whether it realises some other more specifically topic-based structure such as the TopP of Rizzi (1997).

The Tensed S Constraint (11.29) has revealing consequences in this regard. As seen in section 11.3.2, any trace of a root fronting in a Discourse Projection IP (a main clause or a RIDE) must have its closest binder in the *Discourse Shell just above IP*, as in (11.43a). Any trace-binding element that precedes a left dislocated phrase is then "too high," as in (11.43b). Antecedent-trace pairs are in bold.

(11.43) a. [My supervisor]$_j$, [$_{XP}$[$_{SPEC(XP)}$ **a man like that**]$_i$ [$_X$ Ø] [$_{IP}$ she$_j$ would never hire **t**$_i$]].
     [Suzanne]$_j$, [$_{XP}$[$_{SPEC(XP)}$ **what else**]$_i$ [$_V$ does] [she$_j$ do **t**$_i$ to relax]]?

  b. *[**A man like that**]$_i$, [my supervisor]$_j$, [$_{IP}$ I don't think she$_j$ would hire **t**$_i$].
     *[**What else**]$_i$, [Suzanne]$_j$, does [$_{IP}$ she$_j$ do **t**$_i$ to relax]?

Consequently the Tensed S Constraint (11.29) explains in advance, as it were, why dislocations ("free-standing topics") must be exterior to landing sites for movements. And given that topics are in fact generally to the left of focus constituents, (11.29) also explains the broad descriptive generalisation of Rizzi (1997: 291): "Focus is quantificational, Topic is not."[39]

In view of these results, we can use iterated Discourse Shell Specifiers as a natural device for multiple left dislocated constituents. When such SPEC(XP) are DP arguments, they are paired with resumptive pronouns, and when they are adverbial adjunct PPs, they are not.

For an example such as (11.44), I thus propose a structure with multiple Discourse Shells such as (11.45):

(11.44) [$_{ZP}$ That guy$_i$, [$_Z$ Ø] [$_{YP}$ after the play, [$_Y$ Ø] [$_{XP}$ according to Sue, [$_X$ Ø] he$_i$ wept]]].

(11.45)
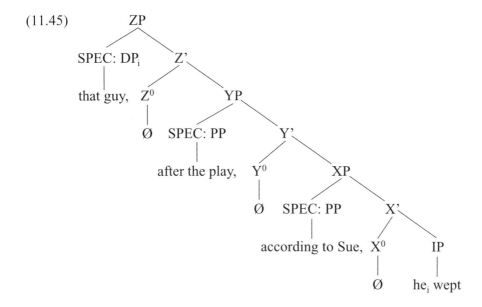

This kind of structure is especially typical of spoken French, perhaps partly because other fronting operations are excluded or marginal, as discussed in section 11.3.3.

(11.46) De nos jours, évidemment, un mec comme ça, amener une fille si riche dans ce genre de bar, sans même penser au qu'en-dira-t-on, ça lui retomberait certainement sur la tête.[40]

I wish now to use the concept of "link" in (11.39) to characterise the comma intonations in left dislocated constructions such as (11.42)–(11.44), which precisely lack such links.

In general, syntax allows (at least non-affixal) categories to be phonologically empty only if they are linked by sub-theories of binding or movement to filled categories; any exceptions to this such as arbitrary PRO require special treatment. Although we do not have a complete theory of empty category licensing, we can take (11.47) as a general statement subscribed to by essentially all current generative theories of syntax:

(11.47) *Empty Categories.* All categories must be phonologically realized except empty categories explicitly permitted by sub-theories such as binding and movement.

In this sense, empty heads that are links according to (11.39) are permitted by a theory of movement, as the definition of "link" is used in computing when the head of a Discourse Shell can be realized as a null allomorph (of *that*). In contrast, the heads X^0 of left-dislocated constructions are *not related to theories of binding or movement.* Hence Empty Categories (11.47) requires that they be phonologically realized.[41]

Now a plausible condition on phonological realization is (11.48), which generative syntax has adhered to even without stating it explicitly:

(11.48) *Morphemes as Categories.* Overt morphemes that are part of syntax must be members of labeled syntactic categories.

In the theory of Discourse Shells, the heads X^0 with left-dislocated constituents in their SPEC(XP) are a-categorial. So these X^0 are required to be phonologically realized – yet they cannot be overt. The only way to meet both these requirements is for them to be realized, at least abstractly, by a silent speech signal, i.e. a pause potential. As a result, the framework of root constructions developed here, supplemented by the uncontroversial statements (11.47) and (11.48), *predicts that the empty heads of Discourse Shells as in (11.45) must be pause potentials.* This corollary actually then explains the earlier tentative proposal for comma intonation in note 12:

(11.49) *Pause Prosody Corollary.* An unlinked, category-less head X^0 must be realised in PF as a pause potential, i.e, as "comma intonation."[42]

All three languages under discussion (English, French and German) widely utilise the configuration of recursive Discourse Shells with pause potentials, as exemplified in (11.45), for both left dislocated DPs and adverbial phrases.

11.5.2 Parentheticals in apparently final position

We have just seen how *initial* or "left-dislocated" constituents set off by commas are generated as Specifiers of Discourse Shells. I next discuss how to generate *final* parentheticals, which can either be right dislocated DPs with resumptive pronouns, speaker-oriented PPs (*to my knowledge, between you and me*), or clausal in form. The system developed here automatically generates such parentheticals in final position, and furthermore correctly limits them to root clauses.

Consider for example a variant of (11.45), in which the intermediate SPEC(YP) is *empty* in the base, and filled by movement of the lowest IP as in the following example.

(11.50)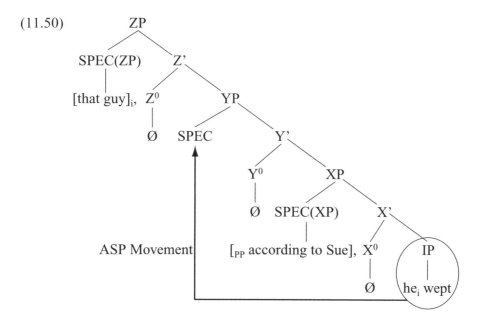

The movement indicated by the arrow causes the PP, which is base-generated as a *left-dislocated* adverbial adjunct, to surface phonologically as a final constituent, as in (11.51).

(11.51) That guy$_i$, [$_{IP}$ he$_i$ wept]$_j$, according to Sue t$_j$.

Section 11.2.2 noted that none of the more familiar root transformational operations exemplified in (11.18) seemed to front an IP. Yet in the tree (11.50) an IP moves to the Specifier of a Discourse Shell, thus filling the gap in the range of root frontings of phrasal constituents. We now can say that maximal phrases XP *of any type* can move to the specifier of a Discourse Shell. The result of moving an IP leftwards over a PP is then a "right dislocated" or "final parenthetical" PP.

The same sequencing of operations also successfully derives right dislocated DPs from left dislocation. For example in an underlying structure (11.52a), a Discourse Shell ZP moves to SPEC(YP), yielding (11.52b) with a right dislocated DP. Y^0 is then phonologically realized with comma intonation, as required by the Pause Prosody Corollary (11.49).

(11.52) a. [$_{YP}$ [$_{SPEC}$ Ø] Y^0 [$_{XP}$ My sister, [$_{ZP}$ never would I want her at a wedding]]].
 b. [[$_{ZP}$ Never would I want her at a wedding] [,] [$_{XP}$ my sister]].

Since these right-dislocated DPs can be generated only in a structure containing Discourse Shells, they require that the fronted IP be a main clause or a RIDE of indirect discourse. These considerations thus correctly exclude examples like (11.53), where the fronted IPs are underlying complements to Ns and hence not potential RIDEs:

(11.53) *Your proposal that [$_{YP}$[$_{IP}$ she be invited] [,] [$_{XP}$ my sister]], fell on deaf ears.
 *The report that [$_{YP}$[$_{IP}$ John was so sad] [,] [according to Sue]], surprised us.

In Emonds (1976), I took this contrast to indicate that right dislocation is a root transformational operation. This conclusion remains valid, but in fact the "root operation" involved is leftward movement of IP, not rightward movement of XP.

The only potential problem with the derivation illustrated in the tree (11.50) is that the trace of the moved IP might seem at first glance to violate the Tensed S Constraint (11.29), because it is not bound inside XP.[43] However, observe that this principle crucially applies only to traces that *are inside a finite complement* of an X^0.

(11.29) *Tensed S Constraint.* A trace inside a finite complement of X^0 must be bound within XP.

Since the IP in (11.50) *is* the finite complement (rather than being inside one), when it moves there remains no finite complement of X^0 to force the binding required by the Tensed S Constraint. Nor is the XP above the IP trace finite, since it has no finite head. The Tensed S Constraint thus correctly *predicts* that the only type of constituents allowed to completely move out of a Discourse Shell XP in one step are (i) the Discourse Projection IP itself, exactly what happens with right dislocated constituents as in the derivation (11.50), or (ii) conceivably the SPEC(XP), as in Rizzi's (1997) Italian examples in which a Focus DP precedes multiple Topics; see again note 39.

Finally, we need to understand why fronting a Discourse Projection leads to a pause potential in examples like (11.50), while the other root frontings in (11.18) do not permit comma intonation. To understand this discrepancy, recall the definition of a link (11.39):

(11.39) *Definition of Link.* An X^0 whose SPEC(XP) binds a trace t_i inside a finite complement of X^0 is called a *link* between SPEC and t_i.

When IP moves out of its XP Shell as in (11.50), neither the X^0 nor the higher Y^0 above the trace qualify as a link, since as just observed (i) the trace of IP is not bound in XP, and (ii) the XP complement of Y^0 is not of itself finite. Hence, the Pause Prosody Corollary (11.49) automatically and correctly requires comma intonation around a right-dislocated XP or a sentence-final parenthetical. In contrast, movement of any other maximal projection into the SPEC(XP) of a Discourse Shell yields an X^0 that is a link, and links are not subject to the phonological realization requirement of Empty Categories (11.47).

Yet another type of sentence-final parenthetical are speaker-oriented PPs associated only with root clauses, of the type studied in Banfield (1982): *between you and me, frankly, for heaven's sake*, etc. These PPs follow not only IPs, but larger structures such as the Discourse Shells YP in (11.54):

(11.54) [$_{YP}$ Not one interesting city did I visit]$_i$, [$_{XP}$ [*between you and me*] – X^0 – t_i].
Mary, [$_{YP}$ why must she always be late]$_i$, [$_{XP}$ [*for heaven's sake*] – X^0 – t_i]?

In (11.54) these YP Shells are base-generated as complements to empty a-categorial X^0 whose SPEC are the speaker-oriented PPs. The crucial factor is that movement of these Shells, which are themselves finite, deprives the

Shell XP immediately above them of finite status. The Tensed S Constraint (11.29) then does not apply. So it seems that without further stipulation, Discourse Shells provide structural positions not only for moved constituents but for both left and right dislocated constituents and final (root) parentheticals as well.

11.5.3 Clausal remnants in apparently final position

The correctness of the Discourse Shells approach is again confirmed by properties of final parentheticals whose form is clausal, italicised in (11.55):

(11.55) Kids pasta really appeals to, *no one can deny.*
John was ill, *it seemed to her.*
How could Mary love John, *I asked Sue.*

Let us call clausal final parentheticals of this type "clausal remnants." Banfield's (1982) detailed study of these remnants finds that, even though their finite verbs may invert with the subject as in (11.56a), they *systematically lack* fronted constituents generally analysed as being in SPEC(CP), as seen in (11.56b):

(11.56) a. This party is so boring, [$_{IP}$ {shouted Sam./don't you think?/can't you see?}]

b. This party is so boring, [$_{CP}$ {*to Mary/ *how often/ *into her ear} Sam whispered].

These facts lead Banfield to conclude that (using today's terminology) remnant parentheticals must be bare IP rather than CP constituents.

Additional evidence for the bare IP status of these remnants comes from the fact that they cannot contain left dislocated adverbials either:

(11.57) John was ill, (*from the obvious symptoms,) it seemed to her.
How could Mary love John, (*a few minutes later,) I asked Sue.

In terms of the present analysis, the asserted left hand clauses as in (11.55)–(11.57) have been raised into the SPEC(XP) of Discourse Shells, while the IP clausal remnants are base-generated IP complements of the X^0

heads of these Shells. The X^0 themselves are pause potentials written as commas.

Observe next that the verbs that occur in Banfield's clausal remnants in (11.55)–(11.57) such as *ask, deny, see, shout, think* are precisely those that accept indirect discourse complements (RIDEs). As throughout, I analyse RIDEs as a-categorial Discourse Shell YPs. This suggests that examples as in (11.55) derive from an underlying structure as in (11.58) by moving one Discourse Shell, namely a RIDE such as [$_{YP}$ *kids pasta really appeals to*], into the SPEC(XP) of another.

(11.58) [$_{XP}$ SPEC [$_{X'}$ X^0 [$_{IP}$ no one can deny [$_{YP}$ kids pasta really appeals to]]]]

As expected, these fronted Discourse Shells can themselves exhibit various root fronting operations; for example the internal shell in (11.58) exhibits topicalisation.[44]

This analysis further correctly predicts that verbs that cannot take indirect discourse IPs (RIDEs) are unacceptable in clausal remnants, even if they pragmatically indicate reported thought or speech.

(11.59) *Bill was poor, Sam {discussed/ talked/ disapproved/ inquired}.

I thus conclude that the surface main clauses in e.g. (11.55)–(11.57) are derived by fronting underlying Discourse Shell RIDE complements of the verbs in the parenthetical clausal remnants.

The range of dislocated constituents analyzed here includes left and right dislocated DPs with resumptive pronouns, left and right dislocated adverbial PPs, and both the speaker oriented PPs and clausal remnants discussed in Banfield (1982). The fact that theory of Discourse Shells (11.16) and the Augmented Structure Preserving Constraint (11.26) taken together account for such a wide range of dislocated elements constitutes very strong evidence for their adoption.

11.6 Summary of proposed hypotheses

The present analysis has provided a unified account of all left peripheral root transformational operations in Standard English, French and German in terms of a generalised Augmented Structure Preserving Constraint on derivations (11.26). A crucial innovation is a single type of iterated and a-categorial functional projection XP at the "top" of root and root-like clauses (RIDES), called Discourse Shells. The framework developed here fully accounts for long known pervasive empirical differences between various types of root constructions: left dislocations, topicalisations, exclamatives, contrastive focus, questions, verb inversions and fronting, and parenthetical formation.

The formal mechanisms proposed in this study include the following definitions and principles. They constitute a proposed fragment of Universal Grammar, in that these principles taken together reduce all the apparently disparate root transformational operations listed in (11.6)–(11.9), including differences among Standard English, German and French, to special cases of structure-preserving substitutions.

(11.10) *Root clauses.* Unembedded finite clauses IP are "Discourse Projections" in all languages.

(11.16) *Discourse Shells.* A series of categorially unspecified projections termed "Discourse Shells" may immediately dominate (only) IPs specified as Discourse Projections.

(11.24) *Definition of Structure-Preservation.* A structure-preserving transformational operation is one in which α substitutes for β, where β cannot be specified for a feature differently than α.

(11.26) *The Augmented Structure Preserving Constraint.* Movements must always be structure-preserving substitutions, as in (11.24).

(11.29) *Tensed S Constraint,* or *"Unique Traces Constraint."* A trace inside a finite complement of X^0 must be bound within XP.

(11.38) *Economy of Derivation.* Among alternative derivations from the same deep structure, prefer the derivation with the fewest insertions of overt free morphemes.

An important issue concerns how to express cross-linguistic variation in the root-embedded asymmetry of syntax. I therefore posed at the outset the three general questions below about how to relate universal grammar and particular grammars. Partial but nonetheless revealing answers have been provided for all three questions, though a certain amount of open-endedness remains. This is natural enough since few investigations have focused on these issues.

Question 1 asked whether different cross-linguistic specifications of grammatical items can account for different behaviours in root and embedded clauses. I have proposed an unambiguous "yes" answer. The telling example is the English null allomorph for the unmarked complementiser, signalled by the parentheses in (11.36a).

(11.36) *Uninterpreted Complementisers*, final version
     a. English: (that), C, Ø, +___IP
     b. German: dass, C, Ø, +___IP

Section 11.4 has argued that this has wide consequences in the differing forms of English and German root clauses; in particular, the lack of parentheses in the above German entry is the cause of its pervasive "Verb Second" pattern.

Question 2 asked whether any other, non-lexical parameterised principles differentiate root and embedded clause syntax for different languages and/or speakers. To answer this, I have looked into two (non-lexical) ways in which languages may plausibly show root-embedded asymmetries. Nonetheless, incomplete analyses rather than language variation may underlie these differences. Most central to concerns here is an idea (11.11) proposed by Ken Hale:[45]

(11.11) *Discourse Projection Parameter.* Particular languages may specify larger classes of finite clauses as Discourse Projections.

For example, the earliest work on structure-preservation suggested that "embedded root phenomena" in English and German fall under the rubric of Indirect Discourse, as in (11.12).

(11.12) *Indirect Discourse.* Standard German and typical idiolects of English permit IPs of indirect discourse to be Discourse Projections

We have briefly examined the possibilities of languages such as Icelandic, Yiddish, Italian and Japanese having larger sets of root-like embedded clauses (RIDEs). Alternatively, the German/ English option may turn out to be the only choice; that is, UG itself may specify that Indirect Discourse is the only possible way to embed Discourse Projections. This question thus remains partly open, but constrained by (11.11).

Finally, a tentative answer has been proposed for *Question 3*: what gives rise to and governs the distribution of comma intonation in root structures? The answer (11.49) is a corollary derived from three principles taken together: this study's analysis of root phenomena in terms of a-categorial Discourse Shells and two other currently uncontroversial tenets of generative syntax methodology:

(11.47) *Empty Categories.* All categories must be phonologically realized except empty categories explicitly permitted by sub-theories such as binding and movement.

(11.48) *Morphemes as Categories.* Overt morphemes that are part of syntax must be members of labeled syntactic categories.

(11.49) *Pause Prosody Corollary.* An unlinked, category-less head X^0 must be realised in PF as a pause potential, i.e, as "comma intonation."

Alternative analyses of root phenomena with labelled functional category heads such as TOP and FOC such as Rizzi (1997) cannot avoid counterparts to the principles and potential parameters reviewed in this summarising section. Precisely because several of these principles can apply to a-categorial Discourse Shells as well as to specified categories, they can be stated here in general rather than ad hoc terms. It is hard to see how proposing special categories at or near the root of trees could eliminate any of these statements; rather, the formulations would become more complex. Moreover, additional statements would then be needed to constrain the appearance of these special nodes. Alternative analyses can thus be questioned on grounds of parsimony, since the properties of root constructions have been accounted for in this study without adding a single category or ad hoc statement to the grammatical inventory. The only statement needed is the statement of the hypothesis itself, namely the existence of a-categorial Discourse Shells (11.16).

Notes

* This essay has appeared in *Peripheries: Syntactic Edges and their Effects*, edited by D. Adger, C. de Cat and G. Tsoulas, 75–120, Kluwer Academic Publishers, 2004. It appears here unchanged except that (i) there are some small editorial clarifications, and (ii) material treating possible rightward movements, including a sizable Appendix in the original, has been omitted. As a result, a few example and footnote numbers don't correspond in the two versions.

1. On the other hand, left dislocations mainly limited to main clauses in English occur more freely in French (De Cat, 2002) – or at least they are more frequent in the structural positions that allow them.
2. Kubo's chart (1994: 190) allows the following constructions in CPs but not IPs: (i) double nominatives, (ii) the *da*-form copula, (iii) topic NPs marked with so-called "exhaustive listing" *ga*, and (iv) emphatic VP fronting associated with morphological "*suru*-support" (partly parallel to *do*-support).
3. The root-like complements of "light verb" expressions such as *make a promise* can be sisters not of N but of V, a result of extraposition as suggested in Ross (1967); cf. (i). Complements unmistakably within NP as in (ii) are not root-like:
   (i) A promise has been made by John that [$_{RIDE}$ defective sets the company will fix].
   (ii) *A promise that [$_{IP}$ defective sets the company will fix] has been made by John.
4. Postal (1998) argues that extraposed clausal complements (of V and perhaps A) are the only constituents that freely tolerate all types of so-called "A-bar" extractions. English clauses of indirect discourse that exhibit root transformations (RIDEs) seem to be a subset of these, i.e., they also must be in final position of VP or AP.
   (i) Bill warned us on time that [$_{RIDE}$ flights to Chicago the company had cancelled].
   It is shocking to Sue that [$_{RIDE}$ never has she heard from her children].
   *Bill's warning that [$_{IP}$ flights to Chicago the company had cancelled] never reached us.
   *That [$_{IP}$ never has she heard from her children] is shocking to Sue.
   Interestingly, the very extractions tolerated in these extraposed clauses (ii) are incompatible with any root transformations in the same domain (iii).
   (ii) [Which company]$_i$ did Bill warn you [t$_i$ had cancelled flights to Chicago]?
   [Who]$_i$ is it shocking to Sue that [Mary has not once heard from t$_i$]?
   (iii) *[Which company]$_i$ did Bill warn you (that) [flights to Chicago t$_i$ had cancelled]?
   *[Who]$_i$ is it shocking to Sue that [not once has Mary heard from t$_i$]?
   Section 11.3.2 shows how the structures in this study explain paradigm (iii).

5. Subsequent treatments sometimes confuse certain distinctions in my original terminology, e.g. between directional PP preposing tolerating at most simple verb inversion and locative PP preposing, where subjects follow possibly complex predicates.
6. If Right node raising is an "across the board" movement (*John has your keys to, and Mary badly wants, my apartment*), it probably belongs under this heading. Like right dislocation, it may be derived by preposing a clause around an initial root constituent (from *My apartment [$_{IP}$ John has your keys to and Mary badly wants]*). However, the construction may result not from movement, but rather from a deletion governed by Ross's (1967) ingenious but unfortunately largely forgotten Directionality Constraint.
7. Saito and Fukui's (1998) strongly motivated revision of the distinction between Move and Merge removes certain apparent counterexamples to structure-preserving movement. Problematic sub-cases of movement such as Heavy NP Shift turn out to be subsumed under Merge in their theory. The appendix to this essay in Emonds (2004) shows how their theory and this essay complement each other.
8. "Unembedded" means a clause that is not an argument or adjunct of an underlying *lexical* X^0, as in Emonds (1985, Ch. 3). We will see as we proceed that a Discourse Projection can be the complement of an *empty* X^0 in a root context.
9. Thus, *Sue knows algebra* commits the speaker to the *reality* of an event based on a knowledge predicate, while *Sue must know algebra* stops short of this commitment; the speaker is only committed to a certain kind of logic, such as "if one understands formulae such as $x^2-y^2 = (x+y)(x-y)$, then one knows algebra."
10. Most data purporting to undermine the structure-preserving constraint in Hooper and Thompson (1973) and other subsequent works are actually already subsumed under (11.12a), a condition stated informally in Emonds (1970). Ensuing discussions expanded the data base, but did little to syntactically formalise the possibilities in indirect discourse. In particular, they rarely acknowledge the several restrictions in (11.2).
11. I am most grateful to my colleague Philip Spaelti for help in constructing all the German and many French examples that appear throughout this chapter.
12. The German examples in (11.13) indicate that "pause potentials," usually indicated by comma intonation, surround the larger Discourse Shell that contains the fronted constituents but not the Discourse Projection itself. Though the English punctuation practice on this point is less consistent, the only possible location for a comma in (11.14) is just after *that* in (11.14a). Hence we can conclude:
    (i) *Tentative Pause Prosody*: Embedded Discourse Shells are set off by pause potentials (= comma intonation).
    This principle is modified and generalised in section 11.5.

13. Discourse Shells are a-categorial counterparts to Rizzi's (1997) FocP and TopP. As I observe at various points, his labels create problems such as necessitating ad hoc distributional statements. However, I have no quarrel with certain arguments he provides for these *structures,* for example his claims that their heads – the X⁰ in Discourse Shells in (11.17) – can interfere with "head government" of I from outside XP.

    A Discourse Shell is also a restrictive reinterpretation of Banfield's (1982) E node in terms of categories with standard bar notation properties. I don't treat all aspects of the syntax of this node in her study.

14. The closest German counterpart to English exclamative WH-fronting seems to be the notorious *was für* construction, which has embedded clause syntax, e.g. a final verb: *Was für schöne Röcke das Mädchen anhabt.* 'What beautiful skirts the girl wears.'

15. Jackendoff (1977: Ch. 6) proposes that subjects of AP and PP, as in traditional grammar, are always external to these categories. This approach to subjects of such phrases, which runs counter to analyses in terms of small clauses, is further developed in Williams (1980), Emonds (2000a), and Chapter 1 of this study.

16. There remain unanalysed restrictions on the outputs of root transformations, which must exclude certain topicalisations, exclamations, narrative sentences, etc.

*A street address Mary should look for.	OK: A new hat I doubt would help her.
*With what a tyrant she works!	OK: What a tyrant she works with!
*The child's poor and run away she has.	OK: I said she'd run away and run away she has.

    Neither my framework nor others I am aware of provide principled reasons for excluding the constructions on the left, while still allowing the ones on the right.

17. Ken Hale first suggested this type of analysis (Emonds, 1976: 6). He felt that even in certain languages with pervasive free word order, structures that are embedded "deeply enough" often reveal fixed order. His examples involved participles akin to reduced relatives, which exhibited fixed word order.

18. In the study cited, non-major or *local* transformations perform operations on a phrase and a non-phrasal constituent adjacent to it. Borer's (1984) influential proposal describes these local transformations as essentially lexical insertion contexts for PF inflections; the inflections themselves correspond to the non-phrasal constituent in the local rule. Much of Emonds (2000a) is an attempt to extend such a model of late lexical insertion.

    However, "inflection" is too narrow a term for the X⁰ that undergo such rules; in Emonds (1976: Ch VI), local rules account for many different free forms of category P, the pro-form *one*, the COMPs *that* and *for*, the French negative *pas*, infinitival *to*, the grammatical A *much* and *so*, etc. In any case, to the extent

some version of Borer's idea succeeds, it subsumes local transformations; only structure-preserving and root transformational operations remain.
19. According to definitions of the crucial construct *root node* in Emonds (1976: Ch. I and 1985: Ch. 3), a root is *not* simply a tree's highest node. These definitions necessarily take into account transformational operations in several non-obvious root domains: **Had John** seen that, ...; Sit down or **must I** call the police; John was late, **as was I**; etc.
20. Criticisms of the SPC have often been based on such misunderstandings. For example, there are other constructions where intermediate traces seem to violate the SPC ($[_{PP}$ *In the garden$]_i$ seems t_i to be safer*). But Emonds (1985: Ch. 3), while indeed claiming that intermediate traces result from substitutions, explicitly states that SPC requirements apply only to *overt* surface constituents. Hence later proposals to move categories through many intermediate SPEC have always been orthogonal to the claims of the SPC framework.

 Another criticism claims that the SPC is defined for "separate rules" and hence can't apply in a modular model of syntax. However, the original SPC (11.21) explicitly applies to operations rather than rules.
21. Lightfoot and Weinberg continue: "Ch[omsky] adds several conditions to ensure that adjunction works appropriately, and they are clearly stipulative enough to require explanation: [they provide a list of 5 such conditions] Moreover, further conditions are required to ensure that adjunction is not used too freely, as we shall see." As doubtful as this analysis is, the SPC (11.21) is simply unrelated to intermediate traces (as pointed out in the text), no matter how many or which adjoined positions are proposed.
22. Under minimalist feature checking, moving α involves "matching features F" on α and some adjacent β that checks α. Occasionally F is independently motivated on *both* α and β, as in subject agreement. More often, there is no support for feature *matching* but only for saying that some functional category requires a certain syntactic context after Move. Indeed, Ndayiragije (1999) argues effectively that feature checking is more motivated as a general process if it is considered as post-Move contextual requirements imposed by (only) functional category elements.

 Going a step further, such contextual requirements (feature matching) on functional categories such as D are plausibly counterparts of the subcategorisation features on corresponding lexical heads such as N (as in Veselovská, 1998), the difference being that contextual features on functional categories are satisfied after Move rather than before. If one accepts both these restrictions, all of feature matching reduces to late lexical insertion for grammatical elements, which is precisely a central hypothesis of Emonds (2000).
23. In a different study, Van Riemsdijk (1998b) defends and develops a conception of *full feature sharing* among the various heads within extended projec-tions. Since this move fully assimilates the features of I to V and of N to D,

it actually implies that the HAP (11.22) and the original SPC (11.21) agree entirely.
24. Permanent reference of N corresponds to what Milner (1978: Ch. 1) discusses under the term "potential reference," and is associated with lexical meaning. By contrast, his SPEC(NP), today's D, acquires "actual reference" according to Milner only by virtue of being used in speech. Thus, a DP with no lexical head N (*something to file bank statements in*) doesn't have the perceived permanent reference of a lexical N, even if that N is a nonce compound (*a bank statement file*).
25. Among other examples, I cannot substitute for C – and it never does in the system here. Nor can D move over material to substitute for an empty P, a structurally parallel scenario which most linguists would consider wildly implausible.
26. If direct objects are always part of a DP, i.e., if object Ns are separated from Vs by an intervening head D, Noun Incorporation skips a head and becomes quite problematic. However, Noun Incorporation languages may be precisely those that tolerate bare NP objects. Cf. Kallulli (1999) for much relevant analysis.
27. Minimalism should not be committed to an a priori design of "extending trees" without landing sites. If it is, it cannot express generalisations of this sort, where several types of constituents compete for a single position even when no specific feature types are involved. In early generative grammar, when structuralism's a priori commitments to the form of permitted scientific descriptions clashed with expressing generalisations found through empirical investigation, these commitments were (correctly, I feel) denounced as dogma and as preventing progress.
28. To allow certain marginal extractions of WH-phrases from within WH-islands, it is sufficient to analyse the (bold) WH-subjects in the constructions (i) as remaining in SPEC(IP). SPEC(CP) is then available to bind a non-subject trace inside the finite clause.
    (i)   ?He is a man who$_i$ I don't know a single person [$_{CP}$ t$_i$ [$_{IP}$ **who** really likes t$_i$]].
          ?Which presents$_i$ did he wonder [$_{CP}$ t$_i$ [$_{IP}$ **who** bought t$_i$]]?
    For a theoretical scenario allowing a WH subject to remain in situ, see Rizzi (1997: 317).
    The Operator Binding constraint of Brame (1981) also prohibits multiple gaps in the same domain from being bound by what today is generally termed different SPEC(CP).
29. Rizzi (1997:296–297) treats this restriction as resulting from an "interpretative clash" involving a proposed construction-specific definition of focus. But the single escape hatch condition generalizes to other constructions such as restrictive relative clause CPs, and so is better treated as due to a general syntactic condition.
30. What is at issue in this study is the Augmented Structure Preserving Constraint (11.26) and how various root transformations conform to it. It would require quite a tour de force to turn the *absence of a movement* in a language (i.e., Mod-

ern French's lack of root frontings) into an argument *against* a proposed constraint on movement.

Standard French may well not tolerate non-phrasal inversions of I either. Subject pronoun enclitics on I may be a form of supplementary agreements on Is that are in situ. That is, French possibly never has a V or an I above IP.

31. An item with a category specification as [B, Ø] cannot satisfy an unmarked subcategorization frame selecting B or BP. For example, the non-locative preposition "*of*, P, Ø" is never selected as a PP with verbs such as *dash, glance, hand, place, put*. Similarly, stative verbs "V, Ø" are not selected as VPs after *try* and *force*; expletives don't satisfy subcategorisation for the category DP. Finally, Ø as a syntactic/ LF feature is *unrelated* to any representation of "null at PF."

32. Emonds (1985: Ch. 7) argues further that the category C is a subcase of P. Among other motivations there, most subordinating conjunctions P in the context ___IP (*before, since, while, when*, etc.) express temporal LOCATION, i.e., they are typical Ps with a feature TIME. The familiar English C *that, if* and *for* differ from them only by being unmarked (and uninterpreted) for the features LOCATION and TIME.

33. This system implies that the feature WH is on SPEC(CP) rather than C. If so, *whether* undoubtedly realises [SPEC(CP), WH], since it differs from *if* in sharing a number of properties with full WH-phrases. (One such property in Old English was the common phonology #hw___.) Locating *whether* in SPEC(CP) then makes WH-movement as a substitution for SPEC(CP) entirely consistent with both the original SPC (11.21) and the ASP (11.26). It furthermore demonstrates clearly how minimalist "feature matching" at the landing site of WH-movement, one of the few contexts where it has independent motivation, reduces to a local subcase of preserving structure.

34. There are some fairly well understood restrictions on when English *that* must also be overt. Briefly, it would seem that Universal Grammar permits a head of a CP such as *that* to alternate with a null allomorph only when CP is (i) governed by a V or an A and (ii) in its *base* position.

35. This reasoning suggests that Economy should also prevent inserting *that* in English dependent clauses as well – should not a null C sanctioned by (11.36a) always be preferred? Since cross-constructional support for formulating Economy of Derivation as (11.38) is so strong, it is likely that some additional factor related e.g. to focus must be forcing *that* to introduce some clauses, even though it apparently alternates optionally with a null allomorph. (There are few cases in language where grammatical morphemes are simply optional.) But as a non-root phenomenon, a full account of the optionality of embedded *that* lies outside the scope of this study.

There may well exist base positions where *that* is obligatory, as in finite subjunctive complements and after manner of speaking verbs: *?Mary insisted the box be wrapped; ?Sue murmured life was short.* In these constructions, the main

verbs seem necessarily focused. Perhaps *that* is required to "de-focus" an IP complement.
36. Visible Links (11.40) is considerably more general than the verb inversion parameter discussed in Roberts (1993), whereby C "is associated with Agr(eement) in Germanic." The term "I to C movement" for subject-auxiliary inversion is in fact also now a misnomer, since its category-less landing site is X^0 rather than C^0.
37. The issue arises as to whether French inversions of subject phrases and of subject clitics in direct questions are ways of satisfying Visible Links. It can be noted that French subject-clitic inversion illustrates perfectly how local adjunctions conform to van Riemsdijk's (1998a) Head Adjacency Principle (11.22a).
38. De Cat (2002, Ch. 3) effectively refutes the widely made claim that French left dislocated DPs with resumptive subject clitics can simply be in SPEC(IP) like other subjects. She shows they are in a position outside IP.
39. Rizzi (1997) claims that topics in Italian can sometimes follow trace-binding constituents (those in "focus"). At issue is the status of examples like (11.43b) and (iii) and (iv) below, which in English are considerably less acceptable than their respective counterparts in (11.43a), (i) and (ii):

(i) I said that John$_j$, this we should tell him$_j$ tomorrow.
     (Topic – Focus – IP)
(ii) ?I said that John$_j$, tomorrow, this we should tell him$_j$.
     (Topic – Topic – Focus – IP)
(iii) ??I said that this, John$_j$, we should tell him$_j$ tomorrow.
     (Focus – Topic – IP)
(iv) *I said that this, John$_j$, tomorrow, we should tell him$_j$.
     (Focus – Topic – Topic – IP)

(i)–(iv) are translations of Rizzi's Italian examples, except that I replace *credo* 'I believe' with *I said*. He gives all four examples as equally acceptable.

The examples (iii)–(iv) can be derived from (i)–(ii) by moving the focused constituent [$_{DP}$ *this*] in the SPEC of the lowest RIDE clauses to the SPEC of a higher RIDE clause; this movement doesn't in itself violate the Tensed S Constraint (11.29) or more generally the overall framework developed here. However, the English judgments suggest to me that such movement incurs a cost by introducing derivational steps that have no syntactic motivation (their only motivation being the pragmatics of indirect discourse). If the Italian counterparts to (i)–(iv) are truly all totally acceptable, perhaps that language has a feature to check in the SPECs of Discourse Shells that is absent in English. It is also possible that Italian sentences with null subjects allow one topic phrase in SPEC(IP), a possibility neither Rizzi nor I have investigated.
40. This style is infelicitous in English, as demonstrated by translating (11.46): *These days, obviously, a guy like that, taking such a rich girl into that type of*

bar, without even thinking about what people will say, that would certainly come back on him. Thanks to C. De Cat for help with the French example.

41. Rizzi (1997: 292) explicitly states that SPEC(TopP) does not involve binding in Italian. Hence his theory of TopP, wherein "Top^0 and Foc^0 are phonetically null in Italian" (1997: 287) violates Empty Categories (11.47), as do theories that express RIDEs with iterated CPs. Violating (11.47) freely leads to vacuous solutions of all sorts of problems; e.g., Japanese can always have null empty final D^0, null agreement everywhere, etc.
42. This proposal has an antecedent in the general principle for comma intonation proposed in my studies on parentheticals in the 1970s, including the formulation in Emonds (1976: Ch. I).
43. This concern could be phrased as a violation of a Minimal Link Condition.
44. In order to maintain the Pause Prosody Corollary (11.49) in unmodified form, the X^0 in examples like (11.58) cannot qualify as a link (11.39). Various ways of modifying the Corollary come to mind, but perhaps the most interesting approach is to consider that bare IP may differ from other constituents in not leaving traces. Without an IP trace, the X^0 in (11.58) is not a link and (11.49) can stand. This move could also explain why IPs seem immune to leftward focus movements, especially when they do not alternate with DPs (e.g., clausal complements of *seem*), and perhaps why CPs with an empty SPEC(CP) are as well.
45. The other possible parameter discussed here is Visible Links (11.40). This parameter is largely orthogonal to the main claims here connecting root phenomena and augmented structure preservation. Visible links may alternatively be (i) a "Conditional Universal" (holding vacuously when the premise is not satisfied), (ii) a part of grammatical lexicons concerning WH and NEG, or (iii) a true non-lexical parameter.

References

Abbott, Barbara
    1976   Right Node Raising as a Test for Constituenthood. *Linguistic Inquiry* 7: 639–642.

Abeillé, Anne and Danièle Godard
    1994   The Complementation of Tense Auxiliaries in French. In: J. Moore (ed.), *Papers from the West Coast Conference on Formal Linguistics* 13. University of California at San Diego, La Jolla.

Abeillé, A., D. Godard and P. Miller
    1997   Les Causatives en Français: Un Cas de Compétition Syntaxique. *Langue Française* 115, 62–74.

Abney, Steven
    1987   *The English Noun Phrase in its Sentential Aspect.* PhD Dissertation, Massachusetts Institute of Technology, Cambridge.

Åfarli, Tor
    1989   Passive in Norwegian and in English. *Linguistic Inquiry* 20: 101–108.

Åfarli, Tor
    1992   *The Syntax of Norwegian Passive Constructions.* Amsterdam: John Benjamins.

Aissen, Judith
    1974   Verb Raising. *Linguistic Inquiry* 5: 325–366.

Aissen, Judith
    1983   Indirect Advancement in Tzotzil. In *Studies in Relational Grammar 1*, David Perlmutter (ed.), 325–366. Chicago: The University of Chicago Press.

Aissen, Judith and D. Perlmutter
    1976   Clause Reduction in Spanish. In V. Edge et al., eds., *Proceedings of the Second Annual Meeting of the Berkeley Linguistics Society,* Berkeley Linguistics Society, Berkeley.

Allerton, D. J.
    1978   Generating indirect objects in English. *Journal of Linguistics* 14: 21–33.

Alsina, Alex and Sam A. Mchombo
    1990   The syntax of applicatives in Chichea: Problems for a theta-theoretic asymmetry. *Natural Language and Linguistic Theory* 8: 493–506.

Anagnostopoulou, Elena
    1993   On the Representation of Clitic Doubling in Modern Greek. [MS. University of Salzburg/University of Tilburg.]

Anderson, Stephen
    1971   On the role of deep structure in semantic interpretation. *Foundations of Language* 7: 387–396.

Aoun, Joseph
    1985   *A Grammar of Anaphora.* Cambridge: The MIT Press.

Authier, J.-M. and L. Reed
    1992   On the Syntactic Status of French Affected Datives. *Linguistic Review* 9: 295–311.

Babby, Leonard H.
    1987   Case, Prequantifiers, and Discontinuous Agreement in Russian. *Natural Language and Linguistics Theory* 5, 91–138.

Baker, Mark
    1985   The Mirror Principle and morphosyntactic explanation. *Linguistic Inquiry* 16: 373–416.

Baker, Mark
    1988a   *Incorporation: A Theory of Grammatical Function Changing.* Chicago: The University of Chicago Press.

Baker, Mark
    1988b   Theta theory and the syntax of applicatives in Chichea. *Natural Language and Linguistic Theory* 6: 353–389.

Baker, Mark
    1989   Object sharing and projection in serial verb constructions. *Linguistic Inquiry* 20: 513–554.

Baker, Mark
    1999   Clitic Climbing and the Boundedness of Head Movement. In Henk van Riemsdijk (ed.), *Clitics in the Languages of Europe,* Berlin/New York: Mouton de Gruyter.

Baltin, Mark
    1982   A Landing Site Theory of Movement Rules. *Linguistic Inquiry* 13, 1–38.

Baltin, Mark
    1987   Heads and Projections. In: M. Baltin and A. Kroch (eds.), *Alternative Conceptions of Phrase Structure.* Chicago: University of Chicago Press.

Barss, Andrew and Howard Lasnik
    1986   A note on anaphora and double objects. *Linguistic Inquiry* 17: 347–354.

Belletti, Adriana and Luigi Rizzi
    1981   The Syntax of *ne*: Some Theoretical Implications. *The Linguistic Review* 1: 117–154.

Belletti, Adriana and Luigi Rizzi
    1988   Psych-verbs and Theta-theory. *Natural Language and Linguistic Theory* 6, 291–352.

Bok-Bennema, Reineke
    1981   Clitics and Binding in Spanish. In: J. Koster and R. May (eds.), *Levels of Syntactic Representation.* Dordrecht: Foris.

Bordelois, Ivonne
    1985   Parasitic Gaps: Extensions of Restructuring. In *Generative Studies in Spanish Syntax*, ed. by Ivonne Bordelois, Heles Contreras and Karen Zagona. Dordrecht: Foris. pp. 1–24.

Borer, Hagit
    1984   *Parametric Syntax.* Dordrecht: Foris.

Borer, Hagit
    1993   *Parallel Morphology.* Cambridge, Mass: MIT Press.

Bresnan, Joan
 1970 On Complementizers: Toward a Syntactic Theory of Complement Types. *Foundations of Language* 6, 297–321.
Bresnan, Joan and Sam Mchombo
 1987 Topic, Pronoun, and Agreement in Chichea. *Language* 63: 741–782.
Burzio, Luigi
 1981 *Intransitive Verbs and Italian Auxiliaries.* PhD Dissertation, Massachusetts Institute of Technology, Cambridge.
Burzio, Luigi
 1986 *Italian Syntax: a Government and Binding Approach*, Reidel, Dordrecht.
Caink, Andrew
 1998 *The Lexical Interface: Closed Class Items in South Slavic and English.* Unpublished Ph.D. dissertation, University of Durham, Durham.
Chomsky, Noam
 1965 *Aspects of the Theory of Syntax.* Cambridge, Mass: MIT Press.
Chomsky, Noam
 1970 Remarks on Nominalization. In *Readings in English Transformational Grammar,* 184–221. R. Jacobs and P. Rosenbaum (eds.), Waltham: Ginn.
Chomsky, Noam
 1972 Deep structure, surface structure, and semantic interpretation. In: *Studies on Semantics in Generative Grammar*, 62–119. The Hague: Mouton.
Chomsky, Noam
 1973 Conditions on Transformations. In: Stephen Anderson and Paul Kiparsky (eds.), *A Festschrift for Morris Halle.* New York: Holt, Rinehart and Winston.
Chomsky, Noam
 1975 *The Logical Structure of Linguistic Theory.* Chicago: The University of Chicago Press.
Chomsky, Noam
 1977 On Wh-Movement. In *Formal Syntax,* 71–132. P. Culicover, T. Wasow and A. Akmajian (eds.) New York: Academic Press.
Chomsky, Noam
 1981 *Lectures on Government and Binding.* Dordrecht: Foris.
Chomsky, Noam
 1982 *Concepts and Consequences.* Cambridge: MIT Press.
Chomsky, Noam
 1986a *Barriers.* Cambridge, MA: MIT Press.
Chomsky, Noam
 1986b *Knowledge of Language: Its Nature, Origin, and Use.* New York: Praeger.
Chomsky, Noam
 1991 Some Notes on Economy of Derivation and Representation. *Principles and Parameters in Comparative Grammar*, ed. by Robert Freidin 417–454. MIT Press, Cambridge, MA.
Chomsky, Noam
 1992 *A Minimalist Program for Linguistic Theory.* MIT Occasional Papers in Linguistics 1. Massachusetts Institute of Technology, Cambridge.

Chomsky, Noam
    1995   *The Minimalist Program*. Cambridge: MIT Press.

Chomsky, Noam and Howard Lasnik
    1977   Filters and Control. *Linguistic Inquiry* 8.425–504.

Chung, Sandra
    1976   An object-creating rule in Bahasa Indonesa. *Linguistic Inquiry* 7: 41–87.

Cinque, Guglielmo
    1980   On Extraction from NP in Italian. *Journal of Italian Linguistics* 5: 47–99.

Comrovski, Ileana
    1989   Verb movement and object extraction in French. In *Proceedings of NELS 20. 19[89]*. Juli Carter, Rose-Marie Déchaine, Bill Philip and Tim Shere (eds.), Graduate Linguistic Student Association, Department of Linguistics, University of Massachusetts, Amherst: 91–105.

Contreras, Heles
    1979   Clause Reduction, the Saturation Constraint, and Clitic Promotion in Spanish. *Linguistic Analysis* 5: 161–182.

Contreras, Heles
    1986   Open and closed A-bar chairs. In *Formal Parameters of Generative Grammar.* Vol. 2: *Going Romance*, Peter Coopmans, Ivonne Bordelois and Bill Dotson Smith (eds.). Utrecht: University of Utrecht.

Contreras, Heles
    1984   A note on Parasitic Gaps. *Linguistic Inquiry* 15.698–701.

Corver, Norbert
    1997   *Much*-Support as a Last Resort. *Linguistic Inquiry* 28, 119–164.

Couquaux, Daniel
    1981   French Predication and Linguistic Theory. In: J. Koster and R. May (eds.), *Levels of Syntactic Representation*. Dordrecht: Foris.

Culicover, Peter
    2001   Parasitic Gaps: A History. In *Parasitic Gaps*, ed. by Peter Culicover and Paul Postal. Cambridge: MIT Press, 3–68.

Czepluch, Hartmut
    1982   Case theory and the dative construction. *The Linguistic Review* 2: 1–38.

Doetjes, J., A. Neeleman and H. van de Koot
    1999   *Degree Expressions and the Autonomy of Syntax,* unpublished paper.

Emonds, Joseph E.
    1972   Evidence that indirect object movement is a structure preserving rule. *Foundations of Language* 8: 546–561.

Emonds, Joseph E.
    1976   *A Transformational Approach to English Syntax.* New York: Academic Press.7

Emonds, Joseph E.
    1978   The Verbal Complex V¢-V in French. *Linguistic Inquiry* 9: 151–175.

Emonds, Joseph E.
    1985   *A Unified Theory of Syntactic Categories*. Dordrecht: Foris.

Emonds, Joseph E.
1986a   Generalized Np-a inversion: Hallmark of English. *Indiana University Linguistics Club Twentieth Anniversary Volume.* Bloomington: Indiana University Linguistics Club.

Emonds, Joseph E.
1986b   Parts of speech in Generative Grammar. *Linguistic Analysis* 16: 247–286.

Emonds, Joseph E.
1987   The Invisible Category Principle. *Linguistic Inquiry* 18: 613–632.

Emonds, Joseph E.
1990   The autonomy of the (syntactic) lexicon and syntax. In *Interdisciplinary Approaches to Language: Essays in Honor of S.-Y. Kuroda*, Carol Georgopoulos and R. Ishihara (eds.). Dordrecht: Kluwer.

Emonds, Joseph E.
1991   The Autonomy of the (Syntactic) Lexicon and Syntax. In: C. Georgopoulos and R. Ishihara (eds.), *Interdisciplinary Approaches to Language: Essays in Honor of S.-Y. Kuroda.* Dordrecht: Kluwer.

Emonds, Joseph E.
1991   Subcategorization and syntax-based theta-role assignment. *Natural Language and Linguistic Theory* 9: 369–429.

Emonds, Joseph E.
1993   Projecting Indirect Objects. *Linguistic Review* 10: 211–263.

Emonds, Joseph E.
1994   Two Conditions of Economy. In G. Cinque et al. (eds.), *Paths toward Universal Grammar: Papers in Honor of Richard Kayne.* Washington, D.C.: Georgetown University Press.

Emonds, Joseph E.
1995   Secondary Predication, Stationary Particles, and Silent Prepositions. In A. Baba et al., ed., *Essays in Linguistics and Philology Presented to Professor Kinsuke Hasegawa,* Kenkyusha, Tokyo.

Emonds, Joseph E.
1999   How Clitics License Null Phrases: A Theory of the Lexical Interface. In H. van Riemsdijk, ed., *Clitics in the Languages of Europe,* Berlin/New York: Mouton de Gruyter.

Emonds, Joseph E.
2000   *Lexicon and Grammar: the English Syntacticon.* Berlin/New York: Mouton de Gruyter.

Emonds, Joseph E.
2002   Formatting Lexical Entries: Interface Optionality and Zero. *Theoretical and Applied Linguistics at Kobe Shoin* 5: 1–22.

Emonds, Joseph E.
2003   Adjectival Passives: the Construction in the Iron Mask. *Syncom Project,* Case 1. Ed. M. Everaert and H. van Riemsdijk. *http://www-uilots.let.uu.nl/syncom/uiltjes/cases.htm*

Emonds, Joseph E. and Rosemarie Ostler
2003   Thirty Years of Double Object Debates. *Syncom Project,* Case 30. Ed. M. Everaert and H. van Riemsdijk. *http://www-uilots.let.uu.nl/syncom/uiltjes/cases.htm*

Engdahl, Elisabet
  1983   Parasitic Gaps. *Linguistics and Philosophy* 6.5–34.
Evers, Arnold
  1975   *The Transformational Cycle in Dutch and German*. PhD Dissertation, University of Utrecht.
Fassi-Fehri, Abdulkader
  1992   *Issues in the Structure of Arabic Clauses and Words*. Dordrecht: Kluwer.
Fillmore, Charles J.
  1965   *Indirect Object Constructions in English and the Ordering of Transformations*. The Hague: Mouton.
Green, Georgia
  1974   *Semantics and Syntactic Regularity*. Bloomington: Indiana University Press.
Grimshaw, Jane
  1979   Complement selection and the lexicon. *Linguistic Inquiry* 10: 279–326.
Hasegawa., Kinsuke
  1968   The Passive Construction in English. *Language* 44: 230–243.
Haverkort, Marko
  1989   Clitic Climbing and Barrierhood of VP. *Current Approaches to African Linguistics* 7: 145–158.
Haverkort, Marko
  1993   Clitics and Parameterization. EUROTYP Working Papers VIII, vol. 2, European Science Foundation, Strasbourg.
Hayes, Bruce
  1990   Precompiled Phrasal Phonology. In: S. Inkelas and D. Zec (eds.), *The Phonology-Syntax Connection*. Chicago: Chicago University Press.
Hendrick, Randall
  1976   Prepositions and the X-bar theory. In *Proposals for Semantic Theory (= UCLA Papers in Syntax 7)*, 95–122. Los Angeles: University of California at Los Angeles.
Hendrick, Randall
  1978   The Phrase Structure of Adjectives and Complements. *Linguistic Analysis* 4: 255–299.
Herschensohn, Julia
  1981   French Causatives: Restructuring, Opacity, Filters and Construal. *Linguistic Analysis* 8, 217–280.
Hoji, Hajime
  1985   Logical form constraints and configuratonal structures in Japanese. Unpublished Ph.D. dissertation, University of Washington, Seattle.
Holmberg, Anders
  1991   On the Scandinavian double object construction. *Reports from Uppsala University* 19: 33–46.
Hornstein, Norbert and Amy Weinberg
  1981   Case theory and preposition stranding. *Linguistic Inquiry* 12: 55–92.
Horvath, Julia
  1992   The anti-c-command and case-compatibility in the licensing of parasitic chains. *The Linguistic Review* 9, 183–218.

Huang, James
    1982   *Logical Relations in Chinese and the Theory of Grammar,* Ph.D. Dissertation. Massachusetts Institute of Technology, Cambridge.

Huang, Li-Yi
    1991   The double object construction of Chinese. Unpublished manuscript, University of California, San Diego.

Jackendoff, Ray
    1972   *Semantic Interpretation in Generative Grammar.* Cambridge, MA: MIT Press.

Jackendoff, Ray
    1973   The Base Rules for Prepositional Phrases. In S. Anderson and P. Kiparsky, eds., *A Festschrift for Morris Halle*, Holt, Rinehart and Winston, New York: 345–356.

Jackendoff, Ray
    1977   *X'-Syntax: A Study of Phrase Structure,* MIT Press, Cambridge, Mass.

Jackendoff, Ray
    1987   The status of thematic relations in linguistic theory. *Linguistic Inquiry* 18: 369–412.

Jackendoff, Ray
    1990   On Larson's treatment of the double object construction. *Linguistic Inquiry* 21: 427–456.

Jackendoff, Ray
    1990   *Semantic Structures*, MIT Press, Cambridge, MA.

Jaeggli, Oswaldo
    1981   *Topics in Romance Syntax.* Dordrecht: Foris.

Jaeggli, Oswaldo
    1986   Passive. *Linguistic Inquiry* 17: 587–622.

Kajihara, Satomi
    1991   *Derivation of the N-suru Construction*, M.A. thesis, University of Washington.

Kayne, Richard
    1975   *French Syntax,* MIT Press, Cambridge, Mass.

Kayne, Richard
    1981a   Unambiguous paths. In *Levels of Syntactic Representation*, Robert May and Jan Koster (eds.), 143–184. Dordrecht: Foris.

Kayne, Richard
    1981b   On certain differences between French and English. *Linguistic Inquiry* 12: 349–371.

Kayne, Richard
    1984   *Connectedness and Binary Branching.* Dordrecht: Foris.

Kayne, Richard
    1983   Connectedness. *Linguistic Inquiry* 14.223–249.

Keenan, Edward
    1985   Passive in the World's Languages. In *Language Typology and Syntactic Description* I, 243–281. Ed. T. Shopen. Cambridge: Cambridge University Press.

Keyser, Samuel J. and Thomas Roeper
  1992   Re: The Abstract Clitic Hypothesis. *Linguistic Inquiry* 23, 89–125.
Kimball, John
  1973   Get. In *Syntax and Semantics* 1, 205–215. Ed. J. Kimball. New York: Academic Press.
Kimenyi, Alexandre
  1980   *A Relational Grammar of Kinyarwanda*. Berkeley: University of California Press.
Koopman, Hilda
  1984   *Verb Phrase Syntax*. Dordrecht: Foris.
Koster, Jan
  1978   *Locality Principles in Syntax*. Dordrecht: Foris.
Kubo, Miori
  1989   Are subject small clauses really small clauses? Unpublished manuscript. Massachusetts Institute of Technology, Cambridge.
Kubo, Miori
  1992   Japanese Passives. *Journal of Institute of Language and Culture Studies (Hokkaido University)* 23: 231–302.
Kubo, Miori
  1996   Some Considerations on Noun Classes and Numeral Classifiers: A Study of (Pseudo)partitives in Japanese and English. *Keio Studies in Theoretical Linguistics* 1, 89–124.
Kuroda, Sige-Yuki
  1965   Generative grammatical studies in the Japanese language. Unpublished Ph.D. dissertation, Massachusetts Institute of Technology, Cambridge.
Kuroda, Sige-Yuki
  1979   On Japanese Passives. In G.Bedell, E. Kobayashi, and M, Muraki (eds.), Exploration in Linguistics: Papers in Honor of Kazuko Inoue, Kenkyusha: Tokyo. Reprinted in In S.Y. Kuroda 1992. Japanese Syntax and Semantics: Collected Papers, Dordrecht; Kluwer: 181–221.
Lamiroy, Béatrice
  1983   *Les verbes du mouvement en français et en espagnol*, Amsterdam: John Benjamins.
Lamiroy, Béatrice
  1991   Binding Properties of French *en*. In: C. Georgopoulos and R. Ishihara (eds.), *Interdisciplinary Approaches to Language: Essays in Honor of S.-Y. Kuroda*. Dordrecht: Kluwer.
Larson, Richard
  1985   Bare NP adverbs. *Linguistic Inquiry* 16: 595–621.
Larson, Richard
  1988   On the double object construction. *Linguistic Inquiry* 19: 335–391.
Larson, Richard
  1990   Double objects revisited: Reply to Jackendoff. *Linguistic Inquiry* 21: 589–632.
Lasnik, Howard and Mamoru Saito
  1984   On the nature of Proper Government. *Linguistic Inquiry* 15.245–289.

Lasnik, Howard and Timothy Stowell
  1991   Weakest Crossover. *Linguistic Inquiry* 22.687–720.
Levin, Beth and Malka Rappaport
  1986   The formation of adjectival passives. *Linguistic Inquiry* 17: 623–663.
Lieber, Rochelle
  1980   On the Organization of the Lexicon. PhD Dissertation, Massachusetts Institute of Technology, Cambridge.
Lieber, Rochelle
  1983   Argument Linking and Compounds in English. *Linguistic Inquiry* 14: 251–286.
Lobeck, A.
  1995   Ellipsis: Functional Heads, Licensing, and Identification, Oxford: Oxford University Press.
Löbel, Elisabeth
  2001   Classifiers and the Notion of 'Semi-Lexical Head'. In N. Corver and H. van Riemsdijk, eds., *Semi-Lexical Categories: The Function of Content Words and the Content of Function Words* Berlin/New York: Mouton de Gruyter.
Marantz, Alec
  1984   *On the Nature of Grammatical Relations.* Cambridge: MIT Press.
Mchombo, Sam A.
  1984   The nonexistence of verb object agreement in Bantu. Unpublished manuscript, San Jose State University, San Jose.
Miller, Philip P.
  1992   *Clitics and Complements in Phrase Structure Grammar.* New York: Garland Press.
Miller, Philip P.
  1992   *Clitics and Constituents in Phrase Structure Grammar*, Garland Press, New York.
Milner, J.-C.
  1978   *De la Syntaxe à l'Interprétation.* Paris: Le Seuil.
Milner, J.-C.
  1982   *Ordres et raisons de langue*, Le Seuil, Paris.
Monachesi, Paola
  1993   Restructuring Verbs in Italian HPSG Grammar. In: K. Beals et al. (eds.), *Proceedings of the 29th Regional Meeting of the Chicago Linguistics Society.* Chicago: University of Chicago.
Napoli, Donna Jo
  1981   Semantic Interpretation vs. Lexical Governance. *Language* 57, 841–887.
Napoli, Donna Jo
  1981   Semantic Interpretation vs. Lexical Governance. *Language* 57: 841–887.
Nespor, Marina
  1990   Vowel Deletion in Italian: the Organization of the Phonological Component. *Linguistic Review* 7: 375–398.
Nespor, Marina
  1993   The Phonology of Clitic Groups. In: L. Hellan and H. van Riemsdijk (eds.), *EUROTYP Working Papers VIII*, vol. 5. European Science Foundation, Strasbourg.

Oehrle, Richard
1976   The grammatical status of the English dative alternation. Unpublished Ph.D. dissertation, Massachusetts Institute of Technology, Cambridge.
Perlmutter, D.
1971   *Deep and Surface Structure Constraints in Syntax.* New York: Holt, Rinehart and Winston.
Pesetsky, David
1982   Paths and Categories. Unpublished Ph.D. dissertation, Massachusetts Institute of Technology, Cambridge.
Plann, Susan
1981   The two *el* + infinitive constructions in Spanish. *Linguistic Analysis* 7: 204–240.
Poser, William
1982   Lexical rules may exchange internal arguments. *The Linguistic Review* 2: 97–100.
Postal, Paul
1986   *Studies of Passive Clauses.* Albany: State University of New York Press.
Postal, Paul
1994   Parasitic and Pseudoparasitic Gaps. *Linguistic Inquiry* 25: 64–117.
Postal, Paul and Geoffrey K. Pullum
1988   Expletive noun phrases in subcategorized positions. *Linguistic Inquiry* 19: 635–670.
Riemsdijk, Henk van
1978   *A Case Study in Syntactic Markedness,* Dordrecht, Foris.
Riemsdijk, Henk van
1998a   Categorial feature magnetism: the endocentricity and distribution of projections, *Journal of Comparative Germanic Linguistics* 2: 1–48.
Riemsdijk, Henk van and R. Huijbregts
1998b   Interface in Space – How Natural Language Expresses Spational Relations. paper presented at the Third International Symposium on Language, Logic and Computation, Batumi.
Rizzi, Luigi
1978   A Restructuring Rule in Italian Syntax. In: J. Keyser (ed.), *Recent Transformational Studies in European Languages.* Cambridge: The MIT Press.
Rizzi, Luigi
1978   A Restructuring Rule in Italian Syntax. In S. J. Keyser, ed., *Recent Transformational Studies in European Languages*, MIT Press, Cambridge, Mass.
Rizzi, Luigi
1978   A Restructuring Rule in Italian Syntax. *Recent Transformational Studies in European Languages*, ed. by Samuel Jay Keyser, 113–158, MIT Press, Cambridge, MA.
Roberts, Ian
1987   *The Representation of Implicit and Dethematized Subjects.* Dordrecht: Foris Publications.

Rosenbaum, Peter
 1967 *The Grammar of English Predicate Complement Constructions.* Cambridge: MIT Press.
Ross, John
 1967 *Constraints on Variables in Syntax.* Ph.D. dissertation, Massachusetts Institute of Technology, Cambridge, Mass. Republished as *Infinite Syntax.* New York: Garland Press.
Rouveret, Alain and Jean-Roger Vergnaud
 1980 Specifying Reference to the Subject: French Causatives and Conditions on Representations. *Linguistic Inquiry* 11: 97–201.
Ruwet, N.
 1990 *En* et *Y*: Deux Clitiques Pronominaux Antilogophoriques. *Langages* 97: 51–81.
Salleh, Ramli Md.
 1987 Fronted constituents in Malay: The base structures and Move a in a configurational Non-Indo-European language. Unpublished PhD Dissertation, University of Washington, Seattle.
Schoorlemmer, Maaike
 1995 *Participial Passive and Aspect in Russian.* Utrecht: Onderzoeksinstituut voor Taal en Spraak.
Selkirk, Elizabeth
 1977 Some Remarks on Noun Phrase Structure. In A. Akmajian, P. Culicover, and T. Wasow, eds., *Formal Syntax* Academic Press, New York.
Siegel, Dorothy
 1973 Nonsources of Unpassives. In *Syntax and Semantics* 2: 301–317. Ed. J. Kimball. New York: Academic Press.
Speas, M.
 1990 Phrase Structure in Natural Language, Kluwer, Dordrecht.
Sportiche, D.
 to appear Clitic Constructions. In: J. Rooryck and L. Zaring (eds.), *Phrase Structure and the Lexicon.* Bloomington: IULC Press.
Stowell, Timothy
 1981 *The Origins of Phrase Structure*, PhD Dissertation, MIT.
Stowell, Timothy
 1985 Licensing Conditions on Null Operators. *Proceedings of the West Coast Conference on Formal Linguistics* 4, ed. by J. Goldberg, S. MacKaye and M. Westcoat. Stanford: Stanford Linguistics Association.
Strozer, Judith
 1976 Clitics in Spanish. Unpublished Ph.D. dissertation, University of California, Los Angeles.
Strozer, Judith
 1981 An Alternative to Restructuring in Romance Syntax. In: H. Contreras and J. Klausenburger (eds.), *Proceedings of the Tenth Anniversary Linguistics Symposium on Romance Languages.* Seattle: University of Washington.
Stuurmann, F.
 1985 *X-bar and X-plain*, Foris, Dordrecht.

Takezawa, Koichi
　1987　　A configurational approach to Case-marking in Japanese. Unpublished PhD Dissertation, University of Washington, Seattle.
Talmy, Leonard
　1985　　Lexicalization patterns: Semantic structure in lexical forms. In *Language Typology and Syntactic Description*. Vol 3: *Grammatical Categories and the Lexicon*, T. Shopen (ed.). Cambridge: Cambridge University Press.
Taraldsen, Knut Tarald
　1981　　The theoretical interpretation of a class of marked extractions. *Theory of Markedness in Generative Grammar*, ed. by A. Belletti, L. Brandi and L. Rizzi Pisa: Scuola Normale Superiore di Pisa.
van Riemsdijk, Henk and Edwin Williams
　1981　　NP-structure. *The Linguistic Review* 1: 171–217.
Veselovská, Ludmila
　2001　　Agreement Patterns of Czech Group Nouns and Quantifiers. In *Semi-Lexical Categories,* 273–320. Ed. N. Corver and H. van Riemsdijk. Berlin/New York: Mouton de Gruyter.
Veselovská, Ludmila and Petr Karlík
　2003　　Analytic Passives in Czech. In Preparation.
Wasow, Thomas
　1977　　Transformations and the Lexicon. In *Formal Syntax*, 327–360. Ed. P. Culicover, T. Wasow and A. Akmajian. New York: Academic Press.
Wasow, Thomas and Thomas Roeper
　1972　　On the subject of gerunds. *Foundations of Language* 8.44–61.
Weissenborn, Jürgen
　1989　　*The Acquisition of Clitic Object Pronouns and Word Order in French: Syntax or Morphology?* Manuscript, Max Planck Institute for Psycholinguistics.
Whitney, Rosemarie
　1982　　The syntactic unity of wh-movement and complex NP shift. *Linguistic Analysis* 10: 299–319.
Whitney, Rosemarie
　1983　　The place of dative movement in a generative theory. Linguistic Analysis 12: 315–322.
Whitney, Rosemarie
　1984　　The syntax and interpretation of A-adjunctions. Unpublished PhD Dissertation, University of Washington, Seattle.
Whong-Barr, Melinda
　2002　　Small Clauses are Bigger. In *Proceedings of the Linguistics Society of Korea International Summer Conference,* Vol. II, 159–170. Seoul: Thaehaksa.
Williams, Edwin
　1981b　　On the notions "lexically related" and "head of a word" *Linguistic Inquiry* 12: 245–274.
Williams, Edwin
　1983　　Against small clauses. *Linguistic Inquiry* 14: 287–308.

Zagona, Karen
 1982 Government and Proper Government of Verbal Projections, PhD Dissertation, University of Washington, Seattle.

Zagona, Karen
 1988 *Verb Phrase Syntax: A Parametric Study of English and Spanish.* Dordrecht: Kluwer.

Zagona, Karen
 1982 Government and Proper Government of Verbal Projections, PhD Dissertation, University of Washington.

Zubizarreta, Maria-Luisa
 1987 *Levels of Representation in the Lexicon and in the Syntax.* Dordrecht: Foris.